Palgrave Studies of Internationalization in Emerging Markets

Emerging market nations such as Russia, Brazil, China, South Africa and India as well as Eastern European territories, are in the process of changes and growth that require specific study and attention. The international business strategies employed in these territories target new opportunities, the study of which provides scholars the opportunity to evolve international business theory.

Covering three main themes - international business, management and marketing – **Palgrave Studies of Internationalization in Emerging Markets** will encompass a multiplicity of topics. Examining the new ways in which firms from emerging economies develop and implement their internationalization strategy, as well as their management and marketing strategies, the series will encompass specific issues such as social entrepreneurship, operations and regional specifics of internationalization. Looking closer at the specifics underlying the development of emerging market nations and their firms, this series aims to shed light on the current and future issues associated with the challenges and opportunities offered by the varying contexts of emerging markets.

The book proposals for this series undergo a single blind peer review by three specialized highly respected established academics out of a pool of 28. The book proposal is sent to the reviewers that are selected based on its specific topic and content taking into consideration the geographic contextual specificity. The reviews with specific comments and recommendations are sent to the authors/editors of the perspectives publication who address them. Afterwards, the revised book proposal is evaluated by the Commissioning Editor of Palgrave Macmillan and Book Series Editor. The final manuscript is single blind peer reviewed. For more information on our peer review policy please see our website: https://www.palgrave.com/gp/book-authors/your-career/early-career-researcher-hub/peer-review-process?countryChanged=true

For information on how to submit a book proposal for inclusion in this series please contact Liz Barlow: liz.barlow@palgrave.com. For details on the book proposal process please visit our website: https://www.palgrave.com/gp/book-authors/publishing-guidelines/submit-a-proposal

More information about this series at
http://www.palgrave.com/gp/series/15456

Suzanne M. Apitsa • Eric Milliot
Editors

Doing Business in Africa

From Economic Growth to Societal Development

palgrave
macmillan

Editors
Suzanne M. Apitsa
University of Poitiers
Poitiers, France

Eric Milliot
University of Nantes
Nantes, France

ISSN 2662-1185 ISSN 2662-1193 (electronic)
Palgrave Studies of Internationalization in Emerging Markets
ISBN 978-3-030-50738-1 ISBN 978-3-030-50739-8 (eBook)
https://doi.org/10.1007/978-3-030-50739-8

This Palgrave Macmillan imprint is published by the registered company Springer Nature Switzerland AG.
The registered company address is: Gewerbestrasse 11, 6330 Cham, Switzerland

Foreword

Publications on entrepreneurship and management in Africa have been growing strongly over the last 20 years, thanks to the economic emergence of the continent, which has one of the best growth rates in the world. The Afro-pessimistic discourses of the 1980s have gradually disappeared in favour of Afro-optimist or Afro-realist discourses. This new context and the diverse dynamics that result from it have given rise to numerous editorial projects, the most recent of which shed diverse and enriching light on entrepreneurial and managerial practices in African contexts. Entrepreneurship and management in Africa are thus gradually becoming a fertile and attractive field of teaching, research, and publication.

The collective work *Doing Business in Africa: From Economic Growth to Societal Development*, edited by Suzanne Apitsa and Eric Milliot, fits perfectly into this editorial dynamic under construction in Africa. This publication, like some of those referenced below, comes at a crucial and critical time for Africa and the rest of the world. The global Covid-19 pandemic will undoubtedly slow down or even halt, for a while, the continuous economic growth curve observed in Africa for the past 25 years. Beyond the negative impacts observed in various fields of activity (health, economic, philosophical, ethical, political, etc.), this brutal and unexpected situation could also create opportunities in the ways of undertaking, managing and doing business in Africa. The subtitle of the book, *from economic growth to societal development*, is a perfect illustration of the transformational process in which African enterprises and economies must imperatively engage in the coming years. While it has already been accepted for years that economic growth is not at all synonymous with societal development, it is even more obvious today that wealth creation that is not accompanied by the creation of collective well-being and *savoir vivre ensemble* is a risky and dangerous situation for social cohesion and the sustainability of enterprises and organizations. The main merit of this book is therefore the challenge addressed to researchers and practitioners interested in entrepreneurship and management in Africa to engage in this paradigmatic transition from economic growth to societal development.

The book explores a few avenues of this transition around four main thematic axes that make up the parties: the process of internationalization, international logistics, cross-border social responsibility, and trust. The 13 chapters present experiences in different national (Algeria, Benin, Burkina Faso, Cameroon, Egypt, Ethiopia, Madagascar, Morocco, Niger, Nigeria, Tanzania) and regional (Central Africa, West Africa, East Africa, North Africa, Indian Ocean) contexts. While one may regret the absence of a contribution from Southern Africa, in this book it is undeniable that the latter is a major edifice that reflects African economic and cultural diversities. It is also a powerful lever for opening African national borders and facilitating the circulation of researchers and practitioners throughout the continent. It is important to recall here the many difficulties encountered by the latter in moving from one country to another, from one geographical region to another. These difficulties are currently illustrated by the reluctance of some African countries to become formally involved in the implementation of the project to create the African Continental Free Trade Area (AfCFTA), which is intended to consolidate the continent's economic integration on a lasting basis. Bringing together in one volume the contributions from all these African diversities is a major challenge that the editors and contributors of this book have successfully met.

Ultimately, this book is a testimony to the capacity of researchers (African and non-African) interested in the experiences and practices observed in African fields to make a useful contribution to the creation of contextualized knowledge in Africa. This creative process enables African publications to gradually break out of the vicious circle of reproducing models and practices imported from elsewhere and not very "actionable" in African contexts. This is not at all a question of holding an exotic or even ethnocentric discourse on the positioning of African research and publications internationally. This kind of discourse is no longer relevant in a world where the digital revolution, teleworking, and tele-research considerably facilitate access to documentary sources (provided that there is a technically reliable and financially accessible Internet connection). The message of this book is that of the African contribution to knowledge creation, in African contexts and in comparison to international contexts beyond Africa. May this book, like those already published, give rise to other editorial projects, in Africa or outside Africa, to ensure better visibility and a brighter image of African research in entrepreneurship and management.

École Supérieure des Sciences Économiques et Commerciales (ESSEC),
Université de Douala, Cameroon
Institut Supérieur de Management et de l'Entrepreneuriat (IME), Douala, Cameroon
Business Sciences Institute (BSI), Luxembourg

Emmanuel Kamdem

References

Adeleye, I., & Esposito, M. (Eds.). (2018). *Africa's Competitiveness in the Global Economy*. New York: Palgrave Macmillan.

Cheriet, F., Beddi, H., Ado, A., & Kamdem, E. (2020). Management international en Afrique: spécificités, strategies des acteurs et enjeux de développement. *Management International*, dossier thématique, Vol. 24, No. 3.

Chrysostome, E. (2019). *Capacity Building in Developing and Emerging Countries: From Mindset Transformation to Promoting Entrepreneurship and Diaspora Involvement*. New York: Springer.

Kamdem, E., Chevalier, F., & Payaud, M. dir (Ed.) (2020). *La recherche enracinée en management: contextes nouveaux et perspectives nouvelles en Afrique, Éditions Management et Société (EMS)*. Caen: Collection Business Science Institute (BSI).

Sègbédji, P. A., Radjabu, M., & Zhan, S. (2020). *Réussir vos projets d'affaires en Afrique*. Laval: Presses de l'Université Laval.

Acknowledgements

Writing a book is always the result of a rich and nourishing collaboration. Therefore, on behalf of all the authors, we would like to extend our heartfelt thanks to the following people for their valuable support and sound advice:

- Professor Victor Harison (Commissioner for Economic Affairs of the African Union)
- Professor Marin Marinov (Series Editor at Palgrave Macmillan)
- Doctor Arkebe Oqubay (Senior Minister and Special Advisor to the Prime Minister of Ethiopia)

Our gratitude concerns particularly all the colleagues who took the time to review the work presented in this book, in particular:

- Professor Jean Biwolé-Fouda (University de Ngaoundéré, Cameroon)
- Associate Professor Foued Cheriet (Montpellier Supagro, France)
- Professor Emmanuel Kamdem (Université de Douala, Cameroon)
- Professor emeritus Jean-Paul Lemaire (ESCPE Europe, France)
- Professor Ulrike Mayrhofer (Université de Nice Sophia Antipolis, France)
- Associate Professor Philippe Mouillot (Université de Poitiers, France)
- Associate Professor Sophie Nivoix (Université de Poitiers, France)

- Professor Frédéric Prévot (Kedge Business School, France)
- Professor Nathalie Prime (ESCPE Europe, France)
- Professor Jean-Pierre Segal (Université Paris Dauphine, France)
- Associate Professor Jan Schaaper (Université de Bordeaux, France)

Finally, we would like to express our gratitude to the Springer and Palgrave Macmillan teams for their efficient and benevolent support in the preparation of this book.

Suzanne M. Apitsa and Eric Milliot

Contents

Notes on Contributors

Hicham Abbad is Associate Professor in Retailing and Supply Chain Management at Nantes University, France. He is a member of the LEMNA laboratory. His major interests are supply chain management, retail operations management, and inter-organizational information systems.

Hachemí Aliouche is Director of the Rosenberg International Franchise Center, the Rosenberg Chair in Franchising, and Associate Professor at the University of New Hampshire, USA. His research has been published in leading academic journals such as the *Journal of Retailing* and the *Cornell Quarterly*.

Suzanne M. Apitsa is a lecturer and researcher of Centre de Recherche en Gestion (CEREGE) Laboratory—University of Poitiers (France). She teaches cross-cultural management, international HRM, international business. She advises some French SMEs in their development in Africa. Her research focuses globally on international management in Africa.

Rodrigue Balima is a lecturer at the University Aube-Nouvelle of Ouagadougou, Burkina Faso. He had managed the dry port of Ouagadougou for almost ten years. He is also the director of a structure (within a private sector support institution) in charge of capacity building of directors and corporate governance promotion.

Dominique Bonet Fernandez is a professor at the IPAG Business School, France. He is also an affiliated researcher at the Transport and Logistics Research Center (CRET-LOG) at Aix-Marseille University. Her research and teaching focus on international trade, logistics, digitalization and new business models of circular and collaborative economy.

Oumaima Chamchati is a PhD student at Cadi Ayyad University of Marrakech, Morocco. She is a member of the Organizational Management Research group. She is also affiliated with ECONOMIA, HEM Research Center. Her research is related to the international development of SMEs, especially in Africa.

Mohamed Nabil El Mabrouki is a professor at Cadi Ayyad University of Marrakech, Morocco. He is a senior researcher associate at ECONOMIA, HEM Research Center. His research focuses on international management, competitive intelligence and corporate social responsibility.

Susan Freeman is Professor of International Business, the University of South Australia Business School, Australia. She provides leadership in the areas of international business research and postgraduate teaching and learning. Her research and teaching focus on international business strategy, entrepreneurship and managerial decision-making.

Clément J. Godonou is General Manager of Roro Terminal Benin, a subsidiary company of the Italian maritime group Grimaldi. He teaches as part of the UNCTAD Train for Trade training and at the Vocational Training Center of PMAWCA in Cotonou. He is a consultant, a researcher at the University of Abomey Calavi (Benin), and an author of scientific articles.

Victor Harison is a professor at the National Institute of Accounting Sciences and Business Administration (INSCAE), Madagascar. He is also the Commissioner for Economic Affairs in Ethiopia. His research focuses on the strategy of SMEs, corporate social responsibility and public management.

Mohamed Kadi is Permanent Researcher at the Centre for Research in Applied Economics for Development (CREAD), Algeria. His research focuses on internationalization of SMEs and more generally on international business development. He is a member of the Euro Mediterranean Network for Economic Studies (EMNES).

Ahmed Kellow is Managing Director and Principal Consultant of First Consult, Ethiopia. He has served as Managing Director of GCS-NCR Ethiopia, CEO of Ethiopian Airlines, and Managing Director (and later Chairman) of Coca-Cola Ethiopia. Previously, he was a lecturer in Business and Finance at Cardiff Business School, University of Wales.

Nebil Kellow is Managing Director of Enterprise Partners, Ethiopia. He is also a Founding Partner at First Consult PLC. Kellow works to supports Ethiopia's industrialisation programme. He previously worked for McKinsey & Co. and in the investment industry in the United Kingdom.

Munoz Pierre Kenmeni is PhD Student at the University of Yaoundé II, Cameroon. He is currently working on environmental management in public administrations and in private corporations in Cameroon

Hugues Valéry Kouakap is a PhD student at the University of Yaoundé I, Cameroon. He is a specialist in impact studies and environmental audits of land use planning projects (buildings, stadiums, road and port infrastructures, engineering structures, etc.).

Messan Lihoussou is Associate Professor in Transport-Logistics at the University of Parakou, Benin. He is also an associate researcher at UMR Idées-Le Normandie. His publications are related to West African ports, corridors and companies' competition in the transport-logistics field.

Sonia Mahjoub is Assistant Professor of Logistics and Industrial Engineering at the ONIRIS Nantes, France. She is also a member of the LEMNA laboratory at Nantes University. Her research focuses on application of game theory in the supply chain. Her work appears in the *International Journal of Production Economics*, *International Journal of Production Research*, and so on.

Narova Barisoa Miasa is a PhD student, lecturer, and researcher at the University of Toamasina, Madagascar. She works on topics linked to corporate social responsibility (CSR). Her research aims to contribute to the implementation of CSR practices.

Eric Milliot is Professor of Management Science at the University of Nantes, France. President of Atlas Association Francophone de Management International (AFMI), he is deputy editor-in-chief of the *International Management* journal and director of the Atlas series at Vuibert. Member of the LEMNA laboratory, he has published several books and academic articles.

Caroline Minialai is Senior Researcher Associate at ECONOMIA, HEM Research Center, Morocco. Her research is dedicated to entrepreneurship, SMEs and family businesses. She is also the cofounder and CEO of an online tutoring firm, Averroes E-learning.

Btissam Moncef is Associate Professor of Supply Chain Management at ISC Paris, France. Her recent research deals with supply chain practices including international and sustainable issues.

Marie Ngolo Bela is Director of Technical Studies for building and other infrastructure at the Ministry of Public Work, Cameroon. She is a civil engineer and holds an MSc in Environmental Management Sciences.

José Kisito Nkenkeu is a PhD student at the University of Yaoundé II, Cameroun. He is Director of the Kisibel-Eco Sarl design office, and an authorized expert in public markets.

Frank Nyamrunda is a lecturer and Topic Coordinator in the College of Business, Government and Law at Flinders University, South Australia. He has taught International Business, Corporate Responsibility for Global Business, and so on, at the University of Adelaide, the University of South Australia and Flinders University.

Gwenaëlle Oruezabala is Associate Professor in BtoB Marketing at Nantes University, France. She is also a member of LEMNA laboratory. Her research interests focus on supplier relationship management, supply chain management and interaction within innovation business ecosystems, more particularly when related to African management alternatives.

Gilde Ralandison is Associate Professor at the National Institute of Accounting Sciences and Business Administration (INSCAE) of Madagascar. Dean for academic affairs, he is a member of the BRAIN laboratory. His research focuses on the internationalization strategy of SMEs and puts the concepts of coopetition and coevolution at the center of analyses.

Mona Shehata is a PhD student and lecturer at the University of Poitiers, France. Specializing in Information and Communication Sciences, her research focuses on the analysis of rumors dissemination on social media in a multicultural context.

Mesmin Tchindjang is Professor at the University of Yaoundé I, Cameroun. His research interests are environmental assessment and management, natural hazards and tourism.

Dora Triki is Associate Professor of International Business at the ESCE International Business School, INSEEC U Research Center, France. Her work focuses on FDI determinants in the MENA region and the performance of international joint ventures.

List of Figures

List of Images

List of Tables

1

Africa, a Continent on the Move

Eric Milliot

Many countries in Africa have been experiencing strong economic growth for several years (World Bank 2019). This growth, focused on market activities, is only a quantitative indicator about the evolution of the production value of a country or a geographical area. On its own, this notion does not make it possible to assess the degree of attractiveness of a territory for local and/or international investors.

In addition to growth, economic and political leaders must take an interest in the development conditions of the studied area. Indeed, development, which is assessed in a more qualitative way, integrates factors that make it possible to identify the economic and socio-cultural changes that accompany the increase in market value created over a period. More than the notion of growth, it is the notion of development that makes it possible to assess the attractiveness of an economy and measure its potential for internationalisation. It is also this notion that makes it possible to

E. Milliot (✉)
University of Nantes, Nantes, France
e-mail: emilliot@poitiers.iae-france.fr

S. M. Apitsa, E. Milliot (eds.), *Doing Business in Africa*, Palgrave Studies of Internationalization in Emerging Markets,
https://doi.org/10.1007/978-3-030-50739-8_1

assess an economy's capacity to cope with a major crisis such as the coronavirus (Covid-19) pandemic in 2020.

The concept of development must therefore be at the heart of research conducted in the field of International Business. The indicators that characterise it are varied. For example, the United Nations Development Programme (UNDP) proposed the Human Development Index (HDI) in 1990. The latter is based on gross domestic product (GDP), life expectancy and the level of education of the population. It thus reflects the multiple forces that combine to contribute to a country's social and economic progress. Although this indicator is now widely accepted and used, it is not without limits; it does not measure the impact of human activities on the natural heritage and does not identify certain social inequalities. This is why many political and economic decision-makers today refer to the notion of sustainable development. With this in mind, 193 countries decided in 2015 to define a plan to achieve this type of development. This plan aims to achieve 17 goals by 2030 (UNDP 2015). Among them are the end of extreme poverty, ensuring inclusive and equitable quality education, ensuring gender equality, ensuring the availability and sustainable management of water, ensuring access to affordable and clean energy, promoting decent work, ensuring sustainable consumption and production patterns, taking urgent action to combat climate change, and so on.

In Africa, a plan to strengthen cooperation and the integration of states was adopted in 2013 to achieve very similar objectives. It is called Agenda 2063, a long-term project that aims to ensure, over the period 2013–2063, the development of the entire continent (African Union 2020). One of the flagship projects of this agenda is the launch in 2020 the African Continental Free Trade Area (AfCFTA), a market of 1.3 billion people.

Some will say that these are partly demagogic and utopian programmes. Nevertheless, these plans have the advantage of providing roadmaps that make it possible to identify the key conditions for ensuring societal development on an international scale; that is, sustainable development combined with governance arrangements (rules, codes and protocols) that facilitate coordination of all the parties involved (states, companies, NGOs, etc.). It is on these different conditions that researchers in

International Business must work to study the potential for action and integration of African countries.

As we indicated at the very beginning of this introduction, the African continent is experiencing strong economic growth. This growth contributes to attracting more foreign capital and accelerating intra- and intercontinental trade, but it is not sufficient to ensure sustainable socio-economic expansion that is beneficial to both states and populations. To better understand the conditions for this expansion, it is also necessary to look at the quality and effectiveness of local regulation. The Doing Business study conducted by the World Bank Group (2019) is interesting in this regard. This survey measures the processes for starting a business, dealing with construction permits, getting electricity, registering property, getting credit, protecting minority investors, paying taxes, trading across borders, enforcing contracts and resolving insolvency. It produces a composite index called the Ease of Doing Business (EODB), which measures an economy's position with regard to the best regulatory practice. Beyond the EODB, the World Bank Group is also interested in the flexibility of employment regulation and various aspects of job quality.

An indicator specific to Africa, more societal than the EODB, should also be considered. This is the Ibrahim Index of African Governance (IIAG) developed in 2007 by the Sudanese Ibrahim Mo. This indicator, used to assess the development of the 55 countries of the African Union, is based on four complementary topics: safety and rule of law, participation and human rights, sustainable economic opportunity, human development (Mo Ibrahim Foundation 2018).

Obviously, the African context—taken here as a field of study—presents very variable socio-economic realities (Subran et al. 2016). This heterogeneity, which is highlighted in the chapters of the book, is not neutral. It reflects the multidimensional nature of the process that enables the transition from growth to development. To illustrate this process and the differences observed across the continent, we can use the five indicators summarised so far (Table 1.1).

- The first two are directly related to economic growth: gross domestic product (GDP) per capita and annual GDP growth rate.

- The last three are associated with societal development conditions: the Human Development Index (HDI), Ease of Doing Business (EODB) and the Ibrahim Index of African Governance (IIAG).

Table 1.1, which presents the data for the year 2018, makes it possible to identify contrasting situations. High-growth countries, such as Rwanda and Benin, are characterised by a relatively low HDI. At the same time, countries with relatively high HDIs, such as Algeria and South Africa, have lower growth rates than many countries on the continent. We can also point out that countries with more flexible regulatory practices and more transparent governance practices, Rwanda and Mauritius, appear to have relatively high growth rates.

These observations illustrate the complex interweaving of the concepts of growth and development, but the indicators generally used to assess this interweaving do not sufficiently highlight the role of enterprises in

Table 1.1 Growth levels and development conditions of selected African countries

Pays	GDP per capita (US dollars)	GDP growth (annual %)	HDI[a]	EODB[b]	IIAG[c]
Algeria	4.115	1.4	0.759	49.65	50.2
Benin	902	6.9	0.520	51.42	58.7
Burkina Faso	715	6.8	0.434	51.57	57.1
Cameroun	1.534	4.1	0.563	47.78	46.2
Egypt	2.549	5.3	0.700	58.56	49.9
Ethiopia	772	6.8	0.470	49.06	46.5
Ivory Coast	1.716	7.4	0.516	58.00	54.5
Madagascar	528	4.6	0.521	48.89	49.0
Mauritius	11.239	3.8	0.796	79.58	79.5
Morocco	3.222	3.0	0.676	71.02	58.4
Niger	414	6.5	0.377	56.08	51.2
Nigeria	2.028	1.9	0.534	52.89	47.0
Rwanda	773	8.6	0.536	77.88	64.3
South Africa	6.374	0.8	0.705	66.03	68.0

Source: World Bank (2019), World Bank Group (2019), UNDP (2019), Mo Ibrahim Foundation (2018)

[a]Composite index (three topics) ranging from 0 (lowest level of development) to 1 (highest level of development)

[b]Composite index (10 topics, 41 variables) ranging from 0 (worst performance) to 100 (best performance)

[c]Composite index (4 topics, 95 variables) ranging from 0 (lowest level of development) to 100 (highest level of development)

the economic and social development of countries. In order to go beyond the regularly published and widely disseminated macroeconomic indicators, this book presents research in Management Sciences to understand how it is possible for firms operating in Africa to contribute to the transition from cyclical growth to more structural development. Even if the concepts of growth and development are not always explicitly mentioned in this book, they are indeed the common threads that give a generic meaning to the chapters.

Before presenting the outline of this volume, it should be noted that the title chosen should not be misleading. The terms *Doing Business* are not a direct reference to the World Bank Group's EODB. To develop the theme of this book, they reflect the need to integrate the various managerial dimensions that condition the operation of various players (governments, companies, NGOs, etc.) in a market. These different dimensions, pillars of societal development, are studied or discussed in four parts.

- The first is concerned with the process of internationalisation. This process strengthens the growth dynamics of economies. In this part, the notions of cooperation, integration, commitment and political relations are particularly studied.
- In the second part, the conditions of economic exchanges are at the heart of the analyses. Trade is at the source of value creation, which is why the concepts of global logistics, supply chain, infrastructure and trade relations are developed here.
- In the third part, we look at corporate social responsibility. This responsibility ultimately ensures the conditions for more sustainable development that respects the stakeholders involved in economic exchanges. In the research presented at this level, we address the themes of ethics, commitment, involvement and ecology.
- In the fourth and final part, we develop one of the key foundations of social responsibility: trust. This psychological state is a key condition for ensuring the commitment and involvement of people and companies in business relationships that often need to be long-term to be successful. Here, issues of governance, communication, partnership relations and rumours are dealt with.

The keywords that we have just cited to characterise the parts of the book (cooperation, integration, supply chain, business relations, involvement, ecology, governance, communication …) reflect the complex and complementary dimensions which form the basis for the societal development of countries.

In this book, 29 academics from 12 countries study how to do business in 11 economies and 5 areas of the African continent. This broad contextualisation is essential for understanding the transition from economic growth to societal development in an area characterised by recurrent and well-known inhibitors (institutional weaknesses, political instability, corruption, etc.). This contextualisation is furthermore enhanced by the preliminary chapter on the notions of culture and ethnicity. The pivotal values that derive from these concepts condition the decision-making and action logics of people and organisations working in Africa. They seem to be indispensable for achieving the objectives of Agenda 2063 established in 2013 by the African Union.

References

African Union. (2020). *Agenda 2063*. Report.

Mo Ibrahim Foundation. (2018). *Index of African Governance*. Report.

Subran, L., Colliac, S., & Kibala, B. G. (2016). *Dix idées reçues sur l'Afrique*. Paris: Euler-Hermès.

United Nations Development Programme. (2015). *Sustainable Development Goals*. New York: United Nations.

United Nations Development Programme. (2019). *Human Development Report 2019*. New York: United Nations.

World Bank. (2019). *GDP Growth (Annual %)*. Washington, DC: World Bank.

World Bank Group. (2019). *Doing Business*. Washington, DC: World Bank.

2

The Dynamics of Ethnic Cultural Interactions in the African Workplace

Suzanne M. Apitsa

1 Introduction

It is now widely accepted that Africa is the centre of attention in the competitive markets of global trade and value chains. Africa is also a mosaic of cultures and ethnicities, a fact that cannot be ignored. Developing activities in this market requires an understanding of the cultural power relations that can alternatively limit or increase the competitiveness of companies operating in this geographical area. These include ethnicity, which is one aspect of cultural anchoring (Eriksen 1991; Abou 2002; Fenton 2010; Seny Kan et al. 2015; Apitsa 2016), and a characteristic of diversity (Kundu and Turan 1999; Ayoko and Härtel 2006; Shore et al. 2009; Ogbanna 2019). Any multinational company setting up in Africa will encounter this cultural and ethnic diversity, which it must manage rather than try to avoid (Apitsa 2013).

S. M. Apitsa (✉)
University of Poitiers, Poitiers, France

S. M. Apitsa, E. Milliot (eds.), *Doing Business in Africa*, Palgrave Studies of Internationalization in Emerging Markets,
https://doi.org/10.1007/978-3-030-50739-8_2

It follows that in Africa, unlike in Europe where it has a negative connotation, ethnicity is involved in the structuring of African peoples. However, it has remained a widely ignored dimension Chanlat's (1990/2007), Kamdem and Fouda Ongodo's (2007) and Apitsa's (2016) work notwithstanding, particularly in the field of management sciences in Africa. In the Anglo-Saxon literature, the term ethnicity conveys the reality of human cultural diversity (Warner and Srole 1945). In this chapter, we define ethnicity as the identity of a social group—recognising itself and in the eyes of other—belonging to a community that shares the same references, whether through language, religion, values, beliefs, customs, traditions, or ways of life. It is a dimension that inhabits an individual (Apitsa 2016).

By including this chapter on the topic of cross-cultural management and diversity management, we wish to shed light on the dynamics of interpersonal cultural and ethnic interactions in companies in Africa. To our knowledge, the cultural interactions of individuals in African workplaces have seldom been studied. Our objective is to understand the logics of individuals in companies in Africa and to see how ethnic cultures can be drawn on in managerial action. Indeed, the relationship to the Other and living together crosses all the issues of management of organisations whatever the context and makes particular sense in Africa in view of its socio-cultural context. In addition, African cultural peculiarity is based on the meaning attributed to each behaviour within an interacting group (Hernandez 2000; Mutabazi 2006; Kamdem 2007; Apitsa 2018a; Diomande and Segal 2019). The cultural and ethnic diversity of African companies is testament to the fact that people who differ in age, dialect (language), ethnic origin, religion, cultural tradition, gender, beliefs, education, occupation, and so on, can cooperate and work together.

In many studies of African companies that focus on the link between African culture and performance, authors conclude that African cultural traits have negative effects on company performance (Easterly and Levine 1997; Kessy 1998; Nizet and Pichault 2007). This representation has been rejected, however, as based on cultural misunderstanding and stereotypes (Mutabazi 2004; Amoako-Agyei 2009; Jackson 2013) or attributed to the implementation of administrative bureaucracy methods or other Western practices and tools without due consideration of African cultural specificities (D'Iribarne 1990; Prinsloo 2000; Yanat and Scouarnec 2005; Henry 2009; Apitsa 2018b). The analysis of Western tools and models and their implementation in Africa is well established. At a time when diversity in the workplace is being promoted (Castles 2000; Prime 2001; Polzer et al. 2002; Carmichael and Rijamampianina 2007; Pierre et al. 2009; Patrick and Raj Kumar 2012; Bentaleb et al. 2012; Kamdem 2017; Gould et al. 2018; Whee Lee and Eunhee 2019), our research objective can be outlined in three questions: How do ethnic cultural elements interact in the logics of individuals in the African workplace? What are their effects on managerial action? How can these ethnic cultural elements be drawn upon in the management of companies in Africa?

To answer these questions, the following text is organised as follows. After describing the theoretical foundations of the research, we present the methodology used and the results of the three case studies carried out in Cameroon and Nigeria. Finally, these results are discussed, and we conclude in terms of their managerial implications.

2 Theoretical Foundations of the Study

Organisations are places where multiple rationalities coexist (Crozier and Friedberg 1977; Milliot 1999). They are places where diversity is integrated and cultural synergies are achieved. The concept of diversity became popular in the United States in the 1960s in anti-discrimination policies. This led in the 1990s to the implementation of diversity management policies in North American organisations. In Europe, the issue of diversity is a more recent concern, for companies and politicians, which can be traced back to the early 2000s. In France, it made a significant contribution to the public debate surrounding the suburban riots of 2005. While its importance appears to be waning, it re-emerges every time immigration problems arise. For example, the death of George Floyd in the United States in May 2020, which sparked a huge global protest. This globally evokes the fight against discrimination. In companies, diversity is a means to act against discrimination and is part of a broader set of corporate social responsibility (CSR) policies. In Africa, the concept of diversity resonates naturally in the socio-historical context. In the literature, many authors have attempted to define the notion of diversity by its characteristics. For Milliken and Martins (1996), diversity within organisations covers ethnicity, age, values and personality, educational background, and functions and/or occupations. According to Thomas (2004), speaking of diversity means considering the differences and similarities that form a whole. He adds that diversity applies to the workforce and can be observed in different dimensions: between customers and suppliers, and positions held within the company and in terms of occupations, age, gender, status, disabilities, ethnic origin, nationality, and so on. The presence of diversity in organisations can be difficult to manage. To understand the logics of individuals in African workplaces, let us first discuss the concept of ethnicity, one element of the diversity around which African societies are built.

2.1 Ethnicity: Emergence of a Concept

Ethnicity cannot be understood outside the overall framework of culture because it carries and shares some of its characteristics (Apitsa and Amine 2014). Culture is tied to the concept of identity, self-perception, and the perception of others. According to Hall (1976), culture is what characterises individuals, giving them their identity regardless of their origin and shaping their behaviour in a specific and lasting way. Thus, in belonging to a specific culture, an individual integrates a certain number of behavioural principles in relation to their social group (Tajfel and Turner 1986).

The first academic reflections on ethnicity were carried out in the United States in the 1940s. To define ethnicity, some authors refer to the concepts of identity, difference, diversity, and human groups (Warner and Srole 1945; Bell 1975; Abou 2002; Kamdem and Fouda Ongodo 2007; Fenton 2010). It should be noted that this concept was born out of a long and fierce intellectual debate in the social sciences on the term ethnicity, which is considered an ambiguous, pejorative term referring—in nineteenth-century secular language—to the words people, nation, tribe, race. It can be used to label particular societies as primitive ("uncivilised"). Ethnic groups are peoples and cultural communities, each with their own language, customs, beliefs, and ways of livings. They form a homogenous group referring to a shared history and territory. It is important not to confuse an ethnic group with a tribe. A tribe is a human grouping within an ethnic group in which several large families obey the authority of the same chief.

It is within this debate that the concept of ethnicity emerged in response to the need for recognition and integration of peoples of different origins in Anglo-Saxon societies. In the United States, it conveys something of the reality of human cultural diversity (Warner and Srole 1945). In Europe, and particularly in France, it is denied in the name of a dogma of national unity and linguistic hegemony ("the Republic is one and indivisible"). In Africa, although the term is unashamedly present in all spheres of society, it is perceived as an expression of economic regression and an obstacle to national construction. However, in the face of repeated structural, economic, and democratic reform failures, ethnicity has emerged as a necessary component to ensure that the various reforms are appropriate to the socio-cultural context.

The definition of ethnicity given in the introduction derives from a literature review (Apitsa 2013, 2016). This definition outlines a human group and expresses the social and cultural singularity of an individual in that group. Individuals, in their relationship with others, experience a sense of belonging to a group with which they assert their identity and values. These elements find a shared meaning within a collective consciousness, because individuals use them as markers of their difference from others and of their ethnic identity. The latter allows them to recognise themselves in their social environment, but also makes them aware of belonging to a community. The notion of ethnicity oscillates between culture and identity. Its different traits shape the behaviour of individuals and condition their existence. Their ways of thinking and acting in the workplace make sense in their own culture (Kamdem 2007; Hall 2017; Apitsa 2018a).

- In Africa, work on ethnicity can be associated with two currents of thought. The first is economic and entrepreneurial, with the concept of ethnicity being used to explain the poor economic performance of the continent. Authors such as Kabou (1991), Hugon (1993), Easterly and Levine (1997) have presented ethnicity as associated with economic and social regression. These authors use macroeconomic and statistical data on the economic growth of African countries to advance their devastating arguments on ethnicity. The current economic emergence of Africa may give lie to these hasty conclusions, however. This line of work has led entrepreneurship researchers to study African businesses in terms of their economic performance. In different academic studies in Africa, the ethnic factor is put forward and cultural traits are seen as having a negative effect on entrepreneurship and performance. How do ethnic realities lead to poor performance in African organisations? This question has never been answered or empirically tested in the literature.

- The second current stems from the fields of cross-cultural and diversity management. It takes the opposite view and presents ethnicity as a dimension that should be mobilised rather than forgotten to ensure successful company development (Chanlat 1990/2007; Nyambegera 2002; Kamdem and Fouda Ongodo 2007). For this approach to be successful, ethnicity has to be understood in the context of the variety of ethnic cultural elements that are expressed in interactions between individuals in the context of diversity. Ethnicity inhabits the individual. This is the very heart of cross-cultural analysis but this perspective has only seldom been adopted in the literature.

2.2 Individuals in Their Relationships with Others: Theoretical Framework for Analysis

In a context of cultural diversity, interactions are at the heart of the meeting between employees, each with their own values and beliefs. However, these interactions have not been the focus of much attention in academic work. Neither the school of Human Relations nor national cultural models explicitly take account of these interactions. The school of Human Relations has shown that an individual at work has complex motivations and does not just aim to maximise profit as the classical economic would have it. It places the individual at the heart of the production process and within a homogenous work group (team), which is a prerequisite for achieving performance. This view of "best practices" has been called into question by advocates of a cross-cultural approach because of the cultural differences between countries (Hofstede 1980, 2001). In spite of their interest, the thought processes of interacting individuals are poorly understood. Moreover, the comparative approach does not allow for an in-depth understanding of the interactions between individuals (D'Iribarne 2004). The sociological approach to organisations (Crozier and Friedberg 1977) offers a clear avenue to understanding the interactions between individuals in the workplace (power, roles, rationality, and opportunism), because by not leaving us outside the company to study interactions, it invites us inside the company to be at the heart of these interactions.

In fact, an organisation is a complex system of relationships between interacting actors (individuals and groups). During these interactions, some will seek to play the role best suited to their individual interests within each collective action (Crozier and Friedberg 1977). For these authors, one of the major challenges of actors is their ability to discover and create opportunities that enable them to improve their situation within their organisation: increasing their satisfaction, margins of manoeuvre, degrees of freedom, influence, ability to make adjustments, and effective reaction to opportunities. Highlighting these situations reveals the individual motivations (individual behaviours and interests) that exist both within and alongside the formal organisation.

Given that there is no theoretical corpus with which to organise the elements of African cultures (Zoogah et al. 2015; Walsh 2015), an empirical classification of the different ethnic cultural elements that characterise the African cultural system has recently been proposed (Apitsa 2018b: 54) (Table 2.1). We use these elements to understand individuals' decisions in their workplace. They provide an understanding of the dynamics of cultural and ethnic interactions (Apitsa 2018a).

The African cultural system is a universe of meanings (Apitsa 2018a). It is characterised by a system of thoughts, values, and rules, whose combination sheds light on the cultural and ethnic realities of individuals in Africa.

The following section sets out the methodology of the study and the results obtained.

Table 2.1 The African cultural system

System of values and meaning	Thought system	
	Community sociability	Ethnicity (ethnic group)
Solidarity and mutual support	Family, clan	Name
Religion	Spirituals entities	Religion
Languages	Dialects	Vernacular languages
Ethic	Ancestors	Values
Respect (age, elder, old, secret)	Relationship to others (human, nature, technology)	Customs and morals
Traditions	Myths, rites, secrets, chieftainship	Occult beliefs, dress codes, greeting habits
Time	Linear time design	Orientation to the past and the future

Source: Apitsa (2018b, p. 54)

3 Study Methodology

The case study was carried out in 2015 and 2017 and involved three French multinationals. Two are established in Cameroon and one in Nigeria, two melting pots of cultures and ethnic groups (approximately 250 and 300 ethnic groups, respectively).

3.1 The Method

We adopted a qualitative approach, allowing us to identify cultural and behavioural landmarks and penetrate the social reality of individuals (Eisenhardt and Graebner 2007). Considering that the results of this case study approach do not allow for statistical generalisation, the reliability and analytical value of the results were increased by comparisons with the existing literature (Eisenhardt 1989). The relevance of this qualitative approach is that it has high internal and construct validity. Construct validity can be achieved through the multiple triangulation of discursive sources. The interviews are complemented by documentary sources and by non-participant observations based on an ethnographic approach (D'Iribarne 2004).

Table 2.2 Elements of the studied multinationals

	Field of investigation: three French multinationals established in Cameroon and Nigeria		
Characteristics	Cas c1	Cas c2	Cas n3
Physical implantation	Cameroon		Nigeria
Year of creation	1950	1980	1995
Business	Bank	Insurance	Distribution of liquid packaging solutions
Subsidiaries in Africa	18 countries	8 countries	13 countries
Number of employees	625	80	70
Number of agencies	29 agencies	2 agencies	1 agency
Number of interviews	22	16	7
	45		

Source: Author's creation

The companies and respondents were anonymised for confidentiality reasons; the cases are simply named c1, c2, and n3 (Table 2.2).

3.2 Data Collection

Forty-five semi-structured interviews, 60 to 90 minutes in length, were organised with executives, senior and middle managers, and employees. The interview guide was organised around five themes: (1) cultural and ethnic diversity, (2) relationships at work (interpersonal and interprofessional), (3) task performance, (4) work behaviour, (5) general atmosphere in the company and in the work team. These themes were chosen based on the literature review. The interviews were conducted in the language of the interviewee (French or English) with the aim of improving the quality of the information collected. In the verbatim transcripts, interviewees were referred to using codes starting with C in Cameroon and N in Nigeria.

3.3 The Data Analysis Process

The interviews were transcribed and then analysed in two stages by two investigators (King 2004).

- The first analysis was a post hoc manual coding performed by the author (Glaser and Strauss 1967). Unlike lexical analysis, which uses the word as the unit of analysis, we chose the sentence or paragraph to avoid truncating discourse and to ensure unity of meaning (Miles and Huberman 2003). The categories of meaning used were derived from the African cultural system described above.
- A second confirmatory analysis was carried out by the second investigator. This double coding (analysis) ensured that the sensitivities and fine nuances in the data were properly captured, to provide a meaningful description and explanation of the data.

Finally, the three cases were analysed using the contextualised explanation method (Welch et al. 2011). This approach is characterised by a strong emphasis on contextualisation and causal relations. Milliot and Freeman (2015) describe it as a praxeological project associated with exploratory and/or causal research objectives. Using abductive inferences, our approach is part of an ontological perspective based on critical realism (Bhaskar 1997, 1998). The analysis starts from factual and interpreted realities (interviews, observations, documentary sources) to propose, using a critical review of the literature, explanations about the facts studied.

4 Results

In this chapter, we set out to understand the logics of individuals in companies in Africa and to investigate how ethnic cultures can be leveraged in managerial action. The aim is to shed light on the dynamics of the cultural and ethnic interactions of individuals in companies in Africa. Three questions structure this objective: How do ethnic cultural elements interact in the logics of individuals in the African workplace? What are their effects on managerial action? How can we take advantage of these ethnic cultural elements in the management of companies in Africa? The results that follow answer these questions.

4.1 The Logics of Individuals in Managerial Action

Our results show that ethnic cultural elements (Apitsa 2018a), such as vernacular languages, age, ethnic origin, gender, and religion, interact in the logics of individuals in the workplace and affect managerial action.

Vernacular Languages in Interprofessional Relationships

Bear in mind that Africa is a diversity of cultures and ethnic groups. Each ethnic group has its own vernacular language. In the multinationals studied, the use of vernacular languages is officially prohibited but widespread in practice.

> *When I took office, I was told that it is not always appropriate to speak one's dialect in the company. I said, I do not mind. "But it is an element of my identity that I will not, for any reason, accept to repress, as it is here"*. (I will not accept the prohibition to speak my dialect in the company). (C, Human Resource Director [HRD], local)

Interview data show that in work teams marked by a strong linguistic bond, the team manager tends to entrust important tasks to employees who speak the same dialect, thus minimising the role of the other team members.

> *I have in my team Douala, Bassa, Bamiléké, Bamenda, Yaoundé people. The ethnic aspect does not come into play. It is just the job. I am Banen. Suppose I have the ability and the power to recruit. If I recruit out of ten accountants, five good Banen and the rest from other ethnic groups, the non-Banens will never be comfortable. Because people in our offices always tend to speak their dialect. So, if there are five good people who are speaking Banen, the others will already*

> *feel left out. I say this because I have experienced it. People speak their 'dialect', and you have to understand what they talk about. If you're completely out of the loop, that hinders work.* (C, Executive senior, local)

This verbatim transcript reveals that during cross-cultural encounters, French and/or English are not the only languages individuals communicate with in the workplace. The behaviours revealed in these interviews show to what extent managers create, in a suitable manner, a qualified climate of trust around themselves with people who speak their own language. Use of the vernacular is instrumentalised and serves as a cover for advancing personal interests (negative effect). The person in charge, in a position of power, creates, through this interplay of interests, a cooperative and affinity group around themselves, with which they are able to operate (Crozier and Friedberg 1977). This kind of behaviour can generate tensions and conflicts, thereby hindering the productivity of the company, since it demotivates the linguistic minority members of the work team.

On the other hand, the use of vernacular language in interprofessional and interpersonal relations can have a positive effect in a context of diversity.

> *We are not asking the company to be a tower of 'Babel' with everyone speaking their own language, but at least to recognise that this diversity brings a certain humanity that can move the company forward.* (N, HRD, local)

> *When we arrive in a department and we have the chance to meet a brother from the village, we speak the 'patois' to share small anecdotes.* (C, Senior executive, local)

> *The 'Persian carpet' is often referred to, with its multitude of colours that contribute to its beauty. We should be able to integrate our diversities into the organisation to help it achieve its objectives; it is a source of enrichment.* (N, Employee, local)

> *As in all African businesses, obviously there are people who express their affinity for each other by speaking their 'dialect'. You cannot stop people in a company, in an African context, from speaking their 'dialect'.* (N, Middle manager, local)

These discourses highlight a call to recognise the diversity of languages in Africa, even within ethnic groups. If it is not used for opportunistic and discriminatory purposes, it can contribute to well-being in the workplace. So, it can increase performance.

Age, an Intergenerational Element that Is Difficult to Overcome in Workplace Relationships

The proportion of ageing staff was high in all three case studies. The age pyramid was shaped like a "spinning top", with an average age of 40. The empirical data highlight difficulties in fostering intergenerational collaboration in the companies.

> *There was a lady in my department, she was over 50 years old. She had habits that she did not want to change and was hostile to any change. She said to me: 'Madame, I am used to working like this, I don't want to change'. I fired her because the department's productivity was declining.* (C, Executive senior, Togolese expatriate)

Another example concerns the training of a young employee by a senior colleague, which was decided by their line manager and proved difficult to manage.

> *I have a collaborator who is elderly. He is not willing to teach newcomers, young people what he does. He prefers to handle all his files himself. He can stay in the office until 11 p.m. and come to work on Saturdays and Sundays. He does not mind. The main thing is that he is the only one able to perform certain tasks in the department. He doesn't want to share.* (C, Executive senior, Togolese expatriate)

> *There is tension between young and old people. Elders say that young people do not respect them even when they are their superiors.* (C, Middle manager, local)

> *In our African cultures, the elder has a special place. I have a lot of respect for people older than me. They are the fathers/mothers of families.* (N, HRD, local)

Our observations show that when an older member of staff is entrusted with training a young person in a specific task, if—in the course of the collaboration—a conflict arises between the younger and the older employee, under the pretext of a "lack of respect for the senior", this brings a premature end not only to the training, but also to any projects to develop activities involving the same two employees.

> *Last year, I decided to include training for younger employees in the major annual objectives of an older employee. There was some tension* (refusal to collaborate) *at this level.* (C, Executive senior, Togolese expatriate)

> *Madame, there is a problem. When we go to see our trainer* (elder), *he says he does not have time, that we don't respect him.* (C, Employee, local)

Age is a culturally meaningful characteristic in Africa. If professional relations between young and old employees are generally strained, this is because they are based on strong cultural cleavages. In Africa, elders hold the keys to the transmission of cultural memory regardless of their social or hierarchical status (positive effect). However, in the workplace, older people do not always trust young people and the latter no longer show the respect to their elders expected in the system of African cultural rules (Apitsa 2018a). This creates tensions that affect goal attainment (negative effect). The behaviour of the senior trainer can also be described as opportunistic and irrational (Crozier and Friedberg 1977). This puts the collectivist spirit of African societies and the achievement of common goals in the company to the test. African sociability is built around the idea of community, and thus on the search for a common interest. Here, however, the trainer seeks rather to pursue their own interests (Apitsa 2018a, b). "This suggests that little value has been obtained from age-associated respect, which stems from the transmission of knowledge".

Ethnic Origin, a Fundamental Element in Individuals' Motivations

Cameroon and Nigeria have about 250 and 300 ethnic groups with different cultures represented by the different employees in the company. Ethnic origin refers here to a shared geographical origin. All three multinationals have the same recruitment policy to respect this diversity and recruit based on competence.

> *The concern for us is to find among the candidates those who correspond to our needs. Therefore, ethnicity is not part of our management system* (ethnicity is not important)*; as an element in the choice of a candidate.* (C, Executive, expatriate)

> *All the employees know that I don't want any ethnic discrimination in this company. I don't want to recruit a person because he/she is the brother/sister of the village brother, because he/she is the boyfriend/girlfriend of someone.* (N, Executive, expatriate)

In reality, ethnicity is a strong factor in how local officials recruit staff. They may decide to recruit a given candidate on the basis of ethnicity rather than ability.

> *If you do not take skills into account, if you choose the ethnic group without skills, then it automatically affects the company's development.* (C, Employee, local)

> *As soon as we recruited him, the first information we got was that this candidate was brought to this position by the Deputy General Manager, because he belongs to the same ethnic group. That's how people here are.*
>
> *This recruitment has created a very difficult situation. The person concerned could no longer stand the label* (protégé of the Deputy General Manager) *that had been stuck on him. The damage caused to his skills led him to resign. He said: "I prefer to use my skills elsewhere than to work in such a climate".* (N, HRD, local)

Ethnicity is a feature of diversity. In the workplace, it fuels suspicions of discrimination. If a recruiter uses ethnicity, he or she runs the risk of making it appear that a candidate's supposed competence is no longer mandatory. This is denounced by other local actors who see a family or ethnic motives behind every recruitment. To avoid these suspicions, some officials avoid recruiting family members. However, this attitude is seen as a lack of respect for the system of thought linked with the family in Africa (Apitsa 2018a, b).

> *I prefer to work with people who are not of my ethnicity. People from my ethnicity are willing, if I may say so, to make you angry. It is different with other ethnicities. The other ethnic groups are afraid of your reaction. They are afraid you might fire them. But the guy in the family, he does what he wants. If you want to kick him out, the grandfather in the village will hear it and you will have to answer for it. Whereas if it is someone, I do not have links with, I don't have to account for it.* (C, Executive senior, local)

The system of thought linked to family in Africa imposes a duty of solidarity and mutual aid on individuals, namely, that a family member who has obtained a job must show recognition to their community or family by integrating other members of their family into the company (Hernandez 2000; Mutabazi 2006; Apitsa 2018a, b).

> *If you put family first, your work will be affected. Now if you want to do things normally, everybody wants to help their family, it's only natural. A brother can bring the same productivity. It can be an extra motivating element contained within the family relationship. But if family can be a hindrance to you in your work goals as well, then you have to go after the one who can meet the goals. You have to be discerning, because there are good and bad things about family relationships at work.* (C, Executive senior, local)

This discourse shows the positive and negative effects of ethnic origin in recruitment practices. The executive's comments show that family ties, if mobilised in a positive way, can facilitate the establishment of a climate of trust that promotes productivity. Family members can sacrifice themselves for the collective interest and boost the company's performance. On the other hand, they can also progressively encourage informal and uncontrolled practices that harm the company (underperformance). For example, managers who recruit family members and entrust them with responsibilities may face difficulties if they misuse them (opportunism, deception, cheating).

Gender, a Complex Component of Professional Equality in Africa

In all three of the studied cases, a number of executives (department director, head of department) were women. In fulfilling their roles, they sometimes find it difficult to be heard by their male colleagues.

> *I inherited the management of a department as a young woman, it's not often easy. Even though I have been used to managing men and women, even older than me, it is often difficult, especially in our African cultures where the woman is not expected to command men. It is frowned upon. In this new responsibility, as a woman, I made it clear from the beginning that their ideas were welcome, but that I was not going to be impressed.* (N, Executive senior, local)

Some employees find the presence of female managers useful in the company's hierarchy and in their progression within the company.

> *My manager is a pretty cool boss. Every year, during the work evaluation, she asks if we need an evaluation and why. She asks you questions, whether we are happy with our work. She always asks the HRD* (Human Resource Director) *to take care of her staff's advancement and can even go to the GM* (General Manager) *if nothing is moving.* (C, Employee, local)

In Hofstede's (1980, 2001) cultural model, the gender dimension measures how unequally roles are distributed between men and women in a country. In Africa, the role of women remains chiefly determined by traditional values. This role is associated with the living environment. Women are generally considered pillars of the family.

Religion, a Sensitive Issue at Work

Cameroon is a secular state. There is no state religion. Christians (Protestants and Catholics) represent the main religious force in the country. A quarter of the population declare themselves to be Muslim and another portion of the population practise their own religion. In Nigeria, the two main religions are Christianity and Islam. In contrast with Cameroon, where Catholics predominate (about 30% of the population), in Nigeria, Islam is the country's majority religion (52% of the population practices Islam). In both countries, the constitution protects religious freedom and prohibits discrimination on the basis of religion and ethnicity.

Our observations show that these religions are expressed by individuals in their workplace behaviour. In our sample of respondents, we interviewed an Evangelical pastor, a salaried employee in Cameroon.

> *I have been able to learn from the employees when I send out meditation prayers from time to time, I see all their reactions. Whoever does not accept them, immediately rejects them.* (C, Employee, local)

> *I did not change the company into a church. I am not spreading my faith around. In my church, there are certain colleagues who come.* (C, Employee, local)

> *I never asked permission to carry out my pastoral work. I do not confuse things. I can pray at night for a sick person and focus on my work the next day.* (C, Employee, local)

We observed that Muslim colleagues were also attached to their religious practices, especially on Fridays, for prayers at 1 p.m. and through the wearing of the boubou on Fridays by Cameroonian employees. In Nigeria, boubous are worn every day, including on Fridays for prayers. In the two geographical contexts of the study, the fasting period of Ramadan imposes adjustments to company working hours.

> *If at 4 p.m. you ask your Muslim colleague who is fasting all day during Ramadan, to be as good as he is at 8 a.m., it doesn't work. If you do not understand that he cannot be productive at 4 p.m., it is a waste of time.* All this will impact the social climate and productivity. (N, Executive senior, local)

The practice of religion here establishes patterns of cultural and social identification between individuals. Some religious practices can irritate certain employees (as illustrated by the pastor's comments), disrupting the social climate and leading to an invitation that they should be left on the company's doorstep. Other practices, such as the practice of Islam, are strongly rooted in the country's culture and are taken for granted as part of a shared set of values.

4.2 Discussion

The results of this study contribute to the literature on cross-cultural management and diversity management in Africa. They provide managers working in Africa with an analytical framework with which to interpret and to understand the ethnic cultural interactions of Africans in the workplace.

Our results highlight the ethnic cultural elements in the managerial action of the three companies. Following the sociological approach of Crozier and Friedberg (1977) and the African cultural system (Apitsa 2018b), our study empirically demonstrates that ethnic cultural elements make both positive and negative contributions to managerial action (Fig. 2.1).

For many authors, cultural synergies in the workplace improve effectiveness and efficiency (Mutabazi 2004, 2006; Jackson 2013; Kamdem 2017; Whee Lee and Eunhee 2019). For others, cultural diversity does not necessarily improve performance but can rather be a source of frustration (Prasad and Mills 1997; Chanlat et al. 2013; Keller et al. 2017). While the results and analysis presented support both these findings, they provide the empirical evidence required to understand the dynamics of cultural and ethnic interactions between individuals in African workplaces.

The elements studied (language, age, ethnic origin, gender, religion) show the extent to which the collectivist dimension (Hofstede 1980/2001) is discussed in Africa in training, recruitment, and team management activities (Hofstede 1980/2001). Role and power games interfere and reveal manoeuvring to satisfy individual interests (Crozier and Friedberg 1977; Henry 2009; Apitsa 2016). Moreover, the interaction of vernacular languages shows that the sole use of French and/or English as the official language for intercultural communication is insufficient to ensure a working climate conducive to productivity growth.

The literature analysing the link between culture and management in Africa has concluded that ethnicity is a factor of economic backwardness and organisational underperformance. Our results suggest that ethnic cultural elements should be considered just like culture, as having positive effects but also as potential sources of difficulties (if poorly managed and controlled) in managerial action.

How can ethnic cultural elements be leveraged in managerial action?

5 Conclusion

The highlighting of the dynamics of ethnic cultural interactions between individuals in managerial action is essential to understand the performance of organisations in Africa. At the heart of these processes is the individual, the quintessential element of culture and diversity. Individuals embody a name, a gender, an age, an ethnic origin, a set of beliefs, a way of life, a mother tongue, other languages, and so on.

Moreover, understanding African organisations and their cognitive functions, as well as the reasons and motivations that underlie them, is insufficient if individuals are not placed at the centre of this dynamic (of their social and cultural truths). Our results allow an in-depth approach, through the elements identified (language, age, ethnic origin, religion, gender), to the hidden elements of any culture, and to meet African individuals in their ethnic cultural truths.

In order to take advantage of ethnic cultures and improve social cohesion, and thereby performance, the positive and negative aspects (see Fig. 2.1) of ethnicity in African companies need to be put into context.

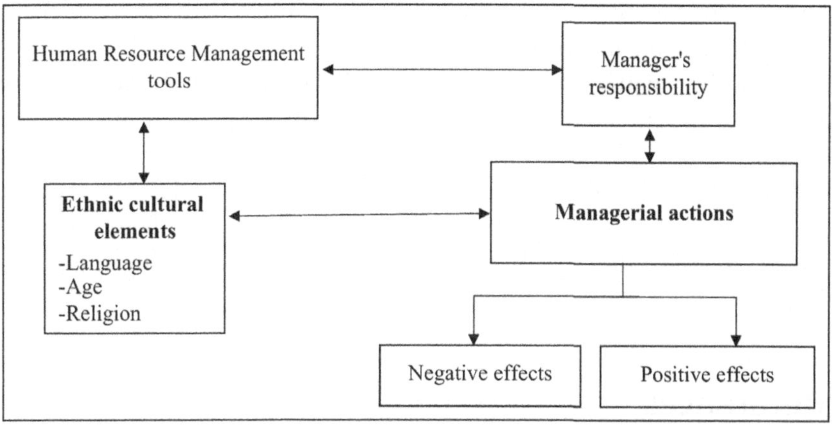

Fig. 2.1 Effects of ethnic cultural elements in managerial action. (Source: Author's creation)

In an environment of cultural and ethnic diversity, the multinationals studied would benefit from setting up transparent communication tools to avoid interference with individual strategies. This transparency in management tools would further guarantee employee motivation and would be beneficial for managerial action.

In African cultures, seniority is valued. Elders are considered to have more experience and knowledge. This age criterion is not mobilised for the common good. In order to create a favourable intergenerational climate, senior employees should be offered a status that would allow them to promote corporate culture. This must be combined with age-related rules and values that make senior colleagues repositories of wisdom, as it is a source of productivity growth and intergenerational and intercultural learning. This should hinder opportunistic reactions and act as a barrier to self-interested behaviours.

We propose to mobilise CSR as a concrete tool for managing cultural and ethnic diversity. This challenge is a real opportunity for collective action, a source of learning about managerial action that is more humane and creates sustainable value. To fully achieve this goal and guarantee certain ethical standards, a company's diversity policy must be translated into visible actions. Giving women responsibilities in key positions is not enough; they should also be afforded the support required to enable them to fulfil their role independently.

Regarding management research in Africa on cultural and diversity issues, studies should evolve towards analyses of the paradox of ethnicity. It is by following this approach that one should be able to understand the internal dynamics of organisations in Africa, question the stereotypical frameworks of thought presented in the literature, and better analyse them. "These studies should not detract from work on the logics governing interactions between individuals".

References

Abou, S. (2002). *L'identité culturelle, suivi de, cultures et droits de l'homme.* Beyrouth: Perrin-PUSJ. Anthropologie.

Amoako-Agyei, E. (2009). Cross-Cultural Management and Organizational Behavior in Africa. *Thunderbird International Business Review, 51*(4), 329–339.

Apitsa, S. M. (2013). L'hybridation des pratiques de GRH à l'international par le truchement de l'ethnicité en Afrique. *Gérer et Comprendre, 113*, 51–61.

Apitsa, S. M. (2016). Renouveler la conception de l'ethnicité pour son ancrage dans le management interculturel en Afrique. In J.-P. Dupuis, J.-P. Lemaire, & E. Milliot (Eds.), *Ancrages culturels dans un monde en mutation* (pp. 37–56). Paris: Vuibert.

Apitsa, S. M. (2018a). Développer les compétences interculturelles à l'aide des systèmes de valeurs dans un contexte spécifique: une plongée dans une multinationale française implantée au Cameroun. *Management International, 22*(3), 24–38.

Apitsa, S. M. (2018b). Les éléments culturels africains pour repenser le management interculturel en Afrique en termes de *crossvergence*. In N. Tournois & P. Very (Eds.), *Internationalisation ouverte* (pp. 41–64). Paris: Vuibert.

Apitsa, S. M., & Amine, A. (2014). L'ethnicité, un levier d'action pertinent du management interculturel des ressources humaines? *Revue Management et Avenir, 70*, 13–35.

Ayoko, O. B., & Härtel, Ch. E. J. (2006). Cultural Diversity and Leadership: A Conceptual Model of Leader Intervention in conflict Events in Culturally Heteregeneous Workgroups. *Cross Cultural Management: An International Journal, 13*(4), 345–360.

Bell, D. (1975). Ethnicity and Social Change. In N. Glazer & D. Moynihan (Eds.), *Ethnicity: Theory and Experience* (pp. 141–174). Cambridge, MA and London: Harvard University Press.

Bentaleb, C., Sahraoui, D., & Sekkak, A. (2012). La diversité dans le contexte du Maroc. In J.-M. Peretti (Ed.), *Encyclopédie des diversités* (pp. 525–532). Cormelles-Le-Royal, EMS.

Bhaskar, R. (1997). *A Realist Theory of Science* (2nd ed. [1st ed., 1975]). London: Verso.

Bhaskar, R. (1998). *The Possibility of Naturalism: A Philosophical Critique of the Contemporary Human Sciences* (3rd ed. [1st ed., 1979]). New York: Routledge.

Carmichael, T., & Rijamampianina, R. (2007). Managing Diversity in Africa. In J. Luiz (Ed.), *Managing Business in Africa: Practical Management Theory for an Emerging Market*. Cape Town: Oxford University Press.

Castles, S. (2000). *Ethnicity and Globalization*. London: Sage.

Chanlat, J.-F. (1990/2007). *L'individu dans l'organisation: les dimensions oubliées*. Québec and Paris: Les Presses de l'Université Laval/Eska.

Chanlat, J.-F., Dameron, S., Dupuis, J.-P., & De Freitas, M. E. (2013). Management et diversité: lignes de tension et perspectives. *Management International, 17*(numéro spécial), 5–13.

Crozier, M., & Friedberg, E. (1977). *L'acteur et le système*. Paris: Seuil.

D'Iribarne, Ph. (1990). L'impossible décentralisation des entreprises africaines. *Revue Française de Gestion*, septembre–octobre, 29–39.

D'Iribarne, P. (2004). Face à la complexité des cultures, le management interculturel exige une approche ethnologique. *Management International, 38*(3), 11–19.

Diomande, M. E. F., & Segal, J.-P. (2019). *Négocier et bien vivre ensemble en contexte ivoirien*. Acte 9ème conférence annuelle d'Atlas AFMI, Le national face au global: nouvelles perspectives pour le management international, Université de Fribourg (Suisse), 17–19 juin, Fribourg, 17p.

Easterly, W., & Levine, R. (1997). Africa Growth Tragedy: Policies and Ethnic Divisions. *Quarterly Journal of Economics, 112*(4), 1203–1250.

Eisenhardt, K. M. (1989). Building Theories from Case Study Research. *The Academy of Management Review, 14*(4), 532–550.

Eisenhardt, K., & Graebner, M. E. (2007). Theory Building from Cases: Opportunities and Challenges. *Academy of Management Journal, 50*(1), 25–32.

Eriksen, T.-H. (1991). The Cultural Context of Ethnic Differences. *Man, 26*(1), 127–144.

Fenton, T.-H. (2010). *Ethnicity* (2nd ed., Revised and updated). Malden and Cambridge: Milton Keynes UK; Polity Press.

Glaser, B., & Strauss, A. (1967). *The Discovery of Grounded Theory. Strategies for Qualitative Research*. Chicago: Aldine.

Gould, J. A., Kulik, C. T., & Sardeshmukh, S. R. (2018). Trickle-Down Effect: The Impact of Female Board Members on Executive Gender Diversity. *Human Resource Management, 57*, 931–945.

Hall, E. T. (1976). *Beyond Culture*. New York: Doubleday.

Hall, S. (2017). *Identités et cultures. politiques des cultural studies* (3è éd.). Paris: Éditions Amsterdam.

Henry, A. (2009). Culture et gestion au Cameroun. In E. Davel, J.-P. Dupuis, & J.-F. Chanlat (Eds.), *Gestion en contexte interculturel: Approches, problématiques, pratiques et plongées*. Québec: PUL. CDROM.

Hernandez, E.-M. (2000). Afrique: l'actualité du modèle paternaliste. *Revue Française de Gestion*, no. 128, mars-avril-mai, 98–106.

Hofstede, G. (1980). *Culture's Consequences*. Beverly Hills, CA: Sage.

Hofstede, G. (2001). *Cultures and Organizations: Software of the Mind*. London: McGraw-Hill.

Hugon, P. (1993). *L'économie de l'Afrique*. Paris: La Découverte.

Jackson, T. (2013). Reconstructing the Indigenous in African Management Research: Implications for International Management Studies in a Globalized World. *Management International Review, 53*(1), 13–38.

Kabou, A. (1991). *Et si l'Afrique refusait le développement?* Paris: L'Harmattan.

Kamdem, E. (1990/2007). Temps et travail en Afrique. In J.-F. Chanlat (Ed.), *L'individu dans l'organisation: les dimensions oubliées* (pp. 231–255). Québec and Paris: Les Presses de l'Université Laval/Eska.

Kamdem, E. (2017). The Challenges of Diversity Management in Africa: The Case of Cameroon. In M. F. Özbilgin & J.-F. Chanlat (Eds.), *Management and Diversity, Perspectives from Different National Contexts International Perspectives on Equality, Diversity, and Inclusion* (Vol. 3, pp. 227–248). Emerald Publishing Limited.

Kamdem, E., & Fouda Ongodo, M. (2007). Faits et méfaits de l'ethnicité dans les pratiques managériales en Afrique. *Gestion 2000, 24*(1), 33–58.

Keller, J., Loewenstein, J., & Yan, J. (2017). Culture, Conditions and Paradoxical Frames. *Organization Studies, 38*(3/4), 539–560.

Kessy, Z. M. (1998). *Culture africaine et gestion de l'entreprise moderne*. Abidjan: NEI-CEDA.

King, N. (2004). Using Templates in the Thematic Analysis of Text. In C. Cassell & G. Symon (Eds.), *Essential Guide to Qualitative Methods in Organizational Research* (pp. 256–270). Thousand Oaks: Sage Publications.

Kundu, S. C., & Turan, M. S. (1999). Managing Cultural Diversity in Future Organizations. *The Journal of Indian Management and Strategy – 8M, 4*(1), 61.

Miles, M., & Huberman, M. (2003). *Analyses des données qualitatives: méthodes en sciences humaines.* Bruxelles: De Boeck.

Milliken, F., & Martins, M. (1996). Searching for Common Threads: Understanding the Multiple Effects of Diversity on Organizational Groups. *Academy of Management Review, 21*(2), 402–424.

Milliot, E. (1999). Les modes de fonctionnement de l'organisation informelle. *Revue Française de Gestion*, no. 125, septembre–octobre, 5–18.

Milliot, E., & Freeman, S. (2015). *Case Study Research in Social Sciences: A Paradigmatic Alignment Framework.* 41st Annual Conference of the European International Business Academy (EIBA), Rio de Janeiro, Brazil, December 1–3, 24p.

Mutabazi, E. (2004). Le management des équipes multiculturelles: l'expérience des équipes afro-occidentales. *Management international, numéro thématique: Cultures, nations et management, 8*(3), 41–54.

Mutabazi, E. (2006). Face à la diversité des cultures et des modes de gestion: le modèle circulatoire de management en Afrique. *Revue Management et Avenir*, no. 10, 179–197.

Nizet, J., & Pichault, F. (2007). *Les Performances des Organisations Africaines. Pratiques de gestion en contexte incertain.* Paris: L'Harmattan.

Nyambegera, M. S. (2002). Ethnicity and Human Resource Management Practice in Sub-Sahara Africa: The Relevance of Managing Diversity Discourse. *International Journal of Human Resource Management, 13*(7), 1077–1090.

Ogbanna, E. (2019). The Uneasy Alliance of Organizational Culture and Equal Opportunities for Ethnic Minority Groups: A British Example. *Human Resources Management Journal, 29*, 309–327.

Patrick, H. A., & Raj Kumar, V. (2012). *Managing Workplace Diversity: Issues and Challenges.* Sage, 1–15.

Pierre, P., Mutabazi, E., & Sadik, Y. (2009). Promouvoir en entreprise des politiques de gestion de la diversité ? Perspectives comparées franco-marocaines. *Revue Camerounaise de Management, 1*(18), 25–44.

Polzer, J., Milton, L., & Swann, W. (2002). Capitalizing on Diversity: Interpersonal Congruence in Small Work Groups. *Administrative Science Quarterly, 47*(2), 296–324.

Prasad, P., & Mills, A. J. (1997). From Showcase to Shadow: Understanding the Dilemmas of Managing Workplace Diversity. In P. Prasad (Ed.), *Managing the Organizational Melting Pot: Dilemmas of Workplace Diversity*. Thousand Oaks: Sage Publications.

Prime, N. (2001). Cultures et mondialisation: l'unité dans la diversité. *Expansion Management Review*, septembre, 53–66.

Prinsloo, E. D. (2000). The African View of Participatory Business Management. *Journal of Business Ethic, 25*(4), 275–286.

Seny Kan, A. K., Apitsa, S. M., & Adegbite, E. (2015). African Management: Concept, Content and Usability. *Society and Business Review, 10*(3), 258–279.

Shore, L.-M., Chung-Herrera, B.-G., Dean, M.-A., Holcombe, E. K., Jung, D.-I., Randel, A.-E., & Singh, G. (2009). Diversity in Organizations: Where Are We Now and Where Are We Going? *Human Resource Management Review, 19*, 117–133.

Tajfel, H., & Turner, J. C. (1986). The Social Identity Theory of Intergroup Behaviour. In S. Worchel & W.-G. Austin (Eds.), *Psychology of Intergroup Relations* (pp. 7–24). Chicago: Nelson-Hall.

Thomas, R. R. (2004). *Diversity Management and Affirmative Action: Past Present and Future*. Thomas & Associates, Inc.

Walsh, J. P. (2015). Organization and Management Scholarship in and for Africa […] and the World. *Academy of Management Perspectives, 29*(1), 1–6.

Warner, W., & Srole, L. (1945). *The Social Systems of American Ethnic Groups*. New Haven: Yale University Press.

Welch, C., Piekkari, R., Plakoyiannaki, E., & Paavilainen-Mäntymäki, E. (2011). Theorizing from Case Studies: Towards a Pluralist Future for International Business Research. *Journal of International Business Studies, 42*(5), 740–762.

Whee Lee, H., & Eunhee, K. (2019). Workforce Diversity and Firm Performance: Relational Coordination as a Mediator and Structural Empowerment and Multisource Feedback as Moderators. *Human Resource Management, 59*, 5–23.

Yanat, Z., & Scouarnec, A. (Eds.). (2005). *Perspectives sur la GRH au Maghreb: Algérie-Maroc-Tunisie*. Paris: Vuibert.

Zoogah, D. B., Peng, M. W., & Woldu, H. (2015). Institutions, Resources, and Organizational Effectiveness in Africa. *Academy of Management Perspectives, 29*(1), 7–31.

Part I

Internationalisation Process

3

The Paradoxes of Coopetitive Integration in Madagascar: An Approach Based on the Actor-Network Theory

Gilde Ralandison, Eric Milliot, and Victor Harison

1 Introduction

Confronted with the turbulences of business circles, some enterprises sometimes decide to cooperate with some of their competitors. Thus, they develop coopetition relationships which are contradictory by nature. Indeed, *coopetition is defined as a paradoxical relationship between two or more actors who are simultaneously involved in both cooperation and*

This chapter has been published in French. The reference is as follows. Gilde Ralandison, Eric Milliot, Victor Harison, "Les paradoxes de l'intégration coopétitive. Une approche fondée sur la sociologie de la traduction", *Revue française de gestion*, 2018, N°270, p. 127–142. Published with the kind permission of Lavoisier SAS.

G. Ralandison • V. Harison
National Institute of Accounting Sciences and Business Administration (INSCAE), Antananarivo, Madagascar

E. Milliot (✉)
University of Nantes, Nantes, France
e-mail: emilliot@poitiers.iae-france.fr

S. M. Apitsa, E. Milliot (eds.), *Doing Business in Africa*, Palgrave Studies of Internationalization in Emerging Markets,
https://doi.org/10.1007/978-3-030-50739-8_3

competition interactions, regardless of their horizontal or vertical dimension (Bengtsson and Kock 2014, p. 25).

Coopetition is particularly interesting to study when it is put in parallel with the logic of integration, even partial, of the parties involved. This integration can be relative to enterprises traditionally in competition, but also some external stakeholders (governmental authorities, intermediaries of international trade, etc.). This type of interactive partnership which is based on relatively stable integration of different protagonists is qualified in this chapter as *integrated coopetition*. In this context, the paradoxes related to the integration of various actors are identified on two levels.

- The relational mode developed within the cluster. The postures can be appreciated on a continuum linking two contradictory notions: competition and/or cooperation.
- The objective of the actors involved in the cluster. This objective can be based on a parallel continuum linking, here again, two contradictory situations: the formal non-integration of legally independent entities and/or the formal integration of legally independent entities.

To empirically analyse these two coopetitive paradoxes, we have studied for three years two clusters of small and medium-sized enterprises (SMEs) of the essential oil industry in Madagascar. These clusters, evolving in a context of geographic proximity, have been developed in 1996 to face the proliferation of intermediaries and the strong asymmetries of means between the actors involved. These two embedded cases convey complementary situations: a cluster is a simple associative structure (formal non-integration) while the other has developed a common structure (formal integration). By putting those two network types in parallel, we try to answer the following research question: How to set up a system of management of the coopetitive paradoxes related to the integration process of different actors within a collective structure?

In this objective, we have adopted as a theoretical framework the sociology of translation (the Actor-Network Theory) which originates from the works of Callon and Latour (1981), Callon (1986), Callon and Law (1997), and so on. This theory helps analyse, in a longitudinal manner, a phenomenon under construction or in evolution. It offers a frame for thinking enabling to distinguish the logic of integration, rationality and managerial coherence.

To structure our thinking, this chapter is divided into four parts. The first one defines the outlines of the concept of integrated coopetition and presents the two cases which enabled its emergence. The second one relates to the theoretical framework mobilised and the methodology retained to establish a model of management of paradoxes linked with coopetitive integration. The third one presents the empirical results from these case studies. The fourth one verifies the relevance of the advanced concept and the solidity of the grid study developed.

2 Outlines of the Concept of Integrated Coopetition and Emergence Context

Adopting both an inductive and an abductive approach at the same time, we have seen the progressive integration of different actors involved in two coopetitive linkups in the essential oil sector in Madagascar, based on archive, interview, and observations analyses.

2.1 The Articulation of the Notions of Coopetition and Integration

In this chapter, we consider that coopetition is founded on interaction modes that are conducive to a more or less formal integration of the parties involved. These modes express a complex network of actors influenced by the intermediation of third-party human actors (representatives of enterprises and external stakeholders) and non-human (a polycephalic governance, a common structure for all members of the agreement, etc.). In this context, integrated coopetition is defined as a relatively stable link-up of directly and/or indirectly competitor actors through common values and under the authorities of a shared formal and/or informal structure. This definition invites us to associate the paradox of the relational mode (competition/cooperation) to that of the objective of the actors involved (non-integration/integration). The dichotomisation of possible options encloses organisations in contradictory forms of logics which mutually nurture each other. Indeed, integrated coopetition leads very often to an uncomfortable situation which results from the opportunism of some coopetitors, of the difficult development of common competitive advantages, of the complex sharing of incomes resulting from it, and so on. Guedri et al. (2014, p. 20) consider that *the existence and the maintenance of paradox can favour a logic of joint construction of a shared vision which will facilitate the adoption and adhesion of different communities of actors*. Hence, as Grimand et al. (2014, p. 146) pointed out, *the management through paradox appears as a relevant mode of regulation* (non-integration/integration) *of these contradictions* (competition/cooperation), *much more than the figure of the dilemma or that of compromise*. In that logic, this research is interested in the management dynamism of joint construction taking into consideration different intra-organisation (coopetitive) and inter-organisation (integrative) paradoxes. To assess the possible impact of this logic of joint construction, we will present the cases selected for our study.

2.2 An Empirical Approach Based on Inductive and Abductive Inferences

To conduct this research, two cases of clusters of small and medium-sized enterprises (SMEs), evolving in a context of geographic proximity and operating in the field of essential oils in Madagascar, have been selected: the Amoron'I Mania (AM) case and the Matsiatra Ambony (MA) case. Table 3.1 shows us the complementarity of selected clusters for the qualitative and longitudinal analysis of the integration of involved parties. In the AM case, SMEs do not have a formal management structure yet; the study is geared towards the capacity of the members to commit to long-term coopetition. In the MA case, an integrated structure called Platform of Consultation and Support to the Field (PCAF) was established; it enables observing the behaviour of the actors in the appropriation or not of a formal device of collective management of the coopetition.

The differences between the two cases help highlight the conditions of transcending the coopetition contradictions (adoption of a competitive

Table 3.1 Comparison of the AM and MA cases

Characteristics	Amoron'I Mania (AM) case	Matsiatra Ambony (MA) case
Products exploited	Geranium	Ravintsara
Historical background	Sector launched in 1996 at the initiative of local producers and exporters to meet the needs of the market	Sector launched in 1996 at the initiative of financial partners within a rural development programme
Organisation	Organisation not formally integrated and made up of 345 farmers	Organisation formally integrated (creation of an integrated structure [PCAF]) made up of 2028 farmers and 32 distillation points)
Strategic orientation	Development strategy focused on a spatial approach (progressive extension of cultivated areas and controlled origin certification)	Development strategy focused on link-up between operators-producers and market operators

Source: Authors' creation

logic [identified essentially in the AM case] and/or a cooperative logic [identified essentially in the MA case]). The similarities emphasise the junction points regarding the integration of actors. Indeed, the problematic to be solved in both cases remains the same: those linked to power asymmetry, to legitimacy, and to the protection of resources and competences (Table 3.1).

3 Mobilised Theoretical Framework and Methodology Selected to Develop an Adapted Model

To study the conditions of transcending of paradoxes associated with coopetition agreements, the theoretical framework offered by the Actor-Network Theory is particularly relevant. Indeed, this theory proposes to understand the social fact as the consequence of successive interactions between human and/or non-human *actants* (objects, practices, management tools, etc.) and is therefore adapted to study in a longitudinal manner collective and reticulated projects. To complement this theoretical framework, we have adopted the method of *contextualised explanation* (Welch et al. 2011), which enables the analytical description of a complex phenomenon based on inductive and/or abductive inferences. From regular participant and non-participant observation, this theoretical and methodological framework allows us to develop a descriptive and causal modelling regarding the management of paradoxes linked to coopetitive integration.

3.1 Recourse to the Actor-Network Theory

To develop our research, we have selected the analysis framework of the Actor-Network Theory adapted by Meier et al. (2012). These authors have taken the classical theory developed by Callon and Latour (1981), Callon (1986), Callon and Law (1997), and so on, by distinguishing the static (non-recurring) and dynamic (longitudinal) aspect of the translation process. This framework enables a description of the emergence of consensus within an inter-organisational network, the consensus over which can be described here as the origin of the stabilisation of that network by transcending the identified paradoxes.

The first step in the framework of Meier et al. (2012) is punctual and consists of carrying out a morphologic study of the *initial* network in order to assess the *degree of convergence* of coopetitors towards a consensus. Thus, it identifies the *poles* which the network is made up of and the intermediaries making the connection between those poles. The latter are clusters of *actants*, both human and non-human (Callon 1986; Callon and Law 1997). Throughout this phase, the roles of the poles within the network are specified. Moreover, the *mandatory waypoints*—the essential phases to be accepted in order to solve problems (Callon 1986)—are identified.

The second step in the framework of Meier et al. (2012) is longitudinal and consists of assessing the evolution of paradoxical relationships within the clusters identified during the integration of actors into a coopetitive structure. For this purpose, the Actor-Network Theory suggests the identification of *controversies* (relating to the asymmetries between actors) and the *spokespersons* (actors involved in the negotiations) associated with the project. The authors of this theory confirm, indeed, that only controversies are likely to evolve the network and change its trajectory by challenging the status quo.

In order to examine the controversies characterising an innovative project, it is possible to take the main phases of the translation chain developed in the theory. These phases are essentially problematisation, incentive, enrolment, and mobilisation (Callon 1986). In this chapter, punctualisation (Callon and Law 1997) is added to ensure the stabilisation of the integrated network within a coopetition agreement (Table 3.2).

This framework of analysis puts into perspective the structure of the network and its components in a static (punctual) and dynamic (longitudinal) way. The static analysis identifies the different clusters which the

Table 3.2 The phases of a translation chain

Phases	Relationships with coopetitive clusters
1. Problematisation (analysis of a problem for which one or many actors suggest a solution)	Cluster(s) of actors in order to deal with the proliferation of intermediaries Strong asymmetries of means between the actors involved
2. Incentive (process of persuasion enabling the stabilisation of the relations between the actors potentially *interested* by the proposed solution)	Identification of the interests of the actors to reach a common project Process enabling the establishment of alliances
3. Enrolment (solutions and relational modes selected to accompany the incentive of relevant actors)	Development of common projects based on an accepted division of roles Alliances leading to the stabilisation of the roles of *actants*
4. Mobilisation (process ensuring that all the enrolled actors represent the interests of all the relevant actors)	Selection of intermediaries (spokespersons) Establishment of a formal and/or informal integration process
5. Punctualisation (the sum of *actants* is considered as a whole, which becomes a referent for the interlocutor)	Management of the interactions between direct/indirect actors and the components of the integrated structure Development of common structures and shared tools

Source: Authors' creation

network is made up of, the (human) intermediaries who can animate the network, as well as the incentive of those actors. Dynamic analysis enables the study of the resolution of controversies and the role of intermediaries (human and non-human) intervening in transcending paradoxes. Concretely, this framework enables the identification of:

- The formal or informal nature of the network by focusing on the clusters, intermediaries, and incentive (static analysis).
- The follow-up of the trajectory of integration of its components by following the process of solving the controversies and the evolution of the roles of intermediaries (dynamic analysis).

The theory mobilised, thus, enables, from successive interactions between human/non-human *actants*, to identify the mechanisms of construction of a collective project.

3.2 Methodological Approach Selected

Regarding the theorisation method based on case studies, we have selected that of *contextualised explanation* (Welch et al. 2011), which emphasises both context analysis and the study of causal relationships. This method is characterised by a praxeological project associated with a descriptive and causal research (Milliot and Freeman 2015). Based on inductive and abductive inferences, our analysis starts thus with the studied reality (archives, interviews, and observations) in order to establish, from a critical literature review, a predictive and explanatory model on the management of paradoxes inherent to coopetitive clusters.

In order to access the most precise information, forty interviews (ten of them open and thirty semi-structured) have been conducted with the main actors of the clusters. The average duration of the interviews was one hour for open interviews and two hours for semi-structured ones. We have interviewed the ten actors considered as leaders of the development poles twice (five for the AM case and five for the MA case). One of the main leaders of each cluster (one for AM and one for MA) has been interviewed on five occasions by following the actual process of integration of coopetitors. These interviews took place from April 2013 to August 2015.

In parallel, we have consulted the archives in order to have a more precise image of the historical background of the studied clusters. Finally, participant and non-participant observations have been carried out regularly to identify the interactions between *actants* within the clusters.

To conduct the static/dynamic analyses of the integration of actors inside coopetitive clusters, we have classified and organised data beforehand. The interviews have been recorded and transcribed. The observations and archive consultations were subject to a logbook. The software Nvivo 10 has been used to process and interpret data.

Putting the two cases in parallel has enabled the identification of saturation points relating to coopetitive paradoxes (asymmetries, legitimacies, polycephalic governance, etc.) related to the Actor-Network Theory, and the links between these points to transcend coopetitive integrative paradoxes. These points and links have enabled us to develop a management model of paradoxes relating to coopetitive integration.

3.3 Proposition of a Management Model of Paradoxes Related to Coopetitive Integration

This research is about the paradoxical logic of integration which can change actor dynamics in terms of objectives, interpersonal relationships, knowledge, and so on. The model which results from that is structured in five fields. These fields represent the phases of translation of the integrative process.

- The *anchoring field* enables the identification of the conditions of management of paradoxes, resulting from the integration of actors. At this level, the consideration of non-human *actants* (relationship between actors, formal and informal aspects of the organisation, etc.) enables an assessment of the coopetitive cluster.
- The *pivot field* enables spotting the actors (direct, indirect, institutional, etc.) who can help face the paradoxes identified in the anchoring field. It aims at *mobilising* intermediaries in the formal and/or informal implementation of the integration process.

- The *impact field* enables the *problematisation* related to the logics of integration. These logics are characterised by the possible multiplication of intermediaries that seek solutions to transcend asymmetries (of means, access to information, etc.) between the actors involved. The intermediaries selected in the pivot field thus *translate* the paradoxes identified in controversies of integration (which can be related to matters of legitimacy, sharing, or protection of resources and competences, etc.) to be managed.
- The *leverage field* involves human and non-human *actants* that enable a solution to the coopetitive paradoxes by referring to different legitimacies (institutional, contractual, or on the market). These *actants* thus bind to enrol the parties potentially involved, by involving the spokespersons (representatives from producers, exporters, institutions, etc.)
- The *action field* aims at institutionalising (under the form of a common structure) the contributions of *actants* in the management of paradoxes. It depends on the *incentive* of the parties involved to reach a common project.

As we can observe, the initial order of translation phases (Callon 1986; Callon and Law 1997) has been changed in order to identify and manage the paradoxes characterising a coopetitive agreement. Indeed, in this specific relational context, another chain of translation can be considered. To justify this new chain, two proposals are brought forward. The first one (that at the beginning), located at the level of the anchorage field of the model, supposes that the capacity of SMEs to adopt a strategy of coopetition is acquired and can be a base of punctualisation for the formed network. The second one (that at the end), located at the level of the action field, states that the adhesion to a common structure is a mandatory waypoint in the management of paradoxes related to coopetitive integration. The association of those two proposals refers to a translation process which enables:

- An understanding regarding how one can go from a cluster of actors in competitions to a body of *actants* which can be perceived as a whole.

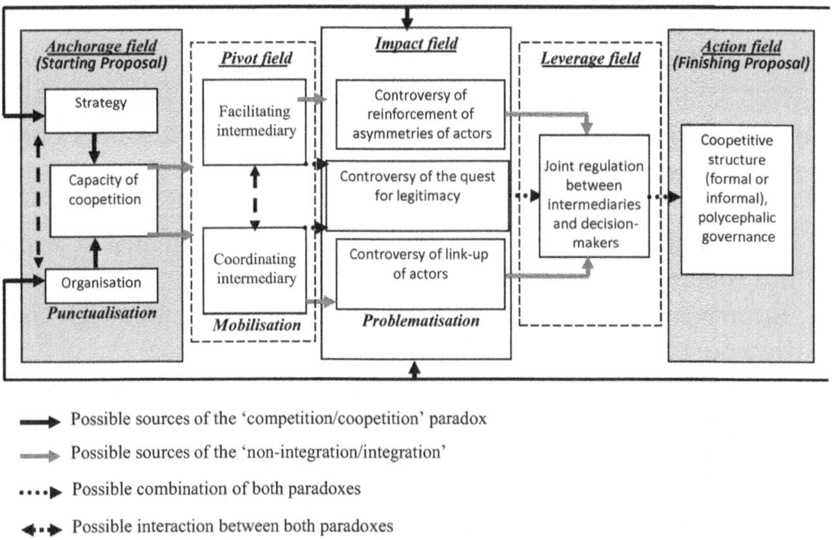

Fig. 3.1 Model for paradox management of the integration into a coopetitive structure. (Source: Authors' creation)

- Identification and management of the controversies of coopetition related to the paradoxical association of logics of competition/cooperation/and non-integration/integration.

The resolution of those controversies concerns mainly three fields: the pivot field which characterises the mobilisation phase, the impact field which made the problematisation emerge, and the leverage field which is associated with the enrolment phase. The model which results from this process is presented in Fig. 3.1. It has been validated by all actors, direct and indirect, of both clusters studied.

4 Main Managerial Contributions of the Model

To measure the managerial implications of this model, it is necessary to highlight the process of punctualisation of the cluster and the management modes adapted to the paradoxes of coopetition.

4.1 A Punctualisation Process Structured in Five Poles

To reach the punctualisation phase, the proposed model identifies a process structured in five poles.

- The *contextualisation* pole outlines the integration potential of actors in a coopetitive cluster.
- The *intermediation* pole measures the degree of potential strategic convergence between the actors involved.
- The *integration* pole identifies the divergence and/or convergence points of the members regarding the resolution of problems related to coopetitive paradoxes.
- The *regulation* pole groups the control operations entrusted to the spokespersons (coordinating and facilitating intermediaries, regulators, representatives of the market, etc.).
- The *shared structure* pole helps find a consensus at the level of relevant actors.

This process offers a structured managerial framework to manage the paradoxical logics related to the coopetitive clusters formally and/or informally integrated. The phases of the process have been subject to a static analysis (punctual state) and to a dynamic analysis (evolution in time) for the two cases selected. The logic of actors observed shows that the first paradox (competition/cooperation) conditions the second paradox (non-integration/integration). Therefore, we will specify this point for each case studied, considering that the AM case fits a static analysis while the MA case is adapted to a dynamic analysis.

Static Analysis of the AM Case

The actors of the AM case are characterised by the adoption of a rather competitive logic that prevents actual progress in the collective project. This trend is illustrated by the words of the direct actors and the facilitating intermediaries (Table 3.3).

Table 3.3 Illustration of the propensity to competition (AM case)

Verbatim	Actors (human)	*Actants* (non-human)	Poles of punctualisation
The producers of green mass can prefer exclusivity contracts (organised proximity) over common-law contracts (cultural proximity) already established	Direct actor (export)	Exclusivity contracts and common-law contracts	Contextualisation
We intervene within link-up—between the market operators and producing operators—dictated by the development plan of the industry. We prohibit any behaviour against this framework	Indirect actor (representative of the Chamber of Commerce and Industry)	Development plan of the industry	Intermediation
We do not hesitate to engage further in this shared structure if we are given the visibility on its contributions in terms of profit and security	Direct actor (producer of leaves)	Specifications proposed to the exporters	Integration
A regulation must be set up between the exporters and the producers. It would enable those actors to reduce the risks on the versatility of partners and to guarantee a better flow of information	Indirect actor (representative of a support organisation)	Rules of procedure governing the existing associations and cooperatives	Regulation
The governance of a structure should enable finding a common ground to anticipate the terms of the negotiation with the decision-makers on the market	Direct actors (oil producer)	Polycephalic governance not formally set up	Shared structure

Source: Authors' creation

To illustrate the propensity to competition of some actors of the AM cluster, we take the three fields that interest us for the static analysis.

- At the level of the anchorage field, integration is mostly influenced by the strategic choice of the managers of the SMEs. On the one hand, this choice results from a relationship of geographic or economic proximity with coopetitors. And on the other hand, this choice depends on the personality traits of the leaders. A manager can be tempted to exploit to their benefit a situation by considering as secondary the impact of this choice on the cluster.
- At the level of the impact field, the members are confronted by a power relation and asymmetry problem (of means, information, etc.). Indeed, some SMEs tend to reinforce their strategic position within the group at the expense of their partners. This reinforcement can be translated into the willingness to control—at least partially—the collective value chain.
- At the level of the action field, the shared structure which encourages integration can be considerably impacted by the presence of coopetitors that want to impose themselves in the governance to serve their own interests.

Characterised by competition behaviours impeding the progressive integration of members, the AM case is well suited to the static analysis of a coopetitive agreement. Indeed, the pivot and leverage fields which enable an assessment of the conditions of evolution of a cluster in terms of practice (competition/cooperation) and engagement (non-integration/integration) are not formally illustrated.

Dynamic analysis of the MA case. As for the actors of the MA case, they develop more collaborative logics. Many direct actors and coordinating intermediaries confirm in verbatim the trend of the involved parties to cooperate (Table 3.4).

To concretely illustrate the evolution of postures in this cluster, we take the three key fields of the model.

- At the level of the anchoring field, the propensity to integration within a coopetitive cluster is influenced by the strategic choices of firms'

Table 3.4 Illustration of the propensity to cooperation (MA case)

Verbatim	Actors (human)	Actants (non-human)	Poles of punctualisation
This industry is marked by many attempts of reorganisation (to facilitate cooperation)	Direct actor (leaf producer)	Common structure	Contextualisation
The common structure has enabled a fruitful collaboration at the level of actor producers by reducing the information asymmetry and by getting them closer to the market operators	Indirect actor (president of the PCAF)	Common structure	Intermediation
The shared structure is supposed to be a place for exchange, valuing and protecting resources and competences between the actors of the industry	Direct actor (oil producer)	Common structure	Integration
We intervene to defend the actors' choice in the pooling of resources and competences by proposing regional decrees protecting the exploited area, the occupants (owner of the land and leaf cultivators), *and the operators* (processors)	Indirect actor (support organisation)	Rules within the existing structure	Regulation
The advantage of the structure is to have representatives for each type of actor in the industry	Direct actor (exporter)	Shared coordination formally established	Shared structure

Source: Authors' creation

managers. The postures, on the continuum from cooperation to coopetition, depend more on the long-term action plan of enterprise members than on the temper of the managers.

- At the level of the impact field, these SMEs are confronted with a situation of uncertainty in terms of protection of resources and competences. They are ready to engage in collective action if the expected advantages are greater than the estimated threats.

- At the level of the action field, the participation of these SMEs in a coopetitive structure is generally considered as positive. Yet, SMEs are sometimes distrustful towards collective governance. They can be confused by the coordination put in place. Moreover, access to information is not egalitarian between the members of the permanent board (that only get the information during general assemblies), the coordinators (that are the emitters of information and are in direct contact with producers), the executive committee (which is the direct connection with exporters and which transmits information from coordinators).

This collaborative spirit, which invites actors to make their cluster evolve together, enables a dynamic analysis of coopetitive integration. Indeed, the *actants* which make up the pivot and leverage fields are formally represented. This formal aspect helps, on the one hand, to follow up on the posture changes of the parties identified in the static approach and, on the other hand, to appreciate the impact of the interventions of these actors/*actants* on the coopetitive cluster.

4.2 Management Modes Adapted to the Paradoxes of Coopetition

As seen earlier, the paradoxes that characterise a coopetition agreement invite us to refer to the five phases of the proposed model. The management modes that come out can particularly be assessed on three levels of the impact field: the reduction of asymmetries between actors, the reinforcement of the connection between the involved parties, and the consolidation of the legitimacies of the collective action.

The Reduction of Asymmetries Between Actors

This first element of the impact field is mostly illustrated in the AM case. It is the result of competitive attitudes identified in the anchorage field. These attitudes show, namely, in a context of asymmetries between actors. As seen previously, the personality of the managers and their intra-group power games sometimes represent an opportunism which impedes coopetitive integration.

Intermediation and regulation can limit, or even reduce, those asymmetries. The decision-making intermediary (member of the cluster) constitutes a pivot representing the members of the cluster to find solutions to the individualist attitudes considered as prejudicial to collective action. At the same time, the joint regulation (Reynaud 1999) is a leverage to manage requests from the matchmaking intermediary (non-member of the cluster). It is at the level of the action field, via a polycephalic governance, that it is possible to control the negotiation power of competitive actors and to limit the denounced asymmetries.

The Reinforcement of the Connections Between the Parties Involved

This second element of the impact field is rather observed in the MA case. The link-up of the members, identified in the anchorage field, is indeed associated with the risks involved by the pooling of some resources and/or competence. Three types of actors/*actants* can intervene in the resolution of disagreement. The first type is about the managers of cooperative SMEs who, by getting closer to competitors, find themselves in a position of vulnerability (collection of sensitive information, identification of potential weaknesses, etc.). The second characterises the managers who must make a strategic choice regarding the pooling or not of resources and/or competences. This point brings us back to the intervention of the third *actant*, which is the system of resource and competence protection.

To facilitate the link-up of actors, two intermediary profiles are identified here: the coordinator and the regulator.

- The coordinator plays a role of pivot (as a spokesperson) of cooperative actors.
- The regulator insures the role of leverage for implementation of a system for protection of resources and/or competences.

This system is an action field aiming at reinforcing the strategic positions of the cooperating members within the shared coordination planned by the structure.

Consolidation of the Legitimacies of the Collective Action

The third element in the impact field is common to both cases studied. It determines the key convergence points for the actors: institutional and contract legitimacies and those related to the market. Four groups of *actants* intervene here.

- The managers of SMEs tend to influence the choice of rules conditioning the coopetition.
- The spokespersons implement the negotiations on the interaction standards within the coopetition.
- The contracts define the limit of the coopetitive relation.
- The market can intervene in terms of standards and objectives to respect.

To reinforce those legitimacies, three groups of intermediaries are sought.

- The facilitating intermediary rationalises the request from actors adopting a competitive attitude.
- The coordinating intermediary defends the strategic position of cooperative actors.
- Double intermediaries (both facilitating and coordinating) encourage dialogue, through a joint regulation, between third-party actors (like importers or standard setters).

From the resolution of paradoxes, the relational mode (competition/cooperation) and the objective (non-integration/

integration), can therefore spring a convergence on the rules of functioning of the structure to be implemented.

5 Discussions on the Proposals Brought Forward in the Model

To grasp all the stakes of the model developed, it is appropriate to take the initial and finishing proposals. The starting proposal is about the context of the management of paradoxes. The finishing proposal advocates the need for an integrative structure. Those two proposals highlight the conditions of punctualisation, that is, the conditions enabling actors/*actants* to be considered as a whole. They also facilitate the identification of a mandatory waypoint, in the process of translation, to formally structure coopetition.

5.1 Adoption of a Joint Regulation: Source of Punctualisation

For the studied clusters, integration is linked to the emergence of rules (spatial and temporal dispatching of exploitations, exclusivity contracts, etc.). This emergence enables viewing integrated coopetition as a dynamic process subjected to social exchanges that are not reduced to individual optimisation logics. The adoption of rules, which conditions the collegial management of the cluster, characterises the punctualisation phase. It also enables the management of controversies related to the construction of a coopetitive structure (asymmetries, resource/competence protection, and legitimacies) and setting up interaction standards involving actors/*actants* (market, decision-makers, and intermediaries) to reach stable, or even irreversible, consensuses.

Regarding the MA case, punctualisation is materialised by a formal collective structure (PCAF) set up in 2013. The dialogues between the facilitating intermediary and the coordinating intermediary (in the upstream part of the integration process) interpret a double intermediation. This double intermediation aims, at the level of the leverage field, to specify the conditions regarding the set-up of joint regulation to *punctualise* the integration of the parties involved.

5.2 Involvement of the Engaged Parties: Mandatory Waypoint

The involvement of the stakeholders entails moving from problematisation (identification and analysis of paradoxes) to mobilisation (setup of an integration process to solve those paradoxes). This involvement thus translates a *mandatory waypoint.*

For the AM case, this waypoint is not located at the end of the translation process because the formal integration is not fully complete. Indeed, for now, this waypoint is only observed in the anchorage field of the model as a result of the initiatives from local actors wishing to reorganise the industry. It should be noted that the actors from the AM cluster have already set shared objectives (EcoCert certification of the products, for instance) without passing through a formally integrated structure.

For the MA case, this waypoint is materialised by a formal coopetitive structure (PCAF) located in the action field of the model. The management of paradoxes within this structure is ensured by a polycephalic governance. In fact, the creation of a coopetitive structure enables limiting the uncertainty areas regarding the management of paradoxes linked to the integration of actors. Indeed, the polycephalic characteristics of the governance sometimes moderate under the authority of an intermediary the competitive attitudes of some actors.

6 Conclusion

As we mentioned at the beginning of this chapter, the paradoxes of coopetition is based on two complementary dimensions:

- The relational mode developed within the cluster (competition/cooperation)
- The objective of the involved actors (non-integration/integration)

In order to understand the way in which those coopetitive paradoxes are managed, we have developed a predictive and explanatory model identifying the development and construction phases of a collective project based on the Actor-Network Theory. Our empirical research shows that the two paradoxical dimensions of coopetition are structured in a sequential way. In the studied clusters, the relational mode conditions the objectives of the actors.

- In the AM case, the competitive logic hinders the community objective. It produces a limited and non-structured integration of the involved parties.
- In the MA case, coopetitive logic facilitates the formal integration of engaged parties. The implementation of a polycephalic governance and the development of a common structure (PCAF) characterise this integration.

The parallelisation of these clusters confirms the need for convergence of the interests of the involved parties, the need for a shared incentive, the importance of intermediation roles and joint regulation. The evolution of integrated coopetition is thus seen throughout the resolution of the identified paradoxes. This resolution passes by a control of competitive behaviours and a rationalisation of cooperative attitudes within the cluster. At the end of the processing of those paradoxes, the strategy of the actors can be redefined, and the management of the integrated coopetition can be adapted.

This research, based on a rich and complex phenomenon, could be complemented on two main levels:

1. The paradoxes analysed in this chapter are part of a specific context: that of the geographical proximity clusters in Madagascar. It would be interesting to study international and multicultural coopetitive agreements.
2. The analysis is only about producers and exporters at the level of the value chain. However, the essential oil industry is not limited to this perimeter and other stakeholders (international standard setters, consumer syndicates, etc.) could be integrated.

The management model of the paradoxes of coopetitive integration proposed in this chapter has been validated by all the stakeholders in both studied clusters. Nevertheless, to check the reproducibility of the conclusions it drew, on the one hand, it should be tested by studying the other forms of coopetition, and, on the other hand, other studies should be conducted on other actor profiles. It would help understand in a more concrete way the multiple interactions experienced within the coopetitive network.

References

Bengtsson, M., & Kock, S. (2014). Coopetition – Quo Vadis? Past Accomplishments and Future Challenges. *Industrial Marketing Management, 43*(2), 180–188.

Callon, M. (1986). Éléments pour une sociologie de la traduction. La domestication des coquilles Saint-Jacques et des marins-pêcheurs dans la baie de Saint-Brieuc. *L'année Sociologique, 36*, 169–207.

Callon, M., & Latour, B. (1981). Unscrewing the Big Leviathan: How Actors Macro-Structure Reality and How Sociologists Help Them to Do So. In K. D. Knorr-Cetina & A. V. Cicourel (Eds.), *Advances in Social Theory and Methodology* (pp. 277–303). London: Routledge and Kegan Paul.

Callon, M., & Law, J. (1997). L'irruption des non-humains dans les sciences humaines: quelques leçons tirées de la sociologie des sciences et des techniques. In B. Reynaud (Ed.), *Les limites de la rationalité, Tome 2: Rationalité, éthique et cognition* (pp. 99–118). Paris: La Découverte.

Grimand, A., Derumez, I. V., & Schäfer, P. (2014). Manager les paradoxes de la RSE. Le déploiement de la norme ISO 26000 dans une ETI. *Revue française de gestion, 40*(240), 133–148.

Guedri, Z., Hussler, C., & Loubaresse, E. (2014). Contradictions, paradoxes et tensions en contexte(s). *Revue française de gestion, 40*(240), 13–28.

Meier, O., Missonier, A., & Missonier, S. (2012). Analyse des systèmes d'interactions à l'oeuvre au sein d'un projet TI: mise en evidence d'une perspective dynamique et relationnelle. *Système d'Informations et Management, 17*(1), 7–48.

Milliot, E., & Freeman, S. (2015). Case Study Research in Social Sciences: A Paradigmatic Alignment Framework. Proceedings of the 41th Annual Conference of the European International Business Academy (EIBA), Rio de Janeiro, Brazil, December 1–3.

Reynaud, J.-D. (1999). *Le conflit, la négociation et la règle* (2nd ed.). Toulouse: Octarès éditions.

Welch, C., Piekkari, R., Plakoyiannaki, E., & Paavilainen-Mäntymäk, E. (2011). Theorizing from Case Studies: Towards a Pluralist Future for International Business Research. *Journal of International Business Studies, 42*(5), 740–762.

4

Factors Influencing the Export Commitment of SMEs: Algerian Case

Mohamed Kadi

1 Introduction

For many authors, quality research in developing countries is difficult to achieve (Daoud 2010; Haddoud et al. 2019). Indeed, researching SME exporters in a country like Algeria, where information is a major barrier, represents a real challenge for researchers. The analysis of the different dimensions of Algerian export SMEs, namely, characteristics such as the commitment to export or their performance, is made difficult due to lack of information and availability of reliable data (Kadi 2019).

In Algeria, although the economy is dominated by 97% of SMEs, their participation in non-hydrocarbon exports remains marginal. In this sense, based on the statistics of the National Agency for Promotion of Foreign Trade and those of the Chamber of Commerce and Industry of 2018, the Algerian economy has nearly 800 SME exporters concentrated mainly in the petrochemicals, agri-food and agriculture sectors. These Algerian export companies regularly encounter difficulties. Moreover, the

M. Kadi (✉)
Centre for Research in Applied Economics for Development (CREAD), Algiers, Algeria

S. M. Apitsa, E. Milliot (eds.), *Doing Business in Africa*, Palgrave Studies of Internationalization in Emerging Markets,
https://doi.org/10.1007/978-3-030-50739-8_4

scarcity of theoretical and empirical work on the theme of the internationalisation of SMEs in developing countries, especially in Algeria, makes any attempt to identify the factors of commitment and success of these companies with regard to export difficult. This research sheds light on this theme in a developing country like Algeria. As part of this work, what are the factors influencing the engagement of Algerian exporting SMEs?

Our objective in this chapter is to identify and analyse the factors influencing the engagement of Algerian SMEs in export. To achieve this, we have structured our chapter into four parts. The first one is dedicated to state-of-the-art concepts with regard to SMEs' exports. The second part is dedicated to the research methodology. The third part is devoted to the main results obtained. The last part is devoted to the examination of the main results obtained, the discussion as well as the main scientific and managerial implications expected.

2 Export for SMEs: Different Ways to Meet Specific Needs

For Cavusgil (1980), going to foreign markets (export) is innovation. Large companies maintain research and development departments at great expense, while SMEs do not always have the financial and human resources. This search for international performance is then carried out through the learning of managers and/or executives belonging to the different departments of the exporting SMEs. The latter form of learning is particularly popular among SMEs (Julien et al. 1999). This adaptation in the strategy to conquer international markets allows the SMEs to maintain their specificity (Bayad and Nebenhaus 1994). This makes it possible to know under which conditions have the notion of the specificity of the SME been accepted in the context of internationalisation (export) and under which conditions does this internationalisation distort the SME?

Several authors indicate that export internationalisation can bring about profound organisational and functional changes in SMEs (Moini 1995). More than that, if we define the internationalisation of the SME as an ultimate stage of its maturation, then it is likely that it adopts strategies and operating modes similar to those used by large companies (Guilhon et al. 1993; Godener 1995). Proponents of this viewpoint of export-related practices believe that greater human and financial resources and management methods are required based on geographical distance. On the other hand, the form of SME seems to be based on a strong geographical and cultural proximity of its activities (the role of the manager in the management and the setting up of the strategies, a functioning which is based on proximity with customers and suppliers, a weak relationship with banks).

Several models have been developed from the 1970s to explain the process of internationalisation of SMEs and to look for the keys to their success. Among these models, the Uppsala model (U-model) was developed by the Swedish school (Johanson and Vahlne 1990; Johanson and Vahlne 2009). Given that the internationalisation of an SME requires the mobilisation of all its resources (resource-based view [RBV]), this concept appears as unifying of different traditional approaches (Laghzaoui 2011). Each of them relies, more or less implicitly, on this concept by favouring certain resources over others to explain the success of SMEs abroad.

Among the traditional approaches that have been mobilised in the internationalisation companies' research, let us quote the integrative model of Etemad (2004). Proponents of this model explain the process of internationalisation of SMEs by three levels: the internal characteristics, the external environment and the profile of the manager. The advantage of this theoretical model lies in its transversal approach that integrates both the internal and the external environment to the company and the characteristics of its manager. As part of this work, we will adopt the Etemad model to study the characteristics of exporting SMEs as well as the factors explaining their commitment to export.

3 Development of Research Hypotheses

To develop our hypotheses, we used studies from developed and developing economies. We have assumed that the factors identified in the various previous studies could explain the factors of companies' engagement in export (Paul et al. 2017; Howard 2018; Haddoud et al. 2019).

The variables used within the framework of our analysis are grouped according to three categories of factors: (1) The profile of the manager through his level of commitment in export (Aaby and Slater 1989; Luong 2011; Chen et al. 2017; Howard 2018; Kadi 2019) and his having to do in export (Chen et al. 2017 ; Kadi 2019). (2) The characteristics of the company through its capacity for innovation and the export marketing advantages it has (St-Pierre and Perrault 2010; Cavusgil 1980; Katsikeas et al. 2000). (3) Factors related to the external environment of the company through infrastructure and the quality of institutions (Jalali 2012; Hashem and Irshaidat 2014; Paul et al. 2017; Haddoud et al. 2019; Kadi 2019).

In order to verify the existence of an effect of the three categories of factors on the commitment of SMEs in export, we propose the following hypotheses:

H1: The profile of the manager expressed by his level of commitment in exporting and his experience in exporting influences the commitment in exporting his company.

H2: The characteristics of the company expressed by the capacity for innovation and by the marketing advantages influence its commitment to export.

H3: The external environment expressed by the quality of infrastructure and institutions influences the company's commitment to export.

4 Research Methodology Adopted

In order to carry out our research, we opted for a quantitative approach based on a field survey by a questionnaire of a sample of Algerian SME exporters. We constructed a questionnaire to quantify the measurement of each of the variables related to the selected research model.

4.1 The Construction of the Research Sample: Difficulties in Identifying Representative Size and Reality Test

According to the definition adopted in the framework of Law 01-18 of 12 December 2001 on the Orientation Law on the promotion of SMEs in Algeria, the choice relates only to exporting enterprises (totally or partially exporting) with a workforce of employees of 250 or less. Only 43 SMEs filled out the questionnaire out of a total of 200 companies constituting the total sample of exporting companies' target. The questionnaire is constructed according to the structure proposed by the Etimad model, in which three levels of analysis are identified. The first level is linked to the identification of the characteristics of the SME manager; the second level is linked to the internal characteristics of the enterprise and the third level is linked to the external environment. The measurement scale used is that of Likert with seven (7) anchorage points.

4.2 Data Collection Methods

We wanted to use the Internet as the preferred method of administering our questionnaire. However, through the directories of exporting companies provided by Algex Anexal and Caci, we have noted the absence of e-mail addresses. Giving all these constraints, we launched the survey in November 2015 with 150 SME exporters using two modes of admission, which are the Internet, with the help of the different organisations with which the exporters have relations like Anexal, Caci and Fce, and the face-to-face mode during field trips in the context of events (fairs and exhibitions, meetings) attended by exporters. In total, we have received 43 completed questionnaires. It should be noted that the acronym EPMEEA-2015 (Algerian SME Export Survey-2015) will be used in the remainder of this work.

4.3 Some Elements of the Algerian Context: The Export Problem Is Still Relevant

The Algerian economy has several specificities in terms of international economic integration: a strong dependence on imports (food, drugs and industrial inputs), a high dependence on hydrocarbons in terms of fiscal resources and foreign revenues, galloping inflation (7.4% in 2018 according to the IMF) and an unstable business climate. This dependence on exports of primary products (oil) influences economic growth (Cnuced 2018) and weakens the industrial fabric. For Daoud (2010), competition is imposed by the implementation of the various regional and international trade agreements (the WTO, the EU, Zale), the bureaucracy, the presence of a large informal sector, the low rates of banking. The difficulty of resorting to a skilled labour force and the insufficiency of innovation are explanatory elements of the fragility and the weakness of the Algerian SMEs for the export. An examination of these factors clearly indicates the importance of the weaknesses and constraints of the initial context (characteristics specific to the Algerian economy). Moreover, and as indicated by Amarouche (2010), Algerian SMEs, as the entire economy, depend on oil export revenues, making the possibility of integration of these companies in international markets very difficult. In total, of the 800 SME exporters, only 100 SMEs (according to Ons data, 2015) in Algeria have a regular and export-oriented activity.

5 Search Results

The descriptive results indicate that the average size of firms in the sample is 96; the average age of the manager is 46 years. More than 70% of executives have a university degree (Table 4.1). The average number of export transactions per year is 21. Nevertheless, the standard deviation values for the averages obtained indicate that we have a very heterogeneous sample of SMEs. Indeed, more than 60% of the SMEs in the sample are in the agriculture sector, 18% in the agro-food industry and 11% in the petrochemical industry and the rest are either in the wood industry or in the mining and quarrying industry (Table 4.1). The types of

Table 4.1 The descriptive elements of the sample

Characteristics	Min	Max	Average	Standard deviation
Firm size (number of workers)	10	230	96.95	78.54
Manager age	28	66	46.58	11.07
Number of destination countries for export	1	6	2.00	1.00
Number of export transaction per year	5	90	21.15	24.39
Level of commitment for export (measuring scale)	1	7	5.414	2.241

Source: Calculated from the survey EPMEEA (2015)

products exported are mainly dates and derivatives, fruit juices, confectionery products and equipment. These companies mainly export 30% to the countries of the European Union, 30% to African countries and 20% to North America.

5.1 SMEs' Size and Activity Sector

Based on our results, we see diversity in the exported products. The sample surveyed indicates that we have a concentration of exporting SMEs in the agriculture sector followed by agribusiness and chemicals. The implementation of various sectoral non-hydrocarbon export promotion schemes such as the National Agency for Agricultural Development and the Special Export Fund, which offer financial advantages, logistics, and technical aspects of export operations, has encouraged SMEs operating in the agricultural sector, particularly those exporting dates, to engage internationally. The first observation that can be deduced is that it does not represent the idea that we have a priori comparative advantage available for Algeria such as for hydrocarbons and fuels. It is expected that exported products will be characterised by the comparative advantage from hydrocarbons such as chemicals and petrochemicals. However, the current trend in exports indicates that more and more agricultural and agri-food SMEs are exporting.

Graphic 4.1 shows that our sample consists largely (60%) of SMEs with a workforce of more than 50 employees. Our survey shows that the

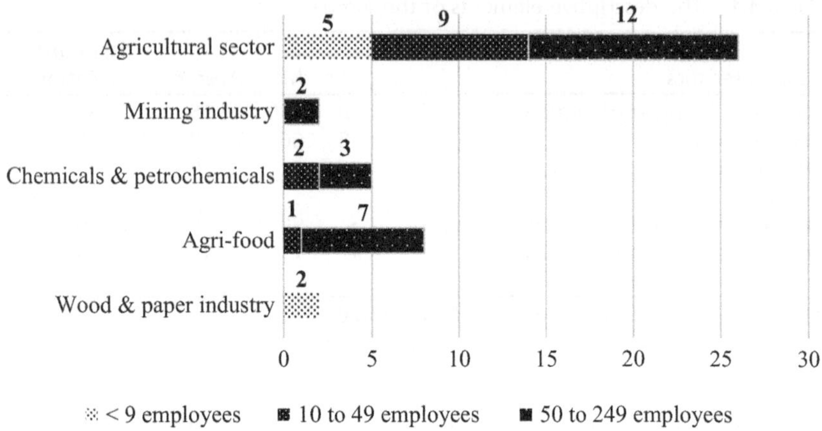

Fig. 4.1 Distribution of SMEs by size and by activity sector. (Source: Adapted from the survey EPMEEA [2015])

size of the company plays a key role in export commitment and performance. In other words, the larger the size of SMEs, the easier the export activity becomes. This is partly due to the benefits of economies of scale and specialisation and the sunk costs of entry into international markets. The chart also shows that more than 80% of SME exporters in the agricultural sector have more than ten employees (Fig. 4.1).

5.2 SMEs' Size and Level of Export Commitment

The strategic choice adopted by companies largely determines the level of export commitment. In some cases, the export strategy is explained by the profit gained from export sales. For others, the export market is a substitute for the domestic market won by products from China, for example, which is characterised by low prices. For others, the export market is an outlet for seasonal production surpluses, as in the case of agricultural products.

Figure 4.2 reveals significant differences between small and very small businesses on one side and medium-sized businesses on the other. Of the 13 SME exporters in Unit 10 and with 49 employees, 9 (70%) are totally exporters compared to only 4 (30%) who are partially exporters

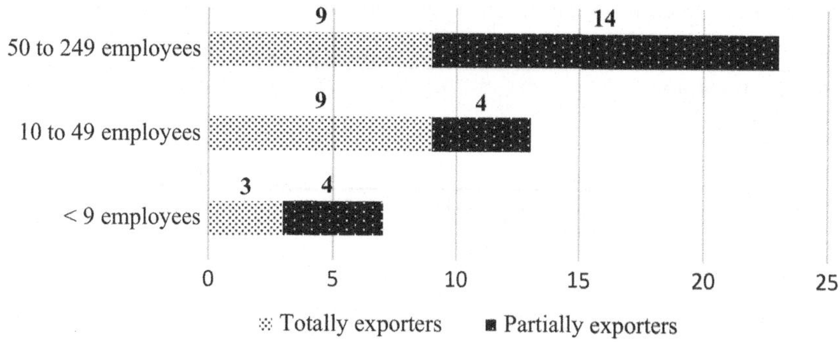

Fig. 4.2 Distribution of SMEs by size and by level of export commitment. (Source: Adapted from the survey EPMEEA [2015])

(Graphic 4.2). Similarly, of the seven small firms (less than nine employees), half are full exporters. On the other hand, out of the 23 enterprises belonging to the 50 to 249 employees group, 14 are partially exporters, and 60% of the SMEs belong to this group of employees. It appears that the size expressed by the number of employees is a factor influencing the level of SMEs' engagement in our sample. Medium-sized enterprises (from 50 to 249 employees) adopt a mixed strategy to minimise the risks associated with export activity by keeping part of their production in the domestic market. On the other hand, small businesses (9 to 49 employees) tend to adopt an entirely international strategy.

5.3 The Training Level of the Exporting SMEs Manager in the Sample

The level of training (level of education) of the manager has a positive impact on the success of SMEs in exporting (Julien et al. 1999). Their knowledge of the field allows the managers to better understand the needs and challenges of the company and the difficulties of the sector, and properly manage the risks associated with the development of their organisation.

We observe that nearly 70% of SME exporting managers in our sample have a university level, nearly 10% have vocational training and more

Table 4.2 The training level of the exporting SMEs manager in the sample

Training level	Frequency	%
University degree	30	69.8
Technical background	4	9.3
No degree	9	20.9
Total	43	100

Source: Adapted from the survey EPMEEA (2015)

than 20% have no degree (Table 4.2). So, from these results, the majority of exporting SME managers have a university degree. However, it remains to identify the existence of a possible relationship between the manager's training and the export activity. This relationship has been dismantled in several studies such as those of St-Pierre and Perrault (2010). These authors have shown that managers who have a technical background are usually at the head of a manufacturing exporting company. According to these authors, another characteristic of the manager can play an important role in the conduct and success of SMEs with regard to export in this case; complementary training on management techniques and international marketing can also be a reducing uncertainty factor through good managerial knowledge and international marketing techniques.

5.4 Experience of SME Leaders in the Sample Export Activity

In addition to the owner-manager's training domain, his sector experience can also be a factor in reducing uncertainty thanks to a good knowledge of the market, the required technologies and the risk factors that can hinder the company's development (Woywode and Lessat 2001).

Table 4.3 shows a relatively similar distribution of experience in the export activity of SME managers in our sample. Indeed, 39.5% of these managers have less than four years of experience in the export business, 32.6% have an experience between five and ten years and nearly 30% of them have more than ten years of experience. It can also be assumed that an SME manager who is an expert in international procedures will also have better geographical, geopolitical and ethnological knowledge, will

Table 4.3 Experience of SME leaders in the sample export activity

Experience/years	Frequency	%
1 to 4 years	17	39.5
5 to 10 years	14	32.6
>10 years	12	27.9
Total	43	100

Source: Adapted from the survey EPMEEA (2015)

not hesitate to travel to discover new markets, will devote more time to exploring new opportunities and will arbitrate in favour of more resources for export (commitment).

5.5 Multidimensional Analysis of Export Activity: Factorial Analysis (PCA)

To test unidimensionality or multidimensionality, it is generally recommended to use principal component analysis (PCA). This consists of reducing the initial variables to a small number of latent factors to reduce the maximum amount of information (the explained variance). PCA tries to identify factors that explain correlations within items. Before starting the factor analysis, the sampling suitability should be measured by the Kaiser-Meyer-Olkin coefficient (KMO), which evaluates the extent of the psychometric relationship of the items. In other words, if the KMO test is above the threshold of 0.5 then we can conclude that the selected items are factorisable. Benraiss (2004) indicates that at this level of analysis, no hypothesis is formulated a priori, neither on the structure of the initial data nor on the significance of the factors emerging from this analysis.

Characteristics of the Manager

The manager sees in the export activity opportunities that can be economically strategic or personal. To illustrate this profile, six items are retained (Chen et al. 2017; Howard 2018). These items, which are listed in Table 4.4, allow us to distinguish between the entrepreneurial leader

Table 4.4 The analysis of the PCA results: the level of his commitment in the export

	Initial eigenvalue			Rotation sums of squared loadings				Varimax rotation	
Components	Total	% de la variance	% cumulated	Total	% de la variance	% cumulated	Items	1	2
1	2.387	39.786	39.786	2.387	39.786	39.786	ENGA1	0.704	0.077
2	1.354	22.566	62.352	1.354	22.566	62.352	ENGA2	0.681	0.121
3	0.828	13.801	76.152	/	/	/	ENGA3	0.790	−0.393
4	0.630	10.496	86.648	/	/	/	ENGA4	0.627	−0.591
5	0.496	8.270	94.918	/	/	/	ENGA5	0.355	0.744
6	0.305	5.082	100	/	/	/	ENGA6	0.532	0.526

Source: Results obtained from the database of the survey EPMEEA (2015)

and the conservative leader. According to Covin and Sievin (1991), an entrepreneurial leader is the one who dares to take risks in foreign markets to ensure the development of his business and the one that combines export activity and the success of his business.

The analysis of the PCA results allowed us to identify two components which restore 62% of the total variance (Table 4.4). To interpret the results provided by the matrix of components, we use Roussel's (2005) two criteria: (1) the elimination of items with contributions greater than 0.40 on several factors, or none contribution at least equal to 0.40 on one of the factors selected; (2) elimination of items with no contribution greater than or equal to 0.50 on one of the main axes identified. The application of these criteria allowed the elimination of two items, which are ENGA4 and ENGA5. It seems that the commitment of the manager of the company in the export business is not associated with competition in the domestic market. In other words, its commitment to exporting is, in this case, a strategic choice that is independent of the level of competition/saturation in the Algerian market. The deletion of the two items yielded a single component that restores 57.5% of the variance. The value of Cronbach's alpha is equal to 0.56.

The Characteristics of the Manager: His Know-How in Export

The accumulation and updating of the various information on the export market allows the SME manager to have a competitive advantage over his competitors. This knowledge, which becomes know-how, enables the SME manager to build an export strategy on the basis of information available on the target market. To measure this variable, we selected five items. The respondent is asked to provide an assessment of his interest in information related to the export market.

Analysis of the PCA's results identified two components that represent more than 74% of the total variance (Table 4.5). The criteria of Roussel (2005) suggest the deletion of items SAVF3 and SAVF5. In fact, the deletion of the two items allowed the obtaining of a single component that returns 71.89% of the variance. In theory, these two items refer to the importance and interest that the manager attaches to information

Table 4.5 The analysis of the PCA results: his know-how in export

	Initial eigenvalue			Rotation sums of squared loadings				Varimax rotation	
Components	Total	% de la variance	% cumulated	Total	% de la variance	% cumulated	Items	1	2
1	2.720	54.405	54.405	2.720	54.405	54.405	SAVF1	0.857	−0.285
2	1.004	20.072	74.477	1.004	20.072	74.477	SAVF2	0.810	−0.239
3	0.692	13.840	88.317				SAVF3	0.527	0.731
4	0.349	6.974	95.292				SAVF4	0.694	−0.388
5	0.235	4.708	100.000				SAVF5	0.756	0.426

Source: Results obtained from the database of the survey EPMEEA (2015)

concerning the evolution of the target market and the regulations and rights in force in these markets. The Algerian exporter, in his strategy, is interested in the accumulation of knowledge on the economic and political stability of the targeted markets, on the customs of business in the export market and on the intensity of competition.

The Characteristics of the Company: Its Capacity for Innovation

Innovation capacity has been identified among the internal characteristics of the SME most influencing its export performance (St-Pierre and Perrault 2010; Luong 2011). To measure this variable, we used five criteria that identify the effects of implementing an innovation policy of the production process, management processes and marketing. The manager evaluates on a seven-point scale the effect of the implementation of the innovation process in the three levels (production, management, marketing) on the improvement of the quality of the exported products, on the increase of the share of production for export, on the increase in the share of production for export. The ease of access to external markets and the adaptability of these products to standards are important factors of a export success.

The factor analysis allowed us to highlight a single component which has an own value equal to 2.088 and returns 52.201% of the total variance (Table 4.6). In addition, the analysis of the contributions of items in the formation of this axis shows that the item (INNOV3) has a small contribution. This item corresponds to the capacity of the innovation strategy (management, production and marketing) adopted by the SME to facilitate access to external markets. Based on this result, it seems that access to foreign markets does not depend on the SME's capacity for innovation but on these relational capacities and the level of development of its network. It would appear that this item does not contribute to the identification of the innovation capacity of the SMEs in our sample. We then decide to delete it.

Table 4.6 The analysis of the PCA results: its capacity for innovations

	Initial eigenvalue			Rotation sums of squared loadings				Components
Components	Total	% de la variance	% cumulated	Total	% de la variance	% cumulated	Items	1
1	2.088	52.201	52.201	2.088	52.201	52.201	INNOV1	0.875
2	0.921	23.030	75.231				INNOV2	0.825
3	0.673	16.829	92.060				INNOV3	0.404
4	0.318	7.940	100				INNOV4	0.692

Source: Results obtained from the database of the survey EPMEEA (2015)

The Characteristics of the Company: The Export Marketing Advantages

We measured the export marketing advantage with four questions about the quality of the exported products, the uniqueness of the exported products, its novelty and its value for money. For each of these benefits, the manager is asked to evaluate, on a scale of seven points, its effect on the ability of the company to place its products in foreign markets.

We observe that all commonalities are high for all items. From these results, we decide to use the three items to measure marketing benefits (Table 4.7). Therefore, the items selected to capture information on the marketing benefits of the company are well specified. It seems that the managers of exporting SMEs are giving importance to the export marketing strategy. Indeed, they consider that the three components of the export marketing strategy, in this case the quality of the products, the unique characteristics and the value for money, play an important role in the conduct and success of their export businesses.

The External Environment: Infrastructure and the Quality of Institutions

The quality of infrastructure and institutions plays an important role in the conduct and development of business in an economy (Hashem and Irshaidat 2014; Haddoud et al. 2019) and can affect even the success of these companies across borders. Indeed, several external business variables explain differences in export performance, such as institutions' infrastructures and legislation (Ben Ayed and Boujelben 2014; Hashem and Irshaidat 2014).

To identify this impact, we have formulated several items related to the quality of infrastructures and institutions. The manager is asked to specify the level of influence (on a scale of seven points) as to the level of development of these elements on the export activity of the company.

The KMO scale suitability test reveals an acceptable psychometric relationship between the items. Indeed, with a KMO equal to 0.642, the selected items are factorisable (Table 4.8). The results of the factor

Table 4.7 The analysis of the PCA results: the export marketing advantages

	Initial eigenvalue			Rotation sums of squared loadings				Components
Components	Total	% de la variance	% cumulated	Total	% de la variance	% cumulated	Items	1
1	1.533	51.088	51.088	1.533	51.088	51.088	MARK1	0.846
2	0.937	31.235	82.324				MARK2	0.736
3	0.530	17.676	100				MARK3	0.524

Source: Results obtained from the database of the survey EPMEEA (2015)

Table 4.8 The analysis of the PCA results: infrastructure and the quality of institutions

	Initial eigenvalue			Rotation sums of squared loadings				Varimax rotation		
Components	Total	% de la variance	% cumulated	Total	% de la variance	% cumulated	Items	1	2	3
1	2.756	34.451	34.451	2.756	34.451	34.451	INFQIST1	0.097	0.749	−0.401
2	1.271	15.883	50.334	1.271	15.883	50.334	INFQIST2	0.128	0.086	0.814
3	1.116	13.950	64.285	1.116	13.950	64.285	INFQIST3	−0.004	0.770	0.378
4	0.891	11.139	75.424				INFQIST4	0.766	−0.113	−0.308
5	0.738	9.221	84.645				INFQIST5	0.686	0.285	0.172
6	0.513	6.413	91.058				INFQIST6	0.539	0.119	0.076
7	0.467	5.832	96.889				INFQIST7	0.701	0.078	0.407
8	0.249	3.111	100				INFQIST8	0.473	0.669	0.260

Source: Results obtained from the database of the survey EPMEEA (2015)

analysis revealed three independent factors. The first corresponds to the external operational aspects that influence the functioning of the company, namely, administrative heaviness, corruption and industrial land. The second is political instability that influences the operation and activity of the company. The third corresponds to the regulation of the foreign exchange market, which also influences the export activity as well as relates to the repatriation of foreign exchange earnings from export operations. All of these elements were identified by interviewees as important elements in the conduct and operation of their business. Moreover, the analysis of the contributions of the items in the formation of the three axes shows that the items (INFQIST1; INFQIST7 and INFQIST8) have a contribution greater than 0.40 on several factors according to the criterion of Roussel (2005). It should also be noted that the interviewees consider that the level of infrastructure development (INFQIST1 and INFQIST7), as well as the availability of raw materials (INFQIST8), is not important.

From the results of the factor analysis (PCA), most of the items retained have been validated. This illustration allows us to validate the three research hypotheses as indicated in Table 4.9.

Table 4.9 Validation of hypotheses

Research hypotheses		Validation of hypotheses
Dimension	Under dimension	
H1: The profile of the manager influences the commitment to export	Manager's level of commitment to export Export know-how	Validated
H2: The characteristics of the company influences the commitment to export	Its capacity for innovation, the export marketing advantages,	Validated
H3: The external environment influences the commitment to export	infrastructure and the quality of institutions	Validated

Source: Author's creation

6 Discussions of Results

The results of this research show that the Etemad (2004) model, through its multidimensional conception of the analysis of the explanatory factors of the commitment of companies in the export sector, has been validated as part of our work. This is indeed an analysis that confirmed the importance of the three dimensions: the profile of the manager's, internal characteristics and external characteristics.

The results of the descriptive and factor analysis (PCA) on the basis of this study show that Algerian SME exporters share the same explanatory factors for their export engagement as those of other developing countries (Howard 2018; Haddoud et al. 2019). Besides, the level of export commitment is a strategic choice that is built independently of the level of competition/saturation in the Algerian market (Narooz and Child 2017; Covin and Sievin 1991 ; Haddoud et al. 2019). Indeed, the profile of the Algerian SME manager through his commitment to export activity and his export know-how positively influences the export engagement of the SMEs in our sample. This result tells us that the entrepreneurial manager is personally committed to achieving financial objectives by increasing export sales, to strategic expansion objectives by increasing the number of countries/markets and to functional objectives by improving the know-how of employees within his company (Covin and Sievin 1991). This result corroborates with those obtained by Luong (2011) and Kadi (2019) concerning the role of the entrepreneurial profile of the manager in export engagement. Indeed, the entrepreneurial manager is the one who takes the risks of conquering new markets and requires more export know-how which will allow the exporting SME to have a cognitive and competitive advantage with regard to the export (Luong 2011; Haddoud et al. 2019). This means that the knowledge accumulated by export market managers helps enhance product benefits.

Also, the results obtained only show that the conditions in the country of origin have a profound influence on the managers of exporting companies in our sample. This result agrees with those obtained by Haddoud (et al. 2019) and Kadi (2019). Indeed, the satisfaction felt by the manager regarding the support of the environment and the quality of the institutions affects his decision to commit to export. These structural conditions can be considered necessary for the success of any export activity. Some variables external to the company, linked to the level of development of infrastructures and local institutions, would explain the differences in terms of the development of exporting SMEs (Jalali 2012; Hashem and Irshaidat 2014). For example, road, port and airport infrastructure, logistics platforms and the quality of institutions (business climate, investment codes, etc.) generate positive externalities that turn into savings in time and costs, which are passed on the competitiveness of exporting SMEs.

Regarding the influence of internal characteristics on export engagement, the results of this research reveal the existence of a positive and significant relationship. Research and development (innovation) and changes in product manufacturing provide competitive products in export markets. The qualification of employees is another source for which the company ensures productivity gains, enabling it to have a self-selection effect. The marketing advantage that is measured in our search by the exclusivity of the product, by the price-quality ratio, allows the company to sell better (more expensive or in more quantity) (Haddoud et al. 2019). It can also easily create a strong connection with clients abroad. This impact has been verified by studies of export engagement (Aaby and Slater 1989; Luong 2011; Kadi 2019). For these authors, the marketing advantages directly affect the product and how it is delivered. Therefore, the export-oriented strategy allows the company to focus its efforts to ensure its sustainability in the markets by adopting a three-dimensional approach.

The corporate strategy in the broad sense, as defined by Porter (1999), consists of defining the general orientations allowing the business to hold a lasting competitive advantage. The results indicate that marketing benefits play a key role in the export commitment decision. These are competitive advantages that the company can build through a better access marketing strategy on the price/quality of the product as well as on innovation (Cavusgil 1980 ; Katsikeas et al. 2000; Luong 2011; Kadi 2019; Haddoud et al. 2019). For some authors, the export marketing advantages are directly linked to the success of SMEs in international markets (Luong 2011). Luong (2011) has identified two types of marketing benefits in his work. The results obtained corroborate those obtained by Luong (2011). The latter measured the export marketing advantage using four questions covering six items: price promotion and distribution, services associated with the products, best selling price, sale on credit, advertising abroad, best selling price.

7 Conclusion

This chapter has focused on the analysis of the characteristics of Algerian SME exporters. To achieve this, we conducted a quantitative questionnaire survey of a sample of 43 exporting SMEs. To highlight this characteristic we performed a factor analysis (principal component analysis) on four variables that characterise the SMEs in our sample, namely, the level of commitment of the manager in the export, the capacity for innovation, the benefits of marketing infrastructure and the quality of institutions.

Moreover, all these characteristics visible in Algerian SMEs are the product of the recent history of the Algerian economy defined by a long transition phase from centralised socialist management to more liberal management where initiative as well as the dynamics of entrepreneurship is encouraged (Redouane 2017; Haddoud et al. 2019; Kadi 2019). We also found that the SMEs in our sample, through their managers, consider exporting as the final step for the development of their activities (Guilhon et al. 1993; Godener 1995).

Nevertheless, this dynamic revolves around an economic environment that is not conducive to the progress of these companies on the organisational and functional levels. These characteristics are also derived from a socio-cultural environment that influences the way of thinking and actions of business managers that have an impact on business growth; this way of thinking is defined by patriarchal management, a very low rate of bank access, the use of support from the family network for financing. In addition, the obstacles related to the business environment (government bureaucracy, financing problem, complexity of procedures related to foreign trade, etc.) can create difficulties for the development of export activity.

Our results thus reinforce the multidimensional conception of the analysis of factors explaining the export commitment of Algerian SMEs. Besides, our results reflect the importance of the role of the manager in the international operations of Algerian SMEs. In this context, the manager uses and develops mechanisms, based on the internal resources of his company and his motivation, his know-how as well as his network, to develop international activities. This strategy is an effective way to circumvent the constraints related to the business climate and the inefficiency of export promotion schemes (Kadi 2019; Haddoud et al. 2019).

We have seen that the first difficulty that must be overcome in the SME study is to provide reliable data. The different organisations with which exporters have relationships such as Anexal Caci and Fce do not produce information regarding export activity. We also mentioned the difficulties on the ground and the excessive costs of field surveys. Indeed, various constraints related to sampling led us to lower our initial ambitions and to resort to a convenience sample.

In terms of the generalisation of the results, we can affirm that they are not necessarily generalisable to all of the Algerian exporting SMEs because of two biases related, respectively, to the size and the heterogeneity of the sampled companies. Furthermore, the descriptive results on the characteristics of SMEs indicate that many seem to be sensitive to the importance of the characteristics of the manager (the profile of the manager). In this sense, it is necessary to know whether the sampled firms had a lower profile or whether the survey covered a larger sample of firms.

However, future research should focus on understanding the relationship between each group of variables and engagement. Besides, future research could use a comparative approach between countries similar (spatial dimension) to Algeria, over several years (time dimension). The elements of comparison will allow a better understanding of the economic, cultural and entrepreneurial specificities which influence the engagement and the success of Algerian exporting SMEs.

References

Aaby, N., & Slater, S. F. (1989). Management Influences on Export Performance: A Review the Empirical Literature 1978–1988. *International Marketing Review, 6*(4), 7–26.

Amarouche, A. (2010). Quelle place pour les PME industrielles dans une économie libéralisée de rente ? Cas de l'Algérie. In A. Joyal, M. Sadeg, & O. Torrès (Eds.), *la PME algérienne et le défi de l'internationalisation* (pp. 123–149). Paris: L'Harmatan.

Bayad, M., & Nebenhaus, D. (1994). Recherche sur la GRH en PME: proposition en vue d'un modèle théorique. In *Vème Congrès de l'AGRH* (pp. 235–242). Montpelier.

Ben, A. O., & Boujelben, Y. (2014). Les déterminants de la performance des petites et moyennes entreprises: cas de la Tunisie. *Economics & Strategic Management of Business Process (ESNB), 2*, 172–178.

Benraiss, L. (2004). Méthodologie de construction d'une échelle de mesure: Application du paradigme de churchill. Paper Presented at the 15éme Congrès de l'AGRH.

Cavusgil, S. T. (1980). On The Internationalization Process of Firms. *European Research, 8*(6), 273–281.

Chen, H. L., Chang, C. Y., & Hsu, W. T. (2017). Does Board Co-Working Experience Influence Directors' Decisions Toward Internationalization? *Management International, 57*, 65–92.

Cnuced. (2018). le développement économique en Afrique. rapport de 2018, Nations-Unis.

Covin, J. G., & Sievin, D. P. (1991). A Conceptual Model of Entrepreneurship as Firm Behavior. *Entrepreneurship Theory and Practice, 16*(1), 7–25.

Daoud, S. (2010). La problématique de l'intégration des PME algérienne aux échanges extérieurs: double handicapes pour des compagnies dynamiques. In A. Joyal, M. Sadeg, & O. Torrès (Eds.), *la PME algérienne et le défi de l'internationalisation* (pp. 124–151). Paris: L'Harmatan.

Etemad, H. (2004). Internationalization of Small and Medium-sized Enterprises: A Grounded Theoretical Framework and an Overview. *Canadian Journal of Administrative Sciences, Vol., 21*, 1–21.

Godener, A. (1995). Les changements de dimensions e l'entreprise en croissance. In Congrès de l'AIMS, Paris, pp. 612–631.

Guilhon, A., Guilhon, B., & Peguin, D. (1993). L'identité de la PME à travers l'activité d'exportation. In Congrès Francophone de la PME, Paris, 25–27 Octobre, pp. 385–401.

Haddoud, M. H. Y., Nowinski, W., Jones, P., & Newbery, R. (2019). Internal and External Determinants of Export Performance: Insights from Algeria. *Thunderbird International Business Review, 61*(1), 43–60.

Hashem, T., & Irshaidat, R. (2014). The Influence of Political-Legal Forces on Jordanian Industrial Exports in the Private Sector. *International Journal of Marketing Studies, 6*(1), 103–115.

Howard, J. D. (2018). The Impact of African Manager's Values on Exporting: Influential Managerial Characteristics and Export Performance. *International Journal of Export Marketing, 2*(2), 141–153.

Jalali, S. H. (2012). Export Barriers and Export Performance: Empirical Evidence From The Commercial Relationship Between Greece and Iran. *South-Eastern Europe Journal of Economics, 1*, 53–66.

Johanson, J., & Vahlne, J. E. (1990). The Mechanism of Internationalization. *International Marketing Review, 7*(4), 12–24.

Johanson, J., & Vahlne, J. E. (2009). The Uppsala Internationalization Process Model Revisited: From Liability of Foreignness to Liability of Outsidership. *Journal of International Business Studies, 40*, 1411–1431.

Julien, P. A., Beaudoin, R., & Njambou, R. (1999). PME exportatrices et information en zones rurales et en zones urbaines. *Revue internationale PME, 12*(1–2), 107–127.

Kadi, M. (2019). *The Factors of Influence in the Export Decision of Algerian Manufacturing SMEs*. In E. Millot & S. Nivoix (Eds.), *Economic Transition and International Business Managing Through Change and Crises in the Global Economy* (240p). New York: Routledge.

Katsikeas, C. S., Leonidou, L. C., & Morgan, N. A. (2000). Firm-Level Export Performance Assessment. *Journal of The Academy of Marketing Science, 4*(28), 493–511.

Laghzaoui, S. (2011). SMEs Internationalization with the Concept of Resources and Competencies. *Journal of Innovation Economics & Management, 1*(7), 181–196.

Luong, T. A. (2011). The Impact of Input and Output Tariffs on Firms' Productivity: Theory and Evidence. *Review of International Economics, 19*(5), 821–835.

Moini, A. H. (1995). An Inquiry into Successful Exporting. An Empirical Investigation Using a 3 Stage Model. *Journal of Small Business Management, 33*(3), 9–25.

Narooz, R., & Child, J. (2017). Networking Responses to Different Levels of Institutional Void: A Comparison of Internationalizing SMEs in Egypt and The UK. *International Business Review, 26*(4), 683–696.

Paul, J., Parthasarathy, S., & Gupta, P. (2017). Exporting Challenges of SMEs: A Review and Future Research Agenda. *Journal of World Business, 52*(3), 327–372.

Porter, M. (1999). *Choix stratégiques et concurrence: techniques d'analyse des secteurs et de la concurrence dans l'industrie*. Paris: Ed. Economica.

Redouane, A. (2017). L'exportation dans les PME algériennes: quelques réalités, illustration à partir de la région de Bejaia. *Marché et organisations, 9*(28), 175–192.

Roussel, P. (2005). Méthodes de développement d'échelles pour questionnaires d'enquête. In P. Roussel & F. Wacheux (Eds.), *Management des ressources humaines: méthodes de recherche en sciences humaines et social* (pp. 245–276). Bruxelles: De Boeck.

St-Pierre, J., & Perrault, J. L. (2010). Motivations et déterminants de l'internationalisation de PME: témoignages du Liban, du Maroc, du canada et de la France. In A. Joyal, M. Sadeg, & O. Torrès (Eds.), *la PME algérienne et le défi de l'internationalisation* (pp. 220–249). Paris: L'Harmatan.

Woywode, M., & Lessat, V. (2001). Les facteurs de succès des entreprises à croissance rapide en Allemagne. *Revue Internationale PME, 14*(3–4), 17–43.

5

Internationalisation of Moroccan SMEs in Sub-Saharan Africa: An Analysis Based on the Uppsala Model

Oumaima Chamchati, Mohamed Nabil El Mabrouki, and Caroline Minialai

1 Introduction

"The empowerment of Africa by itself": this expression comes from Ahmed Arafa's speech at the 43rd session of the Royal academy of Morocco and summarises one of Africa's major orientations for the next 40 years: the promotion of intra-African trade and investment. The 2019 World investment report underlines that the reinforcement of intra-African integration and the development of free trade areas are at the core of

O. Chamchati • M. N. El Mabrouki
Cadi Ayyad University of Marrakech, Marrakech, Morocco

ECONOMIA, HEM Research Center, Rabat, Morocco

C. Minialai
ECONOMIA, HEM Research Center, Rabat, Morocco

S. M. Apitsa, E. Milliot (eds.), *Doing Business in Africa*, Palgrave Studies of Internationalization in Emerging Markets,
https://doi.org/10.1007/978-3-030-50739-8_5

structural changes in Africa. This orientation was confirmed in July 2019 when the African Continental Free Trade Area (ACFTA) came into force, which aims to facilitate intra-African movement of goods, capital and people.

Morocco has been involved in this dynamic since the early 2000s. The African continent is a priority in its strategic choices in terms of trade and foreign investment. The latest figures from the Moroccan foreign exchange office show that sub-Saharan African countries represent Morocco's first destinations in Africa. Over the 2008–2016 period, Morocco's commercial exchanges with sub-Saharan Africa recorded an annual average growth rate of 9.1%. Similarly, direct foreign investment to the continent accounts for most of the outward investment. The same organisation mentioned above states that over the period from 2003 to 2017, an average of 60% of these investments were made in sub-Saharan Africa, distributed across its four regions: West Africa (55%), North Africa (25%), Central Africa (15%) and Southern Africa (5%).

Large private Moroccan companies played a pioneering role in achieving this, particularly in the service sectors (banking, insurance, telecommunications operators). However, the Moroccan strategy in sub-Saharan Africa is not limited to the participation of only large companies. It also aims to encourage and enhance the presence of small and medium-sized enterprises (SMEs), which represent more than 90% of the Moroccan economy. The Ministry of Economy and Finance and the French Development Agency (2018) underlined that the involvement of SMEs is essential to ensure that Moroccan companies are better positioned on the continent. We have therefore chosen to focus on this category of business in this chapter.

From a theoretical perspective, this phenomenon has been little studied in literature. The existing theoretical models were primarily developed in European or North American countries (Angué and Mayrhofer 2010). Moreover, very few studies have tested their applicability in the context of developing countries/economies (Paul et al. 2017).

Among these theoretical frameworks, the Uppsala model is the most popular. It is a model initially developed on the basis of Swedish companies that are expanding internationally into other European or North American countries (Johanson and Vahlne 1977; Johanson and Wiedersheim-Paul 1975). The model provides a complete description of the process of internationalisation for companies by answering two main questions: which country to choose? Which entry mode to adopt? (Meier and Meschi 2010). This theoretical framework has been applied in many studies that have attempted to answer these questions (Angué and Mayrhofer 2010; Cheriet 2010; Coviello and Munro 1997). Even though it was initially developed on the basis of the internationalisation process for large manufacturing companies, this model is also suitable for studying the internationalisation of SMEs (Johanson and Vahlne 2009; Paul et al. 2017). In order to align it with advances in research and developments in the business world, it has undergone several transformations since its initial version was published (Johanson and Vahlne 2009; Vahlne and Johanson 2013, 2017). However, there are still some unresolved questions about its applicability in other contexts that differ from Western countries in terms of socio-economic, institutional and cultural aspects (Shamba and Livian 2014).

Based on these considerations, the purpose of this chapter is to discuss the relevance of the Uppsala model in explaining the internationalisation of Moroccan SMEs in sub-Saharan Africa. Can it be applied to the analysis of choices made by a Moroccan SME in sub-Saharan Africa? Are there any characteristics specific to this African context that are not taken into account in Uppsala's model? Can the universality of the model be questioned? In general, this chapter attempts to answer the following question: To what extent does the Uppsala model explain the internationalisation of Moroccan SMEs in sub-Saharan Africa?

To answer this problematic we will first present chronologically the evolution of the Uppsala model through the main contributions of its authors. The purpose of this presentation is to summarise how they explain the choices of destination and entry mode. After presenting the research methodology, we will then discuss similarities and differences between the proposals of the Uppsala model and the outcomes of our research.

The value of this research is twofold. From a theoretical point of view, it allows us to see how this context, which has been little studied to date, can provide new insights and enrich the Uppsala model. It may also have considerable managerial implications for African SMEs seeking to do business in other African countries.

2 The Uppsala Model: A Dynamic And Evolutive Model

The aim of this section is to provide a chronological overview of the construction of the Uppsala model and its explanation of the choice of host country and entry mode.

2.1 The Initial Version of the Uppsala Model (1975–1977): A Gradual Trajectory Model

The initial version of the Uppsala model is based on a longitudinal study by Johanson and Wiedersheim-Paul (1975), in which four Swedish companies were studied. The results of this research show that companies first develop in their domestic market and gradually expand their horizons and activities abroad.

The model was theorised in 1977. It is based on the intention to provide a model of the basic mechanisms that explain a firm's international choices. According to Johanson and Vahlne (1977), the degree of experiential knowledge accumulated by the company and the psychic distance are at the origin of the incremental characteristic of the model.

For the choice of host countries, Johanson and Vahlne (1977) state that the perceived psychic distance between the country of origin and the host country is a relevant factor in this decision. Psychic distance is "the sum of factors preventing the flow of information to and from the market. Examples are differences in language, education, business practices, culture and industrial development" (Johanson and Vahlne 1977, p. 24). As a result, a company seeking to expand abroad is first oriented towards neighbouring countries, countries that are relatively well known or similar in terms of business practices and then gradually towards more distant countries.

For the choice of entry modes, the authors suppose that companies first prefer those that do not require a significant commitment of resources. They adopt what they call an establishment chain, in four stages: (1) they start with irregular export activities, (2) afterwards they export in collaboration with independent local agents, (3) later they establish their own commercial subsidiaries, (4) then they end up producing locally.

2.2 The First Revision of the Uppsala Model (2009): Integration of the Network Approach

In this revised version of Uppsala's model, Johanson and Vahlne (2009) associate the internationalisation of companies with the integration of business networks, which are defined as "all the varied, close and lasting relationships with important suppliers and customers" (Cowley 1988; Hakansson 1989, quoted in Johanson and Vahlne 2009, p. 1414).

In this version, the authors admit that "the correlation between the time the company takes to enter a foreign market and the psychic distance has weakened" (Johanson and Vahlne 2009, p. 1421). For a firm seeking to expand internationally, the problem is no longer to identify countries that are psychically close to it, but to identify those where it has relevant business relations. It therefore moves from the challenge of entering a market or the liability of foreignness to the challenge of entering a business network or the liability of outsidership (Dominguez and Mayrhofer 2017; Meier and Meschi 2010; Odlin and Benson-Rea 2017). Business relationships are particularly important for companies that do not already have operations in potential host countries (Coviello 2006; Oehme and Bort 2015; Santangelo and Meyer 2017), since they facilitate access to opportunities, information and key partners.

Similarly, the company does not necessarily follow an establishment chain for the entry mode choice. The characteristics of the market, the level of the company's resources and the nature of the relationships with the members of its business networks play a major role in this decision. However, the authors acknowledge that the firms need to know each other well enough by conducting initial operations together that are less binding before proceeding to a higher level of commitment. Such an approach is more profitable for SMEs that, despite their limited resources, can succeed in their international expansion due, among other things, to their position within their business networks (Laghzaoui 2009).

2.3 The Latest Version of the Uppsala Model (2017): Towards a Non-linear and Discontinuous Trajectory Model

On the occasion of the fortieth anniversary of their initial model, Vahlne and Johanson (2017) proposed an alternative model of the eclectic paradigm to explain the evolution over time from a national firm to a multinational firm. They argue that, in contrast to the vision of Dunning and Lundan (2008), today's multinationals are:

> process rather than structure oriented; a network rather than a stand-alone unit; business exchanges rather than production; pro-active and entrepreneurial rather than passive; heterarchical (decentralised) rather than hierarchical. (Vahlne and Johanson 2017, p. 1088)

One of the main proposals of Vahlne and Johanson (2017) is that there is no linear and predefined internationalisation process. The model is built based on the opportunities that each firm identifies and develops. The heterogeneity of companies and their resources on the one hand and the exposure of firms to different levels of risk and uncertainty on the other hand mean that a firm's international commitment cannot be linearly sequenced (Santangelo and Meyer 2017; Vahlne and Johanson 2017) and that there are as many companies as processes.

These points lead the authors to rethink their model in terms of the choice of host country and entry mode. When choosing the host country, the company first refers to its business relationships to determine which countries to target: "It is the firm-specific characteristics of the partner that matters. These in turn are, of course, more or less dependent on the characteristics of the partner's home country" (Vahlne and Johanson 2013, p. 204). For the choice of entry mode, Vahlne and Johanson (2017) consider that this decision no longer represents a factor in measuring the level of commitment and the evolution of a firm internationally. Different modalities can lead to the same results. Only the company's ability to coordinate its relations with members of its internal and external networks, who are involved in its international operations, can make the difference and generate results. The company therefore makes its choice

Table 5.1 Choices of host country and entry mode in the Uppsala model

	1975/1977 version	2009 version	2013/2017 version
Choice of host country	Choice of psychically close countries before targeting more distant countries	Choice of countries where the company has relevant business relationships to facilitate its local integration	Choice of countries according to the characteristics of the local partner and those in the country of origin
Choice of entry mode	Adoption of a gradual establishment chain, from low-commitment modes to more binding modes	The choice is based on the characteristics of the target market, the company's resources and the nature of its relationship with the local partner company	The choice is based on the company's preferences (costs and potential for future profitability) and the characteristics of its local partner (credibility, long-term mutual interest and home country regulation)

Source: Authors' creation

according to its resources, the perceived potential for future profitability in the target country and the characteristics of the local partner (its credibility, the existence of a long-term mutual interest and the regulations in its country of origin).

The Uppsala model has gradually evolved to adapt to both companies that are making their first sales abroad and those that have a global presence (Santangelo and Meyer 2017). Table 5.1 summarises the Uppsala model's proposals for the choice of host country and entry mode.

We realise that the explanation provided in each new version of the model does not represent a rupture with the previous one. It is more a feedback loop, an expression we borrow from Cheriet (2015), where the concepts of the previous version are reconsidered in light of criticisms of the model and developments in the business world, in order to enable it to evolve.

In fact, the Uppsala model has been the subject of much criticism since its inception (Andersen 1993; Chetty 1999; Coviello and McAuley 1999). The main criticism relates to its linear and deterministic nature, its universality, the existence of other international alternatives and the nature of the variables it mobilises, which provide a partial explanation of the phenomenon (Cheriet 2010). Some of these critics still raise questions, including the validity of the model in other geographical contexts, particularly in developing and emerging countries.

3 Research Design

The research conducted included interviews with managers and executives of Moroccan SMEs that operate in sub-Saharan Africa, as well as representatives of key overseas business support organisations. The comprehensive nature of our research work justifies our choice of a qualitative methodology. Moreover, as pointed out by Marschan-Piekkari and Welch (2004), qualitative research may be preferable in developing countries, where secondary data is difficult to access and where the cultures place value on trust and social relationships.

We conducted an interview in each of the seven selected SMEs. In the following paragraphs, they are listed from one to seven. Five of the interviews were with the founder-manager. Due to the unavailability of the founder-manager, the other two interviews were conducted with the sales manager in charge of export activities (SME6) and the director of exports (SME7). We insisted on the importance of meeting a person directly involved in the international activities of SMEs in order to have a proper and updated overview of their different choices in sub-Saharan Africa.

The selection criteria for the chosen SMEs are: (1) Having activities in sub-Saharan Africa with different levels of engagement was the most important criterion. (2) All the selected SMEs comply with the Moroccan definition of an SME, that is, a company with a turnover of MAD 175 million or less[1]; except for SME3, which is undergoing a structuring phase to become a large company. Its experience in sub-Saharan Africa is interesting to us and deserves to be explored, especially since its case allowed us to evaluate the behaviour in sub-Saharan Africa of a more financially successful Moroccan SME. (3) Diversity of business sectors. The selected SMEs operate in media and communication, manufacturing and information technology (Table 5.2).

[1] Approximately equivalent to 16 million euros.

Table 5.2 SMEs description

	SME1	SME2	SME3	SME4	SME5	SME6	SME7
Inception date	2004	2010	1979	2006	1986	1977	2010
Industry	Agri-food industry	Web and mobile solutions	Agri-food industry	Media and communication	Software development	Heating, ventilation and air-conditioning industry	Automotive and industrial battery production
Operating countries in sub-Saharan Africa	Nigeria; Ghana; Sudan; Senegal; Cameroon; Mali; Ivory Coast; Togo	Senegal; Gabon; Ivory Coast	South Africa and Tanzania	Senegal; Burkina Faso; Niger; Ivory Coast; Togo; Central African Republic; Gabon; Burundi; Congo	Ivory Coast; Cameroon; Senegal; Gabon	Senegal; Ivory Coast; Equatorial Guinea; Guinea; Burkina Faso	Mauritania; Senegal; Ivory Coast; Mali; Gabon; South Africa and Angola
Year of first activity in sub-Saharan Africa	2013	2010	2014	2010	2008	2007	2011
Year of first international activity	2009	2014	1979	2007	1987	2007	2010

Source: Authors' creation

We also held five interviews with representatives of the main public and private overseas support organisations which are active in Morocco: INFORISK, MAROC EXPORT, the Moroccan Exporters' Association, the National Council for Foreign Trade, the French Chamber of Commerce and Industry of Morocco.

Overall, we conducted 12 interviews, 10 face-to-face and 2 by phone. The average length of these interviews was 60 minutes. They were conducted during the year 2017–2018. Respondents were allowed to speak in the language in which they felt most comfortable. Some of them answered exclusively in French and others by combining Moroccan dialect and French. The interviews were recorded with the permission of the respondents and then we started with the full transcript.

During the interviews, we used open-ended questions, in order to give the respondents the possibility to express themselves freely. In the first part, the questions were related to the history of the firm, its activities and its international development. In general, the second part was dedicated to the reasons that led the company to focus on sub-Saharan Africa, the choice criteria of the host country and entry mode and, finally, the challenges faced and support opportunities offered.

Since our research attempts to compare the proposals of the Uppsala model with the choices of Moroccan SMEs in sub-Saharan Africa, open coding seems to be the most appropriate choice to identify similarities and differences (Corbin and Strauss 1990). In fact, this coding enables "immersion in the material and the discovery of characteristics of the phenomena analysed" (Lejeune 2014, p. 41). To do so, we followed the advice of Lejeune (2014) by conducting this immersion work in two stages: a micro-analysis phase where we carefully read the interviews in order to explain all the possible meanings of the words, lines or episodes. Then the coding phase where we labelled fragments of text. In this way, we were able to identify the most revealing properties of the company's experiences and aggregate them into categories. The latter are presented and discussed in more detail in the next section.

4 Results and Discussion

In this part of the chapter we examine the choice of host countries and entry modes of Moroccan SMEs in sub-Saharan Africa. We then compare the results with the proposals of the Uppsala model in order to identify similarities and differences between them.

4.1 The Choice of Host Countries

All Moroccan SMEs interviewed have recently shown interest in sub-Saharan Africa. They all started activities in this region over the last two decades. This interest is driven by the will to find new opportunities and growth drivers. Respondents argue that the local market constraints and ongoing regulatory restrictions in other foreign countries, particularly European countries, have led them to seek new markets to boost or consolidate their development:

> In 2013, we were confronted with Europe's protectionist measures, which made it impossible for us, from one day to the next, to export into Europe. So it was, of course, necessary to re-position the company in other markets. (SME1)

This is in line with the initial proposals of the Swedish researchers. Johanson and Vahlne (1977) assume that a company becomes international in order to seize new business opportunities and/or to cope with growth constraints in its home country or in other foreign countries.

The demographic growth of populations in sub-Saharan Africa and the change in their consumption habits represent considerable potential for several industries. Such is the case of SME2, which has targeted Senegal, Ivory Coast and Gabon in order to take advantage of digitalisation projects launched by local companies:

> In Senegal, we sold a customer relationship management solution to a Hyundai distributor. We also automated the sales force for Sigalli, Yoplait's

distributor in Gabon. Besides that, we are working with MOOV, IAM's telecom operator in Abidjan. (SME2)

The same applies to SME6 and SME7, which have focused on sub-Saharan African countries in order to extend their international distribution network.

In terms of host country selection in sub-Saharan Africa, we note that, in most cases, French-speaking countries are the gateway for Moroccan SMEs (Table 5.2). This choice is explained by various factors (Table 5.3).

We first note that a driving effect is generated by the royal visits made by King Mohamed VI to sub-Saharan Africa since his ascension to the throne in 1999. The king's main destinations were Senegal, the Ivory Coast, Gabon, Guinea, Ghana, Zambia, but also English-speaking countries such as Tanzania. The manager of SME1 explained that they followed the path of the royal visits as part of their development strategy in sub-Saharan Africa, by prospecting new distributors in the countries visited by the king or participating in the caravans organised after these

Table 5.3 Selection criteria for host countries in sub-Saharan Africa

	The choice of host countries in sub-Saharan Africa
SME1	**Prospecting in trade fairs and BtoB meetings** "We participate in trade fairs, export caravans and all occasions to make export connections. These are excellent opportunities to develop our customer portfolio." **Consumption habits** "Specifically, due to our positioning as specialists in Halal baby food, we target countries that are 100% Muslim or that have a strong dynamic towards Halal products." **The driving effect of royal diplomacy** "We have followed the rhythm of the royal strategy i.e. focusing on African countries by participating in all the export caravans in Africa in order to be much more present there, because this was not the case beforehand." "We do not accompany the king on his tours, but in terms of prospecting we subsequently approach distributors in each country he visits." "When people see the picture of King Mohamed VI during his visit to Dakar, for example, obviously everyone hears about it. It generates a dynamic and trust."

(*continued*)

Table 5.3 (continued)

	The choice of host countries in sub-Saharan Africa
SME2	**Prospecting in trade fairs and BtoB meetings** "Even if there are no ongoing projects, we develop relationships, we participate in trade fairs, we receive delegations, we visit them, we try to maintain relationships ... there are people we met 3 years ago in Gabon and recently they called us back to request our services." **Country accessibility** "We targeted French-speaking Africa, the others are very far away and small. We are currently exploring the English-speaking region, Kenya and Rwanda. It has potential, but we mustn't be too dispersed either. Covering these two countries requires a lot of flight hours." "If you want to travel to Abidjan it's 12,000 Moroccan dirhams, for Senegal it's a minimum of 8,000, Gabon it's even worse 13,000 or 14,000, it's very expensive ... not to mention the flight schedules which are not tailored to us." **Ease of communication** "People in Mauritania don't understand French, they speak a strange Arabic. Maybe if we were selling traditional products it would work but when you sell intelligence, you have to talk to people, you have to understand their needs, you have to understand to be able to offer things."
SME3	**External requests** "It was a Tanzanian company that contacted us and said: we would like to develop a luxury tea brand, but we don't know how to do it, can you launch it with us?" **The driving effect of royal diplomacy** "Our investment project in Tanzania has been ongoing for a long time but was signed during last year's royal tour. This tour gave a lot of credibility to the project and accelerated many things."
SME4	**Country regulations** "It's a licence issue. For example, Ethiopia is a dream country for me, but the broadcasting sector is not liberalised. They don't allow private radio stations." **Country accessibility** "You are a businessman, you take flights at 4 am, so if you want to be efficient you have to add 2 or 3 days there. These schedules are not tailored to an exporter." "The contact with people is important, you have to go 3 times a year, i.e. 3 visa applications per year, each visa is 1,500 to 2,000 Moroccan dirhams and you need different visas for each country. Why do we need a visa to go to Burundi or Togo?" **Security risks** "Honestly, who dreams of going to Bangui when it' s war every day, to Burundi when there are protests every day, to Togo or Congo when they almost had a coup d'état, to the Ivory Coast when there was a war not long ago, they are not countries that my teams would like to visit."

(continued)

Table 5.3 (continued)

	The choice of host countries in sub-Saharan Africa
SME5	**Countries engaged in reform measures** "What has also driven our approach in Sub-Saharan Africa is identifying countries engaged in reforms: budget reforms, reforms in the structuring of public services or administrative reforms in general." **Ease of communication** "Language is an important factor, it facilitates communication, because all our resources within the company speak French, it is much easier to start with French-speaking countries. English-speaking countries are more promising than French-speaking countries, but events naturally lead us to devote more energy, more time and more resources to countries where we have a natural facility than to countries where we must make a much greater effort before we achieve our goal." **Corruption practices** "In Gabon, considering the scale of the project, I initiated an evaluation mission to determine whether they expect things that we couldn't offer, including corruption." **Security risks** "In Gabon we interrupted our activity for more than six months, we had to take our team out because of the political tension over the presidential elections." **Stability of political decisions** "A change in the political system or the fact that key people involved in a project are promoted elsewhere and replaced by others who may not know much about the project or may not have the same vision, are not insignificant risks in terms of our operation."
SME6	**Prospecting in trade fairs and BtoB meetings** "We participate in South-South caravans with Morocco Export." **Stability of political decisions** "We talked to our banker and he told us that there are risk countries in Sub-Saharan Africa, in particular Benin and Mali. These are countries where the regime can suddenly change and we may no longer be paid."
SME7	**Prospecting in trade fairs and BtoB meetings** "We attended the Morocco Export caravan, we did the tour with them, we had BtoB sessions with those who participated in the caravan, we prescribed our products, then we followed up by e-mail. We even arranged visits to our factory and we were then able to sign with some of them."

Source: Authors' creation

official visits. According to him, having the king's photo posted everywhere after his visit generates trust and creates a dynamic among Moroccan companies. Similarly, the managing director of SME3 explained that they were negotiating a partnership with a Tanzanian company to construct a tea packaging factory in Tanzania. This SME was invited to join the Moroccan Royal Tour of Tanzania in October 2016 to sign the partnership contract. The manager of SME3 stated that their participation in this tour gave more credibility to the project and accelerated the local procedures. This phenomenon refers to a reduced political distance between Morocco and the sub-Saharan African countries visited by the king. However, the definition of distance initially proposed by Johanson and Wiedersheim-Paul (1975) is a psychic distance limited to differences in language, culture and managerial practices.

Moalla and Mayrhofer (2019) distinguish in their definition of distance between the subjective approach, proposed by Johanson and Wiedersheim-Paul (1975), and the objective one by referring to Ghemawat's (2001) model. The latter includes in its definition both the cultural dimension, which takes into account differences in languages, and the geographical, economic and administrative/political dimensions. For Ghemawat (2001), political distance is determined in terms of historical and political links, institutional and legal differences, as well as the existence of a common currency between two countries. In the North-South context, researchers often refer to the existence of a colonial relationship between home and host countries when defining political distance (Burt 1993; Dow and Karunaratna 2006). However, in a South-South context, as in our study, political distance is approached differently. It is based on the diplomatic ties established between Morocco and sub-Saharan African countries, with the aim of developing a supportive South-South cooperation.

Following these diplomatic visits, caravans and BtoB meetings are organised by public overseas support organisations such as MOROCCO EXPORT, ASMEX or other private organisations. The representative of MOROCCO EXPORT explained that their activities are mainly organised in French-speaking African countries, which partly explains the orientation of SMEs: "[I]t is countries such as the Ivory Coast, Senegal, Burkina-Faso, Mali. We are beginning to work on countries in East

Africa, but in a limited way." These events may represent a real opportunity for SMEs wishing to develop their international network (Evers and Knight 2008). In the Uppsala model, we noted that the explanation of host country choice has evolved so as to put the network and business relationships at the centre of this decision (Johanson and Vahlne 2009; Vahlne and Johanson 2013, 2017). In fact, our respondents underlined the importance of having relevant business relationships in a country in order to be able to operate there. They explain that these relationships are essentially built during caravans and BtoB meetings in which they participate (Table 5.3).

Ease of communication is also an essential factor in the choice of host country. In Morocco, French is the first foreign language used in the business world. The manager of SME5 explained that his team is all French-speaking, so it is easier for them to start with French-speaking countries first. Moreover, the company's activity—the development and sale of integrated management systems—requires regular interaction with the customer during the integration and system use phases. Ease of communication is also important for SME2, which operates in the same sector and thinks that *understanding each other* is essential for selling intelligence. This is in line with Johanson and Vahlne's (2009) proposal. They assume that business relationships are socially constructed and that people tend to be more interested in those with whom they find it easier to communicate. Therefore, differences in languages can represent a real obstacle to building relationships.

For the SME2 and SME4 managers, country accessibility also plays an important role in the choice of host country, since they often have to travel in order to prospect and supervise their projects. Johanson and Wiedersheim-Paul (1975) assume that there is generally a positive correlation between psychic distance and geographical distance, but we find it important to distinguish it in order to appreciate more clearly the role it can play. For Ghemawat (2001), this accessibility is not only measured in terms of kilometres; it also refers to freedom of movement within countries and the quality of the transport facilities available. For Moroccan SMEs, these elements have represented, up until now, a major obstacle to their expansion in sub-Saharan Africa. The manager of SME2 claims that, despite the fact that Senegal is one of the closest countries to

Morocco, the price of a direct flight costs at least 8000 Moroccan dirhams[2] and the flight schedules are not tailored to entrepreneurs. SME4 also thinks that requiring a visa to travel in African countries is unjustified and represents a major obstacle to their expansion.

In the Uppsala model, Vahlne and Johanson (2013) explain that the choice of host country is strongly influenced by the local partner's characteristics and those of its country of origin, without clearly clarifying the nature of these characteristics. In the African context, these refer primarily to security aspects related to political turbulence, civil wars and corruption (Boso et al. 2016; Ibeh et al. 2012). For SME4 and SME5, wars and political tensions represent an alarming and real justification for abandoning or interrupting their activities in a country. They explain that these risks can put their teams in danger and have a negative impact on payment deadlines. The instability of political decisions was also noted by SME4 and SME6. They explained that in some countries this can take the form of a change in the political regime or the arrival of another person in power who is unaware of previous projects or who does not share the same vision as the previous person. This specific characteristic increases the company's level of uncertainty and may lead it to abandon a project despite its potential. In addition, the manager from SME5 reports that corruption practices are quite common in certain countries. They were sufficient justification for them abandoning a major project in Gabon.

Other country characteristics can also influence the choice of host country, such as the population's consumption habits and the country's legislation. We use the example of SME1, which targets 100% Muslim countries or those with a strong presence in the Muslim community, as it offers Halal food for babies; or SME4, which was forced to give up in countries such as Ethiopia, because local policies did not allow private radio stations to enter the market.

To summarise, we find that the choice of host country is influenced by a combination of factors related to distance and country characteristics. In the Uppsala model, we believe that the impact of political distance is almost absent. This could enrich the model and strengthen its

[2] Approximately equivalent to 750 euros.

inclusiveness, especially in the African context where there is an intense overlap between political and economic agendas (Ibeh et al. 2012).

Furthermore, Vahlne and Johanson (2013) argue that the choice of host country refers to both the characteristics of the partner and those of its country of origin. We believe that these dimensions must be sufficiently detailed in the model in order to alert SMEs, or anyone who refers to the Uppsala model as a guide for making international decisions, about some risks that could have a fatal impact on their activities, such as security risks and the political stability of the country. Developing these elements could even lead to new extensions of the Uppsala model specific to each continent or region, for example.

4.2 The Choice of Entry Mode

An SME may use various entry modes in a foreign country. These can be classified into three categories: export activities, cooperation with foreign partners or the creation of a subsidiary controlled by the firm (Urban and Mayrhofer 2011).

Export activities are either direct or indirect. The first option consists in self-selling abroad or via a foreign intermediary. Indirect exports imply that the SME outsources its foreign sales to a company in its home country. The second category consists of concluding cooperation contracts, having financial stakes in a foreign company or setting up a joint venture with other companies abroad. The SME may also have subsidiaries over which it has full or majority control. These can be created from scratch or as a result of M&A transactions.

Using this classification, we identify, in Table 5.4, the entry modes used by SMEs and how they explain their choices.

Overall, Moroccan SMEs choose to export directly when it comes to sub-Saharan Africa. However, this choice is not only justified by the lack of resources; other factors also have an impact.

SME2 decided to export directly from Morocco because it considers that sub-Saharan African countries are not sufficiently mature to absorb all the services they provide. For now, they only work on occasional projects in partnership with local companies. The choice to export directly, by

Table 5.4 Selection criteria for the entry modes

	Selected entry mode	Reason(s) for the choice
SME1	Direct export	**To be able to invest in local development of the firm** "This choice allows us to finance our development because, for example, when we receive an order of 5 containers from Cameroon, it represents around 2 million Moroccan dirhams. The distributor will pay us 30% when we place the order and the rest before shipment, so we are almost paid immediately." **To be closer to the consumer's needs and facilitate the firm's expansion** "The distributor knows eating habits and which communication media to use, so I mean he already distributes a lot of other products. He already has his sales representatives and network there, so it's much easier for us than doing an in-depth market study country by country. Is it possible to communicate in the same way with a Togolese as with a Senegalese? Of course not!"
SME2	Direct export	**Market maturity** "These are countries that are not yet fully absorbing what we propose, we are working on projects, it is strategic for us, we have to be there when the market is ready." **Qualifying opportunities** "It is important not to go alone, we know of companies that were with us in the caravans and who were swindled. Somebody can come to you wearing a suit and tie and with 5 business cards and you tell yourself that he is the owner of some company, when in reality he has a cyber-centre in the neighbourhood ... In addition, the sales cycles are very slow, you risk getting worn out, but the local partner will help you qualify opportunities, people and companies."

(*continued*)

Table 5.4 (continued)

	Selected entry mode	Reason(s) for the choice
SME3	Cooperation with foreign partners (creation of a joint venture)	**Having a local basis** "Ultimately, we find that the most appropriate model in Sub-Saharan Africa, in our own industry, is to work with local partners, because it is very difficult to have a local basis and work alone." **Coping with entry barriers** "Our partner in Tanzania could have told us: we want to launch a tea brand, package it at your factory in Morocco and send it directly, but the problem is that there are so many customs barriers that it is very difficult to produce in Morocco and export to Tanzania."
SME4	Direct export or creation of a subsidiary fully controlled by the firm	**Adjust to local legislation** "It's an imposed choice. We use licences when it's allowed and when we're forced to create a local company, we also do that. We adjust to local legislation."
SME5	Creation of a subsidiary controlled by the firm	**Nature of the company's activity** "We manage extremely sensitive elements, such as budgets, salaries, agents, careers, benefits for government employees. The extent of what we are managing is such that we cannot afford to have an onsite structure. From a practical point of view, it is essential to have a technical-functional structure locally and it is also an important trust-building element. It reassures the customer and enables him to realise that he does not depend on another country."
SME6	Direct export	**Market maturity** "Air treatment is not mandatory in real estate projects in Sub-Saharan Africa, it is not a necessity, it is just a luxury. We are currently considering whether to continue working only with distributors or to set up our own sales offices where we will have our own stock, but we are still hesitant ... because when it comes to inventories we are dealing with idle money, especially since it's a new market there."
SME7	Direct export	**Adjust to the specific situation of the target country** "It's only commercial representation contracts or free commercial exchanges ... in countries that are politically unstable, we always have agents who will prospect directly."

Source: Authors' creation

contracting with local companies, may be more advantageous when the company considers that the political situation in the target country is unstable. This is the case with SME7, which prefers to work in this manner in order to cope with the perceived risks in some sub-Saharan African countries.

The legislation of the target country also plays an important role in the choice of entry modes. Some sectors are highly controlled and regulated in sub-Saharan Africa. SME3 operates in the teas and infusions sector. It packages tea brands for companies in more than 50 countries around the world. In general, it manufactures the products in Morocco and exports them directly to its customers. However, in sub-Saharan Africa, when it was approached by a Tanzanian company, it was not possible to proceed in the same way as with the others. Tanzania is a tea producing country and this raw material represents one of its main natural resources. Protectionist measures are therefore implemented in order to prevent any foreign company from importing tea products into Tanzania. To address this situation, SME3 and the Tanzanian company decided to jointly build a production unit in Tanzania. This will enable them to trade in Tanzania and other East African countries, since there is a free trade flow of goods and people between them. Similarly, SME4 explains that the choice of entry mode is decided by the target country. The process of launching a radio in sub-Saharan Africa differs from one country to another. Some require the creation of a local company and others simply grant a licence to the Moroccan company to manage the radio broadcasting.

For other SMEs, the choice of entry mode may just indicate a personal preference. SME1 operates in the agri-food industry sector and prefers to work exclusively with distributors in sub-Saharan Africa. Firstly, in order to fund its domestic development, and also to easily identify people' needs through the experiences, networks and know-how of its distributors.

The type of partner may also influence the choice. SME5 generally works in sub-Saharan Africa with public institutions on sensitive issues. The manager of this SME considers that it is essential to have a local office. On the one hand, it allows the company to be immediately available to handle technical and functional emergencies. On the other hand, it strengthens the sense of pride of those in charge, since they do not want foreign companies to manage their country's national businesses.

Overall, we note that the initial approach of the Uppsala model, which considers that the company adopts an establishment chain abroad which evolves according to accumulated experience (Johanson and Vahlne 1977; Johanson and Wiedersheim-Paul 1975), is wrong. We believe that the latest proposals of the model (Vahlne and Johanson 2013, 2017) are more consistent with our results. The preferences of the company, the characteristics of the partner and its country of origin are all, more or less, considered by Moroccan SMEs when choosing their modes of entry into sub-Saharan Africa.

5 Conclusion

In this chapter, we discussed the relevance of the Uppsala model in studying the internationalisation of Moroccan companies in sub-Saharan Africa. By referring to the various contributions of the model since the publication of its initial version, we have identified how Johanson and Vahlne explain the choice of host country and entry mode. We then compared and discussed their proposals with the results of our empirical study.

In choosing the host country, our analysis shows that the model must give more importance to, and broaden its definition of, distance in order to better assess its impact on the construction of business relationships and automatically on the choice of host countries. In the intra-African context, we found that royal diplomacy is particularly important. It creates a driving effect among Moroccan SMEs, by orientating them towards countries visited by King Mohamed VI during his official tours. The role of such relationships is absent in the Uppsala model and not much explored in literature (Angué and Mayrhofer 2010). In addition, the political stability and security risks of countries are key factors in selecting the host country. These issues are now outdated in the context of intra-European trade, but in terms of intra-African trade they are significant and constitute major obstacles to the expansion of African companies (Boso et al. 2016; Ibeh et al. 2012).

For the choice of entry mode, we consider that the revisions of the Uppsala model (Johanson and Vahlne 2009; Vahlne and Johanson 2013, 2017) are consistent with the behaviour of Moroccan SMEs in sub-Saharan Africa. They adapt their entry mode according to their preferences, the characteristics of the partner and those of its country of origin. However, we think it would be interesting, from a theoretical and managerial perspective, to be more specific about the characteristics of the host country, since they may differ from one geographical context to another. It might even be possible to suggest specific extensions of the Uppsala model for each homogeneous geographical context.

The Uppsala model is a pertinent reference for analysing companies' internationalisation. Through this chapter, we have tried to highlight some specificities of the African context that are absent or unclear in the model. By expanding them, the model could be better adapted to the analysis of intra-African trade and investment. However, the role of these specificities must be the subject of a longitudinal study in order to evaluate their impact over time. It could also be interesting to duplicate this work among other countries or regions in Africa. Finally, instead of focusing on the Uppsala model, further research could explore other theoretical frameworks that explain the international behaviour of SMEs, such as studies on international entrepreneurship.

References

Andersen, O. (1993). On the Internationalization Process of Firms: A Critical Analysis. *Journal of International Business Studies, 24*(2), 209–231.

Angué, K., & Mayrhofer, U. (2010). Le modèle d'Uppsala remis en question: Une analyse des accords de coopération noués dans les marchés émergents. *Management International, 15*(1), 33–46.

Boso, N., Adeleye, I., & White, L. (2016). Africa-to-Africa Internationalization: Emerging Trends and Key Issues. In I. Adeleye, L. White, & N. Boso (Eds.), *Africa-to-Africa Internationalization: Key Issues and Outcomes* (pp. 3–34). Cham: Palgrave Macmillan.

Burt, S. (1993). Temporal Trends in the Internationalization of British Retailing. *The International Review of Retail, Distribution and Consumer Research, 3*(4), 391–410.
Cheriet, F. (2010). Modèle d'Uppsala et implantation des firmes multinationales agroalimentaires. La présence de Danone en Algérie. *Revue française de gestion, 36*(201), 45–64.
Cheriet, F. (2015). Est-il pertinent d'appliquer le modèle d'Uppsala de l'internationalisation des entreprises à l'analyse des nouvelles implantations des firmes multinationales? *Management International/International Management/Gestiòn Internacional, 19*(4), 121–139.
Chetty, S. K. (1999). Dimensions of Internationalisation of Manufacturing Firms in the Apparel Industry. *European Journal of Marketing, 33*(1/2), 121–142.
Corbin, J. M., & Strauss, A. (1990). Grounded Theory Research: Procedures, Canons, and Evaluative Criteria. *Qualitative Sociology, 13*(1), 3–21.
Coviello, N. (2006). The Network Dynamics of International New Ventures. *Journal of International Business Studies, 37*(5), 713–731.
Coviello, N., & McAuley, A. (1999). Internationalisation and the Smaller Firm: A Review of Contemporary Empirical Research. *MIR: Management International Review, 39*(3), 223–256.
Coviello, N., & Munro, H. (1997). Network Relationships and the Internationalisation Process of Small Software Firms. *International Business Review, 6*(4), 361–386.
Dominguez, N., & Mayrhofer, U. (2017). Internationalization Stages of Traditional SMEs: Increasing, Decreasing and Re-increasing Commitment to Foreign Markets. *International Business Review, 26*(6), 1051–1063.
Dow, D., & Karunaratna, A. (2006). Developing a Multidimensional Instrument to Measure Psychic Distance Stimuli. *Journal of International Business Studies, 37*(5), 578–602.
Dunning, J. H., & Lundan, S. M. (2008). Institutions and the OLI Paradigm of the Multinational Enterprise. *Asia Pacific Journal of Management, 25*(4), 573–593.
Evers, N., & Knight, J. (2008). Role of International Trade Shows in Small Firm Internationalization: A Network Perspective. *International Marketing Review, 25*(5), 544–562.
Ghemawat, P. (2001). Distance Still Matters. The Hard Reality of Global Expansion. *Harvard Business Review, 79*(8), 137–147.

Ibeh, K., Wilson, J., & Chizema, A. (2012). The Internationalization of African Firms 1995–2011: Review and Implications. *Thunderbird International Business Review, 54*(4), 411–427.

Johanson, J., & Vahlne, J.-E. (1977). The Internationalization Process of the Firm—A Model of Knowledge Development and Increasing Foreign Market Commitments. *Journal of International Business Studies, 8*(1), 23–32.

Johanson, J., & Vahlne, J.-E. (2009). The Uppsala Internationalization Process Model Revisited: From Liability of Foreignness to Liability of Outsidership. *Journal of International Business Studies, 40*(9), 1411–1431.

Johanson, J., & Wiedersheim-Paul, F. (1975). The Internationalization of the Firm—Four Swedish Cases. *Journal of Management Studies, 12*(3), 305–323.

Laghzaoui, S. (2009). Internationalisation des PME: Apports d'une analyse en termes de ressources et compétences. *Management et Avenir, 22*(2), 52–69.

Lejeune, C. (2014). *Manuel d'analyse qualitative—Analyser sans compter ni classer*. Louvain-la-Neuve: DE BOECK SUP.

Marschan-Piekkari, R., & Welch, C. (2004). Qualitative Research Methods in International Business: The State of the Art. In R. Piekkari & C. Welch (Eds.), *Handbook of Qualitative Research Methods for International Business* (pp. 5–24). Cheltenham: Edward Elgar.

Meier, O., & Meschi, P.-X. (2010). Approche Intégrée ou Partielle de l'Internationalisation des Firmes : Les Modèles Uppsala (1977 et 2009) face à l'Approche "International New Ventures" et aux Théories de la Firm. *Management international/Gestiòn Internacional/International Management, 15*(1), 11–18.

Moalla, E., & Mayrhofer, U. (2019). How Does Distance Affect Market Entry Mode Choice? Evidence from French Companies. *European Management Journal, 38*(1), 135–145.

Odlin, D., & Benson-Rea, M. (2017). Competing on the Edge: Implications of Network Position for Internationalizing Small- and Medium-Sized Enterprises. *International Business Review, 26*(4), 736–748.

Oehme, M., & Bort, S. (2015). SME Internationalization Modes in the German Biotechnology Industry: The Influence of Imitation, Network Position, and International Experience. *Journal of International Business Studies, 46*(6), 629–655.

Paul, J., Parthasarathy, S., & Gupta, P. (2017). Exporting Challenges of SMEs: A Review and Future Research Agenda. *Journal of World Business, 52*(3), 327–342.

Santangelo, G. D., & Meyer, K. E. (2017). Internationalization as an Evolutionary Process. *Journal of International Business Studies, 48*(9), 1114–1130.

Shamba, P. B., & Livian, Y. F. (2014). Le management africain introuvable. *économies émergentes/économies matures, enjeux pour le management international.* In P. X. Meschi & F. Prévot (Eds.), *Économies émergentes: Quels enjeux pour le management international?* (pp. 249–262). Paris: Vuibert.

Urban, S., & Mayrhofer, U. (2011). *Management International: Des pratiques en mutation.* Paris: Pearson.

Vahlne, J.-E., & Johanson, J. (2013). The Uppsala Model on Evolution of the Multinational Business Enterprise—From Internalization to Coordination of Networks. *International Marketing Review, 30*(3), 189–210.

Vahlne, J.-E., & Johanson, J. (2017). From Internationalization to Evolution: The Uppsala Model at 40 Years. *Journal of International Business Studies, 48*(9), 1087–1102.

Part II

International Logistics

6

Internationalisation of West African Transport-Logistics SMEs Facing the Crushing Weight of MNCs

Messan Lihoussou, Suzanne M. Apitsa, and Clément J. Godonou

1 Introduction

Globalisation reflects the speed of trade in goods and services through the gradual removal of trade barriers. Adda (2007) considers that generalisation of capitalism abolishes physical and regulatory borders. For Cavusgil et al. (2008, p. 4), "globalization of markets refers to the ongoing economic integration and growing interdependency of countries worldwide". In Africa, this phenomenon has encouraged the emergence of a new form of corporate internationalisation, which has traditionally been characterised by North-South (Northern Hemisphere countries to

M. Lihoussou (✉)
University of Parakou, Parakou, Benin

S. M. Apitsa
University of Poitiers, Poitiers, France

C. J. Godonou
Roro Terminal Benin, Cotonou, Benin

S. M. Apitsa, E. Milliot (eds.), *Doing Business in Africa*, Palgrave Studies of Internationalization in Emerging Markets,
https://doi.org/10.1007/978-3-030-50739-8_6

Southern Hemisphere countries), South-South, that is, interregional (Southern Hemisphere countries to Southern Hemisphere countries), and South-North (Southern Hemisphere countries to Northern Hemisphere countries) (Boston Consulting Group 2010; African Development Bank [AfDB] Report 2019). Numerous studies note that there is an emergence in Africa of interregional foreign direct investment (FDI) from African multinational corporations (MNCs) in various sectors of the economy (banking, cement, telecommunications, energy, retail, aviation) (Ngwu et al. 2015; Boso et al. 2018; Omokaro-Romanus et al. 2019; Apitsa 2019). However, little is reported on small and medium-sized enterprises (SMEs). South-South internationalisation (Africa to Africa) plays an important role in this research, particularly that of West African transport and logistics SMEs. The latter operate in a competitive sector dominated by the ubiquitous presence of large, highly organised global companies in the port territory, with financing capacities that exceed the budgets of African states, even when pooled (Debrie 2014; Lombard et al. 2014; Lihoussou 2014; Mareï 2017). About 92% of the continent's trade is carried by sea (UNCTAD 2018). Ports are a central node at the heart of national, regional, and international freight flows that are carried by water, rail, and land (Qu et al. 2019; Tchindjang et al. 2019). They are compulsory and value-added crossing points of transport centres and logistics platforms for international trade (Morvan 2014; Godonou 2019). Fredouet and Le Mestre (2014) add that ports are both an essential link in logistics chains and a privileged location for companies seeking to develop their import/export operations. This competitive environment offers an interesting framework for the analysis of the strategic choices of internationalisation which are made in the West African port territory by the companies operating there.

The West African port territory covers the Dakar (Senegal)-Lagos (Nigeria) row. It is made up of its hinterland, which serves the landlocked territories of Burkina Faso, Benin, Mali, and Niger. Niger is the main hinterland of the port of Cotonou in Benin. Hence, these states are at a higher stake with regard to economic competition for all the ports that are seeking to obtain market shares in them, in a continuous trend towards the growth of flows, dissociated from the sovereignties inherited and now installed (Charlier and Tossa 1996; Lihoussou 2014). Benin, through the port of Cotonou, a port with a regional vocation, is geographically positioned as a real gateway to the hinterland. Until recently, Mali, Burkina Faso, and Niger depended on this or that port, created by colonisation in a territorial logic of internal penetration and resource capture, framed by political power. This vigorous competition drives the policies of port authorities and actors who seek to capture traffic destined for inland territories and states without coastlines. This competitive space can constrain the capacity of SMEs to develop on the local and continental port hinterland and, on a large scale, to open internationally. In this perspective of internationalisation, Leonidou (2004) points out that the SMEs face, in their internationalisation trajectories, more constraints. These constraints concern their vulnerability in financial and human resources (Coviello and Jones 2004; Mtigwe 2006), the lack of managerial skills (Buckley 1997; Pantin 2010), and the poor knowledge of foreign markets (Johanson and Vahlne 2009).

From this observation, our research objective is to analyse the factors that influence the strategic choices of internationalisation of West African transport and logistics SMEs on this market characterised by the dominance of MNCs. The existing literature in the African context does not provide a framework for understanding these strategic power relations. Considering the rate of increase of SMEs in the international scene, in Africa, research on the internationalisation of transport-logistics SMEs is still limited. Existing work, which is not exhaustive, focuses on analysing the operational, organisational, and managerial aspects of transport-logistics activities of African SMEs (Abbad and Paché 2013; Godonou 2019).

This leads us to focus on the following research questions: (1) How can the presence of MNCs hinder the international expansion of West African SMEs in transport and logistics? (2) What are the distinctive characteristics that can promote the internationalisation of the two local SMEs studied? (3) Can the career path of the manager be a distinguishing factor for the internationalisation of the SMEs? To sum up, the choice of the mixed empirical study (Ragin 1987; De Meur and Rihoux 2002).

To answer these questions, we mobilised a mixed methodological approach (Ragin 1987; De Meur and Rihoux 2002) over the period from 2012 to 2017. This time frame is deliberately chosen to eliminate any risk of political support in business, as it spans two political regimes in Benin, that is, with different governments. Our methodological approach is justified by the fact that it grasps the complexity of the reality under study and gives more meaning to the emerging objective data. Thus, the data collection by questionnaire is carried out among the actors of transport-logistics in the port of Cotonou (PAC). It is facilitated by the availability of statistical traffic data and the establishment on the Cotonou port platform of the same global operators present in neighbouring ports. It is complemented by qualitative data based on nine semi-directive interviews conducted with two international SMEs established in Benin (Ellram 1996). These two SMEs are the Compagnie d'Affrètement et de Transit Logistics (CAT-Logistics) and the Société Internationale de Transit Touré (SITT).

The structure of our chapter is based on three sections. The first section presents the literature review. The second is devoted to the methodology chosen and the presentation of the firms studied. The third section, which presents the results and their analysis, provides an empirical framework for understanding the exacerbated competition between SMEs and large global transport-logistics operators in the West African port hinterland. It sheds light on the attitude of local international SMEs to cope with it and to develop "timely" strategies to open up at the intercontinental level. It shows that the career path of the manager is a key strategic dimension of the internationalisation of the SMEs studied. We conclude with the potential managerial implications.

2 Literature Review

The internationalisation of firms, both large and small, has been the subject of much research over the past several decades, attempting to show the motivations and modalities of firms' involvement in their foreign operations as well as their effects on organisational performance (Hymer 1960/1976; Bowersox and Sterling 1982; Andersen 1993; Dunning 1988; Oviatt and McDougall 1997; Bell et al. 2003; Lu and Beamish 2006; Luo and Tung 2007; Bandeira-De-Mello et al. 2015; Paul et al.

2017). In this chapter, our attention is focused on the internationalisation of West African transport and logistics SMEs.

2.1 Internationalisation of West African Transport-Logistics Companies

Transport and logistics in their operational, organisational, strategic, and managerial components are crosscutting lines of research at the crossroads of various disciplines (geography, management, economics, history, etc.). They are an essential sector for the economy given the activities that make them up. In fact, these activities, at the heart of national and global trade flows, are part of the strategic stakes for companies that excel in the sector.

In reviewing the work in the field of transport and logistics (Mentzer and Kahn 1995; Cheaitou and Cariou 2017; Schoenherr 2009; Baron and Apitsa 2017; Qu et al. 2019; Goldsby et al. 2019), we very quickly realised that economic and systems approaches largely inspire the research and concepts developed in this field, which is at the crossroads of several disciplines: transaction cost theory, resource-based view, systems theory, integrated logistics, and so on. Because the elements structuring logistics and supply chain management (SCM) focused on design, planning, execution, the control of physical information and system flows, management of inter-organisational relations is associated with an approach of cost minimisation and profit maximisation. These two indicators demonstrate the importance of resource optimisation and the strategic approach for the operational performance of the supply chain (creation of value for the customer through service) and ultimately for the global performance of the company. Therefore, and in order to evaluate them, research issues concern questions of management and optimisation of flows and stocks, coordination between actors in the supply chain, integration of actors, modelling to facilitate decision-making, governance and structuring of multi-actor chains, the impact of globalisation on the supply chain, opportunities provided by information and communication technologies (ICT), sustainable development (Hammami et al. 2008; Miller and de

Mattra 2008; Lee and Wilhelm 2010; Ellram and Cooper 2014; Fabbe-Costes et al. 2018; Lihoussou 2020).

In a context more focused on the strategic choices of internationalisation of logistics and transport players, researchers are less interested. The literature review of articles published in the *Journal of Business Logistics* (Goldsby et al. 2019), which was celebrating its 40 years of existence, and the database of 7636 ABI/INFORM articles show that research is not very focused on the study of strategic choices for the internationalisation of logistics and transport operators (Nelson and Toledano 1979; Bowersox and Sterling 1982; Morgan and Arnold 1990), even less so in the context of internationalisation in Africa. However, the expansion of companies into new markets abroad (Bandeira-De-Mello et al. 2015), offshoring, and the development of outsourcing (Bellin-Munier 2013) have led to changes in global supply chains that have a particular mode of integrating activities (Hülsmann et al. 2008). In these global logistics chains, competition is exacerbated between the various players present and in networks.

In West Africa, which concerns us in this chapter, the port system is dominated by MNCs organised into networks. This presence creates a crumbled offer of local small and medium-sized enterprises (SMEs) (Lihoussou 2014). These globalised players have penetrated African markets thanks to the development model imposed by the Bretton Woods international financial institutions (World Bank and International Monetary Fund). For Brunel (2004), the turning point came in the 1980s with the advent of liberal doctrines in the United States and Great Britain. Senegal is the first country in the African continent and in the region to have a Structural Adjustment Plan (SAP). The debt crisis has just begun for developing countries, forced to adopt "market-friendly development strategies", according to the formula imposed by these institutions. The first productive tools impacted are the transport and logistics activities on the port platforms by the strategic location of the major world operators, given that the management of West African ports was deemed inefficient in contributing to sustained economic growth.

At the port of Cotonou, transport and logistics services are provided by an oligopoly of these MNCs that are organised into networks (Lihoussou 2017), undermining the strategic position of local SMEs to develop within the region. Hence our first proposition. P1: West African transport-logistics SMEs face enormous difficulties in internationalising because of the overwhelming presence of MNCs.

Numerous studies demonstrate the difficulties inherent in the specific resources and skills that force SMEs to develop in foreign markets (Mtigwe 2006; Laghzaoui 2011). To overcome these weaknesses in resources and skills, some research suggests that SMEs should resort to inter-firm cooperation (Haahti et al. 2005; Wu et al. 2007; Milliot and Tournois 2010). According to Haahti et al. (2005), this approach is a key strategic resource for expanding into the foreign market because it increases the knowledge portfolio. For Wu et al. (2007), international cooperation is a necessary information resource for entering an international market. Some authors have questioned this strategic perspective, pointing out the difficulties of their implementation by SMEs (Leonidou 2004), which may be linked to the behaviour of the partner and cultural differences (Prime et al. 2009). Several theories on the internationalisation of SMEs such as the Uppsala model (Johanson and Vahlne 2009) put forward the international experience and the position within a business network as key variables of international engagement of SMEs. In this vein, Oviatt and McDougall (1997, 2005) note that the individual characteristics of the SME manager may also be a factor in facilitating entry into a foreign market. This leads to our second proposition. P2: The successful internationalisation of West African transport-logistics SMEs is linked to the career path of the manager.

2.2 The Theoretical Framework of Analysis

In order to meet research expectations, this section discusses the theoretical framework that provides the basis for our empirical data analysis grid.

The Resources and Skills of the SME Manager

The use of resource and skills theory (Penrose 1959) is particularly fruitful in the study of the internationalisation of SMEs (Bakunda 2003; Laghzaoui 2011) and especially in the analysis of the behaviour of managers of successful SMEs abroad. This theory helps to understand why resources are a critical element in obtaining competitive advantages abroad. The SME literature emphasises the skills of the owner-manager as an intangible resource for international development (Llord-Reason and Mughan 2002). Emphasis is on the concept of international human capital as important for successful business leadership and internationalisation. For Manolova et al. (2002) and Goxe (2010), this capacity increases the propensity to internationalise. These authors point out that the concept of human capital helps to explain the behaviour of firms in the conduct of their international activities. Dichtl et al. (1990) show that in their strategic choices of internationalisation the stronger the international orientation of the firm, the less the leaders are hindered by barriers related to internationalisation and the less they adopt proactive attitudes towards market opportunities. As for Stoian and Rialp-Criado (2010), skills are the result of experience gained through travel, experience that provides a positive view of internationalisation. Johanson and Vahlne (2009), who base their Uppsala model on behaviourist theory (Cyert and March 1963), argue that this accumulated experience, thanks to market information and knowledge, makes it possible to cope with resource constraints. In revisiting this model, they rely on the network approach and show the importance of cooperation between companies. They consider that they can create opportunities in foreign markets through the position within a relational network.

The Position Within a Network

The network approach emerges from the founding model of Johanson and Mattsson (1988) and from empirical work on SMEs (Holmlund and Kock 1998). According to this approach, internationalisation is a process by taking a position in the network of local actors, located abroad, rather than a sequential decision-making process. Researchers agree that inclusion in networks significantly improves the ability of SMEs to internationalise (Johanson and Mattsson 1988; Oviatt and McDougall 2005; Apitsa and Milliot 2019), thereby reducing the associated risks that may hinder opportunities in the targeted international market (Johanson and Vahlne 2009).

Global logistics chains are interdependent and geographically dispersed units that require the development of modes of transport between each location. This generates additional complexity. The units are legally bound by ownership, or by holding a share of the shares, or by a more or less complex supply or subcontracting contracts. Their integration is based on coordination, communication, and control. To have these mechanisms in place, a strong informational capacity is required. This is because, according to Hülsmann et al. (2008), global supply chains are hyper-competitive. Activities run at cruising speed in the price/quality field, in knowledge creation, in protection as well as in market penetration, in the formation of inter-firm cooperation. In such a context, customer loyalty is difficult to achieve. As a result, supply chain operators need to be proactive to create competitive advantages. This perspective can be understood through Dunning's OLI model (ownership advantages, location advantages, internalisation advantages) (1988). This author invites three sets of advantages to constitute an FDI. Borrowing from Hymer (1960/1976) the specific advantage (ownership advantages) and from Williamson (1975) the internalisation advantage (internalisation advantages), he adds a third advantage, which is the location advantage (location advantages). This paradigm makes it possible to understand how actors excel in their choice between internalisation and externalisation.

Thus, the exercise of an activity abroad requires certain intrinsic specificities of the SME: specific resources, skills, mastery of external factors, knowledge of the foreign market, capacity for innovation, and so on.

3 Research Methodology

Theoretical analyses of the internationalisation of firms have up to now focused on one type of determinant (demand, cost) and a geographical level of empirical observations, which is generally the country. In this study, we attempt to broaden and enrich this literature by also integrating the phenomena of port and maritime territories, a space where we can explicitly grasp the issues of competition between MNCs and transport and logistics SMEs, players in national and global trade flows.

West Africa is a market of 350 million inhabitants spread over an area of more than 6 million km-square, organised within a regional grouping: the Economic Community of West African States (ECOWAS). The companies surveyed operate in ECOWAS. The mission of this institution is to promote regional cooperation and integration with the objective of creating an economic and monetary union of West African countries.

Let us now present the socio-economic characteristics of the enterprises studied and the methodological approach used.

3.1 Presentation of the MNCs and SMEs Studied

Transport and logistics activities are carried out within maritime and port basins. They are organised around several players, the main ones being shipowners or shipping companies, stevedores or terminal operators, shippers, customs agents, freight forwarder companies (FFCs) or forwarding agents, land carriers, the Port Authority, and public authority services. These different actors intervene in the logistics chain either on the ship or on the goods. In the case of FFCs they act in the name and on behalf of shippers. The latter have a more decisive say in the choice of port as regards the goods, while the decision to call the ship at a port is taken by the shipowner (or consignee). That is why this research focuses on six major multinational maritime and port logistics firms (MNCs) present in all West African ports in the Dakar-Lagos range: Maersk, Mediterranean Shipping Company (MSC), the CMA CGM Group, Grimaldi, Necotrans, and Bolloré Transport Logistics (BTL). Operators such as COSCO, PIL, Nile Dutch, Dubai Ports World, and others are not dominant in the port of Cotonou, nor in other ports in the subregion. It should be noted that these six MNCs, which are shipowners and ship consignees, do not all have transit companies (FFCs). In the port of Cotonou there are three FFCs directly linked to these MNCs. The focus is on the port of Cotonou because it is a privileged hub of the West African hinterland. For example, some flows of goods re-exported from Niger to northern Nigeria originate from the port of Cotonou.

These large operators dominate the activity of the sector. It should be remembered that a large global operator can integrate all the activities of the global supply chain with a consignment company that handles its ships, a terminal operator that handles cargo at the port, a customs brokerage company (freight forwarder) to assist the shipper, or even a trucking or rail transport company to ensure the overland transport of cargoes. These activities are naturally part of an internationalisation process decided by headquarters, which appoints expatriate managers to run the agencies or sometimes promotes local executives.

In the Beninese customs database of authorised customs agents (2017), we have listed 129 FFCs. They were created from 1978 to 2017. In order to constitute our sample of SMEs under study, we exclude, de facto, forwarding agents from this database. A clearance of this list eliminated the subsidiaries of MNCs and Beninese public transit and service companies or the local industry. SMEs belonging to a large company (Anonymous Society) were also excluded from the study, since they naturally benefit from the traffic of the group's consignment company, reducing our database to 76 SMEs. The characteristic legal form of these SMEs is the limited liability company (LLC), which has certain advantages unlike other SMEs that follow the treaty of the Uniform Act of the Organisation for the Harmonisation of Business Law in Africa (OHBLA). All these companies share the local port traffic with only 14 SMEs (31%) that have a representative in neighbouring ports. This can be explained by the fact that some SMEs are subcontractors to large global operators and the huge investments required by the activity constitute a real barrier to entry in order to develop.

The SMEs studied operate on the port platform of Cotonou. They have between 10 and 100 employees (permanent and contractual). They are most often run by owner-managers or their representatives. They are very protective of their vision, their professional secrecy, and above all the profits to be made from a very profitable and highly capital-intensive activity, which reduces any possibility of opening up capital. The level of education of managers varies from a bachelor's degree (45%) to a professional master's or master's degree in law (25%), with a clear trend emerging: more than 80% of companies going international have managers at master's level: 75% of owner-managers are aged between 45 and 65. They

Table 6.1 West African hinterland companies studied

Characteristics	MNCs for maritime and port logistics		FFCs listed in the Beninese customs database			
	Shipowners or consignors		FFCs of MNCs	Large FFCs state-owned companies	FFCs of SMEs industrial companies and state-owned utilities	FFCs of SMEs
Number	06	03	28	22	76	
Legal form	Anonymous society (AS)	AS	AS	LLC	LLC	
Annual traffic volume as % of total	69	39	61			
Business revenues	Unlimited		Unlimited		−250 million FCFA	
Share capital	+50 million FCFA		+50 million FCFA		1 to 10 million FCFA	
Number of employees (permanent and contractual)	100 to 500		100 to 500		10 to 100	

Source: Benin Customs database

are predominantly married with several women and are perfectly familiar with the realities of neighbouring countries and ports. These company managers have a certain professional maturity and undeniable know-how. Table 6.1 presents these companies in the West African hinterland.

3.2 The Method

The empirical approach adopted is mixed (quantitative and qualitative) (Ragin 1987; De Meur and Rihoux 2002). It is a reasonable choice that is justified by the comparison of a so-called "small number" of cases, and precisely by the analysis of the effects of independence and complexity within the studied phenomenon (Greckhamer et al. 2008). The objective is to be able to generate a multiplicity of explanatory routes for the phenomenon under study. This approach offers a wide range of possibilities in the choice of units of analysis (individuals, organisations, countries) and the variables used (binary, multinomial, fuzzy sets). This last variable makes it possible to go beyond the restrictive vision of the dichotomisation of the membership scores of each case within an interval [0,1]. An iterative process has been put in place to ensure in-depth analysis of the observed evidence (Eisenhardt and Graebner 2007; Yin 2014).

We sent 135 questionnaires to managers and their close collaborators (three questionnaires per SME); 95 questionnaires were collected, and 75 valid questionnaires were used, that is, 55.55%. In view of the material and financial difficulty of reaching all the managers, a nonprobability sample of 45 SMEs was drawn in a reasoned manner, that is, 59.21%, which corresponds to the valid questionnaires used. The processing of the data was done with an Excel spreadsheet. In order to deepen our questionnaire study, the qualitative approach was adopted for two cases of local international SMEs (CAT-Logistics and SITT Benin). A previously established interview guide (according to the rules of the qualitative approach) was used to conduct nine semi-directive interviews with managers and their close collaborators. A content analysis was carried out to identify the salient points of the study. These results are presented, analysed, and discussed below.

4 Results, Analysis, and Discussion

Our empirical observations put into perspective two important elements that make it possible to answer the research questions and validate the propositions put forward: the dominance of MNCs in the transport-logistics activity and the success factors of SMEs that are internationalising at the level of the West African subregion.

4.1 Domination of Transport-Logistics MNCs in West Africa

At the port of Cotonou (PAC), the privileged gateway to the West African hinterland, we can therefore see a strong presence of the major world operators in logistics and transport: MAERSK, MSC, CMA CGM, COSCO, BOLLORÉ, GRIMALDI, and so on. These MNCs dominate the market. This can be seen in the activities of container and vehicle carrier port calls, containerised high-speed vessel traffic, and Roll-on/Roll-off (Ro-Ro) traffic.

Container and Vehicle Ships Calling at the PAC

Empirical evidence shows that on West African maritime routes, the port of Cotonou is the main port of call for container and vehicle ships for MNCs (Fig. 6.1).

Figure 6.1 shows that from 2012 to 2017, an average of 70% of container and vehicle ship calls were handled at the port of Cotonou. The port of Cotonou is a hub for second-hand vehicle traffic in West Africa (Godonou 2019). This is due to the high containerisation of maritime traffic in this port. The processing chain for the various types of traffic (containerised and Ro-Ro) is almost exclusively dedicated to the shipping agencies, stevedores, and forwarding agents of the major world operators.

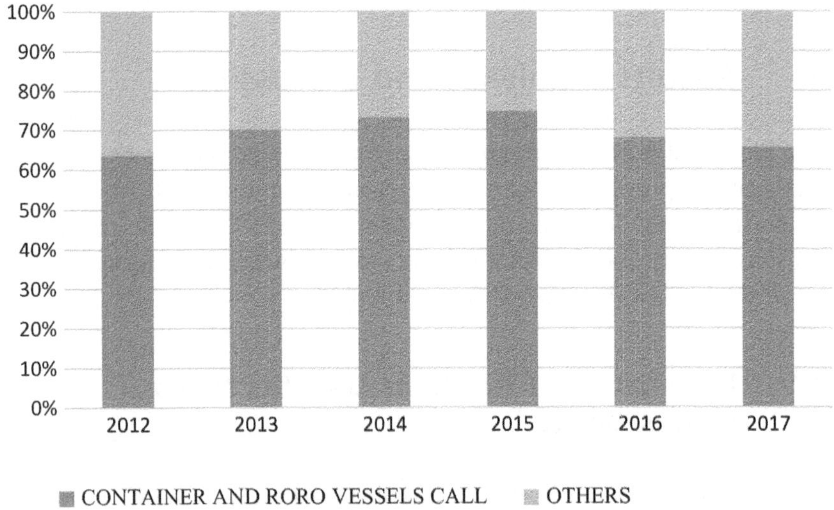

Fig. 6.1 Container and vehicle vessel calls (2012–2017). (Source: Data from the "*Direction Commerciale et Marketing/Port Autonome de Cotonou*" [DCM/PAC])

Containerised and Ro-Ro Traffic at PAC

The importance of the vessels operated by MNCs varies when it comes to containerised or Roll-on/Roll-off (Ro-Ro) traffic.

- Containerised high-speed vessel traffic

The major containerised traffic is operated by the world's three major shipping lines (MAERSK, MSC, and the CMA CGM Group) and handled by their local subsidiaries through integration of activities or in joint ventures with multinational partners (Figs. 6.2 and 6.3).

As shown in Figs. 6.2 and 6.3, from 2012 to 2017, the volume of traffic represents on average 65% of container ship calls. This volume is also handled by other logistics players (consignee or shipping agent, stevedore, and authorised customs agent).

- Ro-Ro traffic

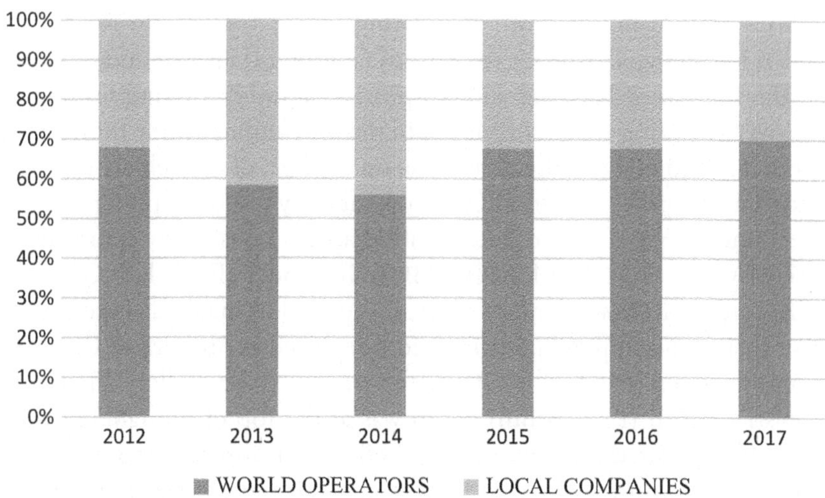

Fig. 6.2 Significant weight of containerised traffic (2012–2017): PAC containerships calls. (Source: Data from the "*Direction Commerciale et Marketing/Port Autonome de Cotonou*" [DCM/PAC])

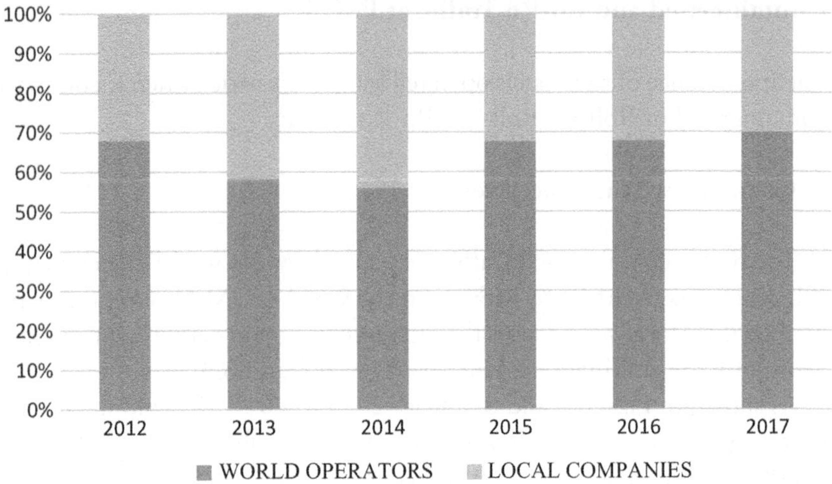

Fig. 6.3 Significant weight of containerised traffic (2012–2017): PAC traffic structure in TEUs. (Source: Data from the "*Direction Commerciale et Marketing/Port Autonome de Cotonou*" [DCM/PAC])

Ro-Ro traffic concerns the transport of heavy goods vehicles or trailers by special vessels (used cars transport, for example). The situation of MNCs' dominance is more stimulating in the case of Ro-Ro traffic, which is a strategic issue for the port of Cotonou (Figs. 6.4 and 6.5).

The analysis of Figs. 6.4 and 6.5 provides a rather striking reading of the overwhelming weight of MNCs in the port and maritime hinterland. From 2012 to 2017, more than 90%, on average, of the vehicle-carrying vessels at the port of Cotonou were operated by global shipping companies and beyond their local subsidiaries (consignee companies): GRIMALDI, SALLAUM, MOL, HOEGH, and THREE KINGS.

According to documentary sources, the world's major operators confirm their leadership in logistics services deployed as Authorized Customs Commissioners (ACC). In 2017, for example, the Bolloré Transport Logistics Benin (BTL-Benin) group was at the top of the ranking with 2372 files declared and more than 17 billion CFA francs (about 27 million euros) in duties collected by Beninese customs. It was followed by DAMCO-Benin (of the MAERSK group) with 647 declaration files and nearly 4 billion CFA francs (about 6 million euros) in duties paid, NECOTRANS-Benin with 295 declaration files and 2 billion CFA

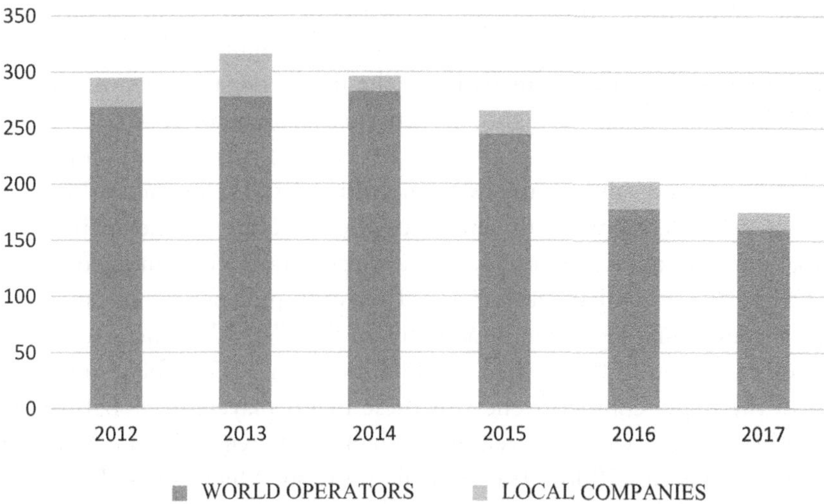

Fig. 6.4 Overwhelming weight of MNCs in Ro-Ro ship calls (2012–2017): PAC Ro-Ro ship calls (2010–2017). (Source: Data from the "*Direction Commerciale et Marketing/Port Autonome de Cotonou*" [DCM/PAC])

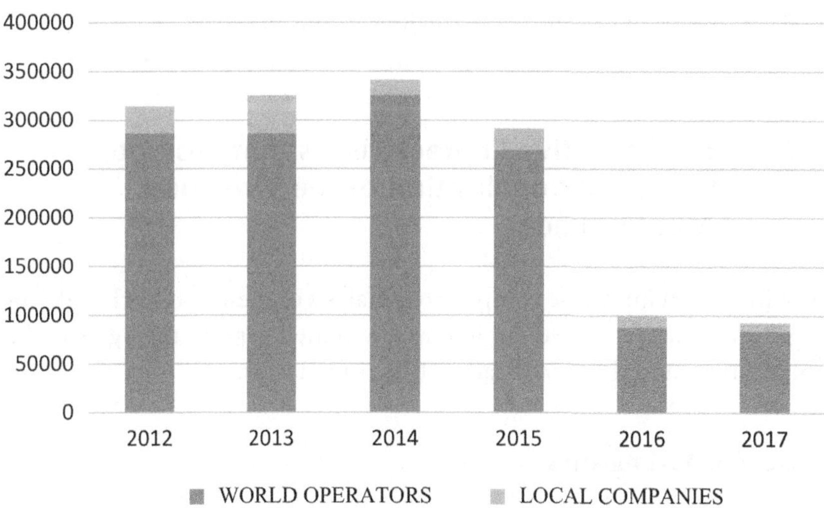

Fig. 6.5 Overwhelming weight of MNCs in Ro-Ro ship calls (2012–2017): PAC Ro-Ro traffic structure in cars. (Source: Data from the "*Direction Commerciale et Marketing/Port Autonome de Cotonou*" [DCM/PAC])

francs (more than 3 million euros) in duties paid, in 2017 to the customs administration. The FFCs' operations are very fragmented in the port of Cotonou and are mostly made up of the transit departments of companies involved in ship consignment activities (Lihoussou 2014).

The behaviour of MNCs activities in the West African port and maritime hinterland validates the first proposition P1. The major world operators (MNCs) significantly influence the structure of the main axes, corridors, or maritime routes, but also port hubs, terminals, or hubs (Debrie 2014; Lombard et al. 2014). Their omnipresence can be explained by a strategy of integrating the activities of these MNCs, which are organised into networks (Schoenherr 2009; Lihoussou 2017). The results confirm the hyper-competitiveness of these major players in global supply chains that are clearly developing adaptive strategies in the sense of Hülsmann et al. (2008). This strategic position, which is based on integration mechanisms supported by resources and a strong information capacity, may hinder the development of local SMEs. Paradoxically, 28% of SME managers surveyed believe that the presence of MNCs challenges local SMEs to improve the quality of their services in order to adapt to international standards. This certainly reflects a need to adapt transport-logistics services but calls for an analysis of the strategies of West African SMEs that take up this challenge of international expansion.

4.2 The Distinctive Characteristics that Promote the Internationalisation of the Two Local SMEs Studied

The inter- and intra-case comparative analysis of these two SMEs offering logistics services is carried out in relation to their genesis, their geographical location, and the career paths of their managers.

Case of CAT-Logistics

Compagnie d'Affrètement et de Transit Logistics (CAT-Logistics) is an SME created in 2010 by a Nigerien who graduated from World Maritime University (WMU) from Malmö in Sweden and moved to Niamey

(Niger) to meet the needs of Nigerien shippers for quality logistics services. It operates as a certified customs agent (FFC). The SME is active in Niger, Burkina Faso, Mali, Benin, Togo, and Ghana in the transit and transport sector. It offers transport, customs brokerage, sea and air chartering, groupage, and warehousing services within this regional network (Image 6.1).

Image 6.1 CAT-Logistics' geographical location network. Note: The market area covered by CAT-Logistics services is in grey. (Source: CAT-Logistics official website, consulted on 4/10/2019)

The owner-manager of CAT-Logistics is a graduate in Maritime Business Administration and Logistics. He managed Compagnie de Navigation Maritime au Niger, a state-owned company of sea-river transport of passengers and goods which chartered several ships, for about ten years. However, this company was dismantled and disappeared like most regional shipping lines of the day after the closure of the shipping conferences, and thus the end of the 40/40/20 cargo allocation law. After the failure of this public establishment, the promoter of CAT-Logistics capitalised on the networks of professional, political, and social contacts to access the various markets of large Nigerien companies and international institutions established in Niger. By relying on these professional networks, it very quickly opened offices in the ports of Cotonou (Benin), Lomé (Togo), and Tema (Ghana), with the aim of expanding its market. Furthermore, his training stays at WMU enabled him to build a network of contacts at the World Bank, in the United Nations system, and with West African port managers. He is very knowledgeable about transport and logistics issues in Africa. His professionalism opens the door to large contracts with UN institutions based in Niger (World Food Programme, UNDP, WHO, etc.) but also with large industrial and distribution companies. Based on the interviews with his partners and other actors, he is defined by the following meaningful adjectives: "rigorous", "strategist", "dedicated and ambitious", "professional", "fighter", and so on.

> CAT-Logistics is our partner since 2014 and this cooperation is still strong because we note that the CEO Ali DJIMBA is rigorous, professional and strategist. (General Manager of CMA CGM Group-Niger)

> I can say that the success story of CAT-Logistics is based on the CEO personality: he is a big fighter, dedicated and ambitious. Director of CNUT. (Conseil Nigérien des Utilisateurs de Transports)

This vision shared and disseminated throughout the company by its leader is a fundamental factor of national and international success. This is reflected in the opening of representations in Burkina Faso and Mali to handle a share of port traffic to or from Sahelian countries. Cat-Logistics provides quality services known for the company's know-how, thus competing with the services offered by major global logistics operators.

From this case of CAT-Logistic an example of interregional internationalisation (Africa to Africa) in the transport-logistics sector can be deduced. Empirical evidence shows that the leader, because of his personal characteristics (Oviatt and McDougall 1997, 2005) and background (Llord-Reason and Mughan 2002), has accumulated professional experience and developed an African business network and international relationships (Johanson and Vahlne 2009; Apitsa and Milliot 2019) which constitute strategic resources for seizing opportunities in a market dominated by MNCs. The skills and resources (Penrose 1959) are acquired through an accumulation of advantages in the sense of the OLI model (Dunning 1988).

Case of the SITT Benin

The *Société Internationale de Transit Touré* (SITT Benin) created in 2003 in Cotonou, Benin, is a company specialising in air, sea, and land transit operations and international transport. Four years after its creation, it has equipped itself with a fleet of 12 trucks for the transport and delivery of goods to customers for whom it carries out customs clearance at the port and airport of Cotonou. In 2010, SITT Benin received the World Customs Organisation (WCO) Merit Trophy, which ranks it among the best transit companies in Benin. The project of SITT Benin, as formulated by its owner-manager, is to open the company to international markets by creating subsidiaries in ECOWAS countries and to associate port handling activities in the port of Cotonou. Its owner-manager holds a master's degree in law and a certificate of training in transit. He was an employee of the Bolloré group in Benin before setting up his own account. This allowed him to gain professional experience. However, competitive rivalries with his former employer Bolloré limited his ability to develop his activities in Benin and open internationally. Indeed, the overwhelming weight of the Bolloré Transport Logistics group, supported by an intense professional and political network, is hindering the development of SITT Benin in its conquest of the interregional market. This competition impacts its market shares. For example, the data collected indicate that in 2010 SITT Benin executed a few transit and logistics transport contracts in the countries of the subregion. Since then, however, it has been struggling to establish itself in these countries. Worse still, our observations show a decline in the company's customer portfolio, which is refocusing its activities on Benin and transit to Niger. In 2017, SITT Benin processed only one-tenth of the declarations compared to its competitor CAT-Logistics (i.e. 36/360).

The analysis of the SITT case, compared to the CAT-Logistics case, suggests a certain difficulty with respect to internationalisation in the face of the weight of the Bolloré group. Interregional internationalisation is limited to a single country, Niger. Beyond the competitive rivalries revealed by the SITT case, our results reveal that this domination encourages the use of direct bills of lading (direct B/L) in an integrated door-to-door offer. It increasingly leads to subcontracting contracts for the land component. This perspective reinforces the literature on overcoming the difficulties inherent in resources and skills through cooperation or the creation of subsidiaries (Haahti et al. 2005; Milliot and Tournois 2010). This is the case, for example, of CAT-Logistics Benin with more than 360 declarations approaching 2 billion FCFA (about 3,048,788 euros) in duties paid and, to a lesser extent, of SITT Benin for 36 declarations with 166 million FCFA (about 256,000 euros) in duties paid to Beninese customs in 2017.

The general manager of SITT testifies to this in this verbatim: "The major world operators (MNCs) are in all ports and do not have the same constraints as we do in terms of financial capacity. Now with the status of Authorised Economic Operator (AEO), Customs Office demands a lot from us, but not from them, because of their status as a multinational corporation, so the competitive game is a bit distorted in my opinion" (General manager, SITT). This is consistent with our survey results, which indicate that 72% of SME managers believe that the overwhelming weight of these groups on port traffic prevents them from accumulating the resources they need to develop and open up internationally.

This empirical discourse corroborates the literature on the financial vulnerability of SMEs in their internationalisation trajectories to MNCs resources (Leonidou 2004; Mtigwe 2006).

Overall, in both case studies, our results validate the second proposition P2. Despite their modest financial capacity, the results show that the backgrounds of the managers of the two SMEs (level of education, professional experience, know-how, market knowledge, integration into a business network, and relational skills) is a key strategic dimension for facing MNCs' competition and developing in the West African port and maritime hinterland. This pathway is useful in reducing the risks associated with a lack of skills and resources and allows for the development of "timely" international development strategies.

5 Conclusion: Managerial Implications and Limitations

The transport-logistics activity is constantly evolving, a logical consequence of the globalisation of activities. The competitive situation, which gives a high concentration of activities to MNCs, limits the integration of local SMEs in the large global transport-logistics chains in West Africa.

Nevertheless, our results show that some local SMEs are succeeding in internationalising. This internationalisation is very recent and reflects the new phenomenon of FDI from Africa to Africa. It is not sequential and is like early internationalisation (born global firm of Oviatt and McDougall [1997, 2005]). Several explanatory factors of distinction (in relation to SMEs that fail) define it: career path of the manager (accumulated professional experience), skills, knowledge of the West African market, integration into a business network, and relational.

Our empirical observations lead us to suggest that large operators should demonstrate responsibility (contribution to the economic development of the country of establishment) by creating a space for integration and cooperation with local SMEs. This can be done through inter-firm cooperation agreements (Haahti et al. 2005; Hülsmann et al. 2008; Milliot and Tournois 2010). Even if this approach is not without its difficulties, it is meaningful and creates jobs, ultimately leading to shared economic and social well-being. For local SMEs, their behaviour shows that their managers have strong skills and accumulated experience.

The integration in business and relational networks should be sustainable as it is a competitive advantage (Johanson and Vahlne 2009; Apitsa and Milliot 2019). Moreover, to meet the competitive challenge of MNCs, we recommend that SMEs capitalise on their resources by mobilising digital tools (Lihoussou 2020) to develop remote international activities via artificial intelligence (development of cooperation with foreign operators under the Born global firms' model) (Oviatt and McDougall 1997; Dominguez and Mayrhofer 2016). This is the strength of the capacity for innovation. Their career path also reveals the strategic dimension of differentiation and value creation for themselves and for loyal and potential customers.

Our research has limits. However, through the field experience to which this research bears witness, the context of studying the internationalisation of SMEs in Africa and more specifically West African transport-logistics SMEs demonstrates a promising framework for research on a sector of activity little explored in the literature. The economic emergence of Africa and more precisely the West African space is inconceivable without better access and control of transport and logistics activities by territorial actors.

References

Abbad, H., & Paché, G. (2013). The Impact of Logistical Criteria in the Selection of SMEs by Large Food Retailers—A Case Study in an Emerging Country. *Problems and Perspectives in Management, 11*(1), 25–35.

Adda, J. (2007). *La mondialisation de l'économie. Genèse et problèmes*. Paris: La Découverte.

Andersen, O. (1993). On the Internationalization Process of Firms: A Critical Analysis. *Journal of International Business Studies, 24*(2), 209–231.

Apitsa, S. M. (2019). Management International en Afrique: Enjeux, Défis et Opportunités de Recherche et Managériales. Actes 9ème conférence annuelle d'Atlas AFMI, *Le national face au global: nouvelles perspectives pour le management international,* Université de Fribourg (Suisse), 17–19, juin, 24 p.

Apitsa, S. M., & Milliot, E. (2019). De l'Intérêt des Réseaux d'Affaires face aux Défis de la Dynamique Economique et Socio-Culturelle des Contextes Nationaux Africains. Actes 9ème conférence annuelle d'Atlas AFMI, *Le national face au global: nouvelles perspectives pour le management international*, Université de Fribourg (Suisse), 17–19 juin, Fribourg, 37 p.

Bakunda, G. (2003). Explaining Firm Internationalization in Africa using the Competence Approach. *Journal of African Business, 4*(1), 57–85.

Bandeira-De-Mello, R., Ghauri, P. N., Mayrhofer, U., & Meschi, P.-X. (2015). Introduction to the Special Issue: Theoretical and Empirical Implications for Research on South-South and South-North Expansion Strategies. *M@n@gement, 18*(1), 1–7.

Banque africaine de développement. (2019). Rapport, *Perspectives économiques en Afrique: Performances macroéconomiques en Afrique et perspectives. Emploi, croissance et dynamisme des entreprises. L'intégration pour la prospérité économique de l'Afrique*. BAD, 234 p.

Baron, M.-L., & Apitsa, S. M. (2017). Le Défi de la Transition Energétique et les Conditions d'adoption des Eco-énergies dans le Secteur du Transport: Le Cas des Tracteurs Electriques. *Logistique & Management, 25*(2), 84–95.

Bell, J., McNaughton, R., Young, S., & Crick, D. (2003). Towards an Integrative Model of Small Firm Internationalization. *Journal of International Entrepreneurship, 1*, 339–362.

Bellin-Munier, C. (2013). Les Défis de la Gestion des Chaînes Logistiques Globales (Global Supply Chain Management). In V. Carbone, S. Nivoix, & J.-P. Lemaire (Eds.), *Nouveaux défis du management international* (pp. 119–135). Paris: Lextenso.

Boso, N., Adeleye, I., Ibeh, K., & Chizema, A. (2018). The Internationalization of African Firms: Opportunities, Challenges, and Risks. *Thunderbird International Business Review, 61*, 1–8.

Boston Consulting Group. (2010). *The African Challengers: Global Competitors Emerge from the Overlooked Continent*, 12 p. Retrieved from www.bcg.com/documents/file44610.pdf.

Bowersox, D. J., & Sterling, J. U. (1982). Multinational Logistics. *Journal of Business Logistics, 3*(2), 15–25.

Brunel, S. (2004). *L'Afrique, un continent en réserve de développement* (235 p). Paris: Éditions Bréal.

Buckley, P. (1997). International Technology Transfer by Small and Medium-Sized Enterprises. *Small Business Economics, 9*(1), 67–78.

Cavusgil, S. T., Knight, G., & Reisenberger, J. R. (2008). *International Business: Strategy, Management, and New Realities*. Upper Saddle River, NJ: Pearson International Edition.

Charlier, J., & Tossa, J. (1996). L'arrière-pays international du port de Cotonou. *Bulletin de la Société Belge d'Études Géographiques, 65*(1), 93–122.

Cheaitou, A., & Cariou, P. (2017). A Two-Stage Maritime Supply Chain Optimization Model. *International Journal of Shipping and Transport Logistics, 9*(2), 202–232.

Coviello, N., & Jones, M. V. (2004). Methodological Issues in International Entrepreneurship Research. *Journal of Business Venturing, 19*, 485–508.

Cyert, R. M., & March, J. C. (1963). *A Behavioral Theory of the Firm*. Englewood Cliffs, NJ: Prentice Hall.

De Meur, G., & Rihoux, B. (2002). *L'analyse quali-quantitative comparée: Approche, techniques et applications en sciences humaines*. Belgique: Academia Bruylant.

Debrie, J. (2014). Portrait d'entreprise. Hubs Portuaires (3): Les Stratégies des Opérateurs sur la Façade Ouest-Africaine. *Flux, 97/98*, 110–117.

Dichtl, E., Koeglmayr, H. G., & Mueller, S. (1990). International Orientation as a Precondition for Export Success. *Journal of International Business Studies, 21*(1), 23–40.

Dominguez, N., & Mayrhofer, U. (2016). Il n'est jamais trop tard pour entreprendre: l'Internationalisation des Born-Again Globals. *Revue de l'entrepreneuriat, 15*(1), 61–80.

Dunning, J. H. (1988). The Eclectic Paradigm of International Production: A Restatement and Some Possible Extensions. *Journal of International Business Studies, 19*(1), 1–31.

Eisenhardt, K., & Graebner, M. E. (2007). Theory Building from Cases: Opportunities and Challenges. *Academy of Management Journal, 50*(1), 25–32.

Ellram, L., & Cooper, M. (2014). Supply Chain Management: It's About the Journey, Not the Destination. *Journal of Supply Chain Management, 50*(1), 13–24.

Ellram, L. M. (1996). The Use of the Case Study Method in Logistic Research. *Journal of Business Logistics, 17*(2), 93–138.

Fabbe-Costes, N., Livolsi, L., & Separi, S. (2018). Le Supply Chain Management. Décloisonner pour créer de la Valeur. *Revue Française de Gestion, 44*(277), 13–24.

Fredouet, Ch.-H., & Le Mestre, P. (2014). Mesure de Performance de Réseau: Le Cas des Places Portuaires. *La logistique*, pp. 243–262.

Godonou, C. J. (2019). Impact Socio-Environnemental du marché de Véhicules d'Occasion en Afrique au sud du Sahara: Le Cas du Port de Cotonou. In

M. Tchindjang, B. Steck, & A. Bopda (Eds.), *Construire la Ville Portuaire de demain en Afrique Atlantique* (pp. 439–465). Caen: EMS.

Goldsby, T. J., Zinn, W., Closs, D. J., Daugherty, P. J., Stock, J. R., Fawcett, S. E., & Waller, M. (2019). Reflections on 40 Years of the Journal of Business Logistics: From the Editors. *Journal of Business Logistics, 40*(1), 4–29.

Goxe, F. (2010). Human and Social Capital Interplay among Internationalizing SMEs. *Journal of Knowledge-based Innovation in China, 2*(1), 73–88.

Greckhamer, T., Misangyl, V. F., Elms, H., & Lacey, R. (2008). Using Qualitative Comparative Analysis in Strategic Management Research: An Examination of Combinations of Industry, Corporate, and Business-Unit Effect. *Organizational Research Methods, 11*(4), 695–726.

Haahti, A., Madupu, V., Yavas, U., & Babakus, E. (2005). Cooperative Strategy, Knowledge Intensity and Export Performance of Small and Medium sized Enterprises. *Journal of world Business, 40*(2), 124–138.

Hammami, R., Frein, L., & Hadj-Alouane, A. B. (2008). Supply Chain Design in the Delocalization Context: Relevant Features and New Modelling Tendencies. *International Journal of Productions Economics, 111*, 641–656.

Holmlund, M., & Kock, S. (1998). Relationships and the Internationalization of Finnish Small and Medium-sized Companies. *International Small Business Journal, 16*(4), 46–63.

Hülsmann, M., Grapp, J., & Li, Y. (2008). Strategic Adaptivity in Global Supply Chains: Competitive Advantage by Autonomous Cooperation. *International Journal of Production Economics, 46*(2), 14–26.

Hymer, S. H. (1960/1976). *The International Operations of National Firms: A Study of Direct Foreign Investment*. Cambridge, MA: MIT Press.

Johanson, J., & Mattsson, L.-G. (1988). *Internationalization in Industrial Systems: A Network* (pp. 468–486). New York: Croom Helm.

Johanson, J., & Vahlne, J. E. (2009). The Uppsala Internationalization Process Model Revisited: From Liability of Foreignness to Liability of Outsidership. *Journal of International Business Studies, 40*(9), 1411–1431.

Laghzaoui, S. (2011). SMEs Internationalization with the Concept of Resources and Competences. *Journal of Innovation Economics & Management, 7*, 181–196.

Lee, C., & Wilhelm, W. (2010). On Integrating Theories of International Economics in the Strategic Planning of Global Supply Chains and Facility Location. *International Journal of Productions Economics, 124*, 225–240.

Leonidou, L. C. (2004). An analysis of the Barriers Hindering Small Business Export Development. *Journal of Small Business Management, 42*(3), 279–302.

Lihoussou, M. (2014). *Ports et Désenclavement Territorial: Cas de l'arrière-pays du Port de Cotonou.* Thèse de Doctorat en Géographie des Transports à l'Université du Havre, 466 p.
Lihoussou, M. (2017). Dysfonctionnements et Entraves à la Circulation en Afrique de l'Ouest: l'exemple du Corridor Abidjan-Cotonou. *Les Cahiers Scientifiques du Transport, 72*, 43–66.
Lihoussou, M. (Ed.). (2020). *Gouverner Ports, Transports et Logistique à l'Ere du Numérique.* Coll. Afrique Atlantique, Caen: EMS, 288 p.
Llord-Reason, L., & Mughan, T. (2002). Strategies for Internationalisation within SMEs: The Key Role of the Owner-Manager. *Journal of Small Business and Enterprise Development, 9*(2), 120–129.
Lombard, J., Ninot, O., & Steck, B. (2014). Corridors de transport en Afrique et intégration territoriale en question. In A. Gana & Y. Richard (Eds.), *La régionalisation du monde, construction territoriale et articulation global/local* (pp. 253–272). Paris: IRMC-KARTHALA.
Lu, J. W., & Beamish, P. W. (2006). The Internationalization and Performance of SMEs. *Strategic Management Journal, 2*, 565–586.
Luo, Y., & Tung, R. L. (2007). International Expansion of Emerging Market Enterprises: A Springboard Perspective. *Journal of International Business Studies, 8*(4), 481–498.
Manolova, T. S., Brush, C. G., Edelman, L. F., & Greene, P. G. (2002). Internationalization of Small Firms: Personal Factors Revisited. *International Small Business Journal, 20*(1), 9–31.
Mareï, N. (2017). Régionalisation entre Maghreb et Afrique de l'Ouest: Regard Géographique. In C. Mballa & I. Mandé (Eds.), *L'Afrique est-elle partie ? Bilan et Perspectives de l'Intégration Africaine* (Transformations Revue Interventions économiques, Hors-série) (pp. 33–36). Transformations.
Mentzer, J. T., & Kahn, K. B. (1995). A Framework for Logistics Research. *Journal of Business Logistics, 16*(1), 231–250.
Miller, T., & de Mattra, R. (2008). A Global Supply Chain Profit Maximization and Transfer Pricing Model. *Journal of Business Logistics, 29*(1), 175–199.
Milliot, E., & Tournois, N. (Eds.). (2010). *The Paradoxes of Globalization.* London: Palgrave Macmillan.
Morgan, I. P., & Arnold, P. M. (1990). International Logistics Management. *Journal of Business Logistics, 11*(2), 140–158.
Morvan, T. (2014). Le Port Maritime de Commerce: Evolutions et Enjeux au sein des Chaînes Logistiques. *La logistique*, pp. 225–242.

Mtigwe, B. (2006). Theoretical Milestones in International Business: The Journey to International Entrepreneurship Theory. *Journal of International Entrepreneurship, 4*(1), 5–25.

Nelson, P. T., & Toledano, G. (1979). Challenges for International Logistics Management. *Journal of Business Logistics, 1*(2), 1–21.

Ngwu, F., Adeleye, I., & Ogbechie, C. (2015). Africa-to-Africa Internationalization: Rhetoric, Reality and Risks of Intra-African Regional Expansion. In S. Nwankwo & K. Ibeh (Eds.), *The Routledge Companion to Business in Africa* (pp. 9–31). London and New York: Routledge.

Omokaro-Romanus, C., Anchor, J. R., & Konara, P. (2019). The Internationalization of Nigerian Firms: Motivations and Location Patterns. *Thunderbird International Business Review, 61*, 75–88.

Oviatt, B. M., & McDougall, P. P. (1997). Challenges for Internationalization Process: The Case of Internationalization New Ventures. *Management International Review, 37*(2), 85–99.

Oviatt, B. M., & McDougall, P. P. (2005). Defining International Entrepreneurship and Modeling the Speed of Internationalization. *Entrepreneurship Theory & Practice, 29*(5), 537–553.

Pantin, F. (2010). Conduire l'Internationalisation des PME: Un Processus porté par les Compétences de l'Equipe Dirigeante. *Revue Internationale PME, 23*(3–4), 13–42.

Paul, J., Parthasarathy, S., & Gupta, P. (2017). Exporting Challenges of SMEs: A Review and Future Research Agenda. *Journal of World Business, 52*(3), 327–372.

Penrose, E. T. (1959). *The Theory of the Growth of the Firm*. New York: John Wiley et Sons.

Prime, N., Obadia, C., & Vida, I. (2009). Psychic Distance in Exporter-Importer Relationships. A Grounded Theory Approach. *International Business Review, 18*(2), 184–198.

Qu, W., Rezaei, J., Maknoon, Y., & Tavasszy, L. (2019). Hinterland Freight Transportation Replanning Model under the Framework of Synchromodality. *Transportation Research Part E: Logistics and Transportation Review, 131*, 308–328.

Ragin, C. C. (1987). *The Comparative Method. Moving Beyond Qualitative and Quantitative Strategies*. Los Angeles and Berkeley: University of California Press.

Schoenherr, T. (2009). Logistics and Supply Chain Management Applications within Global Context: An Overview. *Journal of Business Logistics, 30*(2), 1–25.

Stoian, M. C., & Rialp-Criado, A. (2010). Analysing Export Behavior through Managerial Characteristics and Perceptions: A Multiple Case-based Research. *Journal of Global Marketing, 23*(4), 333–348.

Tchindjang, M., Steck, B., & Bopda, A. (Eds.). (2019). *Construire la Ville Portuaire de demain en Afrique Atlantique*, coll. Afrique Atlantique, Caen: EMS, 681 p.

UNCTAD. (2018). *Review of Maritime Transport*. Geneva, Switzerland: United Nations, 116 p.

Williamson, O. (1975). *Market and Hierarchies: Analysis and Antitrust Implications. A Study in the Economics of Internal organization*. New York: Free Press.

Wu, F., Sinkovics, R. R., Cavusgil, S. T., & Roath, A. S. (2007). Overcoming Export Manufacturers Dilemma in International Expansion. *Journal of International Business Studies, 38*(2), 283–302.

Yin, R. K. (2014). *Case Study Research: Design and Methods* (5th ed.). Thousand Oaks: Sage.

7

Highlighting Performance Indicators for Dry Ports in Landlocked Countries: The Case of Burkina Faso

Gwenaëlle Oruezabala and Rodrigue Balima

1 Introduction

In West Africa, transport infrastructure is an essential tool in the territorial development process. However, numerous dysfunctions hamper the fluidity of circulation between countries and disrupt the logistical links necessary for regional integration (Lihoussou 2017). Port areas regularly experience many operating difficulties, including recurrent congestion of infrastructure and various disturbances in the transit of goods, which cause long delays and exorbitant costs (Dinangue 2017). According to this author, the dysfunctions reveal poor logistical organisation by the operators—carriers and their auxiliaries—and a lack of knowledge of terminals' performance indicators. In landlocked countries, the obstacles

G. Oruezabala (✉)
Nantes University, Nantes, France
e-mail: Oruezabala-g@univ-nantes.fr

R. Balima
University Aube-Nouvelle, Ouagadougou, Burkina Faso

S. M. Apitsa, E. Milliot (eds.), *Doing Business in Africa*, Palgrave Studies of Internationalization in Emerging Markets,
https://doi.org/10.1007/978-3-030-50739-8_7

and constraints to the fluidity of traffic are further increased due to these nations' isolation and dependence on the logistical organisation of their hinterlands. In Burkina Faso's case, its dry port Ouagarinter plays an interesting role in the country's logistical network.

According to European authorities, a dry port is an inland intermodal terminal directly connected by road or rail to a seaport (UNECE 2001). This definition of a dry port is particularly broad, and many logistics terminals could theoretically fit this description because their roads link to seaports. It is therefore necessary to better define the concept of dry port by focusing on academic work in supply chain management (SCM). For Roso et al. (2009), a dry port is an intermodal terminal that operates as a centre for the transhipment of sea cargo to inland destinations, which implies that users can leave and/or collect their goods in intermodal loading units, just as they may at a seaport.

In addition to these conventional transhipments, dry ports offer value-added services such as storage, consolidation, traceability and customs clearance (Notteboom and Rodrigue 2012; Roso and Rosa 2012; Andersson and Roso 2016).

On the basis of these observations, the empirical study presented in this chapter analyses the contribution of a port in Burkina Faso's hinterland—the dry port of Ouagarinter—to the performance of global logistics chains. It is not so much a question of measuring this performance as of analysing the determinants of value creation in the supply chains of landlocked countries.

The first section of this chapter is dedicated to a literature review focused on the contribution of a dry port to value creation in SCM. The second section highlights the context of Burkina Faso's relationship to the globalisation of logistics chains. The third section details an empirical study conducted with Burkinabé actors in the port ecosystem. Finally, the fourth section suggests several elements of a dry port that contribute to value creation in global supply chains.

2 Contribution of the Port Ecosystem to the Creation of Global Value

Recent research in SCM has analysed the performance of transport corridors in sub-Saharan African countries, highlighting dysfunctions with regard to global standards, which limit the capacity of these countries to integrate major global logistics chains (Pelletier 2012; Lihoussou 2017). Few academic works, however, have focused on the contribution of an internal port link to the added value of global logistics chains. The attractiveness of a dry port remains, therefore, a subject that requires further research. It is important to first define the concepts and actors involved before discussing their potential contributions to value creation through performance indicators.

2.1 Actors and Concepts Within a Port Ecosystem

A port link, as described by Barkadleh (2016), comprises a community of actors generally linked by logistics activities but specifically oriented towards port logistics services. Fredouët and Guérin (2002) note the multitude of actors operating in a port, beginning with the port authority, the companies providing logistics services (carriers, forwarders, handlers, etc.), public administrations (customs, sanitary control, security services, etc.) and, of course, the shippers who import and/or export goods. All of these actors are integrated into one or more global logistics chains. These chains can be defined simply by the multiplicity of intermediaries between a supplier and an end customer that makes it possible to design, manufacture and deliver the right product to the right location, at the right time, at the right price (ASLOG 2020). However, some authors refine this general definition by studying supply chains from four perspectives—strategic, systemic, structural and relational (Brindley 2017). From a strategic perspective, Ketchen et al. (2008) see the supply chain as a key competitive weapon for the company insofar as the operations go beyond the simple movement of materials so that the shipper's customers benefit from a higher total value in terms of speed, cost, quality and flexibility. From a systemic perspective, Saikouk and Spalanzani

(2012) consider supply chains to be dynamic and complex systems made up of autonomous enterprises that interact with each other to achieve a common goal. From a structural perspective, the supply chain is organised into networks of actors as entities involved in the production and delivery of a finished product to the end customer (Sanders 2020). Finally, from a relational perspective, Ketchen and Giunipero (2004) see in the supply chain 'a relatively sustainable inter-enterprise cooperative which uses the resources of the participants to achieve the shared and independent objectives of its members'. Zouaghi (2013) offers a procedural and functional fifth dimension based on the work of Zhang et al. (2003), who define the supply chain as a set of synergistically managed activities and functions. For her part, Fabbe-Coste (2007) suggests organisational and technological factors with the aim of integrating supply chains from a lean and agile perspective. Concerning more specifically the maritime activity sector, De Noray (2015) claims that the main challenges for dry ports on the African continent relate to the logistical components that complement the port infrastructure. Moreover, Barkadleh (2016) maintains that supply chains are built around the port ecosystem and that the contribution of this link to the performance of the global supply chain is identifiable and measurable (see Fig. 7.1).

2.2 Performance Indicators for a Port Ecosystem

The previous section established that each stakeholder can potentially contribute to the creation of value in supply chains. For some authors, however, the challenges of improving logistics performance in the face of dysfunctions and the risk of disruption stem in part from joint efforts to optimise logistics chains (Kleindorfer and Saad 2005). In addition, since the latter are systems composed of interdependent and evolving elements, disturbances in one of the links can negatively influence the performance of the whole chain (Craighead et al. 2007). According to Van der Horst and De Langen (2008), the performance of a dry port largely depends on the quality of the road and/or rail interfaces necessary to access the desired seaport. The authors stress, however, that the flow of traffic within a

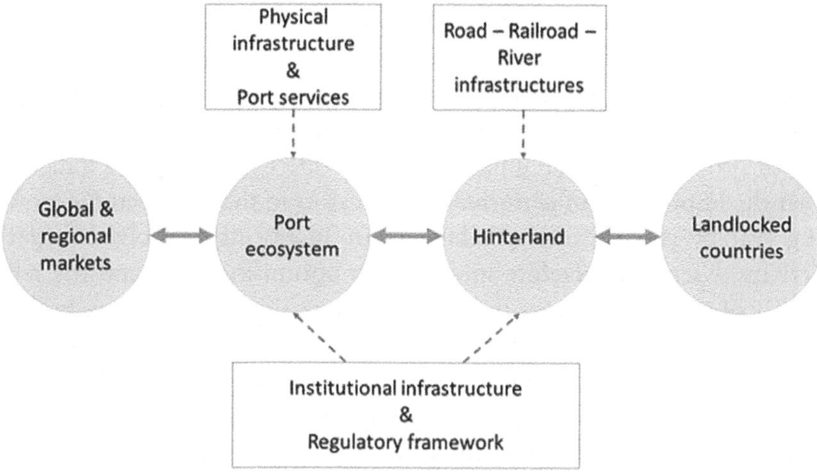

Fig. 7.1 Port ecosystem at the heart of global supply chains. (Source: Adapted from 'African development report 2010: ports, logistics and trade in Africa', The African development bank)

hinterland depends on the behaviour of a wide variety of logistics intermediaries and requires coordination between all the actors involved.

In this multidimensional context of supply chains, Zouaghi (2013) outlines the necessary classification of performance indicators. These indicators are generally of three types: alert indicators, which indicate an abnormal state of the controlled structure; indicators of balance, which make it possible to read the state of the system compared to the objectives followed; and indicators of anticipation, which allow the development of forward-looking strategies. With regard to the sector of ports specifically, De Monie (2012) distinguishes four categories of performance measures. First, production measures express the quantities processed (product, production, turnover, number of visits, etc.). Second, productivity measures report the quantities processed per production unit (production line, worker, machine, square metre of storage, etc.). Third, measures of use express the actual use of production resources in the form of ratios. Fourth, measures of the quality of service offered to the customers of a port or terminal (shipowners, shippers, recipients of goods, logistics service providers, etc.) are indicators of satisfaction and attractiveness.

Finally, Pichot (2006) argues that the success of the overall management of a supply chain is mainly dependent on three factors: new technologies to process a large volume of data, the human/organisational aspect whose objective is to break down the functional barriers and transverse operational processes to make links inseparable. De Langen (2008) indicates that the importance of performance indicators in the port sector is growing year by year because stakeholders are increasingly involved in port activity. Users are therefore interested in optimising costs and the reliability of operations. From the examination of these performance indicators, users will choose a port that will increase both the efficiency and the sustainability of their operations. In addition to the elements of cost and reliability, decision-makers are also increasingly sensitive to the port's employment rate and carbon footprint, that is to say, its social and environmental impact. Frédouët and Le Mestre (2005) argue that it is by minimising the costs and transit times of goods that the port contributes to the value of the chain for customers of the port and beyond the port community. Barkadleh (2016) identifies the geographic location and security of the global supply chain as particularly effective determinants of the port supply chain's value contribution. This last author proposes to deploy a port performance model, the SCOFS model, which incorporates Security, Commercial, Operational, Financial and Service dimensions. This model highlights the measurable nature of the quality of supply chain management. Considering this diversity of indicators, the following section examines their use in the context of Burkina Faso, which does not have a maritime facade but, nonetheless, takes advantage of two so-called dry ports.

3 The Managerial Context of Burkinabé Inland Ports and Their Contribution to the Performance of Global Logistics Chains

In 2018, the annual report of the United Nations Conference on Trade and Development (UNCTAD 2018) estimated that twenty ports handled 9 billion tonnes of world maritime trade, that 752 million twenty-foot equivalent units (TEUs) had been moved to ports around the world, figures which therefore established that 90% of world trade takes place by sea transport. Although one-third of African countries have no coastline, maritime transport remains the principal means of access to the global market. Yet African ports represent only 4% of the volume of world port traffic of containerised goods, a large part of which is made up of imports of manufactured products. Africa's weak presence in the world maritime trade then raises questions towards the political and economic authorities of the African continent. The latter are, in fact, aware that container ports and hinterland transport networks must rely on efforts to modernise infrastructures in order to improve their performance and thus take part in world trade. Responses to these challenges could emerge from subregional bodies. Since 2000, 50 billion dollars have been injected into the port interfaces so that the port terminals have platform lines and fleet areas adapted to new sizes of ships. The models of public/private partnerships, mainly in the forms of concessions or build operate transfers, accompanied the changes in the interfaces and changed the relationship between the port authorities, on the one hand, and the operators on the other. The Ports Management Association of West and Central Africa (PMAWCA) annual council, held in Lomé in June 2019, addressed the question of metropolitan logistics fluidity in Africa. This association predicts that in 2020 the terminal projects completed should make it possible to offer forecasted reception capacities of 25 million TEUs in southern, central and eastern Africa and 13 million TEUs in West Africa. And of these 38 million TEUs, two-thirds will operate in the ports of Bagamoyo in Tanzania (10 million TEUs), Durban in South Africa (9.6 million TEUs) and Tema in Ghana (3.5 million TEUs).

In such a context, how can a landlocked country take part in global supply chains? In Burkina Faso, the Directorate General of Land and Maritime Transport provides transport administration at the technical level. It relies on the Chamber of Commerce and Industry of Burkina Faso (CCI-BF), which performs the services necessary for trade and industry to function and which is the exclusive concession holder for management of warehouses (stores and customs clearance areas). This consular institution has two dry ports (Ouagarinter and Bobointer) where 85,000 square metres of shops are located and 180,000 square meters of transit and customs clearance areas represent borders in these two cities.

The Ouagarinter dry port (ODP) represents an important element in the logistics network of Burkina Faso. Indeed, it is an economically important platform for logistics activities since it contributes to the opening of this landlocked country. ODP processes 10,000 weighed trucks on the weighbridge each year, 7000 international freight vehicles, 10,000 TEUs on the container terminal and a total of 800,000 tonnes of goods. The six main components of the ODP are (1) a 21.7-ha customs area consisting of such elements as administrative buildings, warehouses, a container terminal and an operating car fleet; (2) a 3.3-ha area consisting of such elements as export halls, freight forwarder buildings, a control building, warehouses and parking lots; (3) a 5-ha commercial area consisting of such elements as meeting rooms, hotels and restaurants, shops, bank counters; (4) a 2-ha vocational school; (5) a 10-ha industrial-free zone and (6) a 4-ha hall for the export of agricultural food products. Ouagarinter can therefore be considered the first West African platform that processes national and international traffic of imported goods by road. This traffic generally produces an annual revenue for the CCI-BF of more than 3 million euros. Ouagarinter also contributes to the collection of 30% to 40% of annual customs revenue, which represents part of Burkina Faso's national revenue. Despite these profitable results, the current surface area of Ouagarinter is not sufficient for extensions necessary to accommodate the increase in traffic, containerisation, storage needs, parking needs and exchange needs.

The interests of shippers in Burkina Faso and neighbouring countries are represented by the Burkinabé Shippers Council in the two transit ports mentioned above. Despite this representation, there are many obstacles and constraints to the flow of traffic into and out of these ports. These include regular non-compliance with the maximum axle load, excessive road checks, imposed customs escorts, the difficulty of applying the Inter-State Road Transit system and inadequate training of carriers and their auxiliaries. In addition, there is no real overall management of the performance of Burkina Faso's inland terminals insofar as the players in the port chain seek primarily to improve their creation of internal value.

4 A Grounded Methodology for Understanding Burkinabé Managerial Practices

We conducted an empirical study to assess the contribution of the Ouagarinter port link to the performance of global supply chains. For the implementation of this study, we opted for the grounded theory methodology recognised as pertinent to understanding managerial logic (Walsh 2015; Gligor et al. 2016). Indeed, the inductive nature of this methodology is relevant for understanding a field in which the economic, social and cultural dimensions are tangled and reflected in the interactions between actors, as is the case for ODP stakeholders. In addition, this rooted methodology makes it possible to understand the managerial realities constructed by the actors through the meaning they give to their experiences of the management of their activities. For the implementation of this study, we opted for a mixed method by combining quantitative data—statistics—with qualitative data from interviews to collect the histories and experiences of the respondents.

As the unit of analysis is an organisation considered to be an individual link in the Ouagarinter dry port ecosystem, we have obtained a diversified sample in terms of size, location and sector of activity. First, we had an in-depth discussion with seven professional logistics experts, including logistics managers, operations managers, supply chain directors and logistics consultants. Then we completed this data collection by emailing

Table 7.1 Sample interviewed by questionnaire

Private sector	% of total sample	Public sector	% of total sample
6 logistics service providers	18.75	3 professional associations	9.38
6 importers	18.75		
5 carriers	15.6	2 maritime institutions representatives	6.25
4 shipowners	12.5		
4 truck drivers	12.5		
1 handler	3.13	1 port authority representative	3.13

Source: Authors' creation

a questionnaire to fifty-one companies during the months of April–September 2019.

Thirty-two companies responded, representing a return rate of 62.74%. It should be noted that we wanted to speak to respondents with high levels of responsibility and that, as a result, we were able to contact them only once. The majority of respondents (twenty-six out of thirty-two) are from the private sector. However, we also collected data from public sector actors (six out of thirty-two respondents), as seen in Table 7.1.

Our questionnaire was organised into two parts. The first part questioned whether the actors of the Burkinabé logistics chains measured the performance of the port ecosystem. The second part focused on the contribution of the Ouagarinter port link to the performance of global logistics chains. Based on the port performance criteria identified in the literature previously presented (Pichot 2006; ESPO 2012; De Langen and Michaël 2015; Barkadleh 2016), we have chosen to retain twenty port performance criteria, which we have divided according to seven dimensions: deadlines, expenses, sustainability, digitalisation, connectivity, security and governance (see Table 7.2).

To process the data collected by this questionnaire, we used statistical data processing software which ordered the responses numerically, with values of one (very strong), two (strong), three (fairly strong) and four (weak).

Table 7.2 Themes and port performance criteria

Dimension	Content
Deadlines	Duration of stay in warehouse
	Transport vehicle unloading time (operational time)
	Operational storage time of goods
	Duration of stay of transport vehicles
Expenses	Climate/ease of business transactions
	Terminal handling cost
Sustainability	Impact of port operations on air quality
	Impact of operations on noise/smell
	Impact of port operations on local resident everyday life
	Impact of port operations on riverside road traffic
Digitalisation	Availability of specific functionalities
	Information system investment
	Information technology system availability
Connectivity	Railway sidings
	Transhipment easiness from one transport vehicle to another
	Quality of connections between port and other links in transport network
Security	Quality of entry and exit control system for people
	Quality of entry and exit control system for vehicles
Governance	Quality of port governance
	Dissemination of information

Source: Authors' creation

5 Results: Ouagarinter Dry Port Determinants Contributing to Value Creation

By summing the numerical responses and dividing them by the total number of respondents, we obtained averages that allowed us to prioritise the dimensions that are important to port stakeholders. We assert that the closer the average result is to one, the more the criterion chosen contributes positively to the logistics performance of the port's customers (see Table 7.3).

Taking into account the number of criteria chosen by a majority of respondents in each dimension, we identified four dimensions whose satisfaction threshold exceeded 50%. This threshold is synonymous with better representation and optimum reliability of the results and allows us to retain the corresponding criteria as those which contribute

Table 7.3 Important dimensions for Ouagarinter port ecosystem actors

Dimension	Digitalisation	Sustainability	Governance	Security	Deadlines	Connectivity	Expenses
Average	2.24	2.43	2.58	2.75	2.84	3.39	3.58
Ranking	1	2	3	4	5	6	7

Source: Authors' creation

the most to the performance of global supply chains. These criteria are digitalisation, sustainability, governance and security. These four dimensions therefore make a positive contribution to the Ouagarinter port link.

It should be noted that in the case of the digitalisation dimension, which was composed of three criteria—investment in information systems, availability of specific functionalities and availability of a computer system—we recorded 100% satisfaction because all the criteria were mentioned by more than 50% of respondents.

For the sustainability dimension, which was initially composed of four criteria—the impact of port operations on the lives of local residents, the impact of port operations on air quality, the impact of port operations on riverside road traffic and the impact of port operations on noise/stench—the 50% satisfaction rate meant that only two criteria should be retained: those mentioned by more than 50% of respondents.

Similarly, for the security dimension, on two proposed criteria—the quality of the system controlling the entry and exit of people and the quality of the system controlling the entry and exit of vehicles—only the second criterion was retained.

Finally, for the governance dimension, only one criterion was retained—that of the dissemination of information.

In view of the above, we created a summary Table 7.4 with regard to the criteria that positively contribute to the performance of the Ouagarinter dry port link.

Table 7.4 Performance indicators of the Ouagaringer dry port link

Dimension	Criteria
Digitalisation	Availability of specific functionalities
	Information system investment
	Information technology system availability
Sustainability	Impact of port operations on riverside road traffic
	Impact of port operations on local resident everyday life
Governance	Dissemination of information
Security	Quality of entry and exit control system for vehicles

Source: Authors' creation

Our study shows that there are indeed measurable performance indicators for Ouagarinter dry port stakeholders. However, our results emphasise that these indicators are internal and do not measure the performance of the entire port ecosystem. Indeed, ODP stakeholders use performance indicators relating to their respective companies and sometimes those of the supply chain stakeholders with whom they are in contact. One of the main reasons for this is the lack of a collective development and design process for these indicators. Despite the controlled nature of these measures, they do not provide information on the quality of execution of key operational processes, nor on the efficiency of the overall chain. The factors recognised as the main determinants are digitalisation, sustainability, governance and security. It is surprising to note that actors in the Ouagarinter port chain do not consider as major determinants factors such as deadlines, expenses and connectivity.

As exposed in the first section, substantial research has been conducted on dry ports, about the concept (Roso and Rosa 2012; Notteboom and Rodrigue 2012) and on their role in effective shipping and port management (Roso et al. 2009). However, research regarding value-added services offered by a dry port and their importance for the actors of the transport system was rather scarce until recent years (Andersson and Roso 2016). The results of our empirical study allow us to identify value-added services that could support the development of regional integration and international connectivity. We suggest several performance indicators that could contribute to the creation of value in the context of Burkina Faso: digitalisation, sustainability, governance and security in the supply chains. Indicators used to assess the digitalisation of the port link could include the cost of information technology as a percentage of turnover, the average time without an available server, the average cost/time of development by functionality and the time/budget required for team training. Appropriate indicators for assessing the sustainability of the Ouagarinter port link could include the carbon footprint of port operations, noise levels of port activities, air quality, level of satisfaction with regard to journey time and its reliability and duration of traffic jams and delays. These indicators would provide an impression of the impact of port operations both on the lives of local residents and on local road traffic. As for the assessment of governance, the actors may be interested in the dissemination of information via the deployment of an information system within the port community.

6 Conclusion

The purpose of this chapter was to analyse how an existing dry port can be further developed through the use of performance indicators linked to value-added services. We have identified in the SCM literature that much of the previous research had focused on the challenges and performance criteria of global supply chains from strategic, systemic, structural and relational perspectives. We have also noted that the main challenges for dry ports relate to the logistical components that complement the ports' infrastructure. With these fundamentals, we conducted an empirical study with Burkinabé actors involved in the management of maritime logistics chains, despite their location in a landlocked country. We identified four important dimensions—digitalisation, sustainability, governance and security—that may be used as performance indicators for the dry port of Ouagarinter in a context of international connectivity.

If the limited size of our sample does not allow generalisation, the use of diverse respondents' profiles as well as the in-depth qualitative analysis of the data collected and its validation by the experts themselves lead to results that are both rich and reliable. They also open some interesting lines of research. We emphasise the need to start by defining criteria for assessing the value expected by the various stakeholders of a dry port before rethinking the processes and activities of supply chains. In developing countries, much work is still needed in this field to solve the emerging traffic-related problems. Future research could integrate moderating variables such as risk management or control variables such as size, and experience of the logistics operators companies. However, these suggested elements should be incorporated at different levels—the port ecosystem, states and regional levels—so that all actors in a global supply chain use similar data to compare the links that best meet their interests.

References

Andersson, D., & Roso, V. (2016). Developing Dry Ports Through the Use of Value-Added Services. In U. Clausen, H. Friedrich, C. Thaller, & C. Geiger (Eds.), *Commercial Transport* (pp. 191–203). Cham, Switzerland: Springer.

ASLOG. (2020). *Qu'est-ce que la Supply Chain ?*. Retrieved January 2020, from https://www.aslog.fr/la-supply-chain/

Barkadleh, H. (2016). *La performance de la chaîne logistique globale: la sûreté et la situation géographique d'un maillon portuaire*. Paris: Édilivre.

Brindley, C. (2017). *Supply Chain Risk*. Routledge editions.

Craighead, C. W., Blackhurst, J., Rungtusanatham, M. J., & Handfield, R. B. (2007). The Severity of Supply Chain Disruptions: Design Characteristics and Mitigation Capabilities. *Decision Sciences, 38*(1), 131–156.

De Langen, P., & Michaël, C. (2015). *Indicateurs de Performance Portuaire (IPP)*. Excerpt from a Training Program on Performance Indicators in Ports in Tema, Ghana.

De Langen, P. W. (2008). Analyzing Port Clusters: Definition, Delimitation and Research Issues. In E. Musso & H. Ghiara (Eds.), *Ports and Regional Economies. The Future of Port Clusters* (pp. 19–30). McGraw Hill.

De Monie, G. (2012). *Performance Indicators in Transport and Maritime Management*. Belgium: Institute of Transport and Maritime Management, University of Antwerp.

De Noray, O. (2015). Les ports africains: une modernisation en marche. *Annales des Mines-Réalités industrielles*, pp. 21–25.

Dinangue, G. (2017). *Management des contraintes du maillon portuaire dans la supply chain*. Paris: Edilivre.

European Sea Ports Organization (ESPO). (2012). « *Port Performance Indicators: Selection and Measurement* ». Project executive report.

Fabbe-Coste, N. (2007). «La gestion des chaînes logistiques multi-acteurs : les dimensions organisationnelles d'une gestion lean et agile». In G. Paché et A. Spalanzani, *La gestion des chaînes logistiques multi-acteurs : perspectives stratégiques*, éditions PUG, pp. 19–44.

Fredouët, C.-H., & Guérin, F. (2002). *Le management portuaire: les nouveaux enjeux*. e-thèque éditions, p. 67.

Frédouët, C.-H., & Le Mestre, P. (2005). La construction d'un outil de mesure de la performance des réseaux inter organisationnels: une étude des réseaux d'acteurs portuaires. *Revue Finance Contrôle Stratégie, 8*(4), 5–32.

Gligor, D., Esmark, C., & Gölgeci, I. (2016). Building International Business Theory: A Grounded Theory Approach. *Journal of International Business Studies, 47*(1), 93–111.

Ketchen, D. J., & Giunipero, L. C. (2004). The Intersection of Strategic Management and Supply Chain Management. *Industrial Marketing Management, 33*(1), 51–56.

Ketchen, D. J., Rebarick, W., Tomas, G., Hult, M., & Meyer, D. (2008). Best Value Supply Chains: A Key Competitive Weapon for the 21st Century. *Business Horizons, 51*(3), 235–243.

Kleindorfer, P. R., & Saad, G. H. (2005). Managing Disruption Risks in Supply Chains. *Production and Operations Management, 80*(4), 53–68.

Lihoussou, M. (2017). «Dysfonctionnements et entraves à la fluidité en Afrique de l'Ouest : l'exemple du corridor Cotonou-Abidjan », *Cahiers Scientifiques du Transport*, N°72, pp. 43–66.

Notteboom, T., & Rodrigue, J.-P. (2012). Dry Ports in European and North American Intermodal Rail Systems: Two of a Kind? *Research in Transportation Business and Management, 5*, 4–15.

Pelletier J.-F. (2012). «Les indicateurs de performance logistique pour les corridors de transport». In Y. Alix, *Les corridors de transports*, Editions EMS, pp. 87–104.

Pichot, L. (2006). *Stratégie de déploiement d'outils de pilotage de chaînes logistiques: Apport de la classification*. HAL. Retrieved from https://tel.archives-ouvertes.fr/tel-00159155

Roso, V., & Rosa, A. (2012). Dry Port in Concept and Practice in Maritime Logistics: A Complete Guide to Effective Shipping and Port Management. In D. Song, P. Panayides, & Kogan publishers (Eds.), *Round Tables Port Investment and Container Shipping Markets* (pp. 179–193). International Transport Forum.

Roso, V., Woxenius, J., & Lumsden, K. (2009). The Dry Port Concept: Connecting Container Seaports with the Hinterland. *Journal of Transport Geography, 17*(5), 338–345.

Saikouk, T., & Spalanzani, A. (2012). *L'évaluation des technologies de traçabilité utilisées dans une supply chain forestière en France*. Cahier de Recherche No. 2012-05 E5, halshs-00849825. Retrieved from https://halshs.archives-ouvertes.fr/halshs-00849825/document

Sanders, N. R. (2020). *Supply Chain Management: A Global Perspective*. 2nd edition, Wiley.

UNCTAD. (2018). *Le commerce maritime et l'Afrique*. https://unctad.org/fr/Pages/PressRelease.aspx?OriginalVersionID=476

UNECE. (2001). *Terminologie en transports combinés*. Retrieved January 2020, from https://www.tarifdouanier.eu/info/abreviations/955

Walsh, I. (2015). *Découvrir de nouvelles théories. Une approche mixte et enracinée dans les données*. Paris: EMS.

Zhang, D., Dong, J., & Nagurney, A. (2003). A Supply Chain Network Economy: Modeling and Qualitative Analysis. In A. Nagurney (Ed.), *Innovations in Financial and Economic Networks* (pp. 195–211). Edward Elgar Publication.

Zouaghi, I. (2013). Maturité supply chain des entreprises: conception d'un modèle d'évaluation et mise en œuvre. Retrieved from https://tel.archives-ouvertes.fr/tel-01015950/document

8

The Role of Interpersonal Relations in Logistical Conflicts Resolution between SMEs and the Food Retailing Industry: The Case of Morocco

Hicham Abbad, Sonia Mahjoub,
Dominique Bonet Fernandez, and Hachemí Aliouche

1 Introduction

Small and medium-sized enterprises (SMEs) have several assets (responsiveness, flexibility, adaptability, etc.) that enable them to adopt development strategies compensating for the disadvantages due to their size. These strategies lead them to integrate into new distribution channels, such as those of the food retailing industry. By food retailing industry, we

H. Abbad (✉)
Nantes University, Nantes, France
e-mail: Hicham.Abbad@univ-nantes.fr

S. Mahjoub
ONIRIS Nantes, Nantes, France
e-mail: sonia.mahjoub@oniris-nantes.fr

D. Bonet Fernandez
IPAG Business School - CRET-LOG Aix-Marseille Université, Paris, France
e-mail: d.bonet@ipag.fr

S. M. Apitsa, E. Milliot (eds.), *Doing Business in Africa*, Palgrave Studies of Internationalization in Emerging Markets,
https://doi.org/10.1007/978-3-030-50739-8_8

mean the forms of self-service trade such as hypermarkets and supermarkets which have developed, particularly in Europe, since the 1960s and which mark a profound break with the isolated independent trade (the small grocery store), but also with the informal trade, which was for a long time dominant in North African countries. The food retailing industry in Morocco today includes powerful national and foreign brands such as Marjane, Carrefour, Carrefour Market, Acima and BIM. Since the emergence of the food retailing industry three decades ago, this economic player has totally disrupted the commercial landscape in Morocco by changing the consumption habits of Moroccans and restructuring the operating methods of its agri-food suppliers. Used to collaborating with traditional archaic trade, these suppliers must now deal with a modern, demanding and increasingly important customer in their turnover (Amine and Lazzaoui 2011). This customer also needs local suppliers to meet consumer needs at his best. This need is expressed explicitly through its support policy, which constitutes a real legitimisation practice (Sabri 2012). Given the interdependent relationships between retailers and suppliers, conflict situations seem inevitable (Mohr and Spekman 1994; Bonet 1999; Abbad et al. 2013; Abbad and Paché 2013). Conflicts between these two actors of the distribution channel can affect various fields. Bonet (1999) discussed the difference between transactional conflicts and logistical conflicts. On the one hand, Bonet (1999) contends that transactional conflicts concern price negotiations (prices and referencing) and marketing (promotional operations and retail brands). On the other hand, she argued that logistical conflicts are inherent in the management of physical flows (distribution of roles in the organisation of physical distribution activities such as transport, handling and storage of finished products) and associated information flows (sharing of information needed to control flows). In this chapter, we focus on the logistical conflicts between retailers and their SME agri-food suppliers.

H. Aliouche
University of New Hampshire, Durham, NH, USA
e-mail: hachemi.aliouche@unh.edu

Generally, logistics conflicts arise as a result of retailers' dissatisfaction (Vu 2009; Cunningham 2013; Butt and Ahmad 2019). This is partly linked to SMEs' poorly mastered logistics skills. Although the logistical criterion is considered in the selection process of suppliers, retailers in Morocco are still confronted with the logistical failure of a large proportion of their suppliers (missed delivery times, non-compliant deliveries, high out-of-stock rates in shelves, etc.) (Abbad and Paché 2013). A logistical conflict, if not resolved, can sometimes lead a large retailer to temporarily or permanently sever the commercial relationship with its suppliers (Paché 2002). Such a decision is not without consequences for these suppliers, particularly SMEs for whom a significant loss of turnover could jeopardise the continuity of their business. The resolution of logistical conflicts can be achieved in different ways, but above all it requires the involvement of the staff of stakeholders, customers and suppliers (Belaya and Hanf 2014; Sharma and Parida 2018). This involvement is most effective when representatives of both parties have interpersonal relationships. Interpersonal relationships are defined here as links developed as a result of social interactions between individuals from the companies involved in an exchange relationship. These links are maintained through communication, that is, formal or informal sharing of significant information between two or more individuals belonging to partner enterprises (Anderson and Narus 1990). In this chapter, which articulates two disciplinary fields, logistics and marketing, we attempt to respond to the following research question: What resolution modalities of this type of conflict are adopted when a personal relationship is present between retailers' and SMEs' staff in the agri-food sector? The objectives of this research are twofold. First, we aim at identifying the modalities and relational mechanisms that enable a representative of an agri-food SME to resolve the logistical conflict arising with his partners in an increasingly important food retailing industry. In the second objective, we verify whether the resolution of this type of conflict is specific to the Moroccan socio-cultural context where managers are naturally conditioned by a certain way of thinking and acting.

The issue of logistical conflicts and the role that interpersonal relations could play in their resolution is important from both a theoretical and a managerial point of view. From a theoretical point of view, while there is an extensive literature on the determinants of transactional conflicts in the distribution channel (Krafft et al. 2015; Sharma and Parida 2018), relatively little work has been done on the case of logistical conflicts, including the question of the contribution of interpersonal relationships to the resolution of this type of conflict. In this sense, this contribution aims at enriching the reflection on the issue by focusing on the specific relations between SMEs and large retailers, which are often characterised by unbalanced power relations. From a managerial point of view, this research would allow managers of large retail chains to identify conflict resolution methods that could be part of their SME support policy.

The chapter is organised in three sections. In the first section, a literature review on the place of personal relationships in inter-organisational conflicts is proposed. A second section outlines the research methodology. The third section presents and discusses the results obtained on the role that interpersonal relationships could play in resolving logistical conflicts between retailers and suppliers in the context of an African developing country such as Morocco.

2 Conflict Resolution Modalities and Interpersonal Relationship: A Conceptual Framework

This section presents a literature review on the conflict resolution modalities in the specific context of the distribution channel and the influence of interpersonal relationships on logistical conflicts resolution.

2.1 Conflict Management Strategies

Although the concept of conflict has been the subject of much research in different fields of the social sciences, it still suffers from a lack of consensus on a clear and precise definition (Thomas 1992; Wall and Callister 1995, Bonet 1999; Sharma and Parida 2018). However, in the management science literature, the most frequently cited definition remains the one proposed by Thomas (1992) for whom conflict is "the process that begins when one party perceives that the other has negatively affected, or is about to negatively affect, something that he or she cares about" (Thomas 1992, p. 653). Although the term conflict covers several meanings such as disagreement (Chung et al. 2006), disharmony (Grewal et al. 2013) or misunderstanding (Peters and Fletcher 2004), the literature analysis reveals three essential characteristics of conflict: interaction, interdependence and incompatibility of objectives (Xie et al. 1998).

As noted earlier, logistical conflicts concern physical flows (management of physical distribution activities such as transport, handling and storage of finished products) and information flows (sharing of information needed to control physical flows). In the results of her research on producer-distributor relations in the French context, Bonet (1999) identifies three sources of logistical conflict: (1) those relating to the negotiation and distribution of productivity gains in the management of operations; (2) those inherent to the sanctions and penalties applied for any malfunction or non-compliance with contractually defined supply procedures; (3) those relating to the definition of roles in the management of the logistics chain.

Many authors have focused on conflict resolution mechanisms (Sharma and Parida 2018). Thomas (1976), in his so-called behavioural approach, defines five methods of conflict resolution based on two dimensions: (1) the degree of consideration that the actors have for themselves; (2) the degree of consideration that they have for the other actors involved in the conflict. Thus, by crossing these two dimensions, we obtain five distinct modes of conflict resolution: neglect, domination, accommodation, compromise and cooperation. This typology proposed by Thomas (1976) reveals two methods of conflict resolution (Thomas 1992; Ganesan 1993). One, of the non-cooperative type, includes domination and negligence and the other, of the cooperative type, includes accommodation, compromise and cooperation.

Regarding the non-cooperative way, domination is used when the party with the strongest power imposes its decisions and solutions on others (authoritarian, oppressive behaviour, lacking any willingness to cooperate) and negligence is used in conflict situations of little importance to the parties involved in the crisis (behaviour based on indifference and lack of cooperation). As for the cooperative mode, we find three methods. First, accommodation, which applies when one of the parties makes concessions to maintain its relationship with its trading partner. Then compromise, which means that the parties in a conflict situation are willing to sacrifice their own interests to find an amicable solution. Finally, cooperation, the most constructive mode, used by the parties to reach a satisfactory solution to all parties. This method of resolution is convincing and effective insofar as the partners have a certain interest in the success of their relationship. To illustrate this mode, Thomas (1976) gives the example of Procter & Gamble, which, for one of its products, has developed packaging that reduces logistics costs for both itself and its retail customers.

Based on a multidisciplinary analysis of the literature on conflict, Dant and Schul (1992) find that there are generally two modes of conflict resolution. The first mode is based on so-called "institutionalised" mechanisms, implemented by the channel's leading members to manage the conflict systematically and continuously (membership in professional associations, staff exchanges, etc.). The second mode is founded on more informal mechanisms used by stakeholders that could make it possible to establish institutionalised mechanisms for conflict resolution. In order to operationalise the conflict resolution process in the distribution channel, Dant and Schul (1992) propose, based on the work of March and Simon (1958), four conflict management strategies: (1) joint problem solving; (2) persuasion; (3) negotiation; and (4) use of the policy or mediation by a third party. Problem solving and persuasion are strategies led by actors who operate in a climate of trust due to the regular exchange of information. Members of the distribution channel use negotiation and third-party intervention when there is a climate of mistrust due to withholding information (Stern et al. 1996). Mohr and Spekman (1994) propose a typology of six conflict resolution modalities to explain the success of the inter-company partnership: joint problem solving, persuasion, smoothing, domination, harsh words and arbitration. Of the three typologies of conflict resolution methods (Table 8.1), we retain the one proposed by Thomas (1976) because it has the advantage of being easily operationalisable while distinguishing between cooperative and non-cooperative methods.

Table 8.1 Different modalities of conflict resolution

Authors	Modalities of conflict resolution
Thomas (1976)	Negligence, domination, accommodation, compromise, cooperation
Dant and Schul (1992)	Joint problem solving, persuasion, bargaining, use of politics
Mohr and Spekman (1994)	Joint problem solving, persuasion, smoothing, domination, harsh words, arbitration

Source: Authors' creation

2.2 The Influence of Interpersonal Relationships on Logistical Conflicts Resolution

Previous works in sociology (Granovetter 1985), political science (Axelrod 1984), economics (Klein and Leffler 1981), organisational theory (Ouchi 1980), marketing (Morgan and Hunt 1994; Murry and Heide 1998) and later in logistics (Charvet and Cooper 2011; Wichmann et al. 2015; Ekanayake et al. 2017; Wang et al. 2018) have identified interpersonal relationships as an important mechanism to structure relationships between parties motivated by their own interests. The notion of interpersonal relationships does not only apply to relationships of kinship or friendship. Indeed, it can also be used in the context of social interactions between members of two or more organisations (Gligor and Esmark 2015). In the dyadic relationships selected for this chapter, it refers to the existence of links maintained and developed between the individuals of the companies involved in an exchange relationship, retailers' managers and SMEs' representatives.

This type of relationship is created and developed through interpersonal contacts (Gligor and Esmark 2015; Schorsch et al. 2017). These involve several functions, different levels of management on both sides and finally visits and meetings of varying frequency. In customer-supplier relationships, "restricted" relationships around a small number of business subjects have to be distinguished from "extended" relationships where managers of both parties exchange on commercial, technical, marketing or logistical issues, quality control procedures, market situation, and so on. Frequency is a measure of the quantity of contacts but not necessarily of the quality of exchanges. In customer-supplier relationships, a certain frequency of contact is necessary to monitor performance, resolve conflicts, demonstrate mutual commitment, exchange information and foster the development of social relationships (interpersonal relationships).

According to the neo-institutional sociological approach, the success of transactional relationships can be facilitated by mechanisms other than those of the market or hierarchy. The social context thus appears to be an effective means of regulation and coordination between the parties to the exchange (Gulati 1995). This context refers to the concept of socially embedded relationships (Granovetter 1985; Frenzen and Davis 1990; Carey et al. 2011) and more precisely to the notion of network. In general, a network is defined as a structure of links between points. These points can be objects, individuals or organisations, which leads researchers to distinguish three types of networks: the technical network, which links terminals (information technology), the interpersonal network, which links individuals, and the inter-organisational network, which links legal persons. These three types of networks are integrated into the framework of inter-company relations.

Based on the idea of social network, authors such as Gulati (1998) and Jones et al. (1997) highlight the impact of personal relationships on relationship stability. The social structure in which both parties find themselves, including the personal relationships developed over time, can reduce the risk of conflict and opportunistic behaviour, increase trust and thus improve relationship performance (Gulati 1998; Whipple et al. 2015; Durach and Machuca 2018). The key argument in the social network literature is that the existence of a strong interpersonal bond reflects previous processes of choice and/or socialisation between the parties (Chatman 1991). The effect of such processes is to align the objectives of the parties in question (Murry and Heide 1998). For Guibert (1996), the importance of interpersonal ties in the relationship depends on several factors: the phase of the relationship, the nature of the interdependence, the economic importance of the customer to the supplier and the complexity of the product. Indeed, the younger the relationship, the greater the mutual dependency, the more complex the product, the more important the customer is to the supplier, the stronger the "risk reducing" property of interpersonal relationships. This property makes it possible to better manage conflicts and thus avoid their sometimes destructive effect on the continuity of the relationship (Murry and Heide 1998; Ekanayake et al., 2017).

Researchers in relationship marketing and logistics recognise the impact of interpersonal factors on outcomes in business-to-business relationships (Morgan and Hunt 1994; Murry and Heide 1998; Gligor and Holcomb 2013; Gligor and Esmark 2015; Durach and Machuca 2018). Ring and Van de Ven (1992, 1994) specify the important role of interpersonal relationships in the success of relationships and in increasing the level of trust between the two parties. Similarly, other authors emphasise the growing interest in the use of social norms and bilateral mechanisms of relational governance as a means of reducing the uncertainties inherent in inter-organisational exchange (Heide 1994; Heide and John 1992; Charvet and Cooper 2011). For Jap (1999), the interpersonal links between staff from both sides of the exchange represent micro-conditions that can potentially positively influence the dyad's decision to exploit particularities of the relationship. In the supply chain context, Butt (2018) notes that the absence of personal relationship between the managers of the purchasing and supply undertakings may lead to a possible break in the commercial relations between the partners.

In their research, Phan et al. (2005) conclude that the quality of interpersonal relationships and communication behaviour are important factors in problem solving. Personal relationships provide a favourable context for a new exchange by reducing the risk of logistical conflict (Durach and Machuca 2018). Butt (2019) found that the lack of personal relationships between supply chain managers in different companies made it difficult to approach and build mutual trust, collaboration and conflict resolution. Kanter (1994) stated that personal relationships between individuals within companies are an important basis for collaboration between managers. He noted that personal relationships help resolve small conflicts before they escalate and stated that there is no good way to resolve problems other than through personal relationships. Kanter (1994) noted that personal relationships encourage the sharing of information and promote cooperative behaviour, thereby overcoming some of the limitations of contracts. Hutt et al. (2000) argued that the lack of interpersonal contact between senior managers leads to a lack of cooperation between them. Based on these developments, it seems possible to develop theoretical propositions linking personal relationships to the cooperative and non-cooperative modalities of conflict resolution inspired from Thomas (1976):

P1: Personal relationships between retailers and suppliers managers lead them to adopt modalities of cooperation to resolve logistical conflicts.

P1.1: *Personal relationships between retailer and supplier managers lead them to adopt accommodation to resolve logistical conflicts.*

P1.2: *Personal relationships between retailer and supplier managers lead them to adopt compromise to resolve logistical conflicts.*

P1.3: *Personal relationships between retailers and suppliers managers lead them to adopt cooperation to resolve logistical conflicts.*

P2: Personal relationships between retailer and supplier managers lead them to reject non-cooperation in resolving logistical conflicts.

P2.1: *Personal relationships between retailer and supplier managers lead them to reject dominance to resolve logistics conflicts.*

P2.2: *Personal relationships between retailers and suppliers managers lead them to reject neglect to resolve logistical conflicts.*

To study the role of interpersonal relationships in resolving logistical conflicts between retailers and agri-food SMEs in the Moroccan context, we propose a conceptual model that synthesises our two main research propositions (Fig. 8.1).

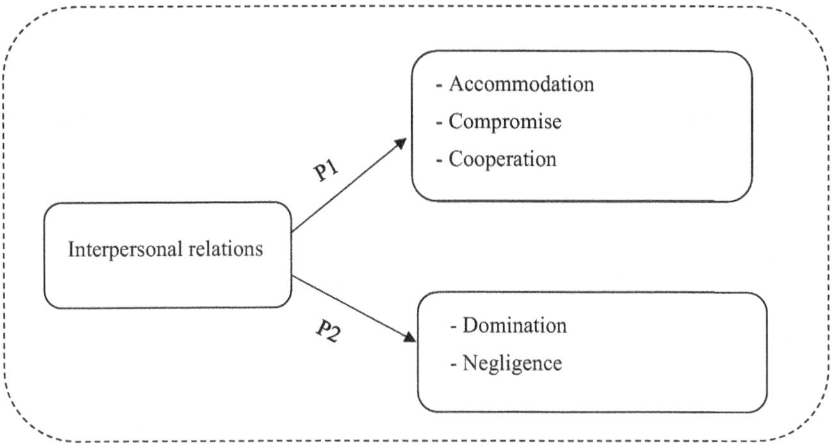

Fig. 8.1 Conceptual model of the role of personal relationship in the choice of conflict resolution modalities. (Source: Authors' creation)

3 Methodological Approach

In order to answer our research question, we chose a qualitative methodology to explore in depth, and to understand interactions and the role of context on its functioning (Hlady Rispal 2002). The empirical survey was conducted with a panel of 30 respondents. Data collection was based on semi-directive face-to-face interviews with managers of three retailers, representatives of ten SMEs (general managers or sales managers) and four experts (Table 8.2). These interviews were fully recorded and transcribed. They were supplemented by a documentary research of internal sources (companies' reports) and external sources (press articles, articles from professional journals, newsletters, etc.). The two sources of information are complementary and allow the cross-checking of data. The interview was used as a privileged means of accessing the facts and interpretations given by the two supply chain actors, retailers and SMEs. The documentation provided a better understanding of the environment of these actors and improved the understanding of the phenomenon studied. The data collected were analysed following a thematic content analysis (Bardin 2013).

Table 8.2 Panel

Retailers • Chairman of the executive board • General manager • Supply chain manager • Two purchasing managers • Three managers of a team of buyers • Eight retail buyers
SMEs • Six general managers • Four sales managers
Experts • University expert in industry/commerce relations • Communication Manager at the National Federation of Food Processing (FENAGRI) • President of the Federation of SMEs (FPME) • Expert at the French Economic Mission of Casablanca

Source: Authors' creation

4 Results and Discussion

Before highlighting the role of interpersonal relations in the management of logistics conflicts between retailers and manufacturers, it is necessary to draw up an inventory of logistics practices in the retailing industry sector. If distribution logistics presents important areas of collaboration between manufacturers and retailers in France, whether in terms of product flows or associated information (Bonet 2000), in the current Moroccan context, it is only on the physical part of the flows that the two channel members coordinate their actions.

4.1 Characteristics of Physical and Information Flows in Morocco

The current system is characterised by the low presence of information systems for exchanging data between the actors of the food distribution channel (Abbad et al. 2012). This situation concerns retailers' relations with not only SMEs but also major Moroccan manufacturers and subsidiaries of multinationals based in Morocco. A large proportion of orders are still sent by fax. It can be explained by the reluctance of large suppliers to open their databases. There are three main reasons for this situation. First, the retailing industry represents only about 11% to 12% of trade and cannot therefore require its suppliers to set up a system such as EDI (Electronic Data Interchange) at a significant cost. Then, the reluctance of Moroccan manufacturers to communicate information on their activities and finally the predominance of oral communication in business practice between suppliers and retailers (Abbad et al. 2013). Unlike retailers who have managed to reorganise their logistics activities quickly using modern techniques, many suppliers lack the IT resources to manage the physical flows of their products.

Currently, the replenishment of the retailers' points of sale operating in the large retail trade is organised in two ways: the "manufacturer-store" logistics model and the "manufacturer-distribution centre-store" logistics model. The transition from the first "manufacturer-store" model to the second "manufacturer-distribution center-store" model is an essential step to avoid conflicts in flow management and thus the way for a real logistical cooperation between retailers and manufacturers. The construction of a clean warehouse or the use of a logistics service provider shows a real willingness on the part of large retailers to cooperate with their food suppliers. The establishment of warehouses has made it possible to reduce transport costs, speed up delivery times, reduce out-of-stocks and achieve productivity gains. Modern distribution has become the lever for the development of logistics warehouses because it is constantly concerned with buying at the lowest prices.

Direct control over the points of sales supply is a preliminary step before delegating the warehouse flows to the manufacturer. However, such an evolution requires an awareness of the importance of logistics and a change in attitudes about how to manage flows. The chairman of the executive board of one of the distributors on our panel sums up the current state of logistics in Moroccan companies: "It is a problem today of the logistics culture which has not yet entered into the habits of producers. (…) the whole question leads to the apprehension of logistics in our culture". Since the retailing industry represents only a small part of national trade and the balance of power does not yet reach the diktat imposed by supermarkets on suppliers in Europe, the change in SMEs' mentalities should be achieved through people and more specifically through strong and sustainable management involvement (Abbad and Paché 2013). If we use the typology developed by Bowersox et al. (1980), differences in perception of the importance of the logistics service and the absence of a real communication process (low number of IT interconnections) remain the main causes of conflict in logistics relations between agri-food SMEs and retailers. However, things are changing rapidly, as logistics processes are progressing at a high speed.

Managers agree on the importance of EDI in the development of the modern distribution sector and their relations with suppliers. The introduction of EDI and its generalisation to all relationships should ensure, in the future, the inevitable transition from push flows (i.e. the point of sale is replenished according to the supplier's production capacity) to pull flows (i.e. the point of sale is replenished according to the needs of the supplier and even those of the final consumer), which has become universal (the Wal-Mart retailer's logistics model).

Some retailers' strategies, modelled on retailers in Europe, is to set up regional distribution centres responsible for the supply of points of sale. For all suppliers, including SMEs, the logistics interface will therefore increasingly consist of a single delivery point (regional distribution centres), even if direct supply of stores is still present (Abbad and Paché 2013). There are two main reasons for direct operations: (1) the absence of distribution centres in the logistics organisation of some retailers operating hypermarkets (the critical size in terms of number of stores has not yet been reached) and (2) the refusal of certain suppliers to pass through distribution centres in view of the importance of the financial participation required by retailers in the logistics contract. This refusal causes conflicts because of the great difficulty for agri-food SMEs, dominated by large retailers, to negotiate an equitable distribution of productivity gains in the management of logistics operations (Bonet 1999).

In addition to the limited competence of agri-food SMEs in the logistics field, the presence of conflicting relationships is also explained by the relatively low weight of logistics service quality criteria in the prior evaluation of suppliers by the food retailing industry. Large retailers are not ignoring these criteria during the selection process, but their impact remains relatively small compared to marketing and financial criteria (sales price, product quality, launch advertising campaign, organisation of promotional operations, etc.) (Abbad and Paché 2013), which confirms the meta-analysis conducted by Nilsson and Höst (1987) and Paché's (1995) findings on the French case and Hansen's (2001) on the Chinese case. Retailers discuss about logistics service quality criteria during the negotiation process with the manufacturer, but with a minimum objective: to ensure that the supplier can set up a delivery system that reduces out-of-stocks to an acceptable level.

The academic literature often pointed out that logistics failures have dramatic impacts on large retailers, threatening to lose customers and therefore market share when out-of-stocks become recurrent (Fernie and Sparks 2014). Not to mention the lasting alteration of the retailer's image when out-of-stocks generate a strong discontinuity in assortment management (Filser and Paché 2006). Moroccan retailers do not give significant weight to logistics performance in the selection process for SMEs (Abbad and Paché 2013). The context of an emerging country that discovered modern distribution in the early 1990s, and consumers used to a low level of service until then, could explain this situation. However, these findings confirm several studies conducted in other national contexts (Hansen 2001), including those where the maturity of food retail companies cannot be questioned.

4.2 Relational and Conflict Resolution Methods

The examination of interpersonal contacts from a hierarchical point of view highlights the existence of functional asymmetries due to structural disparities on both sides. In a large part of agri-food industries, SMEs working with the retailing industry, the company manager is the only interface for all functions in the distribution company. SMEs are characterised by an embryonic management structure in which the company manager alone assumes the functions of manager, technical director, administrative and financial manager and commercial manager (Allali 2003).

Interpersonal relations are a variable that nuances the definition and explanation of its development in the Moroccan context. Most retailing industry managers have a poor understanding of the definition of interpersonal relationships and a specific representation of their role in maintaining relationships. These managers have a poor understanding of the role of interpersonal relationships in exchange in general, and in dispute resolution, since they immediately insist on the non-existence of privileged client-centred relationships. In Morocco, the speeches of both parts of the supply chain indicate some confusion between interpersonal relationships that are established as a result of business and social interactions and clientelist relationships that lack all rational reasoning and choices (belonging to a family, a social group, an ethnic group, etc.). This borrows a significant part of its substance from a Moroccan socio-economic space, both traditional and specific (Brown 1977; Geertz 1986; Tangeaoui 1993; d'Iribarne 2002; Abbad et al. 2013).

The existence of personal ties appears, in the Moroccan context, as a factor that facilitates the establishment of trust guarantying the parties' commitment to the relationship. Trust is associated with "speaking the word", which is more important than the written word. The spoken word and trust are therefore crucial in the social relations that SME representatives have with the staff of large retailers. These social relations are established and developed through frequent and high-quality exchanges, which are themselves facilitated by strong socio-cultural proximity. Generally, trust is built through repeated interactions over time. However, it is worth mentioning that some managers of SMEs benefit from an initial trust because they belong to the economic oligarchy, made up of large traditional families from the city of Fez who monopolise much of the national wealth. The central role played by the manager within his structure makes him the privileged interlocutor of all the representatives of large retailers. Indeed, the head of the agri-food company is called upon by the staff of the retailers to discuss logistical problems, but also to exchange views on questions relating to commercial, marketing, technical areas. These so-called "extended" relations explain the frequency of contacts and the quality of exchanges between the two parties. Interactions are mainly through oral communication (telephone and face-to-face), which has the advantage of being quick and efficient in the conflict resolution process.

The respondents, retailers' and suppliers' managers together state that knowing the interlocutors personally facilitates communication (mainly oral) and thus improves the flow of exchanges by offering more possibilities in conflict management. Relationship in trade is essential since it allows agri-food SMEs and retailers to unblock conflict situations that could be detrimental to both supply chain actors. "Relationship in trade is very important. (…) when you have two people working in the same direction and getting along, I think it's easier to unblock situations and move things forward", explains a retail buyer.

Many of the conflicts inherent in the agri-food SME's logistics service are settled amicably. Accommodation (when the supplier makes concessions to maintain his relationship with his customer) and, to a lesser degree, compromise (parties in conflict situations are willing to sacrifice their own interests to find an amicable solution) remain the most common methods used to solve problems in the supply chain. While the choice of accommodation can be explained by the economic dependence of agri-food SMEs on their customers, compromise mainly refers to the willingness of some retailers to support these SMEs in order to improve their legitimacy in the face of political and social institutional pressures (Sabri 2012). The cooperation modality, which presupposes a mutually satisfactory solution, is very rarely adopted by managers. Also, the interviewees state that they never resort to non-cooperative methods such as neglect and domination. These results confirm the research of Kanter (1994) for whom personal relationships favour the adoption of cooperative behaviour to resolve conflicts between partners.

Aware of the importance of interpersonal relations between their staff and that of their customers, some agri-food SMEs offer professional buyers' positions of responsibility (sales and/or logistics manager) with better financial conditions than those offered by food retailing industry companies. We had the opportunity to meet two sales managers who have worked for many years as professional buyers. Thanks to this experience, these two managers have an important social capital. This type of recruitment makes it easier for "visionary" SMEs to manage crisis and thus stabilise their relationships with a customer who represents an increasingly essential part of their turnover. It is an informal mechanism used by the manufacturer to make it possible to establish institutionalised dispute resolution mechanisms for the logistics service (Dant and Schul 1992).

It is necessary to clarify that interpersonal relationships are essential in the process of resolving logistical conflicts only when the supplier's logistical failure is acceptable, that is, the out-of-stock rate does not exceed the threshold tolerated by the customer. SMEs who fail in terms of logistics are faced with a series of financial penalties. Despite this penalty system and the financial contributions imposed on suppliers, particularly in the context of commercial cooperation contracts, many suppliers are only concerned with maintaining their exchanges with the retailing industry. Professional buyers all consider that if SMEs continue to work with them, it is because they are financially satisfied with their relationships. "Nowadays, the producers also benefit from working with us because at least there is the certainty of reaching the consumer directly with us and seeing the turnover grow", a retailer's manager explains.

In short, the results obtained show that for resolving logistical conflicts, retailers' and suppliers' managers in personal relationships use only cooperative modalities, and more specifically accommodation and compromise. These results seem to argue in favour of accepting the two proposals P1.1 and P1.2 but reject proposal P1.3 (proposal P1 can therefore be considered partially accepted). Also, personal relationships lead managers to reject the uncooperative way (neglect and domination) when confronted with logistical conflicts. In this sense, proposals P2.1 and P2.2 seem to have a good degree of acceptance. Proposal 2 is therefore accepted. Overall, we can consider that our research model is validated, with cooperative resolution modalities favoured on non-cooperative resolution modalities.

5 Conclusion

The purpose of this chapter is to understand the ways in which logistical conflicts are resolved in the specific context of relations between agri-food SMEs and large retailers in Morocco. We have focused on showing the role of interpersonal relationships in resolving this type of conflict. In the absence of a real modern logistics infrastructure (sites and information systems) optimising exchanges, the quality of the logistics service is not a main criterion for referencing and, in case of failure, it does not constitute a factor for dereferencing. We have observed that interpersonal relations are characterised by frequent contacts and quality exchanges. These social relations, which bind the staff of business partners, who prefer essentially oral communication, make it possible to maintain exchanges and a stable climate of relations by ensuring the implementation of "acceptable" methods of logistical conflict resolution. Interpersonal relations guide companies involved in logistical disputes towards the choice of cooperative resolution methods (accommodation and compromise) in the sense of Thomas (1976). We outline that communication is nourished by interpersonal trust to become better and of higher quality, which gives interpersonal relations an even more effective role in the resolution of logistical conflicts. Our main theoretical contribution is to extend the mobilised theories of conflict resolution to the specific cultural context of Morocco, in the field of logistics. Our managerial contribution is to underline a set of actions that will allow logistic managers to improve their logistics interfaces through better controlled logistic skills and human interactions.

In the face of rapid changes in the competitive environment of SMEs (increasing imports of food products mainly from Europe), a sustainable and stable relationship with the ever-growing and fast-growing supermarkets is an objective of great importance for the heads of these companies. Cooperation, as an effective way to avoid potential conflicts, could become a real strategy if stakeholders seek commitment over time, based on trust, communication, shared values and equity (Morgan and Hunt 1994; Jap and Ganesan 2000; Abbad et al. 2013). Cooperation enables the most dynamic SMEs to adapt their environment to reduce uncertainty, better manage the long term (Marchesnay and Julien 1990) and "build spaces of stability" (Delapierre 1991). However, we note that cooperation requires SME managers to have a good business vision (Allali 2003).

As an extension of this contribution, it would be appropriate to focus on other Maghreb and comparable countries, given that this research is geographically limited to the Moroccan context. A comparative approach would be relevant insofar as the countries on the southern shore of the Mediterranean basin (Morocco, Algeria, Tunisia, Egypt) certainly share a common cultural background (geographical belonging, history, language, customs, religion, etc.) but also present points of divergence, particularly in terms of the influence of politics in the economic and social spheres (Perrin 2002).

References

Abbad, H., & Paché, G. (2013). The Impact of Logistical Criteria in the Selection of SMEs by Large Food Retailers – A Case Study in an Emerging Country. *Problems and Perspectives in Management, 11*(1), 25–35.

Abbad, H., Senkel, M.-P., & Dari, L. (2012). Understanding the Non-adoption of EDI in the Modern Moroccan Food Retailing Industry. *Supply Chain Forum: An International Journal, 13*(3), 82–91.

Abbad, H., Paché, G., & Bonet, F. D. (2013). Building a Long-term Relationship Between Manufacturers and Large Retailers: Does Commitment Matter in Morocco? *Journal of Applied Business Research, 29*(5), 1367–1380.

Allali, B. (2003). *Vision des dirigeants et internationalisation des PME marocaines et canadiennes du secteur agro-alimentaire*. Doctoral dissertation in Management, Université de Montréal, Ecole des HEC Montréal, Canada.

Amine, A., & Lazzaoui, N. (2011). Shoppers' Reactions to Modern Food Retailing Systems in an Emerging Country: The Case of Morocco. *International Journal of Retail & Distribution Management, 39*(8), 562–581.

Anderson, J. C., & Narus, J. A. (1990). A Model of Distributor Firm and Manufacturer Firm Working Partnerships. *Journal of Marketing, 54*(1), 42–58.

Axelrod, R. (1984). *The Evolution of Cooperation*. New York: Basic Books.

Bardin, L. (2013). *L'analyse de contenu*. Paris: PUF.

Belaya, V., & Hanf, J. H. (2014). Power and Conflict in Processor-Supplier Relationships: Empirical Evidence from Russian Agri-Food Business. *Supply Chain Forum: An International Journal, 15*(2), 60–80.

Bonet, D. (1999). *Conflit et coopération dans le canal de distribution: l'analyse du discours des acteurs comme révélateur des comportements stratégiques*. Doctoral dissertation in Management, Université d'Aix-Marseille II, France. Disponible sur. Retrieved from https://tel.archives-ouvertes.fr/tel-02448480.

Bonet, D. (2000). Conflit et coopération dans le canal de distribution: une analyse du discours des acteurs. In P. Volle (Ed.), *Etudes et recherches en distribution* (pp. 231–246). Paris: Economica.

Bowersox, D. J., Cooper, M. B., Lambert, D. M., & Taylor, D. A. (1980). *Management in Marketing Channels*. New York: McGraw-Hill.

Brown, K. (1977). *Changing Forms of Patronage in a Moroccan City*. In E. Gellner & J. Waterbury (Eds.), *Patrons and Clients in Mediterranean Societies* (pp. 309–328). London: Duckworth.

Butt, A. S. (2018). Personal Relationships and Higher Agency Costs: Study of Buyers and Suppliers in Australian Manufacturing and Service Sector. *Operations and Supply Chain Management – An International Journal, 11*(3), 140–150.

Butt, A. S. (2019). Absence of Personal Relationship in a Buyer-Supplier Relationship: The Case of Buyers and Suppliers of Logistics Services Provider in Australia. *Heliyon, 5*(6), 1–8.

Butt, A. S., & Ahmad, A. B. (2019). Personal Relationship and Conflicts in Supply Chains: Exploration of Buyers and Suppliers in Australian Manufacturing and Service Sector. *Benchmarking: An International Journal, 26*(7), 2225–2241.

Carey, S., Lawson, B., & Krause, D. R. (2011). Social Capital Configuration, Legal Bonds and Performance in Buyer–Supplier Relationships. *Journal of Operations Management, 29*(4), 277–288.

Charvet, F. F., & Cooper, M. C. (2011). Key Contact Employees and Supply Chain Collaboration: A Literature Review and Research Agenda. *Supply Chain Forum: An International Journal, 12*(2), 4–18.

Chatman, J. (1991). Matching People and Organizations: Selection and Socialization in Public Accounting Firms. *Administrative Science Quarterly, 36*(3), 459–484.

Chung, J. E., Sternquist, B., & Chen, Z. (2006). Retailer–Buyer Supplier Relationships: The Japanese Difference. *Journal of Retailing, 82*(4), 349–355.

Cunningham, M. K. (2013). Reducing Channel Conflict. *Journal of Marketing Development and Competitiveness, 7*(1), 78–83.

d'Iribarne, P. (2002). Les ressources imprévues d'une culture: une entreprise 'excellente' à Casablanca. In P. d'Iribarne et al. (Eds.), *Cultures et mondialisation: gérer par-delà les frontières* (pp. 225–253). Paris: Seuil.

Dant, R., & Schul, P. (1992). Conflict Resolution Processes in Contractual Channels of Distribution. *Journal of Marketing, 56*(1), 38–54.

Delapierre, M. (1991). Les accords inter-entreprises, partage ou partenariat ? *Revue d'Economie Industrielle, 55*, 135–161.

Durach, C. F., & Machuca, J. A. D. (2018). A Matter of Perspective – The Role of Interpersonal Relationships in Supply Chain Risk Management. *International Journal of Operations & Production Management, 38*(10), 1866–1887.

Ekanayake, S., Childerhouse, P., & Sun, P. (2017). The Symbiotic Existence of Interorganizational and Interpersonal Ties in Supply Chain Collaboration. *The International Journal of Logistics Management, 28*(3), 723–754.

Fernie, J., & Sparks, L. (2014). *Logistics and Retail Management: Emerging Issues and New Challenges in the Retail Supply Chain* (4th ed.). London: Kogan Page.

Filser, M., & Paché, G. (2006). La dégradation du service logistique comme source d'avantage concurrentiel: l'étrange paradoxe de la distribution française. *Gestion, 31*(3), 36–45.

Frenzen, J. K., & Davis, H. L. (1990). Purchasing Behavior in Embedded Markets. *Journal of Consumer Research, 17*(1), 1–12.

Ganesan, S. (1993). Negotiation Strategies and the Nature of Channel Relationships. *Journal of Marketing Research, 30*(2), 183–203.

Geertz, C. (1986). *Savoir local, savoir global: les lieux du savoir*. Paris: Presses Universitaires de France.

Gligor, D. M., & Esmark, C. L. (2015). Supply Chain Friends: The Good, the Bad, and the Ugly. *Business Horizons, 58*(5), 517–525.

Gligor, D. M., & Holcomb, M. (2013). The Role of Personal Relationships in Supply Chains: An Exploration of Buyers and Suppliers of Logistics Services. *International Journal of Logistics Management, 24*(3), 328–355.

Granovetter, M. (1985). Economic Action and Social Structure: The Problem of Embeddedness. *American Journal of Sociology, 91*(3), 481–510.

Grewal, R., Kumar, A., Mallapragada, G., & Saini, A. (2013). Marketing Channels in Foreign Markets: Control Mechanisms and the Moderating Role of Multinational Corporation Headquarters – Subsidiary Relationship. *Journal of Marketing Research, 50*(3), 378–398.

Guibert, N. (1996). *La relation client-fournisseur et les nouvelles technologies de l'information: le rôle des concepts de confiance et d'engagement*. Doctoral dissertation in Management, Université des Sciences et Techniques du Languedoc-Montpellier II, France.

Gulati, R. (1995). Social Structure and Alliance Formation Patterns: A Longitudinal Analysis. *Administrative Science Quarterly, 40*(4), 619–652.

Gulati, R. (1998). Alliances and Networks. *Strategic Management Journal, 19*(4), 293–317.

Hansen, K. (2001). Purchasing Decision Behaviour by Chinese Supermarkets. *International Review of Retail, Distribution and Consumer Research, 11*(2), 159–175.

Heide, J. B. (1994). Interorganizational Governance in Marketing Channels. *Journal of Marketing, 58*(1), 71–85.

Heide, J. B., & John, G. (1992). Do Norms Matter in Marketing Relationships? *Journal of Marketing, 56*(2), 32–44.

Hlady Rispal, M. (2002). *La méthode des cas: application à la recherche en gestion.* Bruxelles: Editions De Boeck Université.

Hutt, M. D., Stafford, E. R., Walker, B. A., & Reingen, P. H. (2000). Case Study: Defining the Social Network of a Strategic Alliance. *MIT Sloan Management Review, 41*(2), 51–62.

Jap, S. D. (1999). Pie-Expansion Efforts: Collaboration Processes in Buyer-Seller Relationships. *Journal of Marketing Research, 36*(4), 461–475.

Jap, S., & Ganesan, S. (2000). Control Mechanisms and the Relationship Life Cycle: Implications for Safeguarding Specific Investments and Developing Commitment. *Journal of Marketing Research, 37*(2), 227–245.

Jones, C., Hesterly, W. S., & Borgatti, S. P. (1997). A General Theory of Network Governance: Exchange Conditions and Social Mechanisms. *Academy of Management Review, 22*(4), 911–945.

Kanter, R. M. (1994). Collaborative Advantage: The Art of Alliances. *Harvard Business Review, 72*(4), 96–108.

Klein, B., & Leffler, K. B. (1981). The Role of Market Forces in Assuring Contractual Performance. *Journal of Political Economy, 89*(4), 615–641.

Krafft, M., Goetz, O., Mantrala, M., Sotgiu, F., & Tillmanns, S. (2015). The Evolution of Marketing Channel Research Domains and Methodologies: An Integrative Review and Future Directions. *Journal of Retailing, 91*(4), 569–585.

March, J. G., & Simon, H. A. (1958). *Organizations.* New York: John Wiley and Sons.

Marchesnay, M., & Julien, P. A. (1990). The Small Business: As a Transaction Space. *Entrepreneurship and Regional development, 2*(3), 267–278.

Mohr, J., & Spekman, R. (1994). Characteristics of Partnership Success: Partnership Attributes, Communication Behavior, and Conflict Resolution Techniques. *Strategic Management Journal, 15*(2), 135–152.

Morgan, R., & Hunt, S. (1994). The Commitment-Trust Theory of Relationship Marketing. *Journal of Marketing, 58*(3), 20–38.

Murry, J. P., & Heide, J. B. (1998). Managing Promotion Program Participation Within Manufacturer-Retailer Relationships. *Journal of Marketing, 62*(1), 58–68.

Nilsson, J., & Höst, V. (1987). *Retailer Assortment Decision Criteria*. Aarhus: Aarhus University Press.

Ouchi, W. G. (1980). Markets, Bureaucracies and Clans. *Administrative Science Quarterly, 25*(1), 129–141.

Paché, G. (1995). Le poids du critère logistique dans les procédures de sélection des fournisseurs: application à la grande distribution alimentaire. *Logistique & Management, 3*(2), 57–66.

Paché, G. (2002). L'évolution des relations logistiques entre industriels et détaillants: coopération ou simple coordination? *Gestion 2000, 19*(1), 109–124.

Perrin, S. (2002). *Les entrepreneurs marocains, un nouveau rôle social et politique face au Makhzen?* Genève: Institut Universitaire d'Etudes et de Développement (IUED).

Peters, L. D., & Fletcher, K. P. (2004). Communication Strategies and Marketing Performance: An Application of the Mohr and Nevin Framework to Intra-Organisational Cross-Functional Teams. *Journal of Marketing Management, 20*(7/8), 741–770.

Phan, M. C. T., Styles, C. W., & Patterson, P. G. (2005). Relational Competency's Role in Southeast Asia Business Partnerships. *Journal of Business Research, 58*(2), 173–184.

Ring, P. S., & Van de Ven, A. H. (1992). Structuring Cooperative Relationships Between Organizations. *Strategic Management Journal, 13*(7), 483–498.

Ring, P. S., & Van de Ven, A. H. (1994). Developmental Process of Cooperative Interorganizational Relationships. *Academy of Management Review, 19*(1), 90–118.

Sabri, R. (2012). *L'accompagnement comme pratique de légitimation en grande distribution: Le cas de Marjane Holding*. Doctoral dissertation in Management, Université Montpellier I, France.

Schorsch, T., Wallenburg, C. M., & Wieland, A. (2017). The Human Factor in SCM: Introducing a Meta-theory of Behavioral Supply Chain Management. *International Journal of Physical Distribution & Logistics Management, 47*(4), 238–262.

Sharma, D., & Parida, B. (2018). Determinants of Conflict in Channel Relationships: A Meta-Analytic Review. *Journal of Business & Industrial Marketing, 33*(7), 911–930.

Stern, L. W., El-Ansary, A. I., & Coughlan, A. T. (1996). *Marketing Channels* (5th ed.). Prentice Hall.

Tangeaoui, S. (1993). *Les entrepreneurs marocains: pouvoir, société et modernité.* Paris: Editions Karthala.

Thomas, K. W. (1976). *Conflict and Conflict Management.* In M. D. Dunnette (Ed.), *Handbook of Industrial and Organizational Psychology* (pp. 889–935). Chicago, IL: Rand McNally.

Thomas, K. W. (1992). *Conflict and Negotiation Processes in Organizations.* In M. D. Dunnette & L. M. Hough (Eds.), *Handbook of Industrial and Organizational Psychology* (Vol. 3, 2nd ed., pp. 651–717). Palo Alto, CA: Consulting Psychologists Press.

Vu, H. L. (2009). *Gestion du conflit et management interculturel dans le canal de distribution: une analyse des déterminants et des effets du conflit sur la satisfaction des acteurs. Application au cas de la grande distribution au Vietnam.* Unpublished doctoral dissertation in Management, Université d'Aix-Marseille II, France.

Wall, J. A., & Callister, R. R. (1995). Conflict and Its Management. *Journal of Management, 21*(3), 515–558.

Wang, B., Kang, Y., Childerhouse, P., & Huo, B. (2018). Interpersonal and Inter-organizational Relationship Drivers of Supply Chain Integration. *Industrial Management & Data Systems, 118*(6), 1170–1191.

Whipple, J. M., Wiedmer, R., & Boyer, K. K. (2015). A Dyadic Investigation of Collaborative Competence, Social Capital, and Performance in Buyer–Supplier Relationships. *Journal of Supply Chain Management, 51*(2), 3–21.

Wichmann, B. K., Carter, C. R., & Kaufmann, L. (2015). How to Become Central in an Informal Social Network: An Investigation of the Antecedents to Network Centrality in an Environmental SCM Initiative. *Journal of Business Logistics, 36*(1), 102–119.

Xie, J., Song, X. M., & Stringfellow, A. (1998). Interfunctional Conflict, Conflict Resolution Styles, and New Product Success: A Four Culture Comparison. *Management Science, 44*(12), 192–206.

Part III

Transborder Corporate Social Responsibility

9

A Review of Corporate Social Responsibility Practices in Ethiopia

Ahmed Kellow and Nebil Kellow

1 Introduction

The concept of corporate social responsibility (CSR) has become noticeably salient in the modern-day global business environment. The interest in CSR, however, is not limited to the world of business and academia as it extends to everyday life. According to Aras and Crowther (2011), a number of factors such as poor business behaviour towards customers, employees and the environment are highlighted to have contributed to the popular consciousness in corporate social responsibility.

Similar articles claim that the issues of climate change and supply chains have also become prominent concerns in driving CSR. Nowadays, people have become more conscious and concerned about issues such as the emission of greenhouse gases, particularly carbon dioxide, and about

A. Kellow (✉) • N. Kellow
First Consult, Addis Ababa, Ethiopia
e-mail: akellow@firstconsultet.com; nebil@firstconsultet.com

S. M. Apitsa, E. Milliot (eds.), *Doing Business in Africa*, Palgrave Studies of Internationalization in Emerging Markets,
https://doi.org/10.1007/978-3-030-50739-8_9

exploitation of people in developing countries, especially in the use of child labour in global supply chains.

From the perspective of corporate management, the expectations of profit making and social responsibility in businesses provides an oxymoron for debate. Business corporations are profit making entities that exist and operate in competitive environments. In these circumstances, they may be limited in their ability to solve a multitude of social problems, particularly considering that more investment in corporate social responsibility comes at the expense of the shareholders (Cavico and Mujtaba 2012).

On the other hand, social responsibility is the fundamental duty of the state that must focus on social justice to its citizens. The state, however, is unable to execute its primary social responsibilities because it is not able to mobilise funds that are adequate against the demand. Consequently, businesses from micro to corporate levels emerge as drivers of economic and social growth.

From a corporate management perspective, the question is no longer whether or not to include corporate social responsibility as part of doing business; rather, it is how to do so. It is more to do with the philanthropic guidelines for corporate contributions and improvements. It relates to how corporate resources should be allocated, who the beneficiaries are, to what extent and in what order of priority.

The chapter starts with an introduction to the basic concepts and definition of CSR. In the following section, global practices of CSR are discussed. Then comes CSR practices in Africa. Finally, CSR practices in Ethiopia and its determinants are discussed with empirical practices by notable corporates.

2 What Is Corporate Social Responsibility?

There is no single commonly accepted definition of corporate social responsibility. Therefore, there is a general consensus of relating CSR to company concerns such as community involvement, socially responsible products and processes, concern for the environment and socially responsible employee relations (Ortiz-Martinez and Crowther 2006, cited by Aras and Crowther 2011).

According to the World Business Council for Sustainable Development (WBCSD 1998), the definition of corporate social responsibility and what it consists of varies across time and place, depending on a range of local contexts including culture, religion, governmental and legal conditions. The WBCSD broadly defines CSR as the ethical behaviour of a company towards society. In particular, this means management acting responsibly in its relationships with other stakeholders who have a legitimate interest in the business—not just the shareholders. The formal definition is as follows: "Corporate social responsibility is the continuing commitment by business to behave ethically and contribute to economic development while improving the quality of life of the workforce and their families as well as the local community and society at large." The WBCSD puts human rights, employee rights, environmental protection, supplier relations and community involvement as priority issues at the centre of corporate social responsibility.

The World Bank also offers its definition, according to which CSR is summed as "the voluntary commitment by company managers to integrate social and environmental considerations in their business operations". This commitment goes beyond normal compliance with the legal, regulatory and contractual obligations, which companies are generally expected to meet. The general concept of CSR encompasses:

1. A collection of policies and practices linked to the relationship with key stakeholders, values, compliance with legal requirements and respect for people, communities and the environment;
2. The commitment of business to contribute to sustainable development.

The World Bank also indicated the following material components to the concept of CSR: (1) environmental protection, (2) labour security, (3) human rights, (4) community involvement, (5) business standards, (6) marketplace, (7) enterprise and economic development, (8) health protection, (9) education leadership and national development and (10) human disaster relief.

3 Global Practices

The concept of CSR came into being in the United States in the 1950s and spread to European companies in the 1990s. Intergovernmental and regional organisations have taken the initiative of developing the concept through publishing guidelines and standards, and establishing a comprehensive CSR reference toolkit for the private sector. Over the last two decades, CSR strategies have evolved towards increasingly standardised frameworks.

The primary international reference framework on CSR matters are the OECD (Organisation for Economic Cooperation and Development) Guidelines that became enforced in 1976 and revised in 2011. These are non-binding recommendations, and they provide an implementation mechanism via a network of National Contact Points (NCPs), which receives complaints and can impose sanctions in every signatory country. These guidelines deal with human rights, employment and industrial relations, the environment, fighting corruption, and so on, and are addressed to companies in 42 signatory countries.

Another international framework in CSR is the UN Global Compact, launched in 2000. It encompasses ten principles in the fields of human rights, labour standards and the environment and anti-corruption measures. Presently, it has more than 8000 signatories in 135 countries.

There are also international standards that companies use as a support structure for implementing them, the most prominent being ISO 26000, which provides guidance on how organisations can operate in a socially responsible way with respect to governance, human rights, labour relations and working conditions, the environment and community relations—among others.

There is a global consensus on the overall notion that CSR is concerned about the responsibilities of companies with regard to other actors in the society. However, it should be recognised that its practices may take a different approach as a result of country differences and it needs to be studied in the context of where it is practised. Matten and Moon (2008) argue that country differences in CSR are a function of a variety of long-standing, historically entrenched institutions such as governmental and legal institutions, norms, incentives and rules.

In major US and UK firms, especially larger ones, CSR is firmly ingrained in their corporate mindset, and the need to align CSR as an integral part of doing business is well recognised. As to other countries, different studies indicate that the proliferation of multinational companies and their expanding global reach has increased awareness of CSR as a global topic.

A study by Robertson (2009) on the state of corporate social responsibility in Singapore, Turkey and Ethiopia—countries that the study selected as representative of varying levels of economic development—illustrates that CSR is responsive to country differences in institutional factors. Accordingly, the nature of corporate social responsibility in different countries is expected to vary based on ownership structure of companies, corporate governance, openness of the economies to international investors and the role of civil society.

Ownership structure, that is, public versus private ownership of firm, matters because it influences how executives make decisions about CSR (Table 9.1).

Sound corporate governance is another necessary condition for CSR to thrive. Corporate governance can be reflected in three dimensions:

- dependence on formal organisations including the government (governmental effectiveness),
- corporate transparency and disclosure, in the form of fair treatment and engagement of all stakeholders (control of corruption) and
- response to informal pressures from stakeholders (voice and accountability).

Openness to international investment is expected to influence the culture of CSR in a country in at least two ways. One is through the impact of multinational companies with reasonably well-developed CSR programmes that may have an impact on local firms. Secondly, multinational firms can act as agents of change in reducing corruption and introducing better business practices. Hence, in economies that are more open, there will be more expectations of CSR engagement by businesses.

Table 9.1 Ownership structures in Singapore, Turkey, and Ethiopia, and implications on CSR

	Ownership structure			
Country	Publicly owned (%)	Individual/ family-owned (%)	Controlled by managers (%)	Implication on CSR
Singapore	13	22	59	• Strong protection of shareholder rights • Emphasis the union of CSR and profitability • Lack of shareholders' and management appreciation for CSR
Turkey	<1	60	19	• CSR modelled as philanthropy reflecting the values and preferences of corporate leaders • The advantage of family ownership is in the relative ease in reaching shareholder consensus on philanthropic decisions.
Ethiopia	<1	44	18	• Firms more concerned with corporate survival than CSR. • More philanthropic than CSR.

Source: Adapted from Robertson (2009: 621)

In this regard, the large presence of multinationals and the level of trade and foreign direct investment (FDI) in Singapore led to CSR in the model of US and UK businesses. In Turkey, an economy that is relatively more guarded regarding international trade and investment, the dominant model of CSR is philanthropy. In Ethiopia, the dominance of international NGOs and development agencies may influence the way CSR develops in the country.

The final dimension is the role of civil societies, which embodies the collective mentality and encompasses pressures brought on firms from its stakeholders, ranging from the expectations of customers, employees and suppliers, to pressures from trade unions, NGOs, political interest groups or social movements.

The global practice of CSR can also be looked at from the perspective of the UN Sustainable Development Goals (SDGs). The SDGs, set in 2015 by the United Nations, present a universally agreed-upon sustainable development vision for 2030. The 17 goals, which have a total of 169 targets, are No Poverty; Zero Hunger; Good Health and Well-being; Quality Education; Gender Equality; Clean Water and Sanitation; Affordable and Clean Energy; Decent Work and Economic Growth; Industry, Innovation, and Infrastructure; Reducing Inequality; Sustainable Cities and Communities; Responsible Consumption and Production; Climate Action; Life Below Water; Life on Land; Peace, Justice, and Strong Institutions; Partnerships for the Goals.

Particularly for Africa, CSR represents an opportunity as it can encourage corporates' contribution to inclusive and sustainable development.

4 CSR in Africa

Business has played a significant place in the development of Africa. The question here is how responsible and ethical have these businesses been. In its positive term, business brings capital, creates employment, is a skills transfer tool, brings about infrastructural development and social responsibility programmes to countries throughout Africa. However, evident cases have been observed where businesses have been involved in political corruption, environmental destruction, labour exploitation and social disruption (Visser et al. 2006).

CSR was conducted in Africa by transnational companies during the colonial period (Honke 2012). This practice also continued after the end of colonial period. As cited in Idemudia (2014), Noyoo stated that in colonial times, though with racial bias, some corporations used to provide housing and hygiene accommodations for their employees in Zambia. He also states that, however, these transnational corporations used these 'CSR' activities as a cover to hide their exploitation of the resources of the continent (Bagire et al. 2010).

CSR is affected by the level of development of a country. CSR activities get wider acceptance in countries with high levels of poverty. It has increased acceptance in companies in Africa, in part due to a weak legal framework and, at the same time, higher acceptability with little effort (Cheruiyot and Onsando 2016).

According to Idemudia (2014), CSR practices in Africa are driven by three main factors: internal factors (local social movements and corporate-community conflict), external factors (adherence to international standards) and transnational factors (collaboration with international NGOs). Ayalew (2018) also identified CSR determinants as firm characteristics, corporate governance characteristics and institutional or industry characteristics. Firm characteristics include factors like size, profitability, capital structure or investments in research and development. Governance characteristics refer to ownership structure and board composition. Industry characteristics refer to the sector of involvement; sectors with higher side effects to the community and environment tend to be highly involved in CSR activities.

In more recent years, the private sector has been in a good position to positively contribute to the socio-economic and environmental conditions in Africa (Visser 2006). Therefore, there should be a shift in the role of business from being the cause to the solution for underdevelopment of Africa (Idemudia 2014). Businesses at present should be tools rather than agents to development in the continent. This could be through the practice of responsible business through public-private partnerships to bring about sustainable economic transformation within communities (Japan External Trade Organization 2009).

CSR comes at a cost to the businesses, brought about with being socially and environmentally responsible. However, reward follows with stable and sustainable growth (Japan External Trade Organization 2009).

CSR is criticised for ignoring local priorities and basic livelihood needs of people in developing countries (Japan External Trade Organization 2009). It is often associated with large companies and particularly with multinational and global enterprises. Some aspects of CSR codes of conduct are not applicable to the wider business community. This is especially true for small businesses that are sometimes conceived as recipients of CSR activities in the codes of conduct and at the same time required to abide by the codes. Besides, small businesses have limited capacity to undertake CSR activities, which creates a barrier to these businesses (Bagire et al. 2010).

CSR in Africa is highly misunderstood and misused by companies. It has different concepts in different regions. Most of what is perceived to be CSR in Africa is actually not in the developed world (Cheruiyot and Onsando 2016). This is because most CSR concepts in Africa are adopted from the developed world, which are not applicable in Africa due to contextual differences (Dartey-Baah and Amponsah-Tawiah 2011). The studies so far on CSR in Africa failed to incorporate indigenous CSR concepts (Cheruiyot and Onsando 2016). Ayalew (2018) suggests blending indigenous and international best practices to bring about better CSR practice.

According to Carroll (1979), businesses have four major spheres of CSR activities: economic, legal, ethical and philanthropic responsibilities. Priority given to these responsibilities differs by context. Visser (2006) found that economic responsibilities are prioritised in Africa followed by philanthropy, legal and ethical responsibilities. Poverty and shortage of foreign direct investment are the main reasons for the priority given to economic responsibilities. In terms of philanthropic responsibilities, this is mainly due to the reliance of African nations on foreign aid. Philanthropy is an expectation from the community in Africa. Higher priority to philanthropy manifests that CSR is at its earliest stages in Africa. The legal infrastructure in Africa is poor and not usually enforceable. Ethical responsibilities are prioritised least due to low enforcement mechanisms and corruption (Visser 2006). Figure 9.1 shows the hierarchy of responsibilities.

As a significant number of Africans live under poor economic conditions, unable to afford the necessities of life (Cheruiyot and Onsando 2016), most CSR practices in Africa focus on the philanthropic like cash, food or other material donations, but which do not contribute towards the long-term betterment of society (Cheruiyot and Onsando 2016; Ayalew 2018). However, CSR is not just a philanthropic activity; it should be inclusive of accountability to moral and legal rules and regulations (Ayalew 2018).

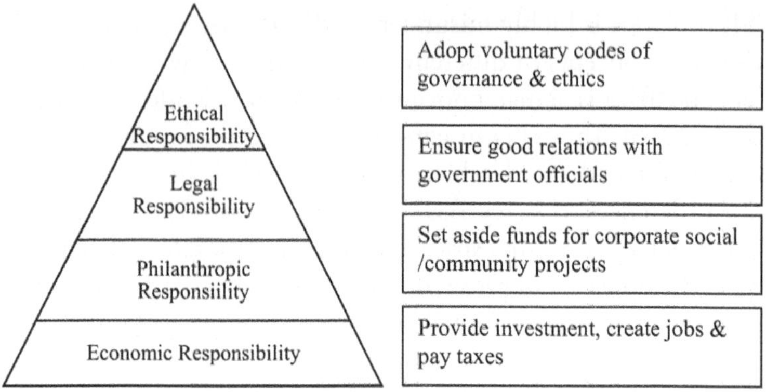

Fig. 9.1 Africa's corporate social responsibility pyramid. (Source: Adapted from Visser 2006)

5 CSR in Ethiopia

5.1 Economic Context

Prior to delving into the status of CSR in Ethiopia, a discussion of the country's economic condition is needed to provide context.

A country with a population of 109 million in 2018, Ethiopia is one of the fastest-growing economies in Africa. The strong and broad-based economic growth averaging 9.9% from 2007/2008 to 2017/2018 has brought with it poverty reduction in both urban and rural areas. Despite these successes, Ethiopia remains one of the poorest countries with a per capita income of USD 790 (World Bank 2019).

The main challenges are sustaining positive economic growth and accelerated poverty reduction, and these require massive work in job creation and improved governance. A high share of the government's budget is devoted to pro-poor programmes and investments.

Given the weak state of the Ethiopian economy, and occurrence of droughts and famines over the last three decades, there is a strong presence of international and local NGOs that are focused on providing relief, as well as working with the government and private sector to improve the country's economic and social resources (Robertson 2009).

5.2 Legal and Policy Framework

According to Steurer (2010), there are critical grounds for governments to care about the issue of CSR. First, particular business endeavours can help meet the government's policy objectives on issues such as sustainable development and environmental protection on a voluntary basis. Besides these, CSR can positively contribute to foreign policy goals such as development assistance.

Second, CSR policies are perceived to positively complement hard-law regulations in cases where hard-law regulations are politically unattractive or infeasible. Therefore, the soft-law nature of CSR policies gives them lower political costs in terms of resistance from special interest groups (Moon 2002).

Other reasons for states' interest in CSR include:

- The soft approach of CSR policies agrees with a broader transition of public governance altogether, leading away from hierarchical regulation towards more of a partnership modality.
- As CSR is concerned with managing business relations with a broad matrix of stakeholders, it reshapes management routines as well as the roles of, and relations between, businesses, governments and civil society.

Therefore, it is recognised that the state has the responsibility to promote public policy with regard to the CSR agenda. Especially in a developing economy like Ethiopia, where government's developmental efforts are far from succeeding to meet the socio-economic needs of the society, the need for corporates to discharge their social responsibility has become a significant concern (Deyassa 2016). Accordingly, public policies as development instruments and facilitators have a vital role in the promotion of CSR.

Policies concerning CSR in Ethiopia are unclear and disorganised, often found scattered in different policy instruments which are usually hard to find.

Despite the widespread application of philanthropic and CSR activities in Ethiopia, the private sector is not taking a leadership in CSR initiatives and for the most part does not have a logical approach to develop their own definition and understanding based on the unique features of the companies. These days, more corporates are initiating their own CSR strategies in Ethiopia. However, most of them do not have their own comprehensive and general policy framework, and the CSR definitions and policies are mere transplantation from developed countries' contexts. The presence of such differing conceptual understandings of CSR by various corporates, each valuable in their own right, leads to inconsistencies and ineffective discharge of obligations.

The largest enterprises in Ethiopia operate without any formal CSR definition and policy document. These conduct CSR on an informal basis and integrate them in their business strategies.

One key aspect in which the lack of CSR policy has shown its effect is the issue of environmental management and health. The Ethiopian constitution declares that all persons have the right to a clean and healthy environment, and that the government has a duty to ensure that all Ethiopians live in a clean and healthy environment. There is also an environmental regulatory framework and the Environmental Protection Authority is mandated with environmental management.

However, environmental governance in Ethiopia does not consider the notion of corporate responsibility and companies also do not think in terms of environmental responsibility. Instead, for the most part, they are concerned about economic survival (Robertson 2009). This is evident by the fact that pollution from the industrial sector is high and rising in Ethiopia with textiles, tanneries, beverage and food processing factors discharging polluting waste into rivers, often without treatment. A study by the Ethiopian Ministry of Environment and Forestry (2014) revealed that, out of 163 factories surveyed, 101 (62%) release their industrial wastes directly to the environment without any treatment.

5.3 Current Practices of CSR in Ethiopia

CSR has been practised in Ethiopia in traditional ways for a long time. There are traditional institutions that embedded social responsibility practices and serve as instruments for socio-economic collaboration and cooperation among people. The most common examples of CSR in Ethiopia are 'Idir', which provides financial support in times of loss of family member; 'Iqub', which supports members by providing a loan with zero interest rate, 'Zeker', which provides food for those in need by Christians; 'Sedeqa', which involves the provision of food for the poor by Muslims; 'Zekat', which entails the contribution of 10% of annual income for the poor by Muslims; 'Asrat', which is the same as Zekat practised by Christians (Ayalew 2018).

CSR is at its earliest stages in Ethiopia as in most sub-Saharan countries (Kassa 2018). As discussed in Robertson (2009), it is at a stage in which it is being pitched by the academics and the government, and has not been implemented as yet.

According to Kassa (2018), most CSR activities in Ethiopia are so only from a philanthropic angle. Ghrmay (2013) argues that this philanthropic culture is an extension from the extended family culture in Ethiopia which grew to business endeavours and practices. Robertson (2009) ties the philanthropic nature of CSR in Ethiopia to the various NGOs in the country. These NGOs are partnering with the government and the private sector to improve the socio-economic conditions of the country by providing foreign aid and investment. They are also addressing democracy and governance issues in the country. Therefore, it can be said that they have a significant stake in government initiatives, which they could use to lobby on the role of businesses in the society.

CSR in Ethiopia is usually undertaken by multinational companies while participation of locally owned companies in CSR is low. However, Kassa (2018) suggests that it is difficult to say that companies in Ethiopia are averse towards CSR. Rather, he argues that the political framework is lacking to practise CSR in a sustainable manner. For instance, Altes (2018) found that there is no concerned government organ on CSR practices in the tourism industry. However, as cited in Nigatu (2018), Asfaw mentioned that the Ministry of Trade and Industry, with support from the World Bank, USAID and other development partners, is developing a CSR programme in order to instil a CSR culture in the national companies.

According to Kassa (2018), local companies usually prioritise economic aspects of their endeavours. Ethical practices towards social and environmental protection are seen as less ranked than economic returns to investment (Altes 2018; Amare 2019). As stated in Desjardins (1998), businesses should also consider their CSR while pursuing profits. However, as cited in Amare (2019), Nukpezah (2010) argued that businesses in developing countries forgo the future at the cost of present benefits. Andualem as cited in Nigatu (2018) identified lack of awareness about CSR by the business community as the main reason for low participation in CSR. Potluri and Temesgen (2008) stated that competition by other businesses is a threat for them. This is due to the additional financial resources allocated for CSR activities, which could reduce their profitability compared to others.

CSR has recently become the agenda of various companies, especially for the large ones (Téllez 2017). Most CSR practices are undertaken by a few companies like Ethiopian Airlines, Heineken, Diageo, BGI Ethiopia, MIDROC, Dangote Cement, Sunshine Group, East Africa Holdings and some others of the same large scale. According to Nigatu (2018), most of these companies were criticised for abandoning these activities. However, in recent years these companies have started establishing a foundation wing for their CSR activities (The Reporter Ethiopia 2016; Ethiopian Business Review 2020; Forbes 2018).

Robertson (2009) cites openness of a country for foreign investment as a contributing factor for CSR practices. An example for this in the Ethiopian context is the CSR activities by Heineken, Diageo and the industrial parks factories, most of which are owned by foreign investors.

Below are some notable practices of CSR in Ethiopia:

- *Heineken Ethiopia*: Heineken Ethiopia's slogan for its CSR activities is "Brewing a Better World". Heineken Ethiopia is involved in various CSR activities including support of local smallholder farmers to supply its breweries by providing them with top-quality seeds, agricultural training, improved access to finance and links to reliable markets to sell their crop, construction of a hospital in Bedele with a maternal wing for mothers and infants, support for mentally ill female patients, creating jobs for a youth group in Shashemene by building a mill house, protecting water resources, reducing CO_2 emissions, advocating responsible consumption and promoting health and safety (Heineken Ethiopia).

- *Diageo*: It forms partnerships with farmers, sources raw materials in a responsible manner (locally and at competitive price), promotes responsible drinking by discouraging drivers from overdrinking; it also has DRINKiQ, a tool that enables people to unlock the knowledge of drinking responsibly (Diageo).
- *Industrial parks*: They have played significant roles, especially in areas where they operate.

  – Industrial parks (IPs) pay a fair price for cotton, integration of local cotton producers' sourcing of cotton, sourcing and training of employees from the region. Besides, IPs through the Industrial Parks Development Corporation support local communities that have been displaced during construction of the IP. They provide schools materials such as exercise books, pens, bags, and so on, to the community children.
  – PVH (PVH Corp., formerly known as the Phillips-Van Heusen Corporation) has a partnership with leading conservation organisation World Wildlife Fund (WWF) to help conserve freshwater resources in Ethiopia's Lake Hawassa. PVH also partners with Save the Children to expand employment opportunities, increasing income and improving working conditions for the young and the female gender living in Hawassa and its surroundings (PVH 2018).
  – Provision of sewing machines, fabrics and threads for various TVET (Technical and Vocational Education and Training) colleges by companies like EPIC, EVEREST and HELA.
  – IPs have played an invaluable role during the COVID-19 response. They have supported the regional governments with PPEs (Personal Protective Equipment) and sanitation tools manufacture. They have also coached their employees to create awareness about the pan-

demic. Besides, the IPs have placed a temperature check-up facility and sanitation tools at the gates of the IPs.

- Other CSR activities by IPs include Mother Theresa alms giving, provision of food for the needy, sponsorship of the world health & safety day.
- However, critics say there is gap between what the companies in the IPs and their brands say and the reality for the people working in the IPs (Kyritsis and Nova 2019).

- *Ethiopian Airlines*: It established its foundation wing: the Ethiopian Airlines Foundation (The Reporter Ethiopia 2016). Through the foundation, Ethiopian Airlines intends to contribute to the development of the country and help Ethiopia achieve Sustainable Development Goals. Ethiopian Airlines CSR activities also extend to a green environmental policy, support to local farmers, planting trees (one for every passenger) campaign, involvement in Boeing's Humanitarian Delivery Flights Program to transport medical and educational donations in Ethiopia and Africa, lunch feeding programme in schools and the community, supporting orphans, supporting the tourism sector by providing stop-over packages in Addis Ababa with no additional fee and contributing to the empowerment of women with all-women operated flights. In response to COVID-19, Ethiopian Airlines deployed its pharma wing to provide medical supplies (including Jack Ma's round of donations) to various countries (Ethiopian Airlines).

In recent years, various initiatives have been undertaken by the Government of Ethiopia to pull the business community into CSR activities like the 'Beautifying Sheger Project', 'The Grand Ethiopian Renaissance Dam', 'Tree Planting Initiative'; recently the business community participated significantly in response to the government's pleas for COVID-19 relief measures, including through donations (in kind and in cash), production of PPE equipment, exemption of rental fees by real estates, reduction in loan interest rates by banks in hard-hit sectors.

5.4 Determinants of CSR in Ethiopia

As described in the previous sections, CSR is contextual in its nature. Below are attributes to CSR in Ethiopia, some of which are applicable elsewhere:

- *Company size*: The larger a company, the larger its participation in CSR activities (Ayalew 2018). Ayalew mentions public image as a factor for this relationship. Besides, larger companies usually have formal proceedings that push them to disclose their CSR activities.
- *Ownership structure*: As cited in Idemudia (2014), Stokes argues that where there is a separation between ownership and control, companies tend to be more active in CSR practices. Within ownership structure types, involvement in CSR activities increases in the following order: sole proprietorship, private limited company and share company.
- *Sector of business*: More CSR activity is expected from companies with more social and environmental impact. Besides, there are some sectors like mining, where limited opportunities are available. This is especially the case in certain sectors such as the extractive industries, where there is the need for competitive advantage. Wiig and Kolstad (2010) found that CSR is strategically critical in such types of sectors to widen their chances of winning contracts.
- *Indebtedness of the company*: The more indebted a company is, the less it involves itself in CSR activities (Reverte 2009). Indebtedness lessens the focus of companies in social activities and pushes them to focus on repayment of their loans.
- *Legal framework*: According to Ayalew (2018), the government is the critical organ to influence businesses to involve in ethical business practices by devising laws, policies and strategies. However, though the government is drafting relevant laws and regulations, its enforcement capability is questionable. Therefore, the stricter the legal enforcement mechanism, the more businesses stick to ethical business practices.
- *Availability of the stock market*: According to the National Bank of Ethiopia, Ethiopia is set to start a stock market. Stock markets push

companies to align to corporate governance systems (Ayalew 2018). This would pressure companies to align to CSR practices.

- *Commitment*: Amare (2019) found that some companies in Ethiopia with official environmental policies have been found to be polluting the environment. They have no commitment to actually apply their policies.
- *Corporate governance*: Companies with established policies, rules and regulations tend to be more sensitive to CSR.
- *Openness of the economy to international investment*: Alderin (2014) found a positive relationship between openness to international investment and CSR activities. Transnational corporations have a value chain from local producers, which requires the local producers to abide by the CSR policies of the transnational corporations. Therefore, the more the number of transnational corporations, the more initiatives by local producers to comply with CSR practices.
- *Role of civil society*: NGOs play a critical role in initiating CSR practices by lobbying with the government (Robertson 2009). These NGOs also support CSR initiatives by supporting companies with interest in the subject.
- *Information and communication technology penetration*: Better information and communication technology (ICT) access and penetration means better access of the society to news of any violations in CSR practices (Smith 2003). This pushes companies to comply with CSR standards.

6 Conclusion

Available empirical evidences on the status of corporate social responsibility (CSR) in Ethiopia indicates the lack of a well-developed culture of CSR and its integration into corporates. CSR is being implemented mostly by multinationals and large local enterprises. However, these are mostly inconsistent philanthropic activities, and not supported by sustainable CSR policies and strategies. There are also companies that have CSR policies but do not comply with their implementation. This is specifically evident in environmental management issues.

Studies attribute the lack of strong CSR practice in Ethiopia to gaps in the necessary requirements. First, there has not been any visible government commitment in the form of national CSR policies and organised efforts to integrate them into its own socio-economic development efforts. Second, most businesses in Ethiopia are privately owned, and corporate governance is at a stage where it is only a centre of academic discussions and not afforded much attention. Therefore, to enhance the contribution of corporate social responsibility to national development, the government needs to have clear policies and strategies. It is also crucial to increase public awareness and strengthen civil society's role in voicing society's needs and concerns, and their expectations from corporates in terms of social contribution.

References

Alderin, C. (2014). *Made in Ethiopia: Challenges and Opportunities in the Emerging Textile Industry in Ethiopia*. Thesis, Uppsala University, Department of Social and Economic Geography

Altes, C. (2018). *Analysis of Tourism Value Chain in Ethiopia*. Center for the Promotion of Imports (CBI Ministry of Foreign Affairs of the Netherlands).

Amare, A. (2019). Corporate Environmental Responsibility in Ethiopia: A Case Study of the Akaki River Basin. *Ecosystem Health and Sustainability, 5*(1), 57–66.

Aras, G., & Crowther, D. (2011). *Global Perspectives on Corporate Governance and CSR*. Routledge.

Ayalew, B. M. (2018). Corporate Social Responsibility Practices, Determinants. *Journal of Investment and Management, 7*(6), 157–165.

Bagire, V. A., Tusiime, I., Nalweyiso, G., & Kakooza, J. B. (2010). Contextual Environment and Stakeholder Perception of Corporate Social Responsibility Practices in Uganda. *Corporate Social Responsibility and Environmental Management, 18*, 102–109.

Carroll, A. B. (1979). A Three-Dimensional Model of Corporate Performance. *Academy of Management Review, 4*, 497–505.

Cavico, F. J., & Mujtaba, B. G. (2012). National and Global Perspectives of Corporate Social Responsibility. *International Journal of Management Sciences and Business Research, 1*(3), 1–21.

Cheruiyot, T. K., & Onsando, P. (2016). Corporate Social Responsibility in Africa Context-Paradoxes-Stakeholder Orientations-Contestations-and Reflections. In: *Corporate Social Performance in the Age of Irresponsibility—Cross National Perspective* (pp. 89–110). Information Age Publishing Inc.

Dartey-Baah, K., & Amponsah-Tawiah, K. (2011). Exploring the Limits of Western Corporate Social Responsibility Theories in Africa. *International Journal of Business and Social Science, 2*(18), 126–137.

DesJardins, J. (1998). Corporate Environmental Responsibility. *Journal of Business Ethics, 17*, 825–838.

Deyassa, K. (2016). CSR from Ethiopian Perspective. *International Journal of Scientific & Technology Research, 5*(4), 299–320.

Ethiopian Airlines. (n.d.). *Press Release*. Retrieved from https://corporate.ethiopianairlines.com/media/Press-Release.

Ethiopian Business Review. (2020). *We Have Plans to Transform in to Multinational Company*. Retrieved from https://ethiopianbusinessreview.net/archives/6873.

Forbes. (2018). *The Ethiopian Multi-millionaire Who Built Africa's First Mariott Hotel*. Retrieved from https://www.forbes.com/sites/mfonobongnsehe/2018/01/01/the-ethiopian-multi-millionaire-who-built-africas-first-marriott-hotel/#6a21b9774666.

Ghrmay, T. M. (2013). *The Nature of Corporate Social Responsibility (CSR) in Ethiopian Business Context*. International School of Management, Paris.

Honke, J. (2012). Multinationals and Security Governance in the Community: Participation, Discipline and Indirect Rule. *Journal of Intervention and State Building, 6*, 57–73.

Idemudia, U. (2014). Corporate Social Responsibility and Development in Africa: Issues and Possibilities. *Geography Compass, 8*(7), 421–435.

Japan External Trade Organization. (2009). *Corporate Social Responsibility: An African Case Study*.

Kassa, F. (2018). The Status of Corporate Social Responsibility in Ethiopia. *Ethiopian Journal of Business Management and Economics, 1*(1), 1–14.

Kyritsis, P., & Nova, S. (2019, April 16). *Doing Well by Doing Good? Ask Ethiopia's Garment Workers*. Retrieved from https://news.trust.org/item/20190412084358-qsrd3.

Matten, D., & Moon, J. (2008). 'Implicit' and 'Explicit' CSR: A Conceptual Framework for a Comparative Understanding of Corporate Social Responsibility. *Academy of Management Review, 33*(2), 404–424.

Ministry of Environment and Forestry. (2014). *Survey on Factories' Environmental Pollution*. Addis Ababa.

Moon, J. (2002). The Social Responsibility of Business and New Governance. *Government and Opposition, 37*(3), 385–408.

Nigatu, T. F. (2018). Corporate Social Responsibility for Social Dimension of Human Development in Ethiopia: A Conceptual Paper. *Journal of Culture, Society and Development, 42*, 25–36.

Nukpezah, D. (2010). *Corporate Environmental Governance in Ghana: Studies on Industrial Level Environmental Performance in Manufacturing and Mining*. Accra.

Potluri, R. M., & Temesgen, Z. (2008). Corporate Social Responsibility: An Attitude of Ethiopian Corporates. *Social Responsibility Journal, 4*(4), 456–463.

PVH. (2018). *Corporate Responsibility Report.*

Reverte, C. (2009). Determinants of Corporate Social Responsibility Disclosure Ratings by Spanish Listed Firms. *Journal of Business Ethics, 88*, 351–366.

Robertson, D. C. (2009). Corporate Social Responsibility and Different Stages of Economic Development: Singapore, Turkey, and Ethiopia. *Journal of Business Ethics, 88*, 617–633.

Smith, C. N. (2003). Corporate Social Responsibility: Whether or How? *California Management Review, 45*(4), 52–76.

Steurer, R. (2010). The Role of Governments in Corporate Social Responsibility: Characterizing Public Policies on CSR in Europe. *Policy Sciences, 43*(1), 49–72.

Téllez, S. J. (2017). Marketing and Corporate Social Responsibility (CSR). Moving between Broadening the Concept of Marketing and Social Factors as a Marketing Strategy. *Spanish Journal of Marketing, 21*(1), 4–25.

The Reporter Ethiopia. (2016, February 27). *Ethiopian Airlines Establishes Foundation.* Retrieved from https://www.thereporterethiopia.com/content/ethiopian-airlines-establishes-foundation.

Visser, W. (2006). Revisiting Carroll's CSR Pyramid: An African Perspective. pp. 29–56. Copenhagen Business School Press.

Visser, W., McIntosh, M., & Middleton, C. (2006). *Corporate Citizenship in Africa: Lessons from the Past; Paths to the Future.* Greenleaf Publishing.

Wiig, A., & Kolstad, I. (2010). Multinational Corporations and Host Country Institutions: A Case Study of CSR Activities in Angola. *International Business Review, 19*, 178–190.

World Bank. (2019). *Ethiopia*. Retrieved from https://www.worldbank.org/en/country/ethiopia/overview.

World Business Council for Sustainable Development. (1998). *Corporate Social Responsibility: Meeting Changing Expectations.*

10

The Perception of the Notion of Corporate Social Responsibility (CSR) in Madagascar: A Representation Through the Cognitive Map of Managers in the Downstream Oil Sector

Narova Barisoa Miasa and Suzanne M. Apitsa

1 Introduction

Since the work of Bowen (1953, 1978), the Brundtland Report (1987) and the European Commission (2001, 2011) on corporate social responsibility (CSR), every organisation is under pressure to be accountable. In terms of managerial literature, the numerous existing works justify the interest of studying CSR in companies (Lépineux et al. 2010; Wang et al. 2016). Indeed, CSR highlights the urgency of responding to economic and social development and environmental protection (Bowen 1953).

N. B. Miasa (✉)
University of Toamasina, Toamasina, Madagascar

S. M. Apitsa
University of Poitiers, Poitiers, France

S. M. Apitsa, E. Milliot (eds.), *Doing Business in Africa*, Palgrave Studies of Internationalization in Emerging Markets,
https://doi.org/10.1007/978-3-030-50739-8_10

Initially, it was a question for companies to voluntarily integrate social and ecological concerns into daily management. In a second phase, CSR became a source of duties towards society (Bowen 1978; European Commission 2011). This second approach, now linked to the notions of obligation and constraint, blurs the conception and understanding of CSR, particularly for African managers.

In Africa, CSR is the subject of public debate (Barmaki and Aitcheikh 2014). In the Malagasy context, Obrecht and Harison (2013) and Harison (2013) study the operationalisation of CSR in extractive industries. Rajaonera and Ramboarison-Lalao (2013) look at responsible human resource management practices. Ramonjy (2009) focuses on ethics and fair trade and Rasolofo-Distler (2010) on stakeholder relations. However, relatively little empirical research has examined the very notion of CSR in Madagascar (Rabekolo 2019) in particular, and in Africa in general (Apitsa 2020).

The abundant literature in the West points to an unstable, ambiguous and evolving concept (Bowen 1953, 1978; Freeman 1984; Carroll 1991; Frederick 1994; CE 2011). Delalieux (2005) sees CSR as commonplace, while Heilbrunn (2004) speaks of an ideology. Still others approach CSR in terms of values (Hamman et al. 2009; Danet 2019). As a commonality and ideology, CSR refers to the cognitive behaviour of an individual or group. This behaviour is influenced by psychological factors including values.

Thus, the values of managers play an important role in the process of planning and implementing CSR. These managers decide and act on the basis of the representations they have of what surrounds them. The diversity of currents of thought that encompass CSR can indeed illustrate the diversity of values and motivations that underpin the activities of organisations. Several studies point in this direction (Bowen 1953; Brady 2003; Hamman et al. 2009). This approach invites one to consider decision-makers as guarantors of the design and/or implementation of the so-called responsible business policy. The study of their representations can therefore help in understanding the decisions that lead to CSR practices. More specifically, what are the values and responsibilities underlying the representation of CSR?

Adopting the interpretive sensemaking method of Welch et al. (2011) and the paradigmatic alignment that characterises it according to Milliot and Freeman (2015), we worked qualitatively on five case studies. This approach made it possible to identify each manager's representation of CSR (Eden 1988, 1992; Cossette 1994). Empirical data were collected over two periods eight years apart (2011 and 2019). The particularity of the responses is that they come from the same respondents (the managers surveyed). An analysis of the personal values and hierarchical responsibilities of each manager was necessary (Brady 2003; Hamman et al. 2009).

This chapter begins by taking stock of this research by examining CSR, the concepts of responsibility and values. It then outlines the methodology used and concludes with an analysis of the results.

2 CSR, a Concept Still in Quest of Understanding

Created in the United States, the term corporate social responsibility refers to related concepts such as ethics, morals, deontology (Gond and Mullenbach 2004), sustainable development (Bowen 1953) and corporate governance (El Mehdi 2013). In Madagascar, it is proposed with reference to Carroll's (1991) pyramid model.

2.1 Social Responsibility: A Legal Object Under Construction in Madagascar

In general, the concept of CSR is criticised because of its imprecision and frequent confusion with other concepts such as corporate citizenship. Allouche et al. (2004) also noted that studies that are continually advancing in the fields of economics and management are still obscuring the understanding of CSR. As for the definition, it may depend on the regulatory, cultural, social, economic and environmental context (Campbell 2007). Each author approaches the concept from a different angle, referring to his or her discipline and context of study. Focusing on the

Malagasy case could then lead to the identification of specificities of interest for Africa.

A recent qualitative study by Rabekolo (2019) mobilises 22 mini-cases of companies from different sectors of activity in Madagascar. It studies the factors favouring the implementation of CSR and its instrumentation via societal reporting. While this study is interesting in terms of the modelling it proposes (Mbengue and Vandangeon-Derumez 2007) for societal reporting, it does not provide elements for understanding the meaning that local officials attribute to the notion of CSR in Madagascar. Furthermore, the proposed model is not sufficient to describe the different perceptions of CSR by local stakeholders in the sense of Freeman (1984). For the latter, a stakeholder is "any individual or group that impacts or is impacted by the pursuit of the company's objectives" (Freeman 1984: 46).

Moreover, at the institutional level, there is still no national regulatory framework for Madagascar defining the content and practices of CSR in the country. It appears that private sector actors are more involved in practice than public sector actors (Obrecht and Harison 2013; Harison 2013; Rajaonera and Ramboarison-Lalao 2013; Apitsa et al. 2020). Firms in different pillar sectors such as telecommunications, mining, oil, logistics and transport or agri-food do not hesitate to communicate on what they call their CSR practices. Despite the absence of national guidelines for public institutions, the adoption of these practices is still in its infancy.

The Malagasy ministry in charge of the environment and sustainable development requires more practices from companies than from public institutions, most often in the form of environmental and social specifications. These companies, convinced that their actions are useful, even necessary, define what should be done by imitating international practices. Above all, they have reservations about a definition of CSR, even if it is contextualised and still opaque. The reason often cited is the lack of control by the Malagasy government. Private sector actors therefore have fairly heterogeneous forms of CSR practices and content, even within a single sector.

Following the logic of Capron and Quairel Lanoizelée (2007), according to which the absence of a single definition mentioned gives everyone the possibility or the obligation to deepen the meaning of the concept, our research aims to reveal the representations of meaning that managers give to CSR. With this in mind, Gond and Mullenbach (2004) undertook a broad review of CSR definitions and concluded that there are three main phases in the broadening of definitions. These phases can be associated with three categories.

- The first category includes visions that focus primarily on the content of CSR: obligations, principles and their scope. Bowen (1953, 1978) is one of the oft-cited authors among the founders of this approach, which focuses more on what the firm should do, taking into account what would be considered desirable by the society in which it operates.
- The second category is more process-oriented. In this logic, the company acts in response to stakeholder pressure and community demands. Davis (1973) had thus considered going beyond the legal framework when he engaged in so-called CSR decisions. Frederick (1994) points out that definitions no longer focus on what is important to do, but on how to act. Within this category, the integrated approach is often cited by Carroll (1991), partly because of its categorisation of responsibilities, which classifies the types of corporate responses to stakeholder expectations as a configuration of several principles of responsibilities and areas.
- Finally, the third category includes broader conceptualisations, incorporating the principles, processes and outcomes of societal behaviour. The notion of corporate social performance then emerges (Wartick and Cochran 1985; Husted 2000).

As we can see, the lowest common denominator in CSR approaches is the attempt to grasp the contours of a phenomenon at the interface of business and society.

2.2 Defining CSR in the Light of Carroll's Pyramid Model (1991)

When we talk about CSR, the purpose assigned to companies is summed up in the notion of responsibility (Ajina et al. 2019). In practice, corporate responsibility translates into multiple practices: governance, citizenship, social performance sanctioned by an evaluation report, socially responsible investment, and so on (Ajina et al. 2019). Given the above panorama of definitions, our discourse is consistent with the work undertaken by Bowen since the 1950s (Carroll 1999). In Madagascar, social responsibility is assimilated to the application of sustainable development in companies, respecting the triple bottom line (3P) Planet-Profit-People. The concept created by John Elkington in 1994 refers to environmental responsibility (Planet), economic responsibility (Profit) and social responsibility (People). This concept is somewhat similar to the work of Frederick (1994) who argues that companies do indeed have various types of powers that imply various responsibilities to society.

The complexity of modern businesses and the imprecise legal context of this study in Madagascar may increase the difficulty of identifying the people involved. Furthermore, the issue of liability invites consideration of the stakeholders of the company (Holme and Watts 2000). Indeed, the relational dimension of responsibility raises the question of to whom it applies. The definition of responsibility proposed by Carroll (1991) may help to identify answers at this level. Carroll refers to several works, from Friedman's (1970) minimalist approach to others that emphasise philanthropic dimensions. He then proposes four categories of responsibilities represented by a pyramid (Fig. 10.1).

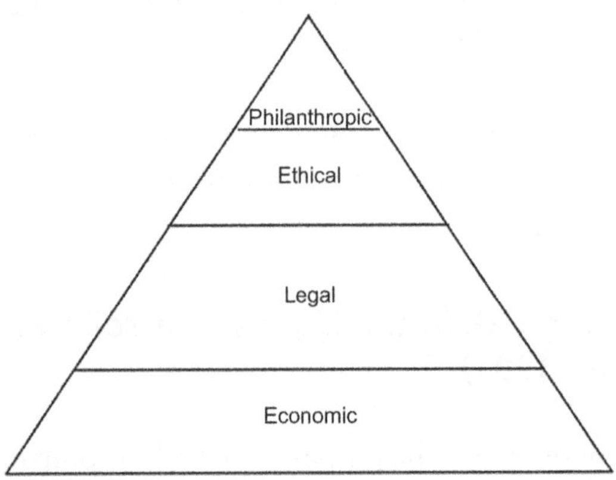

Fig. 10.1 Carroll's pyramid of responsibilities. (Source: Carroll 1991)

1. Economic responsibilities relate to the traditional economic roles of a company such as obtaining profits, manufacturing products that meet quality and safety standards, and so on.
2. Legal responsibilities refer to the company's obligation to comply with the laws in force.
3. Ethical responsibilities refer to actions that conform to principles that go beyond legal requirements and are therefore consistent with the company's principles, beliefs and moral standards.
4. Philanthropic responsibilities correspond to acts of charity and/or a willingness to be charitable.

Each level of responsibility depends on the one that precedes it: the satisfaction of a level goes through the level that is at its base. The application of the first two responsibilities is required; the third is expected and the fourth is desired by the company. However, this hierarchical division ignores the possible interactions between the different levels. Cross-referencing their work with this pyramid modelling framework, Attarca and Jacquot (2005) demonstrate that each form of responsibility proposed by Carroll can be broken down into the three levels of Wood (1991; Table 10.1).

We will use this reading grid to analyse the perception of CSR by Malagasy leaders in the oil sector. Indeed, it facilitates the identification of the type(s) of responsibility to which each manager refers in his speech.

2.3 The Influence of Values on the Perception of CSR: A Universal Reach

Since CSR is an ideology (Heilbrunn 2004), practices are also influenced by psychological factors, including values (Weber 1965). In order to ensure the coherence of CSR policy with the general policy of the firm, it is interesting to turn to decision-makers by focusing on the type of values (Hamman et al. 2009; Danet 2019) that they take into account in their implementation of CSR. From this perspective, Schneider and Angelmar (1993) observed that the logic of the paradigm that leads to the definition of managerial cognition is as follows:

Table 10.1 Levels and nature of social responsibilities

	Institutional scale	Organisation scale	Personal scale
1. Economic responsibilities	Produce goods and services, offer jobs, create wealth for shareholders	The prices of goods and services reflect the real costs of production and integrate all externalities	Produce using non-polluting technologies, reduce costs by promoting recycling
2. Legal responsibilities	Comply with laws and regulations	Work for public policy by defending *enlightened* interests	Innovate based on regulatory instructions
3. Ethical responsibilities	Follow fundamental ethical principles (e.g., honesty)	Provide accurate and complete information to increase safety of use beyond legal requirements	Develop user information for users as a product benefit
4. Philanthropic responsibilities	Act as a model citizen in all areas: beyond regulations and ethical rules. Return part of the turnover to the company	Invest the company's resources in charitable actions	Choose charitable investments that are profitable in terms of solving social problems

Source: Attarca and Jacquot (2005) based on Carroll (1991) and Wood (1991) typologies

- individuals think (= cognitive psychology),
- managers are individuals, which is why they have to think (= managerial cognition),
- and managers also think about the organisation while engaging in different organisational tasks (= organisational behaviour) such as strategic decision-making (cognition in the organisation).

From this perspective, managers will focus on a specific dimension of their actions according to their value system, which makes value an interesting concept in the representation of CSR by managers. There has been no real consensus on the definition or reliable, unanimously recognised methods for measuring them. This is reflected in the different conceptions of the very concept of value (Hamman et al. 2009). However, it seems reasonable to think, as I did, that decision-making is largely influenced by values: they influence the way people, and therefore leaders, represent the world. For Weber (1965), values are fundamental in explaining organisation and change, at the level of society and individuals. Values can influence the attractiveness of an action even if the consequences are not consciously weighed (Brady 2003; Barrena-Martinez et al. 2016).

Several studies attempt to explain these relationships between behaviours, particularly responsibilities, and values in the context of CSR. The work of Reynaud and Roques (2007) argues that the types of social responsibilities that individuals assume depend on the values they consider important. Long before this, Bowen (1953) attempted to identify the values underlying CSR. Weber (1965) deduced from this the influence of values promoted by the Protestant religion, which is crucial to the very origin of CSR. Martinet and Payaud (2008) observed that individuals who believe only in corporate economic responsibility have values close to their own interests. Reynaud and Roques (2007) found that individuals who opted for economic responsibility chose values aimed at enriching work, while those who behaved in a socially responsible manner were guided by altruistic values. This view reinforces our case study on CSR in Madagascar. These authors examined in detail the CSR practices that respondents considered to be either within or outside the company's duty, and then highlighted the links between employees' values and their judgement of the implementation of corporate responsibility according to Carroll (1991). To do so, they used the value grid of Schwartz (1992) and Schwartz et al. (2012).

According to this theory, the fundamental values of individuals are recognised as such in all cultures, which makes it an interesting framework to use to address values in the Malagasy context. Schwartz (1992) and Schwartz et al. (2012) distinguish ten different basic values that are universal, with a dynamic of oppositions and compatibilities between them: *autonomy, stimulation, hedonism, success, power, security, conformity, tradition, benevolence* or *kindness, universalism*. These values are universal because each of them meets at least one of the three necessities of human existence: satisfying the biological needs of individuals, enabling social interaction and ensuring the proper functioning and survival of social groups. The 1992 version of Schwartz's theory hypothesised an 11th, almost universal fundamental value: spirituality. The objective of the values of spirituality is meaning, coherence and inner harmony, obtained by transcending everyday reality; but more recent research has led the author to no longer reconsider this value. Finally, this theory of values also attributes characteristics to them. First of all, values are beliefs inseparable from affects; when values are *activated*, they combine with feelings. A very concrete example is that of people for whom *independence* is an important value, who are on the alert if their independence is threatened, who are desperate when they cannot preserve it, and who are happy when they can exercise it. The notions of motivation and value are therefore interdependent and sometimes confused. Second, values transcend or provoke, but do not really describe specific actions and situations. Values also guide the selection or evaluation of actions, policies, events, so that they serve as desirable criteria and objectives that motivate action (Hamman et al. 2009). In Africa, they explain the cultural behaviours of individuals (D'Iribarne 2003, 2012). Every action, attitude and behaviour is guided by the relative importance of multiple values. However, although Schwartz describes the structure of values as being similar in groups belonging to different cultures, individuals and groups differ in the priorities they give to these values. They therefore have their own ranking or degree of importance of values, which is different: a particular value may be particularly important to one person but not to others.

3 Methodology

To meet the expectations of our research, we used a qualitative case study methodology. This choice is justified because this research is intended to study revealing cases. The study is based on the interpretive sensemaking method (Welch et al. 2011). This approach emphasises context analysis to identify the meanings given to facts by precisely identified actors. It refers, according to Milliot and Freeman (2015), to an idiographic project associated with a descriptive and/or exploratory research objective.

Based on a logic of inductive inference, our approach is part of an ontological perspective based on interpretativism. The interviews were conducted in two phases: 2011 and 2018.

We considered a limited number of cases to develop an in-depth analysis of the perception of CSR within the downstream oil sector in Madagascar. This fast-developing sector is characterised by numerous entities claiming to be involved in CSR, making it an interesting sector to explore. These entities are presented below.

- Importers: the Galana refinery terminal, and so on.
- Distributors: Total, Shell, Jovenna and Galana Distribution.
- Local regulatory authorities: The Ministry of Mines and Hydrocarbons, the Malagasy Hydrocarbons Office, the National Environment Office, and so on; and international regulatory authorities (representatives of the French Standards Association, etc.).
- Prestataires de services: Logistique Pétrolière SA, Plate-forme Terminal Pétrolier SA, and so on.
- Consumers: companies of all sizes and individuals, public works, natural or legal persons working in non-commercial sectors (schools and hospitals), local authorities, households, and so on.

Since the research focuses on the representation of executives who practise CSR in their organisations, the consumer profile was not taken into account in the interviews. Five executives, representing the first four stakeholder profiles, were solicited. Each respondent was contacted by mail. Table 10.2 gives details of their status.

An individual's representations are usually expressed through oral or written speech. Thus, an interview guide structured around semi-open-ended questions was administered individually face to face in 2011, then remotely (audio and/or video calls) in 2019 with the same people and with the same questions. The responses obtained were initially in French, which were then entered into the data processing software Decision Explorer® developed by Colin Eden et al. (1992) before being translated into English.

As for cognitive mapping techniques, they are used by researchers from a wide variety of disciplines (Langfield-Smith 1992) to paint a picture or a graphic summary of cognition (Cossette 1994). The mapping technique used in this study is based on the work of Eden (1988, 1992, 2004)

Table 10.2 Details about the interviewed managers

Managers	Type of actor	Responsibility in the organisation
A	Importer	Director General: coordinates all activities in the organisation and make final decisions on general policy, including CSR policy
B	Distributor	CSR Manager: primarily responsible for the design and implementation of the organisation's CSR practices
C	Regulatory authority	Director: he is responsible for enforcing the law with regard to business practices in the sector
D	Service provider	Director of Operations: ensures that the company's actions respect its common values and the law. He develops and validates the CSR policy before presenting it to his superiors.
E	Distributor	Sales and logistic Director: at the same time, he is responsible for the CSR policy and its diffusion within the company

Source: Authors' creation

and Cossette (1994) because it makes it possible to highlight particular concepts in managers' thinking that would otherwise be difficult to bring out (Eden et al. 1992). Cognitive maps reveal the pattern of influence in an individual's cognitive universe, helping to visualise many ideas and beliefs. The manager is in a double position: he is the source and thus the constructor of a personal cognitive map, while being the user or the actor of the maps obtained (Mintzberg et al. 1999).

Concerning data processing, the phases of the coding protocol of Decision Explorer® are as follows: exploration, coding, semantic analysis and feedback. The first phase will collect the information needed to create each cognitive map: the respondent explores his or her ideas and communicates them in a discursive manner. Then comes the phase of coding the information collected on the basis of the transcripts of the interviews, which aims to identify and list the concepts and the links of influence between them once they have been entered into the software. Concepts are treated as variables; each exposes a distinct idea. Once the concepts have been identified and formulated, they are assigned a unique identifier (number), and each influential relationship between the concepts can then be listed. The sign and meaning of each influence is also identified and synonymous concepts are merged. The concepts and links are then presented in the form of a coding sheet, and a map is finally sketched. For the semantic analysis, three steps are essential: first, complexity analysis to see the general organisation of the cognitive schema in the map; identification of the key concepts; content and structure analysis to highlight possible awareness points (the influence factors and those influenced). Discussion will focus on this step.

However, Simon (1980) observes that there is sometimes a transformation by adding or reducing information between the schema suggested by the respondent (cognitive product) and the final representation or cognitive map that emerges from it (material product). This is the representation (of the researcher) of a representation (of the respondent) (Cossette and Lapointe 1997) caused by the subjectivity of the researcher. To avoid this, the validation phase ensures the accuracy of the information: the results of the survey are presented to the managers interviewed for their approval. In addition, mapping and other cognitive approach methods are criticised because they use a written method without oral recording. Hence the choice of recorded interviews to facilitate transcription and to remain as faithful as possible to the meaning given by the interviewee.

4 Perception of CSR: Results and Discussions

Madagascar's downstream oil sector is part of the energy sector, making it a strategic area for the country's economic development. It is also subject to several controversies regarding the scope of corporate responsibility on a global scale, which makes it interesting to focus on it.

4.1 Realities of the Downstream Oil Sector in Madagascar

Since the privatisation of the sector in 2004, the five interviewees argue that the actors in this sector have applied what they call *CSR practices*, which can be broken down into several names and levels depending on the entity concerned. The contents are not perfectly identical: HSE (health, safety and environment) or QHSHE (quality, hygiene, safety, health and environment) policy, ethical charter, commitment charter, values charter, and so on. Malagasy legislation does not specify any required format. Only the principles of sustainable development are translated into areas of intervention through, for example, the environmental impact study and its environmental and social specifications. It is then up to the company to respect its commitments or the conditions involved to obtain its operating permit. So far, therefore, for the Malagasy state, respect for this context, combined with respect for other texts in force in other fields, seems sufficient to speak of the effective application of CSR by companies. However, respect for the environment remains at the heart of these concerns before talking about social issues.

4.2 Intensity and Organisation of CSR-Related Discussions

The complexity analysis step reveals the extent to which the thoughts of the manager being interviewed are differentiated according to the number of concepts in the map (Cossette 1994).

In 2011, it varies from 23 concepts to 67 concepts with links ranging from 23 to 84 between them. In 2019, the differences between the minimum and the maximum number of concepts were reduced to 35 and 45 concepts with links ranging from 35 to 50.

- These variations show that the development of reflection on the concept of CSR (Caroll 1991) does not have the same intensity from one manager to another.
- The cognition maps with the greatest number of concepts have the most differentiated visions. That means that the manager has sufficient information or data to communicate on CSR. Import manager A and one of the distributors B are the only two well-informed managers in 2011: they have developed more details than the others on practices, explaining situations, and so on (example of manager A's card in Fig. 10.2).
- In eight years, the visions of managers C, D and E have been enriched and also became more differentiated. This is seen, for example, in

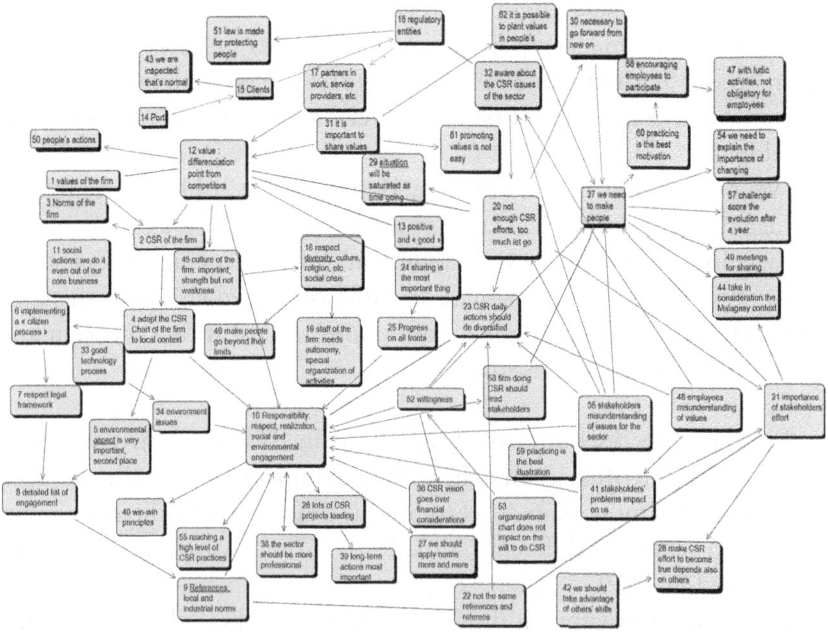

Fig. 10.2 Cognitive map of manager A in 2011. (Source: Authors' creation)

greater communication on the importance of anchoring CSR activities in the overall policy of each entity:

- C insists on the importance of seeing the long-term effects,
- D gives more positive consequences linked to the activity of those who do CSR,
- E mentions more results and at the same time proposes many options or possibilities for action.

Those differentiated visions refer to more extensive thinking structures and thus a greater involvement in CSR. However, it does not allow the relevance of opinions or concepts to be inferred.

We also need to interpret the number of concepts in their context: the main reasons for the decrease of the maximum and increase of the minimum in 2019 are the way the surveys were administered. This had an impact on the average length of interviews, which varied according to the evolution of the manager's speech: from 25 to 90 minutes in 2011 and from 16 to 35 minutes in 2019. Managers seem less comfortable or more rushed when conducting surveys remotely, so their vision of CSR is less developed.

We also noticed in 2011 that A, B and C have a higher number of influencing than influenced factors but all five cases show a dominance of influencing factors in 2019. A dominance of influencing factors shows structures with cognitively simple and well-organised visions of the CSR topic; they present a multiplicity of options to deal with a problem and are more oriented towards solutions.

- In 2011, the discourses of A and B go in this direction given their experience in this sector where their companies have already been working for more than 30 years at that time and have therefore experienced many different situations. This structure has not changed in 2019.
- For C, as a regulatory authority, he also cited other solutions, arguing that they exist, that they are not always difficult to implement, but that it is all about will.
- The two maps of D and E show many received influences in which it is necessary to put some order; they are more problem-oriented. This may be due to the difficulty of integrating the demands of a wider set of different stakeholders, which are then perceived as difficult or even contradictory to achieve, or as a result of particular professional experiences that are considered to be laborious. We have drawn the main conclusions in Table 10.3.

Finally, in 2019, it appears that the five respondents are more focused on solutions, probably because they now have more experience with CSR and are more aware of the realities or *challenges that are not always easy* to deal with (as D and E put it).

Table 10.3 Overview of general organisation, dominant factor and interview duration

Manager	General organisation (differentiated vision)		Dominant factor		Interview duration	
	2011	2019	2011	2019	2011	2019
A	More differentiated vision = more involvement		Influencing factors = simple and well-organised visions, solution-oriented	Influencing factors = simple and well-organised visions, solution-oriented	00:40:16	00:20:39
B					01:30:04	00:35:39
C	Less differentiated vision = do not have much information on CSR	Vision of effects in the long term			00:25:35	00:29:59
D		More positive consequences	Influenced factors = received influences, problem-oriented		00 :32 :23	00:23:23
E		More results and options/ possibilities for action			00:42:08	00:16:09

Source: Authors' creation

4.3 Shared Personal Values Associated with CSR

In both phases of data collection, there is always more than one value per cognitive map, showing that values are essential for cognitive modelling of CSR. However, the ten Schwartz values are not necessarily all present at the same time in the same person's responses.

Besides, four values were often mentioned in the first survey in 2011: *universalism, ethics, morality* and *benevolence*. In 2019, these values still exist with a fifth that was explicitly stated by A, B and D as a common value: *sharing*. This means that every manager feels it is necessary to involve all stakeholders for the success of a *true* CSR, that is, a more effective CSR.

It is also interesting to note that in 2011 and 2019, there are Schwartz's values that have not been ranked: human and environmental values for A; personal commitment, humility, integrity and ethics for B; morality for C; ethics and the human being for D; will, personal conviction, human and environmental values and the three pillars of CSR for E. The limitations on the theory of Schwartz are due to the heterogeneity of the perception of CSR by the interviewees. Once again, each manager associates the concept with what seems most relevant to him or her. For the value of universalism, it is particularly considered in terms of the company's survival, the fear of the future if there is no social peace or if the environment is destroyed, or fear of punishment. Cases of cooperation and solidarity or win-win benefits and compliance come to the same conclusion in both 2019 and 2011. Finally, in 2011, manager B considers that values motivated by profit-making objectives cannot be qualified as values in CSR, while, in contrast, D considers that concepts aimed at purely profit-making objectives reflect values such as success. The latter changed his mind in 2019 and considers that value is not motivated by economic objectives. For C, personal conviction and will are the keys to implementing CSR, while E talks about ethics and morality. Table 10.4 gives an overview of these values.

Finally, we can say that consideration of values can change over time, and some leaders believe that CSR values should not be motivated by profit (Schwartz and Carroll 2003).

Table 10.4 Overview of CSR values and comparison with Schwartz' list

	Considered values in CSR		Values not in Schwartz's list	
Managers	2011	2019	2011	2019
A	Benevolence, universalism, ethics and morality	Sharing	Human and environmental values	Sharing
B		Values motivated by lucrative goals = not values Sharing	Personal commitment, humility	Integrity and ethics, Sharing
C		Ethics and morality	Morality	
D	Values motivated by lucrative goals = success values	Sharing value, values motivated by lucrative goals = not values	Ethics	Ethics Human being
E	Ethics, morality		Will, personal conviction and the three pillars of CSR	Human and environmental values

Source: Authors' creation

4.4 Responsibilities and Practices of CSR

As the surveys were conducted in French, there is a slight confusion between the terms social and *societal* for managers; although there is a preference for *societal*, which is better known or at least more quoted. The same preference prevails in 2019. Only D highlighted the difference between the two terms in 2019, due to more experience in the last eight years as he has changed sector since 2016 but his current position is still linked to CSR. Moreover, Carroll's four responsibilities are found in all the managers' representations at each survey period, but each one has its own hierarchy which does not follow the logic or the hierarchical sequence of the author. In addition, each manager makes his or her own categorisation, which is not systematic. For the differentiations in 2011: A designates social and environmental responsibilities; C designates social,

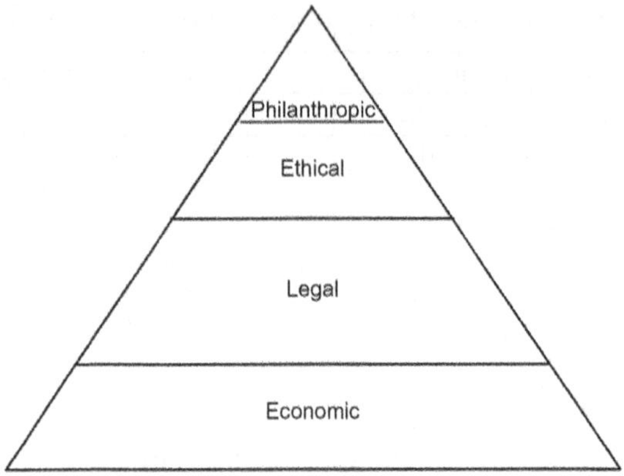

Fig. 10.3 Representation of manager A's responsibility in relation to Carroll's pyramid (1991): Carroll's four responsibilities. (Source: Carroll 1991)

societal and environmental responsibilities; E designates social and societal responsibilities and B designates functional and personal responsibilities. For C and E, CSR therefore refers to actions that respect the three pillars of sustainable development (economic, social, environmental), particularly internally. Whereas in 2019, A, B, C and D insist that whatever classification or names are given to these responsibilities, the most important thing is that they must be shared among stakeholders. They referred to the Malagasy proverb *three pillars for a perfect kitchen* to mark the need for combined efforts in CSR, but not only the responsibility of the Malagasy State or of companies alone (Manager A outlined in Figs. 10.3, 10.4 and 10.5). According to them, the efforts made to set up and operate discussion platforms and participation in national events bringing together stakeholders (Freeman 1984) demonstrate the will to do so.

5 Conclusion

The use of a cognitive mapping technique made it possible to highlight important values and prioritise responsibility according to the manager's knowledge of CSR and to see how the surveyed manager ultimately

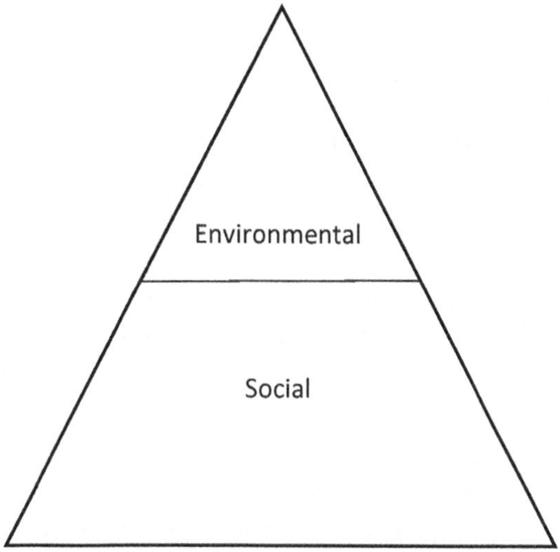

Fig. 10.4 Representation of manager A's responsibility in relation to Carroll's pyramid (1991): responsibility consideration by manager A in 2011. (Source: Authors' creation)

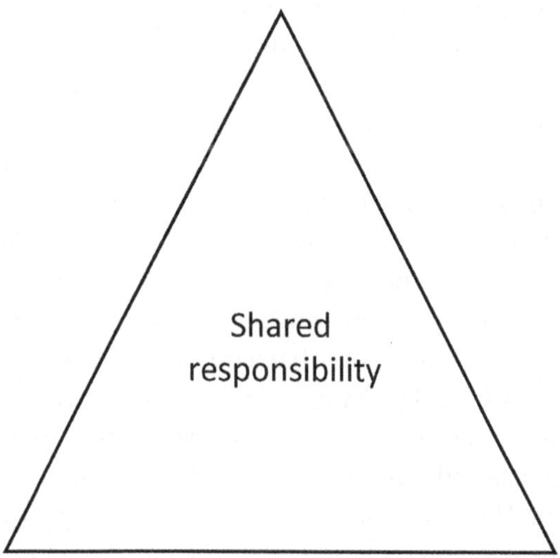

Fig. 10.5 Representation of manager A's responsibility in relation to Carroll's pyramid (1991): responsibility consideration by manager A in 2019 (classification and names does not matter). (Source: Authors' creation)

defines CSR. We should stress that a large number of concepts and links may indicate a fairly in-depth reflection on a topic but do not guarantee its relevance, just as a small number does not automatically indicate a lack of relevance or interest in the topic. In this case, the high number of concepts reflects the fact that well-informed managers are able to communicate with structures that show cognitively simple and well-organised visions at the subject of CSR. However, the opposite does not necessarily indicate a lack of involvement in the topic or a lack of information. Moreover, a cognitive map that is more complex than another does not imply better decision-making or higher social performance for the company: these measures only take into account the complexity of the structure and not the meaning. It is therefore not essential to try to make a manager's map complex, but to be attentive to the relevance of the ideas that are presented in the analysis of the contents or the concepts themselves. This is what we have done with a more in-depth analysis of the representations in CSR for each map.

The representations are quite different when it comes to combining concepts, reflecting the specific definitions of each respondent, but there are, nevertheless, commonalities in terms of value and legal responsibility considerations, for example. In general, we also noted that the logics change over time, probably due to experience, and those motivations might also change at two different periods.

The tendency to focus on one particular responsibility over another among four Carroll's (1991) responsibilities changes the individual's representation of the concept of CSR, and the manager's value system also has an impact on his or her conception of social responsibility (definition, classification and prioritisation). Executives who demonstrate *altruistic values* have CSR concepts that emphasise concerns about ethical responsibility—in Carroll's sense—more than other types of responsibility. Similarly, managers whose CSR concepts prioritise philanthropic and economic responsibilities have primarily values related to *altruism*, *safety* and *compliance*. The values of *security* and *personal conviction* or *commitment* also influence representations towards more economically oriented patterns. The value of *caring* appears in many combinations of values in 2011, whereas in 2019 they generally recognise the importance of combining the efforts of all stakeholders in the sector to achieve a truly effective CSR with mention of the value of *sharing*. The latter can therefore be seen as specific to the design or definition of CSR in this research context.

Apart from this, legal responsibility is not a priority but it is well known as they give details about it. Legal pressure through national legislation or standards set by the organisation pushes these managers to comply with CSR requirements in order to avoid problems with the law. However, as there is a lack of CSR legislation in Madagascar, this situation tends to suggest that the regulatory context prior to the arrival of CSR or at least its dissemination was not yet ready to consider the subject in legislation. We then assume that the current national regulatory framework is under construction and can draw on the results of this study.

We also noted that the representation of CSR through the three pillars of sustainable development is present in two cases but not for the others, so this conception is not generalised. Indeed, as it concerns the oil sector, companies are attentive to environmentally sensitive products. One would think that this should lead them to justify themselves against the environmental pillar when discussing CSR achievements and responsibilities, but only two of the five managers really value this.

Above all, the managers present concrete examples of CSR practices even if the cognitive complexity is less intense in 2019. However, the voluntary nature of CSR motivation is not systematically observable in the discourse in 2011, but more explicit thereafter.

Finally, cognitive mapping and the use of Decision Explorer® enriched our understanding of realities, whether individual or collective (Cossette and Lapointe 1997), but the results must be reconsidered in each context and within the limits of the method. We also assume that we can talk about the contributions of this study to the respondent himself or herself, who can now access their own reflections, become aware of their content and make them evolve. In this way, we hope to pave the way for raising awareness among managers, for example, by giving an image of the issues inherent in the dimensions of CSR management. In any case, the positive reactions of the managers interviewed during the two validation phases (feedback) and the absence of rejection suggest a good level of validity of the results, even if the interviewees retain some information because, in their opinion, they do not want to give an impression of judgement.

However, remaining in the same sector with its specificities, this study limits itself to describing the relationships between the variables we have chosen without studying the intensity of these relationships or searching for them. It therefore appears that in order to get an overview of the reality of CSR in Madagascar, it is interesting to extend the study to other sectors. Similarly, deepening the notion of CSR in Africa presupposes a structuring study in other countries.

References

Ajina, A., Faten, L., & Sabrine, A. (2019). Does Corporate Social Responsibility Reduce Earnings Management? The Moderating Role of Corporate Governance and Ownership. *¿La responsabilidad social corporativa reduce la gestión de las ganancias? El papel moderador de la gobernanza y la propiedad, 23*(2), 45–55.

Allouche, J., Huault, I., & Schmidt, G. (2004). Responsabilité sociale des entreprises: la mesure détournée?. *15e Congrès annuel de l'AGRH*, Montréal, Septembre.

Apitsa, S. M. (2020). Enjeux et défis de la RSE et du développement durable en zone portuaire: Cas des ports du Havre, de Douala et de Kribi. 10ème conférence annuelle Atlas Afmi, *Management des ressources à l'international: Enjeux, configurations et impacts.* 1AE—Université de Poitiers, 18–20 mai, Poitiers, France.

Apitsa, S. M., Ramboarison-Lalao, L., & Gannouni, K. (2020). La GRH socialement responsable d'une multinationale dans ses filiales malgache, camerounaise et tunisienne: une réponse aux tensions stratégiques et managériales? *Management International, 24*(3), 92–106.

Attarca, M., & Jacquot, T. (2005). La RSE en représentations: Quelle convergence entre vision académique et vision managériale ?. Document de travail AIMS, XIVème Conférence Internationale de Management Stratégique, Pays de la Loire, Juin.

Barmaki, L., & Aitcheikh, D. (2014). Responsabilité sociétale des entreprises en Afrique: approche comparative (Afrique du Sud, Maroc, Sénégal et Tunisie). *Revue dossiers de recherches en économie et gestion,* 3ème numéro, Septembre, pp. 153–169.

Barrena-Martinez, J., Lopez-Fernandez, M., & Romero-Fernandez, M. P. (2016). Socially responsible human resource policies and practices: Academic and professional validation. *European Research on Management and Business Economics, 23*, 55–61.

Bowen, H. R. (1953). Social Responsibilities of the Businessman. In: Buchloz, R. A. (1977), An Alternative to Social Responsibility. *MSU Business Topics*, Vol. 25, No. 3.

Bowen, H. R. (1978). Social Responsibilities of the Businessman 'Twenty Year Later'. In E. M. Epstein & D. Votaw (Eds.), *Rationality, Legitimacy, Responsibility: The Search for New Direction in Business Society* (pp. 116–130). Santa Monica, CA: Goodyear Publishing Co..

Brady, A. K. O. (2003). How to Generate Sustainable Brand Value from Responsibility. *Journal of Brand Management, 10*(4/5), 279–289.

Brundtland, G. H. (1987). *Brundtland Report: Our Common Future, The World Commission on Environment and Development*. UK: Oxford.

Campbell, J. L. (2007). Why Would Corporations Behave in Socially Responsible Ways? An Institutional Theory of Corporate Social Responsibility. *Academy of Management Review, 32*(3), 946–967.

Capron, M., & Quairel Lanoizelée, F. (2007). *La responsabilité sociale d'entreprise*. Paris: Éditions la Découverte.

Carroll, A.-B. (1991). The Pyramid of Corporate Social Responsibility: Toward the Moral Management of Organizational Stakeholders. *Business Horizons, 34*, 39–48.

Carroll, A. B. (1999). Corporate Social Responsibility: Evolution of a Definitional Construct. *Business and Society, 38*(3), 268–295.

Cossette, P. (1994). La carte idiosyncrasique. Étude exploratoire des schèmes personnels de propriétaires-dirigeants de PME. In Cossette (dir.), *Cartes cognitives et organisations* (pp. 113–154). Les Presses de l'Université Laval/ Éditions ESKA.

Cossette, P., & Lapointe, A. (1997). A Mapping Approach to Conceptual Models: The Case of Macroeconomic Theory. *Canadian Journal of Administrative Sciences / Revue Canadienne des Sciences de l'Administration, 14*(1), 41–51.

D'Iribarne, P. (2003). *Le Tiers-monde qui réussit, nouveaux modèles*. Paris: Odile Jacob, 288 p.

D'Iribarne, P. (2012). *Managing Corporate Values in Diverse National Cultures: The Challenge of Differences*. London: Routledge.

Danet, Th. (2019). Déployer une culture RSE en Afrique. *Annales des Mines—Réalités industrielles*, vol. Août 2019, No. 3, 76–79.

Davis, K. (1973). The Case for and against Business Assumption of Social Responsibilities. *Academy of Management Journal, 16*, 312–322.

Delalieux, G. (2005). L'influence des idéologies dans le développement de la RSE. *Actes du 23ème Congrès de l'IAS*, Lille.

Eden, C. (1988). Cognitive Mapping: Invited Review. *European Journal of Operational Research, 36*(1), 1–13.

Eden, C. (1992). On the Nature of Cognitive Maps. *Journal of Management Studies, 29*(3), 261–265.

Eden, C. (2004). Analyzing Cognitive Maps to Help Structure Issues or Problems. *European Journal of Operational Research, 159*(3), 673–686.

Eden, C., Ackermann, F., & Cropper, S. (1992). The Analysis of Cause Maps. *Journal of Management Studies, 29*(3), 309–324.

El Mehdi, I. K. (2013). Les questions de gouvernance dans les entreprises socialement responsables. *Management International, 17*(2), 31–47.

European Commission. (2001). *Green paper – towards a European strategy for the security of energy supply*. Brussels: European Commission, Technical document.

European Commission. (2011). *Corporate Social Responsibility: A new EU strategy for 2011–2014*. Brussels: European Commission, Technical document.

Frederick, W. C. (1994). From CSR1 to CSR2. *Business & Society, 33*, 150–164.

Freeman, R. E. (1984). *Strategic Management: A Stakeholder Approach*. Boston: Pitman.

Friedman, M. (1970). The social responsibility of business is to increase its profits the new york times magazine, September 13, The new york times company.

Gond, J. P., & Mullenbach, A. (2004). Les fondements théoriques de la Responsabilité Sociétale de l'entreprise. *Revue des Sciences de Gestion, 205*, 93.

Hamman, E.-M., Habisch, A., & Pechlaner, H. (2009). Values That Create Value: Socially Responsible Business Practices in SMEs—Empirical Evidence from German Companies. *Business Ethics: A European Review, 18*(1), 37–51.

Harison, V. (2013). RSE: des principes internationaux à la mise en pratique locale. Le cas de deux entreprises malgaches. In U. Mayrhofer & P. Very (coord.), *Le Management international à l'écoute du local* (pp. 299–317). Paris: Gualino.

Heilbrunn, J. R. (2004). *Anti-Corruption Commissions: Panacea or Real Medicine to Fight Corruption ?*. World Bank Institute/IBRD.

Holme, R., & Watts, P. (2000). *Corporate Social Responsibility: Making Good Business Sense*. World Business Council for Sustainable Development, janvier, Genève.

Husted, B. (2000). A Contingency Theory of Corporate Social Performance. *Business & Society, 39*(1), 24–48.

Langfield-Smith, K. (1992). Exploring the Need for a Shared Cognitive Map. *Journal of Management Studies, 29*(3), 349–368.

Lépineux, F., Rosé, J.-J., Bonanni, C., & Hudson, S. (2010). *La RSE—La responsabilité sociale des entreprises. Théories et pratiques*. Paris: Dunod.

Martinet, A. C., & Payaud, M. A. (2008). Formes de RSE et entreprises sociales: une hybridation des stratégies. *Revue Française de Gestion, 34*(180), 199–214.

Mbengue, A. (s. d.), & Vandangeon-Derumez, I. (2007). Analyse causale et modélisation, in Méthodes de recherche en management, coord. par R.A. Thiétart, Paris, Dunod.

Milliot, E., & Freeman, S. (2015). Case Study Research in Social Sciences: A Paradigmatic Alignment Framework. 41st Annual Conference of the *European International Business Academy* (EIBA), Rio de Janeiro, Brazil, December 1–3.

Mintzberg, H., Ahlstrand, B., & Lampel, J. (1999). *Safari en pays stratégie: l'exploration des grands courants de la pensée stratégique*. Paris: Village mondial.

Obrecht, J. J., & Harison, V. (2013). Essai d'évaluation de la RSE dans les industries extractives: le cas du Projet Ambatovy (Madagascar). In V. Carbone, S. Nivoix, & J.-P. Lemaire (Eds.), *Nouveaux défis du Management international*. Paris: Gualino.

Rabekolo, F. (2019). *Modélisation du processus d'adoption de la démarche RSE et de son instrumentation via le reporting sociétal Cas des entreprises localisées à Madagascar*, Thèse de doctorat, IAE—Université de Poitiers, décembre, 332 p.

Rajaonera, I., & Ramboarison-Lalao, L. (2013). Pratiques RSE dans les pays en développement: premiers résultats de terrain dans les entreprises malgaches. *Revue Camerounaise de Management, 26*, 19–33.

Ramonjy, D. (2009). Ethique et responsabilité sociale des organisations du commerce équitable. *Revue Management & Avenir, 29*, 71–90.

Rasolofo-Distler, F. (2010). Opérationnalisation d'une stratégie de développement durable par un système de tableaux de bord: une démarche innovante qui combine 'Méthode OVAR' et 'Balanced Scorecard'. *Actes du 31ème congrès de l'Association Francophone de Comptabilité*, Nice.

Reynaud, E., & Roques, O. (2007). Les pratiques de responsabilité sociale de l'entreprise confrontées aux valeurs des salariés. *Acte du Congrès AGRH*, Fribourg.

Schneider, S. C., & Angelmar, R. (1993). Socially Responsible Behaviour: Developing Virtue in Organizations. *Organization Studies, 16*, 63–77.

Schwartz, M. S., & Carroll, A. B. (2003). Corporate Social Responsibility: A Three Domain Approach. *Business Ethics Quarterly, 13*, 503–530.

Schwartz, S. H. (1992). Universals in the Content and Structure of Values: Theory and Empirical Tests in 20 Countries. In M. Zanna (Ed.), *Advances in Experimental Social Psychology* (Vol. 25, pp. 1–65). New York: Academic Press.

Schwartz, S. H., Cieciuch, J., Vecchione, M., Davidov, E., Fischer, R., Beierlein, C., Ramos, A., Verkasalo, M., Lönnqvist, J., Demirutku, K., Dirilen-Gumus, O., Konty, M., & Konty, M. (2012). Refining the Theory of Basic Individual Values. *Journal of Personality and Social Psychology, 103*(4), 663–688.

Simon, H. A. (1980). Cognitive Science: The Newest Science of the Artificial. *Cognitive Science, 4*(1), 33–46.

Wang, E., Tong, L., Takeuchi, R., & George, G. (2016). Corporate Social Responsibility: An Overview and New Research Directions: Thematic Issue on Corporate Social Responsibility. *Academy of Management Journal, 59*(2), 534–544.

Wartick, S. L., & Cochran, P. L. (1985). The Evolution of the Corporate Social Performance Model. *Academy of Management Review, 10*, 758–769.

Weber, M. (1965). *Essai sur la théorie de la science (Recueil d'articles publiés entre 1904 et 1917)*, Plon.

Welch, C., Piekkari, R., Plakoyiannaki, E., & Paavilainen-Mäntymäki, E. (2011). Theorizing from Case Studies: Towards a Pluralist Future for International Business Research. *Journal of International Business Studies, 42*(5), 740–762.

Wood, D. J. (1991). Corporate social performance revisited, *Academy of management review, 16*(4), 691–718.

11

State of the Art on Environmental Management in the Cameroonian Public Administration: The Case Study of the Desk Management Activities in the Ministerial Central Services

Munoz Pierre Kenmeni, Hugues Valéry Kouakap, Mesmin Tchindjang, Marie Ngolo Bela, and José Kisito Nkenkeu

1 Introduction

Since the cave man, antiquity and the medieval century, environmental management (EM) problems have always been seriously posed, but with less acuteness. Today, these problems constitute a major concern in public and private management worldwide. EM really took shape in the

M. P. Kenmeni (✉) • J. K. Nkenkeu
University of Yaoundé II, Yaounde, Cameroon

H. V. Kouakap • M. Tchindjang
University of Yaoundé I, Yaounde, Cameroon

M. Ngolo Bela
Ministry of Public Work, Yaounde, Cameroon

S. M. Apitsa, E. Milliot (eds.), *Doing Business in Africa*, Palgrave Studies of Internationalization in Emerging Markets,
https://doi.org/10.1007/978-3-030-50739-8_11

twentieth century in the most advanced countries of Northern America and Western world (Shifrin 2019). The evolution of EM accelerated in the second half of the twentieth century with the famous "Stop for growth" known as Meadows Report and the first environmental conference at Stockholm in 1972. Therefore, the number of consultations at the international level devoted to the environment grew and took an annual pace, to the point where, as early as 1980, there was a real intensification of public actions in the field of environmental protection and in the direction of enterprises. In the 1990s, the adaptation of corporate structures to the environmental issue was the subject of lengthy developments in the management literature. Since 2000, there has been a strong competition from both private and public organizations that are moving in a voluntary way toward obtaining an eco-label/green label in order to satisfy customers and citizens or residents. Integration of the environment into any organization strategy or management system is a pragmatic key in the invention of EM (Reverdy 2005). However, such an experience is slowly showing growing interest in public sector administrations. However, environmental management is being included more and more in the program of these administrations at several levels worldwide.

Indeed, it is known that administrative governance in Africa (CPIA 2017) has many bottlenecks that make it poorly performing and of low quality compared to private organizations. The public administration machinery and practices in Cameroon like elsewhere in sub-Saharan Africa are beclouded by internal (self-inflicted) and external (environmentally induced) problems (Mukoro 2005), impacting the performance and the management quality and competitiveness in public institutions negatively (CPIA 2017; Molina-Azorín et al. 2009; Pertusa-Ortega et al. 2017). As it stands, public administration is cumbersome and awfully expensive. The weight of public organization suffocates the economic system. A new thinking about public management and its complexity as a result of globalization (Mathiasen 1999) influences its modern view in public administration.

In addition, the synergistic link between public sector management and the content of public administration can contribute to addressing critical skills shortages in the public service (Subban and Vyas-Doorgapersad 2014). The public administrations of developing countries are assigned a task far beyond that which is incumbent upon them in the developed countries, and, as such, they are notoriously insufficient for their tasks (construction, health).

Thus, the managerial and organizational deficiencies in the management of bureaucratic activities constitute a lagging factor on the triple economic, social and environmental efficiency. In Cameroonian public administrations, energy and water consumption are enormous and uncontrolled; the same is the case with the management and consumption of paper. Also, the management of the acoustic environment (air and noise) does not meet any standard in this area. Purchases do not take into account environmental considerations, waste is produced in large quantities and is poorly managed, no sustainable transport policy is encouraged, standards for the construction and renovation of buildings (sustainable architecture, etc.) are not yet respected and no social responsibility policy is put into practice in a formal way. Therefore, an EM approach can allow these administrations to control the costs and contribute toward a substantial and consequent reduction in all kinds of nuisances.

Many authors consider the EM approach like a global system. Most of the researches in this field are directed toward the private sector (corporations) and focused on EM as a coordinated or organized activity within the organization and its multiple functions (Boiral 1990, 2007; Jolly 1992; De Baker 1992). Some other studies carried out on an environmental management system (EMS) and tools have mainly focused on: (1) the reasons that push organizations to adopt such a system (Nash and Ehrenfeld 2001; Morrow and Rondinelli 2002; Boiral and Dostaler 2004); (2) giving importance to contingency factors that may influence its location in firms (Nash and Ehrenfeld 2001; Marquet-Pondeville 2003; Andrews et al. 2003, etc.); (3) the impacts it may have on the environmental performance of firms (Berry and Rondinelli 2000; Florida and Davison 2001; Melnyk et al. 2002, 2003; Janicot 2007) (4) and its use to decline and improve the environmental strategies of enterprises (Dohou-Renaud 2009).

Nowadays, with awareness regarding climate warming, most responsible private companies and some administrations try to reduce their footprint. Thus, economic actors and public services that care about their energy impact can set up within their organization EM whose implementation requires a certain number of complementary and integrated tools. Indeed, environmental management in any organization, as a global approach, is characterized by a myriad of tools (Nel and Kotze 2009; NEC-Bhutan 2011), nine of which have been tested: corporate social responsibility, energy and water efficiency, green purchasing, the sustainability budget, sustainable mobility, the environmental impact assessment/environmental audit, the ecological footprint and the ISO 14001 certification known as EMS. Likewise, the uniqueness of this chapter is drawing up an inventory of these tools, even if it is necessary to examine their application in the desk management activities in the central departments of 36 ministries in Cameroon.

Private enterprises considered such an approach in their industrial, technical and managerial choices as not only an obligation, but also a major asset for their development and sustainability. Public administrations must not be left behind because they have the responsibility to manage the territorial policy and to decide to implement an EM approach allowing them to respond to the growing environmental concerns of their citizens. As well as business for customers, these administrations are, in turn, obliged to play an exemplary role with the public and the society. Indeed, how can they ask the citizen to be environmentally responsible and live in a sustainable way if they don't set the tone by better controlling their own managing methods?

Given that the fact these tools are beneficial in terms of environmental performance and socioeconomic improvement in private organizations, the public administrations that wish to use them could derive a great benefit in terms of governance and environmental or societal performance. From this statement and based on the nine test tools used, the following question deserves to be formulated: what is the state and the application of the tools of the EM in public administrations and what can be its contribution in their environmental policy in Cameroon?

It is paradoxical to notice that the Cameroon environmental Framework Law N° 96/12 of 5 August 1996 does not explicitly mention environmental management. But, it, nevertheless, emphasizes the following: (1) All public and private institutions are required, within the scope of their competence, to sensitize all populations to the environmental problems. (2) They must therefore integrate in their activities programs to ensure a better knowledge of the environment. It is only with the recent Ministry of Environment, the protection of the nature and sustainable development (Minepded) decree of 2013, that the environmental audit and the EMS were clearly clarified even though some private companies had been carrying out audits since 2008. It is a loophole because the Interministerial Committee (composed of about 15 technical ministries) validates these audits and environmental evaluations without expert advice. Therefore, the realization of the present survey is an initial and indispensable step in collecting information on the actual environmental situation of these institutions in order to define a public environmental policy in the next steps.

Because desk activities in public administrations have direct and indirect impacts on the environment, it is useful to assess their level of knowledge of EM and its practice by describing the state of arts of the initial situation of the EM of office activities in the Cameroonian administration. The objective of this chapter is to establish an inventory of the application of EM tools in these institutions and in terms of results to draw some conclusions that should be used in their environmental policy. Thus, it is assumed that considering, applying or implementing EM tools requires environmental responsibility, management transparency and communication on the impacts as well as economic constraints that will improve the environmental performance and governance of these public administrations.

2 Literature Review

Environmental management has a long history that can be recognized in several major periods but with an essential emphasis on the twentieth century. The first recognized step of adequate EM is the caveman (Shifrin 2019), who took only the essential until antiquity. Many changes have been recorded with demographic pressure and the industrial revolution, which brought economic and technological advances, but also a little ignorance on the ecological side. In the early 1970s, companies began to take into account environmental concerns in their policies and management (Gendron 2004). This turning point also concerns a breakthrough in EM legislation by various OECD countries in particular. Advances were rapid between 1970 and 2000 (Gendron 2004). Since the 1980s awareness, a lot has been done and the appearance of the ISO 14000 standard in 1996 constitutes a significant, undeniable and unavoidable revolution. Consequently, EMS, the outlet of which is often certification, has gained the attention of entrepreneurs who have made a real commitment, reflected in the performance of their companies. With the post-industrial era, which can be described as the era of technological acceleration, global changes and digital performance, the environment has taken pride of place where its management is carried out by interposed or even intertwined systems.

EM is difficult to define. Thus, the concept needs a broad review of its meaning before defining the tools and processes accompanying its implementation. This difficulty is linked to the complexity of the terms environment and management that are part of the term EM, which is also elusive. As stressed by Colby (1989), the concept "environment" encompasses green issues (biotic and abiotic elements of the earth system including their interactions) associated with brown issues (sociocultural, political and economy) as expressed also by Nel and Kotze (2009). *Management is the art of maximizing value from natural resources and human capital. It reflects the results of political, social, economic, and environmental policies adopted by national leaders* (Kairouz et al. 2016). Both definitions mean that EM implies the understanding of the structure and function of the earth system, as well as the ways in which humans use or exploit their environment.

Several definitions collected on EM are complementary and show that EM is a subject that combines science, policy and socioeconomic applications. It primarily stresses on finding a solution to practical problems that people face in cohabitation with nature and its protection, resource exploitation and its equitable distribution, sustainable economic growth and waste production. Indeed, EM involves many stakeholders at many spatial scales (from the local to the global) and requires a multidisciplinary perspective. According to Barrow (2005), it implies diverse goals, *including the desires to control the direction and pace of development, to optimize resource use, to minimize environmental degradation and to avoid environmental disaster* (https://www.soas.ac.uk › unit1 › page_10). To this extent, Table 11.1 gives an overview of some definitions retained.

Table 11.1 Environmental management definitions

Authors and dates	Definitions of environmental management	Observations
Colby (1989:33)	*The field that seeks to balance human demands upon the Earth's natural resource base with the environment's ability to meet these demands on a sustainable basis*	Anthropocentric view and utilitarian perspective
PA Consulting Group USAID—EAST (2001: 1)	*A systematic approach to finding practical ways for saving water, energy and materials, and reducing negative environmental impacts. A win-win-win proposition helping a property saving money, getting recognized for environmental leadership and preserving and protecting unique destinations*	Put emphasis on touristic, desk perspectives and benefits
French norm NFX30200 in Gendron (2004 :58)	*The set of management activities that determine the environmental policy, the objectives and the responsibilities, and that implement them by means such as the planning of the environmental objectives, the measurement results and control of the effects on the environment*	Responsibilities and policy aspects are concerned
Barrow (2005: 15)	*A process concerned with human-environment interactions, which seeks to identify what is environmentally desirable, what are the physical, economic, social and technological constraints to achieving it and what are the most feasible options*	Human-environment interface, implying that choices and trade-offs are needed
Barrow (2005), https://www.soas.ac.uk › unit1 › page_10	*Refers to a goal or vision, to attempts to steer a process, to the application of a set of tools, to a philosophical exercise seeking to establish new perspectives toward the environment and human societies, and to much more besides*	Imply EM tools and processes

(*continued*)

Table 11.1 (continued)

Authors and dates	Definitions of environmental management	Observations
Nel and Kotze (2009: 5)	*The planning, doing, checking and acting activities of managers and governing agents as they relate to either the green environment or combinations of green and brown environmental elements*	Both human and physical environment using Deming model or management perspective
NEC-Bhutan (2011: 1)	*A subject that combines science, policy, and socioeconomic applications. EM is a response to human actions considering the increasing seriousness and significance of today's disastrous human impact on natural ecosystems*	Broad definition from decision-makers

Source: Compilation by the authors

The EM concept has evolved and is still evolving from the

> initial polarized positions of 'economics and development' versus 'ecology and conservation', to a continuum of environmental management paradigms that range from frontier economics, environmental protection, resource management and eco-development, to a deep ecology paradigm that reintroduces the principles of ethics into the environmental management debate. (Colby 1989: 15)

Such an evolution increases complexity and creates awareness on its extent to various tools and paradigms (sustainability, corporate social responsibility, corporate governance, ecological footprint).

Undertaking EM is important and requires the use of these tools (Table 11.2) to which are attached some advantages including cost savings, ensuring legislative compliance, anticipating future legislation, reducing environmental risk, meeting supply chain requirements, improving relations with regulators, improving public image, increasing market opportunities, employee enthusiasm (NEC-Buthan 2011). EM tools brought many perspectives depending on the need of the country or enterprise implementing it. Also, any tool has a close link with the EM principles borrowing from the Rio de Janeiro principles (Table 11.2).

Table 11.2 Environmental management tools and possible link with it principles

Type of tools	Tools	Principles concerned
Analytical and planning	EIA, life cycle assessment, SEA, risk assessment, disaster planning, biodiversity impact assessment, social impact assessment, environmental labeling, environmental management program	Precautionary, uncertainty, prevention, recognition and preservation of diversity
Criteria and standards	Law, ISO and Occupational Health and Safety Assessment Series (OHSAS), accountability, sectorial environmental performance standards, environmental policies, environmental indicators, ecological footprint	Internalization of costs, polluter pays, prevention, protection and promotion of health and safety
Doing, management	EMS, emergency plans, EMP, CSR, administrative tools and operating procedures, disaster management plan	Intra-generational equity, inter-generational equity, multi-sectorial integration, subsidiarity
Checking and acting (corrective actions)	Environmental and social monitoring and measuring, inspection, analysis and records, environmental and social auditing, EMP performance monitoring, continual improvement tools, improvement management, energy efficiency, water efficiency, green procurement, sustainable mobility, sustainability budget, eco-balances	Intra-generational equity, inter-generational equity, multi-sectorial integration, subsidiarity
Communication and report	Environmental and social reporting, triple bottom line reporting, environmental and social communication, statutory reporting, public participation, risk communication	Precautionary, uncertainty, prevention, protection and promotion of health and safety

Source: Adapted from NEC-Bhutan (2011: 7–14) and Nel and Kotze (2009: 11)

Giving these tools and benefits related, EM may be practiced by individuals, public administrations, corporations, enterprises and groups holding conflicting views (Barrow 2005). These practices may result in the description and monitoring of environmental changes, the prediction of future changes, and the maximization of human benefits as well as the minimization of any environmental degradation due to human activities. From this point of view, EM is considered as a system that anticipates and avoids, or solves, environmental and resource conservation issues (Colby 1989; Barrow 2005).

The nine tools chosen were the most affordable for the understanding of public administration and the most known considering the daily activities of the civil servants and institutional administratives responsible. The following section will emphasize on these tools and methodology.

3 Methodology

Built around a hypothetic-deductive approach, the methodological corpus that guides this work has four components.

- *The main sample*

This research was conducted in all central services of 36 Cameroon ministries based in Yaoundé City, Mfoundi Division, and Centre Region, from 2 July to 30 September 2012. In each ministry and depending on the level of responsibility, five managers (General Affairs, Personnel, Budget, Heritage and Contract Services) were interviewed, totaling 180 persons.

- *Questionnaire and interview guide methods*

A nine-part questionnaire with 66 questions was designed and structured. Excluding the first section of ten questions dedicated to the identification of the respondent, these questions concerned the various tools of the EM and their application to bureaucratic activities in public administrations, as shown in Table 11.3.

Table 11.3 Criteria or indicators used for interview

Tools	Number of questions	Criteria/indicators used for this chapter
Corporate social responsibility	8	– Human resources governance – Management strategy for natural resources – Environmental policies
EMS/ISO 14001	3	– Eco-manager in charge of environmental policy – Environmental regulations – ISO 14001
Energy efficiency	9	– Number of electric devices in the computer base – Number of air conditioners and functioning mode – Energy consumption – Energy economy policy – Low-cost energy devices – Energy saving strategy when building – Use of renewable energy
Water efficiency	11	– Water consumption – Plan of water fitting – Environmental characteristics of cleaning detergent – Water efficiency strategy
Green purchases	9	– Life cycle products – Type of paper used – Biodegradability of the material – Tools identifying green purchasing, interest in such approach
Sustainability budget	3	– Knowledge about – Participative budget management – Gender issue consideration

(*continued*)

Table 11.3 (continued)

Tools	Number of questions	Criteria/indicators used for this chapter
Sustainable mobility	7	– Distance for supply – Eco-mobility strategy – Incentive measures to walking, cycling, carpooling – Visio, teleconference room, Internet, Skype use – Parking for staff/employees – Car using renewable energy
Environmental impact assessment (EIA) and environmental audit assessment	7	– Environmental audit and EIA of the premises – Reducing environmental impacts measures – Air quality, visual and acoustic comfort – Waste typology and management – Management of packaging
Ecological footprint	9	– Knowledge about – Green space and landscaping – Electricity devices functioning – Number of cars, carpooling frequency

Source: Authors' creation

- *Pretest*

Before forwarding the questionnaire to the administrative managers, three semi-structured interviews were conducted with (1) an ISO 14001 expert, (2) an environmental manager in an ISO 14001 certified company, (3) a quality manager in a company undergoing certification and nine ministerial managers for better identifying the contours of these tools before their application to these administrative departments. These round-trip interviews between theory and practice constituted a pretest.

- *Survey treatment and analysis*

The 66 questions were subject of an input mask in an Excel database, which is characterized by its flexibility of use, interoperability and clarity of the post-processing graphic rendering. Almost 59 were processed in Excel and the authors chose to include in this text what they consider to be significant in relation to the objectives of the study. Admittedly, the tools analyzed have an average of eight variables and the authors have chosen to present the graphs of those that better reflected the results of their analysis.

4 Findings and Interpretations

The main results are presented below according to the characteristics of EM tools used during the survey.

4.1 Application of CSR to Public Administrations of Cameroon

Corporate social responsibility (CSR) can simply be understood as the relationship between global corporations, governments and individuals citizens with an ethical stance (Wan Saiful Wan-Jan 2006; Crowther and Aras 2008). Most of the studies in Cameroon (Wamba Tiona 2009; Boubakary and Moskolaï Doumagay 2016; Ndzi Gheyoh 2016; Awang Ollong and Ndzi 2016) show that private corporations applied CSR with lukewarm results. But, public administrations are still lagging. CSR includes sustainable development and such a consideration led the authors to verify the management of human resources, the relations of the ministries with the neighboring and local communities as well as their environmental policies.

- *Human resources management*

Human resources management concerns policies, initiatives and actions related to the following domains among others: education, training and skill of the staff; empowerment and involvement of staff;

improvement of the communication process information; balance between work, family and leisure; equal opportunities also in terms of remuneration policies and the approach and modalities of management of the professional integration phase. Out of the 36 ministries, 86% possess and implement a human resources management policy (Fig. 11.1).

- *Management strategy for the environmental impacts on the natural resources*

In this area, 56% of the surveyed population do not manage the effects of their activities on the environment and natural resources (Fig. 11.1). This is due to ignorance or a great lack of sensitization among civil servants and citizens. Also, 75% think that activities have an impact on local communities (Fig. 11.1).

CSR appears as the appropriation by companies of sustainable development logics and refers to their commitment to ecological and social registers. In reality, in Cameroon public administration, the treatment of

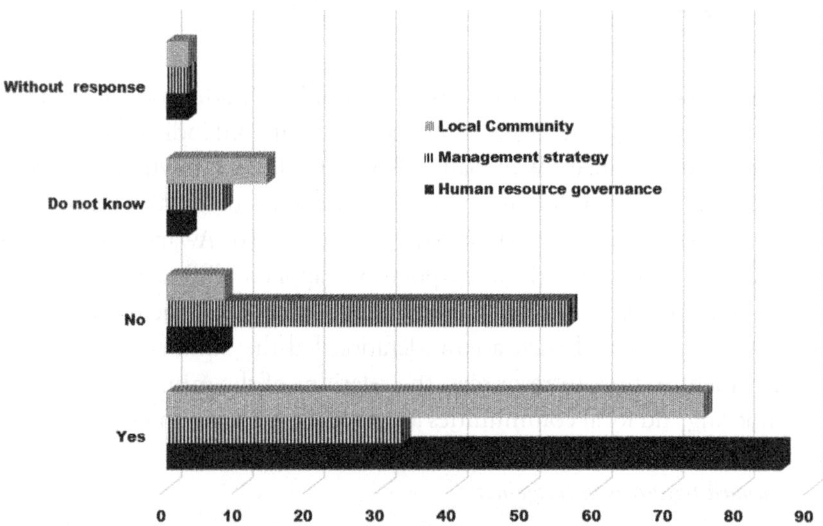

Fig. 11.1 Percentage of ministries holding a human resources governance policy, a management strategy for their environmental impacts on the natural resources and the relationship with local community. (Source: Field survey, August 2012)

human resource problems from a CSR perspective is in fact nothing original compared to what had been done a century earlier when labor problems were being studied. CSR practices for civil servant or any employees are, above all, a corporate strategy. They consist of defending "internalist" solutions while supervising employees. In the Cameroonian context, public authorities remain hesitant about the level of regulation they must provide. Regarding the merits, the idea that both employers and employees would benefit from the implementation of socially responsible practices remains to be checked.

Whereas public administrations are engaged in actions improving community life and participating in its development, the relationship with local community is always stringent, because local communities are aware of the impacts of public activities. Finally, a CSR approach promotes the overall performance of the concerned administration by anticipating and controlling risks related to the depletion of natural resources and biodiversity, pollution, climate change, disappearance of ecosystems services and the degradation of human settlements.

- *Global environmental concerns*

This CSR dimension is based on the findings that ecological problems have no geographical boundaries, let alone legal ones. Of the surveyed ministries, 33% say they have an environmental policy on the one hand, and on the other hand the same number claims to have environmental concerns at the local level and the global level (Fig. 11.2). In fact, this claimed environmental policy is merely a guide for activities in favor of environmental protection.

These results show the gap between CSR strategies and the management of the local and global environment in which Cameroonian public administrations operate (social inequalities, air pollution, environmental degradation, water contamination, etc.). It confirms the light implementation of CSR in Cameroon as well as in African countries (Apitsa 2019). The conclusion raised the difficulty experienced by the Cameroon ministries to integrate this process because of their limited concerns being purely economic. However, it would be better to encourage them to pursue the implementation of actions initiated and leading to CSR.

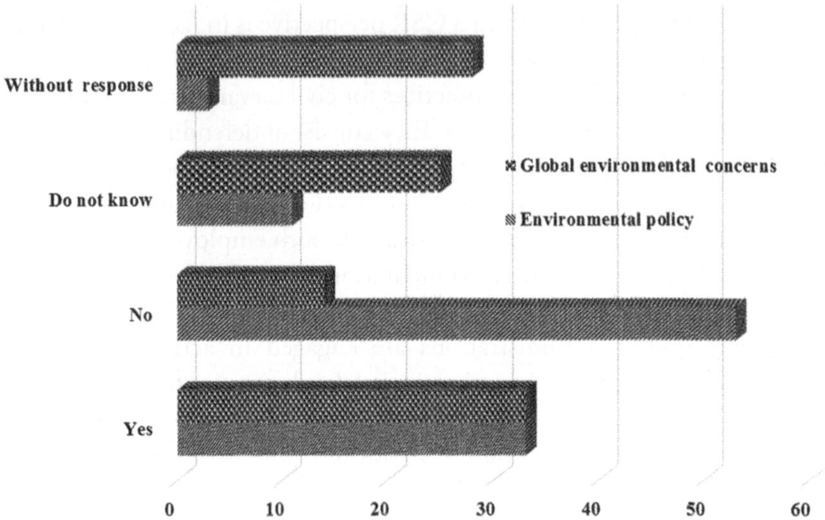

Fig. 11.2 Distribution of ministries according to the existence of global environmental concerns and policy. (Source: Field survey, August 2012)

4.2 Energy and Water Efficiency

These EM tools provide the opportunity to check the way public administration managed water and energy as well as the equipment fitted. The survey on energy efficiency illustrates that 90% of the ministries do not consider the energy consumption of equipment when purchasing. Also, 72% turned on light and air conditioners all day long (Fig. 11.3).

Most of the surveyed approve getting knowledge on energy and water efficiency (Fig. 11.4), but, it is a loophole because:

- All electrical appliances in offices are turned on even when the premises are empty for long periods (lunch break, meeting).
- The lack of awareness campaigns on eco-gestures (10% of the ministries).
- The lack of energy diagnosis.
- The non-use of renewable energy as an alternative to energy efficiency.

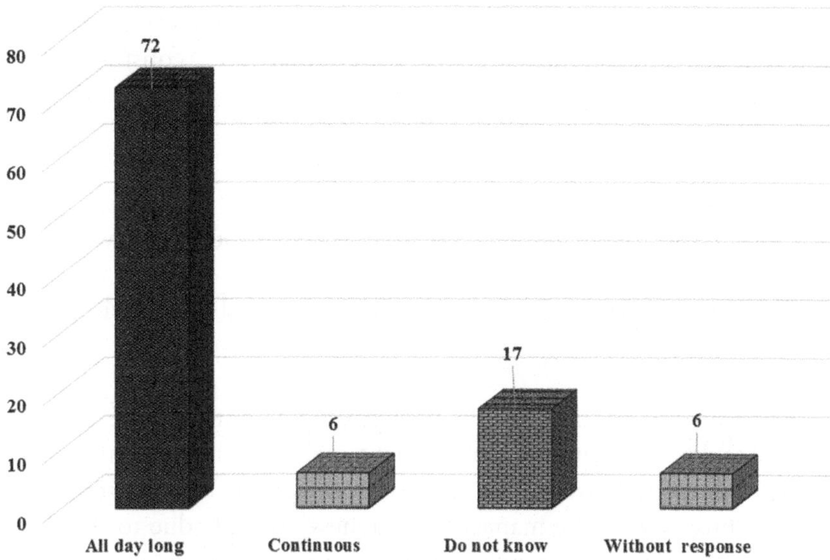

Fig. 11.3 The pace of operation of air conditioners in ministerial departments. (Source: Field survey, August 2012)

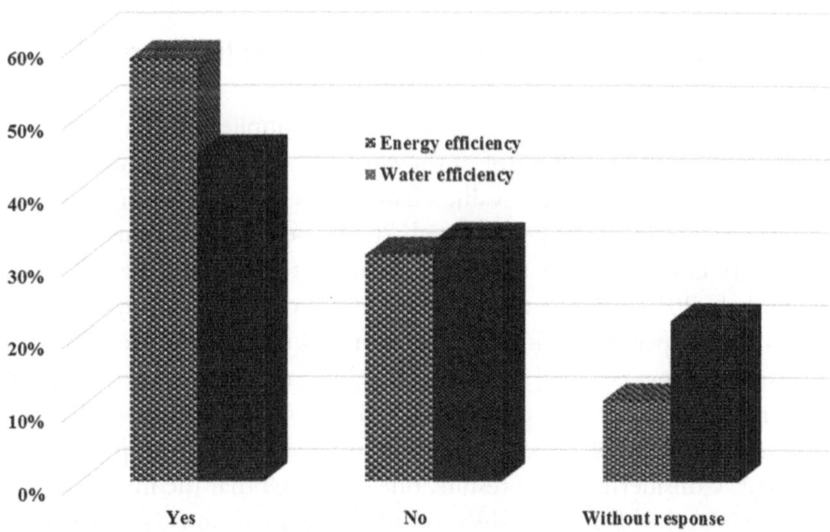

Fig. 11.4 Energy and water efficiency. (Source: Field survey, August 2012)

About water efficiency, 61% admit not using economical materials in the toilets. Few respondents (17%) believe that water consumption is high. Complementary observations show that:

- The diagnosis for water fittings was never made.
- None hold a sketch diagram of these facilities.
- Only 25% encourage staff to save water through a few awareness messages.
- 70% are unaware of office cleaning detergents and their environmental characteristics.

Finally, it can be seen that the fittings used do not promote water or energy saving. The current management and handling systems are not compatible with a strategy of rational and optimal use of energy and water. Thus, despite the managers' awareness probably due to the additional costs generated by this situation, any ministry possesses a real water/energy efficiency strategy. Also, the distribution of water in the ministries is not regular and probably transforms toilets into a waste storage facility.

4.3 Green Procurement and Sustainability Budget

The green purchasing approach aims at using supplies (product and services) that are more respectful of the environment and integrating environmental aspects into the value chain of the production and the life cycle of any product (Appolloni et al. 2014). Better still, it considers and values its environmental aspects in relation to its complete life cycle (Coulibaly 2012). Public administrations are characterized by a significant use of paper. As far as printing paper is concerned, few respondents (6%) are using certified paper while 3% are using recycled paper. Nevertheless, the use of certified paper ISO 9001/14001 is widespread even though 61% of respondents have no idea of the green purchasing concept. Considering these results, one can argue that the ministries are not aware of the life cycle of the products purchased. Consequently, these products are polluting, entail health risks, result in huge waste generation and are not likely to be fully or partially reused.

Participatory budgets are the “flagship” of participatory democracy and have a large and fast diffusion nowadays (Porto D’Oliveira 2010, 2016). Sustainability budget surveys provide a full record of great ignorance (100%), due to the centralized descending hierarchy and condescension in assigning tasks. Thus, the budgets of these ministries are not participatory, although few lines are oriented toward the poorest. There are no gender budgets, despite the existence of a Ministry of Women and Family Affairs in which there are some actions funded for addressing the gender issue. But, they are not developed accordingly and therefore do not arise from an established approach. Also, one can notice the absence of gender-responsive budgeting, which aims at promoting gender equality (Labourie-Racapé 2002; Moreau 2002).

4.4 Sustainable Mobility

As a result of energy crises and global warming, green or eco-mobility (Coiffard and Figuière 2012; Perschon 2012) encourages a green environment by reducing pollution from motorized fuel-consuming devices. There is no strategy, no car pool, no transport or commuting. The ministerial minibuses are used for out-of-town trips or tourist events. Among the surveyed:

- 76% hold internet facilities with a poor use of Skype.
- 100% don’t take into account the distances for delivering the supplies.
- 100% have car parks dedicated to staff vehicles only.
- None have usual vehicles operating other than gasoline/diesel.
- None of them takes steps to encourage employees to travel smoothly (walking and cycling).

There is no formal strategy, policy and program action for sustainable mobility in these ministries. New behaviors with soft modes of transportation and carpooling are not encouraged, public transportation vehicles where existing are used only occasionally and teleworking is still unrealistic if not unclear.

4.5 Environmental Impact Assessment and Environmental Audit

From 2005 to 2008, none within Cameroonian administration could ignore what Environmental impact assessment (EIA) and environmental audit are. Both tools are helpful for decision-makers as well as in waste and risk management. Unfortunately, the usual practices and documentary research show that none of the Cameroonian ministry has carried out an environmental audit of its activities yet. Some ministries (31%) performed an EIA study during the extension of their premises or the accomplishment of certain projects (Fig. 11.5), but it is a loophole because none of them has so far carried out EIA of their fittings.

Moreover, 70% of respondents are not satisfied with the quality of air and 50% with acoustic comfort. Less than 20% are satisfied with the visual comfort, and 52% maintained a ventilation system regularly; 72% of the office waste produced is transferred to the landfill by *Hygiène et salubrité du Cameroun* (HYSACAM). In fact, by burning unnecessary documents (Images 11.1 and 11.2), some ministries contributed to the

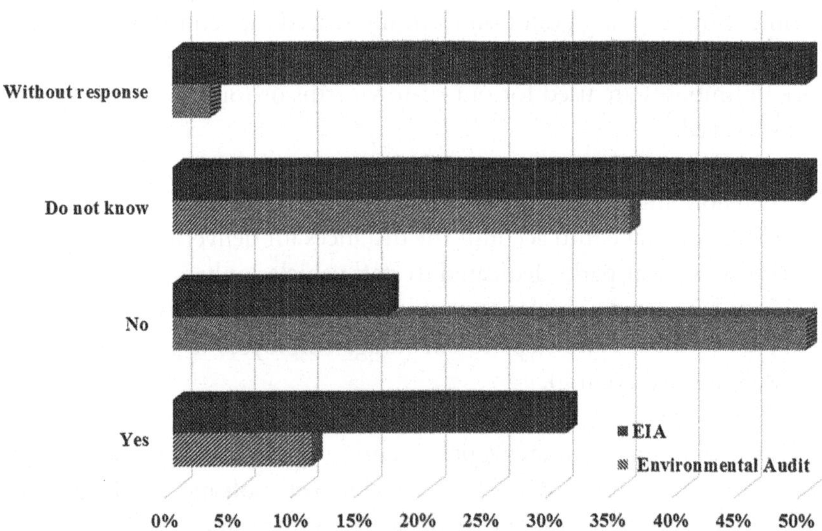

Fig. 11.5 Ministries completing an EIA or environmental audit during the extension of their premises. (Source: Field survey, August 2012)

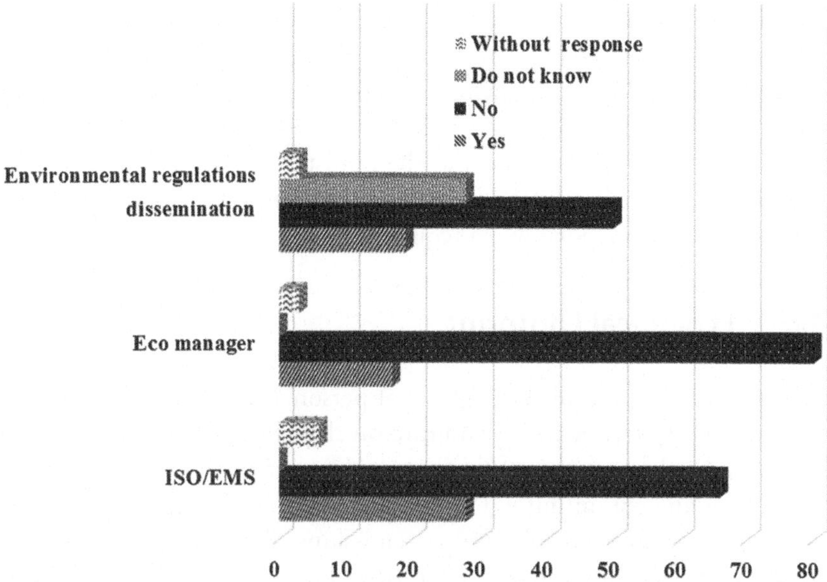

Image 11.1 Waste destruction/trash in a ministry. (Source: Field survey, August 2012)

Image 11.2 Waste destruction/trash in a ministry. (Source: Field survey, August 2012)

greenhouse gases emission and its corollary. In addition, useless computer devices and consumables (D3E) are fully trashed without sorting.

The legal provision requiring EIA and environmental audit studies when carrying out projects is not included in the Cameroonian ministries policies, even though most of the ministers and staff attend impact assessment reports' validation at the Environmental Interministerial Committee in Minepded when required.

4.6 Ecological Footprint

The footprint counts all the impacts of personal spending as well as the business and government expenditure on their behalf (Calcott and Bull 2007) and it became a tool for measuring sustainable development of individuals and communities (Sonu et al. 2011). It aims at assessing individual or collective greenhouse gas emissions. We notice that 81% of respondents have any ecological footprint knowledge while 52% affirm keeping the light turned on all day in case of good or bad weather. Also, the narrowness of the office reduces the comfort level, which impedes performance. Concerning transportation, the number of vehicles available per ministry is significant, compared to a public transit strategy or the soft travel model. In the waste domain, there is no strategy to reduce, recycle and reuse. Also, the lack of selective waste sorting contributes to increasing the poor quality (70%) of the ministerial landscape environment in which green spaces are uncommon.

4.7 ISO Certification and EMS

The survey reveals that 67% of the ministries have some knowledge of the existence of ISO 14001 certification (Fig. 11.6). Such a situation shows the gap between the law regulations and practices. Only private organizations have voluntary realized ISO certification in Cameroon: *Les Brasseries du Cameroun* (ISO 9001v2000 in 2008 and FSSC 22002 in 2013) and HYSACAM (ISO 9001v2000 in 2008).

Nevertheless, 75% of the ministries are interested in setting up an ISO 14001 certification process. But, there is no trained environmental manager (Fig. 11.6) for coordinating environmental policy in almost all

Fig. 11.6 Distribution of the ministries according to their knowledge of ISO 14001, the existence of an eco-manager and their knowledge and dissemination of environmental regulations. (Source: Field survey, August 2012)

ministries (81% of respondents). Similarly, environmental laws and regulations available are unknown or poorly disseminated (ISO 14001 standard). EMS does not exist in Cameroon ministries, whereas 72% expressed their interest on its implementation. The same is the case with knowledge on environmental regulations (50%, Fig. 11.6). Nevertheless, no environmental regulation report related to the management of office activities is available in any Cameroonian public administration.

5 Discussion

Although efforts are being made to reform the civil service in most African countries (CPIA 2017), the present chapter shows that the Cameroonian public administration seems to ignore the environmental and sustainable development tools it is supposed to manage or implement in laws, programs and policies. One can also notice great resistance to change. Three main issues are discussed: CSR, EMS and water/energy efficiency.

CSR establishes the appropriation by enterprises of sustainable development logics and refers to their commitment to ecological and social registers (Ivanaj and McIntyre 2006). CSR is based on two principles (rights and effects; Cazal 2005) and a triple bottom line (people, planet and profit of Shnayder et al. 2015) known as three Ps, which have sometimes also been referred to as the social, environmental and financial dimensions of a company's CSR performance (Slaper and Hall Tanya 2011). Diawara and Lavallée (2014) think that CSR is to reconcile economic objectives with respect to social ethics and environmental concerns. CSR is also part of the theory of global governance that seeks to conceive governance without government: a regulatory system that operates without official authority (De Woot 2004). In this sense, it brings together companies and, more importantly, multinationals, with organizations representing civil society (Igalens 2004), by resolving conflicts of interest between stakeholders and then mitigating practices that generate a loss of confidence (Aymen et al. 2018). Stressing on this, Pesqueux (2011) thinks that CSR carries ambiguities and presents a mixed character, legal and voluntary, as shown by Wamba Tiona (2009) in Cameroon. These considerations were checked in the management of human resources, the relations of the ministries with neighboring communities and the environmental policy. Taking the case of human resources management, approaches from Lascoumes (1994), Deligne (2004) and Semal (2005) simultaneously emphasize social benevolence (CSR) and the informed realization of the company's interests. However, in addition to specific actions concerning the environment or safety, the credibility and effectiveness of any organization depend on an integrated management system (Lesourd and Schilizzi 2001) geared toward risk prevention and the satisfaction of interested parties including customers, local residents and public authorities. Better, Danet (2019) recommended boosting CSR culture in Africa based on seven key questions: *governance, human rights, labor relations and working conditions, the environment, fair operating practices, community involvement and development, and consumer issues.*

Concerning ISO 14001, private enterprises are willing to set it up. But, it met resistance to change in public administrations, which is inherent to the nature of public administration in Africa. It is worthmentionning that these resistances are linked to the lack of interest of public servants and, to their bad perception or representation of the public service. We can also underline the fact that these tools are not an emanation of the administrative staff who take pleasure in their laxity (Boiral 2008). Therefore, the communication tool not taken into account in the surveys appears not only essential for understanding the interest, the stakes and the means of change, but it also makes it possible to overcome the differences in perceptions and representations among the various groups of actors (Brénot and Tuvée 1996; Bernoux 2004). Indeed, the conception of the public service in Cameroon keeps the logic of the descending hierarchy and the condescension in the attribution of the tasks. Such a logic does not guarantee the satisfactory participation of officials in the tasks. Therefore, the staff is also obliged to achieve objectives to which he adheres little because of his lack of involvement. This has been observed in Tunisia where the implementation of ISO 14001 in public enterprises has failed (Ben Yedder and Farhoud 2014) whereas in Marrakech city in Morocco it has succeeded (Daddi et al. 2011).

In both cases, the projects come from public administration with different results. It can be deduced that the participation of employees in thinking about implementation methods is part of the EM/EMS tools as suggested by Reverdy (2005). It is a sine qua non and objective condition. The feeling of precariousness of the recruited officials is far from provoking their mobilization. Staff autonomy is almost non-existent. Likewise, the lack of communication and the retention of information amplify conflicts within the organization.

Without underestimating some changes and improvements observed here and there, the avatars of administrative management in Africa usually reside only on the strength of the managerial discourse which underlines the precariousness of actual achievements. However, where these tools still open up a few spaces of freedom, the managers cautiously turn away, decline in fact the responsibilities they liked to claim in words and reproduce in total the logic that the instrument claimed to question. This is why human resources management was first observed in CSR.

The temptation is great, then, to conclude that EM is likely to be reduced in Cameroon to the state of ideological discourse, insofar as it equates the state to the company and the citizen to the customer, both participating in the way to the deregulation of public service and the decline of the rule of law. Merit, fairness, responsibility, mobility would constitute threats to a return to arbitrary power; they would call into question essential social gains such as equal treatment and the universality of public service. These barriers show that the structural and cultural dimensions as well as the distribution of power appear as key elements to take into account during organizational change (Aubert et al. 2005, Crozier and Friedberg 1977). The failure to take ownership of these tools also comes from the lack of accountability and the rise of mismanagement of the public administration in Africa and Cameroon. All things contrary to the principles of EM and even public management applicable in a democracy. Appointments, assignments, awarding of public contracts, recruitments are rather tools of retribution for *electoral soldiers* (Kakdeu 2014).

The administrative reforms necessary to support the development and democratization of Africa work by depoliticization of public administration to avoid the spoil system linked to the political meeting days; human resources management in public administration through the establishment of a merit system when appointing civil servants like that practiced in the USA (Kakdeu 2014). Ndi-Zambo (2018), embracing the pace, talks about refocusing the role of public administration in relation to the state and the society; move from traditional bureaucratic thinking to organic proactive thinking; fostering within the civil service a transforming and visionary leadership in place of traditional authoritarianism. After the analysis, these breakdowns in the EM in Cameroonian public administration underlined the desired changes which have to deal with ethics, professional standards, competence, motivation/passion for excellence, effectiveness and personal qualities.

Energy crisis is at the heart of the three major challenges faced by humanity today. Energy efficiency is the main solution being implemented nowadays to reduce CO_2 emissions and overcome the problem of climate change (Abolhosseini et al. 2014). Thus, focusing on water and energy efficiency, any EM program is based on practical steps to conserve water and energy and minimize waste (PA group 2001). Typical strategies include efficient equipment for water conservation devices, energy-efficient lighting and lighting controls with new less consumed lamp, weather-stripping and insulation of refrigerant lines, air-conditioned areas and better energy efficiency governance (Jollands and Ellis 2009).

6 Conclusion

The objective of this chapter was to establish an inventory of the application of EM tools in Cameroonian public institutions and to draw some conclusions that should be used in the environmental policy of these administrations. Thus, it is assumed that considering, applying or implementing EM tools requires environmental responsibility, management transparency and communication on the impacts as well as economic constraints that will improve the environmental performance and governance of these public administrations.

This research was conducted in the central services of 36 Cameroon ministries based in the City of Yaoundé. In each ministry and depending on the level of responsibility, 5 managers (General Affairs, Personnel, Budget, Heritage and Contract Services) were interviewed, totaling 180 persons. From the starting assumption postulated, both direct observations and semi-directive interviews allowed us to notice that none of the EM tools are formally implemented in the public services of Cameroon. Choosing and using nine tools characterizing EM, the results revealed managerial and organizational shortcomings in the management of office activities. Also, the EM concept is unknown, let alone regulated. This confirms the initial hypothesis.

Thus, EM with all its processes and tools seems to meet an obstacle in its implementation in public administrations, not only in Cameroon, but also in most of the African countries due to politicization and resistances related to the lack of interest of public servants, bad perception and laxity. In such a spoil system, it is hoped that extensive research on the implementation of each instrument individually may lead these administrations to adopt a progressive step approach to good EM practices. Similarly, the establishment of a legal framework integrating all aspects of EM is advisable.

References

Abolhosseini, S., Heshmati, A., & Altmann J. (2014). *A Review of Renewable Energy Supply and Energy Efficiency Technologies*. Discussion Paper No. 8145, 35 p.

Andrews, R., Amaral, D., Darnall, N., & Rigling, D. (2003). *Environmental Management Systems: Do They Improve Performance?* The University of North Carolina at Chapel Hill.

Apitsa, S. M. (2019). La Responsabilité Sociétale des Entreprises (RSE) des acteurs portuaires en Afrique: une grille de lecture en termes de défi environnemental. In M. Tchindjang, B. Steck, & A. Bopda (Eds.), *Construire la ville Portuaire de demain en Afrique Atlantique* (Chap 16; pp. 405–428). Collection Afrique Atlantique, Editions EMS 2019.

Appolloni, A., Sun, H., Jia, F., & Li, X. (2014). Green Procurement in the Private Sector: A State of the Art Review Between 1996 and 2013. *Journal of Cleaner Production, xxx*, 1–12.

Aubert, N., Guerre, J.-P., Jabes, J., Laroche, H., & Michel, S. (2005). *Management, aspects humains et organisationnels*. Paris: PUF.

Awang Ollong, K., & Ndzi, E. (2016). Analysing The Corporate Social Responsibility Strategies by Extractive Multinational Corporations in Cameroon. *Social Science and Humanities Journal, 5*, 359–397.

Aymen, A., Lakhal, F., & Ayed, S. (2018). Does Corporate Social Responsibility Reduce Earnings Management? The Moderating Role of Corporate Governance and Ownership. *Management International, 23*(2), 45–55.

Barrow, C. J. (2005). *Environmental Management and Developing Countries*. London: Routledge.

Ben Yedder, M., & Farhoud, M. (2014). Le développement durable est-il bienvenu dans les organisations ? Cas de l'implantation d'un Système de Management Environnemental en Tunisie. *Développement durable et territoires*, Varia (2004–2010).

Bernoux, P. (2004). *Sociologie du changement dans les entreprises et les institutions*. Paris: Seuil.

Berry, M. A., & Rondinelli, D. (2000). Environmental Management in the Pharmaceutical Industry: Integrating Corporate Responsibility and Business Strategy. *Environmental Quality Management, 9*, 21–33.

Boiral, O. (1990). *Du développement durable au management écologique: une étude de cas sur les actions environnementales de sept entreprises québécoises*. Essai de maîtrise, Faculté des sciences de l'Administration, Université Laval.

Boiral, O. (2007). Corporate Greening Through ISO 14001: A Rational Myth? *Organisation Science, 18*(1), 127–146.

Boiral, O. (2008). Les pays du sud à l'épreuve des normes ISO: vers un sous-développement durable? *Management International, 12*(2), 49–63.

Boiral, O., & Dostaler, I. (2004). *Gestion environnementale et ISO 14 001: une approche néo-institutionnelle*. Québec: ASAC.

Boubakary, B., & Moskolaï Doumagay, D. (2016). The Influence of the Implementation of CSR on Business Strategy: An Empirical Approach Based on Cameroonian Enterprises. *Arab Economic and Business Journal, 11*, 162–171.

Brénot, J., & Tuvée, L. (1996). *Le changement dans les organisations*. Paris: PUF.

Calcott, A., & Bull, J. (2007). *Ecological Footprint of British City Residents*. UK: Carbon Plan, WWF.

Cazal, D. (2005). RSE et parties prenantes: quels fondements conceptuels? *Les cahiers de recherche du CLAREE*.

Coiffard P., & Figuière C. (2012). Mobilité durable et "imbroglio" institutionnel: quelle compatibilité ? Le cas de l'agglomération grenobloise. XXVIIIème journées du développement ATM 2012 "*Mobilités internationales, déséquilibres et développement: vers un développement durable et une mondialisation décarbonée?*", Association Tiers-Monde, Laboratoire d'économie d'Orléans, France. halshs-00713065.

Colby. (1989). *Environmental Management in Development: The Evolution of Paradigms*. Retrieved from http://wds.worldbank.org/servlet/WDSContentServer/WDSP/IB/1989/11/01/000009265_3960928125138/Rendered/PDF/multi_page.pdf.

Coulibaly, N. (2012). *Analyse du cycle de vie (ACV) et impact sur le consommateur*. Mémoire de Maîtrise en Environnement. Université de Sherbrooke, Centre Universitaire de Formation en Environnement (CUFE), Sherbrooke.

CPIA Afrique. (2017). *Évaluation des politiques et des institutions en Afrique*. Washington: Groupe de la Banque Mondiale.

Crowther, D., & Aras, G. (2008). *Corporate Social Responsibility*. Ventus Publishing ApS.

Crozier, M., & Friedberg, E. (1977). *L'acteur et le système*. Paris: Seuil.

Daddi, T., Frey, M., Iraldo, F., & Nabil, B. (2011). The Implementation of an Environmental Management System in a North-African Local Public Administration: The Case of the City Council of Marrakech (Morocco). *Journal of Environmental Planning and Management, 54*(6), 813–832.

Danet, T. (2019). Déployer une culture RSE en Afrique. *Annales des Mines—Réalités industrielles*, vol. Août 2019, (3), 76–79.

De Baker, P. (1992). *Le management vert*. Paris: DUNOD.

De Woot, P. (2004). *Responsabilité sociale de l'Entreprise: Faut-il enchaîner Prométhée ?* Paris: Economica.

Deligne, C. (2004). Histoire longue et prospective environnementale. Le cas d'une rivière périurbaine (Maelbeek, région bruxelloise). In P. Leveau & J. Burnouf (Eds.), *Fleuves et marais, une histoire au croisement de la nature et de la culture. Sociétés préindustrielles et milieux fluviaux, lacustres et palustres: pratiques sociales et hydrosystèmes* (pp. 285–290) Les éditions du CTHS.

Diawara, K. & Lavallée, S. (2014). La responsabilité sociale de l'entreprise (RSE) dans l'espace OHADA: pour une ouverture aux considérations non économiques. « *Revue internationale de droit économique* » 2014/4 t. XXVIII, pp. 431 à 451.

Dohou-Renaud, A. (2009). *Le système de management environnemental comme moyen de contrôle de la déclinaison et de l'émergence des stratégies environnementales*. Université de Poitiers, Thèse de doctorat en sciences de gestion, Poitiers.

Florida, R., & Davison, D. (2001). Gaining from Green Management: Environmental Management Systems Inside and Outside the Factory. *California Management Review, 43*(3), 64–84.

Gendron, C. (2004). *La gestion environnementale et la norme ISO 14001*. Montréal: PUM.

Igalens, J. (2004). La mise en œuvre de la responsabilité sociale de l'entreprise: modalités, enjeux et limites du partenariat firme-ONG. In E. Quéinnec & J. Igalens (Eds.), *Les organisations non gouvernementales et le management* (pp. 111–128). Paris: Vuibert.

Ivanaj, V., & McIntyre, J. (2006). Multinational Enterprises and Sustainable Development: A Review of Strategy Process Research. International Colloquia: "*Multinational Enterprise and Sustainable Development: Strategic Tool for Competitiveness*", 19–20 Oct, Georgia Tech Center for International Business Education and Research (CIBER), Atlanta, USA.

Janicot, L. (2007). Les systèmes d'indicateurs de performance entre communication et contrôle. *Comptabilité Contrôle Audit, 1*(13), 47–68.

Jollands, N., & Ellis, M. (2009). Energy Efficiency Governance: An Emerging Priority. *ECEEE 2009 Summer Study: Act! Innovate! Deliver! Reducing Energy Demand Sustainably* (pp. 91–100).

Jolly, D. (1992). La politique environnementale d'un groupe industriel: le cas d'Elf-Aquitaine. *Revue Française de Gestion*, juin-juillet-août, N° 89, 117–121.

Kairouz, A., El Hokayem, J., & El Hage, U. (2016). Sustainability of Public Management in the Developing Countries: The Case of Lebanon. *Procedia—Social and Behavioral Sciences, 221*(7), 378–387.

Kakdeu, L. M. (2014). Les cinq réformes nécessaires dans l'administration publique en Afrique. Retrieved from www.libreafrique.org/KAKDEU-administration-171114.

Labourie-Racapé, A. (2002). Femmes-Hommes, la longue marche vers l'égalité professionnelle. *Entreprises Formation, 129*, 19–34.

Lascoumes, P. (1994). *L'éco-pouvoir: environnements et politiques*. Paris: La Découverte.

Lesourd, J. B., & Schilizzi, S. G. M. (2001). *The Environment in Corporate Management New Directions and Economic Insights*. London: Edward Elgar Publishing Limited.

Marquet-Pondeville, S. (2003). *Le contrôle de gestion environnemental*. Thèse de Doctorat en Sciences de Gestion. UCL, Presses Universitaires de Louvain, Belgique.

Mathiasen, D. G. (1999). The New Public Management and Its Critics. *International Public Management Journal, 2*(1), 90–111.

Melnyk, K., Sroufe, R., & Calantone, R. (2003). Assessing the Impact of Environmental Management System on Corporate and Environmental Performance. *Journal of Operations Management, 21*, 329–351.

Melnyk, K., Sroufe, R., Calantone, R., & Montabon, F. (2002). Assessing the Effectiveness of the US Voluntary Environmental Programs. *An Empirical Study, 8*, 1853–1878.

Molina-Azorín, J. F., Tarí, J. J., Claver-Cortés, E., & López-Gamero, M. D. (2009). Quality Management, Environmental Management and Firm Performance: A Review of Empirical Studies and Issues of Integration. *International Journal of Management Reviews, 11*(2), 97–222.

Moreau, T. (2002). *Egalité des sexes et développement, concepts et terminologie*. Paris: Organisation internationale de la Francophonie. Agence intergouvernementale de la Francophonie.

Morrow, D., & Rondinelli, D. (2002). Adopting Corporate Environmental Management Systems: Motivations and Results of ISO 14001 and EMAS Certification. *European Management Journal, 20*(2), 159–171.

Mukoro, A. (2005). The Ecology of Recruitment and Seclection of Personnel in the Federal Civil Services of Nigeria. *Journal of Human Ecology, 17*(1), 31–37. https://doi.org/10.1080/09709274.2005.11905754.

Nash, J., & Ehrenfeld, J. R. (2001). Factors that Shape EMS Outcomes in Firms. In: C. Coglianese & J. Nash (Eds.), *Regulating from the Inside. Can Environmental Management Achieve Policy Goals? Resources for the Future* (Chapter 3, pp. 61–81). Washington, DC: RFF Press.

National Environment Commission-Bhutan. (2011). *Environmental Management Tools and Techniques. A Learning material.* Bhutan.

Ndi-Zambo, B. (2018). Towards a Culture of Cooperation and Quality in African Public Administration. https://africainstitute.info. *Africa News.* Retrieved from https://africainstitute.info/culture-cooperation-quality-african-public-administration/.

Nel, J. G., & Kotze, L. J. (2009). Environmental Management: An Introduction. In H. Strydom & N. King (Eds.), *Fuggle and Rabie's 9 Environmental Management in South Africa* (2nd ed., pp. 1–33), Ed.Juta, 2009.

Ndzi Gheyoh, E. (2016). Corporate social responsibility in Cameroon: The Hydro Electricity Sector University of Hertfordshire, United Kingdom. *African Journal of Business Management, 10*(7), 151–161.

PA Consulting Group. (2001). Environmental Management, a Win-Win-Win Proposition. USAID Environmental Audits for Sustainable Tourism Project (EAST), p. 5.

Perschon, J. (2012). *Sustainable Mobility. Recommendations for Future-Proof Transport Strategies.* Policy Paper 36. Stiftung Entwicklung und Frieden (SEF)/Development and Peace Foundation.

Pertusa-Ortega, E. M., López-Gamero, M. D., Pereira-Moliner, J., Tarí, J. J., & Molina-Azorín, J. F. (2017). Antecedents of Environmental Management: The Influence of Organisational Design and Its Mediating Role Between Quality Management and Environmental Management. *Organisation and Environment, 31*(4), 425–443.

Pesqueux, Y. (2011). La responsabilité sociale de l'entreprise (RSE) comme discours ambigu. *Innovations*, 2011/1 n°34, pp. 37 à 55.

Porto D'Oliveira, O. (2010). *Le budget participatif: pourquoi le modèle de Porto Alegre ?* Dans *Le transfert d'un modèle de démocratie participative: Paradiplomatie entre Porto Alegre et Saint-Denis Chapitre 2; pp. 61–89* [en ligne]. Éditions de l'IHEAL, Paris.

Porto D'Oliveira, O. (2016). La diffusion globale du budget participatif: le rôle des « ambassadeurs » de la participation et des institutions internationales. *Participations, 1*(14), 91–120.

Reverdy, T. (2005). Management environnemental et dynamique d'apprentissage. *Revue Française de Gestion, 31*(158), 187–205.

Semal, N. (2005). Le développement durable est-il l'héritier du mouvement proenvironnement?. *Esprit critique*, Hiver 2005, Vol. 07, N° 1.
Shifrin. (2019). *Environmental Science and it History*. https://www.environmentalscience.org/environmental-management-history.
Shnayder, L., Van Rijnsoever, F., & Hekkert, M. P. (2015). Putting Your Money Where Your Mouth Is: Why Sustainability Reporting Based on the Triple Bottom Line Can Be Misleading. *PLoS ONE, 10*(3), e0119036. https://doi.org/10.1371/journal.pone.0119036.
Slaper, T. F., & Hall Tanya, J. (2011). The Triple Bottom Line: What Is It and How Does It Work? *Indiana Business Review (IBR), 86*(1), 4–8.
Sonu, G., Patro Binod, P., & Raj Sonika, G. (2011). Ecological Footprint: A Tool for Measuring Sustainable Development. *International Journal of Environmental Sciences, 2*(1), 140–144.
Subban, M., & Vyas-Doorgapersad, S. (2014). Public Administration Training and Development in Africa: The Case of the Republic of South Africa. *Journal of Public Affairs Education, 20*(4), 499–514.
Wamba Tiona, H. J. (2009). *Pratiques de responsabilité sociale des entreprises industrielles au Cameroun*. Mémoire de DIPET 2, Université de Douala.
Wan Saiful Wan-Jan. (2006). Defining Corporate Social Responsibility. *Journal of Public Affairs, 6*, 176–184. Wiley Interscience.

Part IV

Trust in Africa

12

Small and Medium Enterprises in Transitional East African Economies: The Case of Tanzania

Frank Nyamrunda and Susan Freeman

1 Introduction

The rapid growth of business-to-business (B2B) relationships between firms from transitional economies and other economies has not only stimulated the introduction of new products and services into international markets, but also provided more opportunities for small to medium-sized enterprises (SMEs) to engage in international business (IB) activities over the past two decades (Chit 2017). The recent International Monetary Fund (IMF) (2018) report on the world economic outlook found economic stagnation and relatively slow growth in

F. Nyamrunda (✉)
College of Business, Government and Law, Flinders University, Bedford Park, SA, Australia
e-mail: frank.nyamrunda@flinders.edu.au

S. Freeman
University of South Australia Business School, Adelaide, SA, Australia
e-mail: Susan.Freeman@unisa.edu.au

S. M. Apitsa, E. Milliot (eds.), *Doing Business in Africa*, Palgrave Studies of Internationalization in Emerging Markets,
https://doi.org/10.1007/978-3-030-50739-8_12

developed economies, which was mainly caused by weak productivity performance in various industries. Furthermore, the IMF report states that the economic growth in emerging economies has slowed down as competition and the cost of production are increasing, while consumer demand and incomes decline. This in turn makes it imperative for many firms from developed and emerging economies to find other potential business partners outside their markets in order to reduce costs and to have sustainable businesses (Narooz and Child 2017). Small to medium-sized enterprises (SMEs) in transitional economies have thus become important business partners (Amoako 2019), and an understanding of how business relationships work in transitional economies is vital yet missing from the IB literature.

2 The Growing Importance of Transitional Economies in Africa

Transitional economies can be understood based on their progress of economic and institutional developments, which are characterised by inadequate legal support and widespread corruption that result from their underdeveloped institutional systems (Maksimov et al. 2017). Generally, transitional economies have faced long-term constraints on their economic development due to their contextual backgrounds (Ramaswamy et al. 2017; Amoako 2019).

Transitional economies in Africa are currently transforming their economies from a centrally controlled economy to a market-based economy (Alemayehu and Van Vuuren 2017). Governments in transitional economies, such as Tanzania, have been implementing free trade policies with other countries and creating conducive business environments for local and foreign firms (Hansen et al. 2018). Transitional economies in Africa are still characterised by high levels of market imperfections and generally suffer from lack of supportive market institutions (McKinsey and Company 2017). As a result, SMEs in a transitional economy, such as Tanzania, lack essential necessities, such as easy access to capital, market information, and managerial skills, compared to their counterparts

(Hansen et al. 2018). While these conditions have contributed to considerable business risk and uncertainty in transitional economies, recent economic liberalisation reforms and growth have encouraged SMEs to engage in IB (IMF 2018).

Transitional economies are generally defined based on the following dimensions. First, their *economic growth rate* is significantly higher than those in advanced and emerging economies (IMF 2018). Transitional economies are experiencing rapid growth in business development and social activities (IMF 2018). For example, recently Tanzania maintained an average annual growth rate above 7% (IMF 2018), but problems of poverty and inefficient institutions persist including territorial disputes, famines, and wars (Hansen et al. 2018). Second, *structural adjustments*—many transitional economies follow policies and programmes which are administered by the IMF and the World Bank and other international financial institutions. Structural adjustment policies aim to ensure internal and external changes and reforms including privatisation and market liberalisation (IMF 2018). Therefore, most national policies in transitional economies are predetermined and are based on the interests of the IMF and the World Bank in which transitional economies have diminutive voting rights (Alemayehu and Van Vuuren 2017). However, structural changes are invariably context-specific. Imposing a similar adjustment framework or conditions such as those imposed by the IMF and the World Bank across largely very different economies can create further economic problems (Alemayehu and Van Vuuren 2017). Hence, there is a need to understand a transitional economy characterised by a constantly changing environment (Kohtamäki et al. 2018; Amoako 2019).

Finally, *political influence*—political factors have significant implications for business and economic development in transitional economies (Maksimov et al. 2017). According to Cavusgil et al. (2015), political risk and instability can undermine the business environment by discouraging confidence among business stakeholders. While many transitional economies tend to be characterised by political instability, Tanzania is among a few transitional economies that continues to have political stability, allowing the country to maintain a favourable business environment in the region of East Africa (IMF 2018). This enables the Tanzanian government to focus on facilitating business environment reforms such as infrastructure, stimulating the SME sector, and maintaining a supportive trade policy (McKinsey and Company 2017). The presence of bureaucracy and corruption, however, continues to create difficulties for Tanzania's SME business environment (IMF 2018). Thus, political influence/power/connections are at least equally important in business dealings in transitional economies (Costa et al. 2017).

3 Challenges Facing Transitional Economies in Africa

Compared to their counterparts in developed and emerging economies, business relationships in transitional economies encounter significant challenges given their unstable business environment (Ramaswamy et al. 2017). For example, Freeman et al. (2013) and Leonidou et al. (2017) found that firms in developed and several emerging economies have the ability to obtain critical resources (e.g. managerial and financial resources) from their local markets during the initial stages of their internationalisation. In contrast, firms in transitional economies lack opportunities to obtain managerial and financial resources and support from their local markets due to underdeveloped institutional systems. Prange and Pinho (2017) suggest that the availability of resources contributes to firms' internationalisation by allowing them to develop a competitive advantage that enhances their business relationships. The main assumption of Prange and Pinho's (2017) study is that firms must not only be internally self-sufficient; they have to depend on resources from external environments. This assumption is feasible in a resource environment such as those in developed and emerging economies, where firms are more dependent on external environments that offer available institutional support. However, firms in transitional economies face challenges attaining resources from external institutions. Thus, they are forced to manage uncertainty and mitigate the impact of the external environment in order to develop their performance (Kohtamäki et al. 2018). For example, the lack of direct support and incentives from governmental institutions reinforces the difficulties encountered by firms when relying upon and trusting formal institutions in their business operations (Freeman et al. 2010; Amoako 2019). We now turn to the region of East Africa and the economy of Tanzania.

4 Tanzania as a Research Setting

Tanzania is a unitary republic state in Eastern Africa with a central government and a semi-autonomous government of Zanzibar. Tanzania shares borders with Kenya, Uganda, Rwanda, Burundi, the Democratic Republic of the Congo, Zambia, Malawi, and Mozambique. The president of Tanzania is the head of state and government and is the country's commander-in-chief of the Tanzanian armed forces. The president is elected by a majority vote to serve for a maximum of two five-year terms (Hansen et al. 2018). Compared to other African transitional economies, Tanzania has experienced strong and sustained economic development (IMF 2018). Its economic development has shown promising growth and outlook, with a population of 49 million (IMF 2018). The agriculture, mining, energy, and tourism sectors are the main contributors to Tanzania's growth (McKinsey and Company 2017). The Bank of Tanzania (2017) continues to invest in infrastructure, construction, and the private and public sectors.

SMEs play a prominent role in Tanzania's economic development, yet supporting the sustainable development of Tanzania's SME sector requires major changes in the social and economic structures. Tanzania's reliance on agriculture and its very low levels of irrigation make it singularly vulnerable to global competition (FAO 2019). In Tanzania, the industrial sector consists of manufacturing (53%), processing (43%), and assembling industries (4%) (FAO 2019). The manufacturing sector consists mainly of food processing (24%), textiles and clothing (10%), chemicals (8.5%), and others (FAO 2019). According to the Tanzania Investment Centre (2020), transforming the economy from a predominantly agricultural to a semi-industrialised economy requires a larger and more diversified industrial structure, but it also requires changes in social structures of societies and in transport infrastructure.

By the year 2025, Tanzania aims to reach middle-income status, as documented through its Tanzania's Development Vision 2025, also known as TDV 2025. TDV 2025 was developed in late 1990 and launched in 2000 to guide economic and social development efforts up to the year 2025 (Tanzania Investment Centre 2020). TDV 2025 envisages an economy with a high-quality livelihood including peace, stability, and unity; good governance; a well-educated and learning society; a competitive economy capable of producing sustainable growth and shared benefits; and a diversified semi-industrialised economy with a substantial industrial sector (International Monetary Fund 2018). Industrialisation is listed as a key priority by the current government and it is currently focusing on improving infrastructure, which is a necessary step in promoting long-term growth in the SME sector (Tanzania Investment Centre 2020). Despite these trends, there is virtually no literature examining East Africa's transitional economies, particularly Tanzania, where growth is occurring rapidly. The few existing studies focus on poverty reduction (e.g. Maksimov et al. 2017) and political instability of the continent (e.g. Chit 2017). These studies are general in nature, lacking a focus on the development of firms' business relationships. To understand the context of East Africa, the next section gives a brief overview of how the historical background of one of its more prosperous economies, Tanzania, has affected its contemporary development and trajectory.

5 Tanzania: Historical Background

This section provides a brief historical background on Tanzania, which helps to better understand the Tanzanian SME business environment. Ong and Freeman (2017) suggest that a country's business environment may be affected or be influenced historically by its economic and structural changes over time. Young (1995, p. 24) argues that an "overall colonial legacy casts its shadow over the emergent African state system to a degree unique among the major world regions". This implies that the context of Africa can be neither explored nor understood without understanding its long colonial influence. To illustrate, there are two historical phases that can be identified to describe Tanzania's present-day transformation. The first phase is the *colonial period*, where the country was mainly subject to German and British administrations. The second phase is the *post-independence period.*

5.1 The Colonial Period in Tanzania: German Administration (1886–1916)

During the period 1886–1916 the German government seized control of East African countries and established its territory, which became known as Germany East Africa comprising countries such as Tanzania, Rwanda, and Burundi (Ndulu 1987). In Tanzania, German colonial administrators promoted the Tanzanian national language (Swahili) as the language of education and administration (Hansen et al. 2018). In the German colonial era, the main focus of the economy was on low-value, labour-intensive agricultural goods (Aminzade 2013), a legacy that has continued.

During this period, Germany introduced cash crops of sisal, coffee, and cotton as the major focus of socio-economic development of the nation (Bagachwa 1992). Transportation proved to be an important and necessary development to support cash crop production. The German government invested heavily in infrastructure projects, such as roads and railway lines. The infrastructural systems contributed immensely to the government's internal and external trade balance (Ndulu 2006). The German administration formed clustered settlements where people were forced to live near major infrastructural projects in order to operationalise these investments in terms of the supply of labour (Aminzade 2013). This was a major social and cultural disruption.

Nevertheless, today, Tanzania and Germany still engage in friendly relationships, with Germany being one of the major trading partners of Tanzania (Hansen et al. 2018). Germany dominates business relationships between the two countries in terms of export/import and inward foreign direct investment (FDI). Over the last five decades, Tanzania-Germany bilateral relations have generated more than AUD 3.36 billion (The World Bank 2017). Coffee and cotton are the largest export crops, which together constitute more than 10% of the country's exports per year and these crops generate earning of approximately AUD 200 million per year (The World Bank 2017).

As well as the ties between Germany and Tanzania in the agriculture sector, Tanzania has its renowned tourist attractions, such as wildlife parks (e.g. Serengeti National Park, Old Germany's historical sites, Ngorongoro National Park, and Mount Kilimanjaro), which have supported the development of the country's tourism industry, attracting tens of thousands of tourists and business investors from Germany annually (IMF 2018). In addition, Germany is among Tanzania's major donors in the sectors of health, water, and renewable energy (McKinsey and Company 2017).

5.2 The Colonial Period in Tanzania: British Administration (1916–1961)

Tanzania (known as Tanganyika at the time) was under British administration after World War I, from 1916 to 1961 (Hansen et al. 2018). The British invasion into East Africa during this period coincided with the end of the German colonial era. In this new colonial era, the British government introduced imports of goods from abroad and began structural changes to emphasise the development of capital goods in Tanzania (Bagachwa 1992). Under the British administration, industrial development involved the production of cotton, sisal, tea, and tobacco (Aminzade 2013). In support of industrial development, more infrastructure systems were built or extended and the structure of health care was established (Temu and Due 2000). During the first few decades of the British regime in the region, Tanzania became a net importer of British industrial goods (Temu and Due 2000) and the industrial sector was dominated by large British companies. Consequently, this distorted the development of the local market and undermined the presence of indigenous entrepreneurship in Tanzania (Hansen et al. 2018). Due to insufficient demand for industrial goods, poor infrastructure, and shortage of skilled workers (Aminzade 2013), the industrial sector in Tanzania did not perform well, with many companies performing well below full capacity (Hansen et al. 2018).

The UK remains one of Tanzania's oldest trading partners and both countries are still engaged in bilateral trade relationships, particularly in the mining, agriculture, and manufacturing sectors (The World Bank 2017). The UK accounts for around 40% of market share in FDI flows into Tanzania, followed by the USA and China (The World Bank 2017). British influence can still be seen today in the Tanzanian education and legal systems. For example, the legal system in Tanzania has evolved mainly from the English common law system (Hansen et al. 2018).

5.3 The Post-Colonial Period in Tanzania

In 1961, Tanzania (formerly Tanganyika) gained independence from the British and merged with Zanzibar in 1964 to form the present state, Tanzania (Aminzade 2013). In the early post-independence period, the new Tanzanian government adopted a capitalist market-led economy, which was inherited from the German and British colony regimes and implemented policies towards indigenous socialism to promote self-reliance, public ownership, and the role of the private sector (Ndulu 1987). To implement these policies, many foreign-owned companies then operating in Tanzania were nationalised in order to ensure the expansion of the public sector and to increase state control (Temu and Due 2000). Ensuring a socialist society and economy, the government established settlement schemes (Village Settlement Scheme, VSS) aimed to bring people together to form more densely populated areas in order to utilise the available land in agricultural production and to create a cohesive community (Hansen et al. 2018).

Moreover, the post-colonial period between the 1960s and 1980s marked the beginning of ties between Tanzania and other socialist countries with anti-Western sentiments, such as China and Russia (Aminzade 2013). For example, China was involved in building more than 100 factories and large infrastructure projects in Tanzania (Hansen et al. 2018). Tanzania's trading relationship with China began in the early 1960s. Strong trading ties between Tanzania and China operated between 1961 and 1985 (see Fig. 12.1). This period is marked by reform measures and the restructuring of institutions in Tanzania to align with the concept of

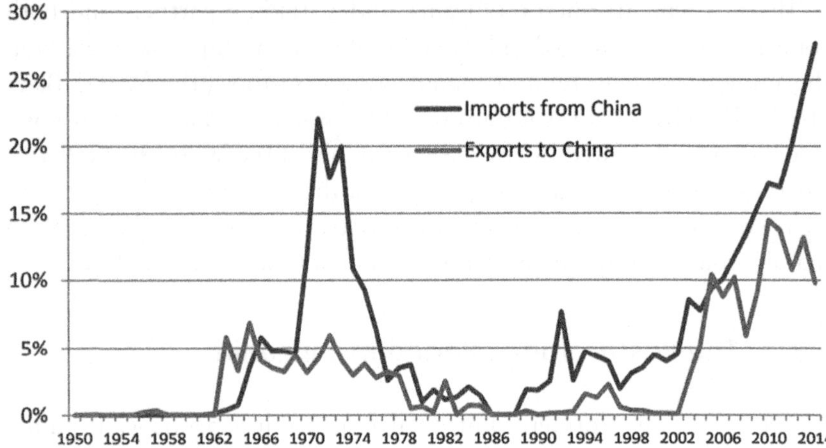

Fig. 12.1 Tanzania-China trade relationships. (Source: IMF 2018)

socialism (Ndulu 1987). China was Tanzania's major trading partner during this period, where Tanzania imported manufacturing goods from China and exported its natural resources (McKinsey and Company 2017). However, in the 1980s, the share of exports to China declined because of a change in the country's socialist economic and political policy and increasing globalisation (Aminzade 2013). In the 2000s, Tanzania began strengthening its trading relationship with China again, and Chinese activities in Tanzania have accelerated ever since (McKinsey and Company 2017).

Since this time period both countries have continued to engage in stronger bilateral relations (McKinsey and Company 2017). However, while the Tanzanian socialist policy was intended to support sustainable economic growth of the country, the government failed to properly implement the necessary reforms (Temu and Due 2000). The decline and final downfall of Tanzania's socialist system was due to a perceived lack of available resources in terms of people and skills to manage and to implement the policies throughout the country (Ndulu 1987). Moreover, some scholars (e.g. Djimeu 2018) argue that the intervention and influence of the IMF and the World Bank contributed to austere and inappropriate economic and structural changes in Tanzania, as discussed below.

6 The Role of the IMF and World Bank in Tanzania in Post-Colonialism

As previously mentioned, in the 1980s and the 1990s Tanzania was characterised by ongoing attempts at economic and political reforms. The reform processes were influenced heavily by the interests of external institutions such as bilateral and multilateral donors, including the IMF and the World Bank (McKinsey and Company 2017). These institutions generally imposed conditions on the implementation of economic and political policies (Djimeu 2018). According to the IMF (2018, p. 7):

> *When a country borrows from the IMF, its government agrees to adjust its economic policies to overcome the problems that led it to seek financial aid from the international community. These loan conditions also serve to ensure that the country will be able to repay the Fund so that the resources can be made available to other members in need.*

The IMF (2018) still argues that Tanzania was and is in an economic crisis due to its inward-looking trade policies including protectionism and subsidies that make its local markets less competitive in terms of IB engagement. The IMF and the World Bank involvement required the Tanzanian government to follow trade liberation policies, particularly an open trading policy, in which the country had to reduce or remove all tariff and non-tariff barriers (Djimeu 2018).

However, one of the arguments against trade liberalisation was based on the costs associated with trade liberalisation for poorer countries such as Tanzania. Trade liberalisation had a significant and crippling negative impact on the fiscal stance of many African countries (Djimeu 2018). In the case of Tanzania, the country has a history of heavy indebtedness including substantial government borrowing from the IMF, the World Bank, and the China Development Bank (which continues to rise). This has put the country under increased financial pressure and it can be argued that it has compromised its economic development and thereby directly and indirectly impacted the growth of the business environment (Cavusgil et al. 2015). Tanzania's total national debt in 2018 stands at approximately USD 19 billion, which is almost 35% of its GDP (The

World Bank 2017). It is important to note that this situation is an outcome of a combination of internal and external factors. From an external perspective, its colonial past with the burden to convert to cash crops, for example, and policies designed to increase the export of manufactured goods into Tanzania from Germany and the UK have all had an impact. This fundamental change, through two prolonged periods of colonialism, has led to low-value commodity production in Tanzania, and continues to make it difficult to build entrepreneurial opportunities for SMEs given their lack of experience in a range of sectors and industries. However, there are signs that this is changing especially in sectors such as agribusiness, construction, information, technology, furniture, retailing, petroleum, and mining (Tanzania Investment Centre 2018).

Today, many transitional economies are still relying on import taxation as their most important source of government fiscal revenue (Hansen et al. 2018). Thus, the removal of tariffs and non-tariffs, as required by the IMF and the World Bank, has negatively impacted their revenue sources (Temu and Due 2000). Moreover, the IMF and the World Bank generally require countries to follow additional conditions, which has further worsened Tanzania's competitive position. These conditions include the following:

- Balancing the national budget by reducing capital spending in order to control the prices of basic needs. However, cutting spending on education, health, and social systems has had a negative impact on the majority of the population as many are heavily dependent on these systems (Aminzade 2013).
- Reduction in government overall spending on economic subsidies in order to increase competitiveness in a market. However, cuts in government social and economic subsidies cause unemployment and poor performance of infant industries (Costa et al. 2017).
- Devaluation of the country currency in order to control the demand for local products in international markets and to control inflation (Djimeu 2018). However, this condition may result in the loss of a local government's power to govern its own currency and economic policy direction (Djimeu 2018).

Resource dependence theory (Gulati and Sytch 2007) posits that the IMF and World Bank conditions have created an increasing dependency of transitional economies on developed and emerging economies. The main criticism of the IMF and the World Bank's financial and monetary conditions placed on poor countries is associated with a lack of credibility. Lack of credibility is caused by the dual role played by these institutions acting as both creditors and monitors (advisors) of economic reforms (Djimeu 2018). Table 12.1 summarises the main historical changes in Tanzania and its impact on SME business development.

Table 12.1 A summary of the historical background of Tanzania and its impact on SME business development

Historical changes in the Tanzanian context	The impact on SME business development in Tanzania
Colonial period	
German administration (1886–1916)	• The German period in Tanzania is marked by the introduction of cash crop agriculture • Focus on developing new infrastructural systems includes roads and railways in order to facilitate transport of raw materials and agricultural products • Introduced labour-intensive production and cash crops such as sisal, coffee, and cottons • Forced Tanzania to produce agricultural goods solely to export to Germany-related markets, thereby lowering the price of agricultural goods
British administration (1916–1961)	• Under British administration, agriculture became increasingly commercialised and industrialised. The British administrators put more emphasis on a few cash crops (cotton, sisal, tea, and tobacco). This made Tanzania reliant upon these agricultural crops and undermined the production of other consumer goods • By exporting selected cash crops and importing extensively manufactured British goods into Tanzania, the British administration undermined the competitiveness of the Tanzanian manufacturing industry, by making it completely reliant upon the British market for its economic development • Improved the infrastructure

(continued)

Table 12.1 (continued)

Historical changes in the Tanzanian context	The impact on SME business development in Tanzania
Post-colonial period	
The role of China (1961–1980)	• After Tanzania gained independence, China became its largest trading partner • Chinese involvement in Tanzania was influenced by socialism, an ideal shared by both countries • Tanzania-China trading dealings were mostly on large-scale infrastructure projects, dominated by state-owned enterprises in the early years after independence • More recently, many Tanzanian SMEs have been participating in export-import business relationships with Chinese firms in diverse industries
The role of IMF and the World Bank from the 1980s	• Provide financing to Tanzania's infrastructure • Imposed structural adjustment policies in Tanzania with the purpose of improving economic development. The IMF and the World Bank policy conditions include trade liberalisation, privatisation, devaluations, and so on • However, the IMF and the World Bank have been subjected to a range of criticisms relating to the imposed conditions and the lack of transparency in poor countries
The current transformation of the economy	• After independence, the Tanzanian government focused on the production of a wide variety of cash crops and consumer goods • Germany and Britain, as former colonial powers, still play a significant role in Tanzania through economic cooperation and business engagement. Both Germany and the UK are the major trading partners in Tanzania • The government encourages the role of the private sector in supporting economic development • Increasing the engagement of SMEs, especially in export and import trade in IB. The Tanzanian government has enhanced the SME sector by introducing the Small and Medium Enterprises Development Policy, launched in 2002, with the aim of improving the competitiveness of Tanzania's SMEs by 2025

Source: Authors' creation

7 Regional Integration

Today, despite its legacy of colonialism, Tanzania is considered one of the most politically stable and peaceful nations, not only in *East Africa*, but also in the *continent* (IMF 2018). The country has a multi-party political system where several political parties are involved in presidential and legislative elections every five years (IMF 2018). However, the political party system is still dominated by the Chama Chama Mapinduzi (CCM), which was the sole operating political party for many years and one of the longest ruling political parties in Africa beginning in 1977 (Hansen et al. 2018). Regarding the culture and customs of Tanzania, the country is characterised by a young population and is one of the most diverse nations in Africa today (McKinsey and Company 2017). Presently, over 45% of the total population of Tanzania is below the age of 20, giving the country a potentially high workforce (IMF 2018). Tanzania has a high diversity of religious and spiritual beliefs with low levels of tension between religious groups and is the most politically stable nation compared to other nations in Africa (IMF 2018). The dominant religious beliefs consist of Christianity 40%, Islam 30%, and various indigenous beliefs (25%) (The World Bank 2017). Tanzania is considered a collectivistic society: arguably, this is contributed by its history with socialism (Djimeu 2018). Tanzanians value their families, extended families, and relationships to a great extent (Temu and Due 2000). In terms of organisational structure, Tanzania is considered hierarchical. This indicates that people accept a hierarchical order/system and the power distance is high (Hofstede 2017). In this case, a top-down management style is preferred, suggesting a greater need to understand the implications of culture in this context.

From a business perspective, Tanzania has slowly moved away from its socialist view (Deloitte 2017). The country is rapidly integrating itself into the global economy as evidenced by the growing number of trading partners including, Brazil, Russia, India, China, South Africa (BRICs), the European Union, the USA, and other African countries (Deloitte 2017). Tanzania is part of several regional economic communities in Africa including the East African Community (EAC), the South Africa

Development Community (SADC), the Tripartite Free Trade Area (TFTA), and other blocs, where each regional bloc provides different opportunities for Tanzanian firms and their business partners as highlighted below.

7.1 East African Community (EAC)

The East African Community (EAC) aims to facilitate trade among its members (i.e. Tanzania, Kenya, Uganda, Burundi, Rwanda, South Sudan) by implementing several integration agendas, such as rules of origin, internal tariff elimination, the common market, and the establishment of the custom union (EAC 2017). According to the IMF (2018), the EAC is the world's fastest-growing regional economic bloc. Tanzania is the largest state in terms of size and population and it is the fastest-growing economy in this community, where the country's GDP grew by 7% in 2016 and is projected to continue to grow in the future (IMF 2018). Tanzania has largely benefited from being a major producer and consumer in the region. Political and economic reforms (e.g. issues of corruption and transparency) initiated by the new president Dr. John Pombe Magufuli have led to greater inward FDI and improved economic competitiveness in comparison to other EAC members. For example, Tanzania has become a major destination for China into Africa, where the current major investment of China in Tanzania is the development of a special economic zone including the construction of the AUD 15 billion (USD 11 billion) new port, which will become one of the largest ports in Africa (The World Bank 2017). In 2016, Tanzania also received an AUD 10.3 billion (USD 7.6 billion) loan from China to construct a railway line that will connect the country to its neighbouring countries (The World Bank 2017). Additionally, Tanzania's recent discovery of 55.1 trillion cubic feet of natural gas has also attracted foreign investors, such as an AUD 1.6 billion (USD 1.2 billion) loan in a natural gas pipeline from China (Tanzania Investment Centre 2018). However, an increased reliance on foreign loans, despite Tanzania's economic growth, has led to many questions and doubts regarding the nature of the loans, and the ability of Tanzania to repay those debts, particularly to China. With this rising external debit has a negative economic impact and more particularly, a direct impact on budget projections, the Tanzanian government's working budget for 2018/2019 has reduced to approximately AUD 19 billion (USD 14 billion) (The World Bank 2017). Djimeu (2018) argues that repaying the debts will significantly increase the burden on the government and will threaten local industries. However, having a relatively stable political environment in this region, Tanzania has the potential to attract more foreign business partnerships compared to other EAC states.

7.2 Southern African Development Community (SADC)

The Southern African Development Community (SADC) is a regional economic community with 15 member states (SADC 2017). The main objective of the SADC is to facilitate and promote the flow of trade and investment among the member states by encouraging economic development and ensuring peace and political stability in the region. The SADC has managed to increase the competitiveness of the region by minimising trade barriers and lowering other costs and risks of doing business in its member states (SADC 2017). Besides its large size of more than 200 million consumers (IMF 2018), the rising middle class and its purchasing power makes this region a prime spot for attracting IB activities (IMF 2018). Intra-regional trade among countries in the eastern African and SADC regions has fostered a stronger participation by SMEs in global markets according to the IMF.

7.3 Tripartite Free Trade Area (TFTA)

The Tripartite Free Trade Area (TFTA) comprises 26 countries in Africa that are members of the East African Community (EAC), the South Africa Development Community (SADC), and the Common Market for Eastern and Southern Africa (COMESA). The objective of the TFTA is to bring together these three major regional economic communities in Africa in order to address the conflict of interests and misunderstandings that are posed by the overlapping of trade blocs (SADC 2017). The TFTA members represent 51% of Africa's GDP, with a combined population of 632 million (SADC 2017). The TFTA has initiated the need for major trade policy reforms among the member countries by promoting tariff liberation and facilitating trade through physical and institutional infrastructures. Tanzania benefits from many opportunities offered by the TFTA arrangements and access to the large, regional domestic market has increased Tanzania's total trade and investment to other TFTA members (SADC 2017).

Generally, the involvement of Tanzania in several regional integrations and its acceleration in its social, political, and economic reforms have improved the business environment and enhanced the country's attractiveness in terms of FDI, business collaborations, and other ventures (McKinsey and Company 2017). The country has benefited from these arrangements in terms of increased openness of trade, removed tariffs and non-tariffs barriers, and strengthened regulatory and legal systems (IMF 2018). Although these regional economic communities are confronted with a number of challenges in the implementation of their agenda, these first steps are enabling SMEs in transitional African economies of East Africa to emerge and become more competitive.

8 Transitional Economies in Africa: The Growing Influence of China and India

As discussed earlier, many transitional economies in Africa are experiencing sustainable growth in the global economy, as these countries are moving to diversify their economies through more industrialisation and manufacturing activities (Alemayehu and Van Vuuren 2017). As the second-largest continent and with its population of 1.2 billion, twice the size of Latin America and similar to the populations of India and China, Africa is on a rapid growth trajectory economically, politically, and in a business context (IMF 2018). The McKinsey Report (2017) indicates that business is booming in Africa, especially in the telecommunications, banking, retail, and construction sectors. There is a transformation of economic relationships in Africa at present, as firms adopt new technological investments in their business relationships and take on an international perspective (Alemayehu and Van Vuuren 2017). Transitional economies are generally characterised by the process of diversifying their source of growth as they traditionally relied on one sector, industry, or commodity that was vulnerable to climate change (Maksimov et al. 2017) given their previous reliance on agricultural commodities (Matanda and Freeman 2009). The diversification of transitional economies in Africa, especially East Africa, in terms of resources, economic potential, and improving macroeconomic conditions and political stability is increasing the attractiveness of the African continent and this particular region of East Africa and is the key reason behind this growth surge (Alemayehu and Van Vuuren 2017).

For example, China remains Africa's largest trading partner, with business relationships between China and Africa growing rapidly over the last two decades (McKinsey and Company 2017), in evidence in East Africa, and illustrated in the case of Tanzania. According to the McKinsey Report (2017), African-Chinese trade has been growing at approximately 20% per year over the past decade. The USA has also strengthened business relationships with Africa through different initiatives such as the Doing Business in Africa Campaign, Power Africa, and Trade Africa, while US trade and investment in Africa has tripled over the past decade (McKinsey and Company 2017). According to the Australian Department of Foreign Affairs and Trade (2017), there is an increase in Australian investment in Africa with more than 170 Australian Stock Exchange-listed firms operating in African transitional economies. These ongoing business dealings highlight the importance of understanding the nature of SMEs and evaluating the existing problems and barriers they are facing from the perspective of a transitional economy. Africa's transitional economies, such as Tanzania, are still characterised as having lower per capita incomes, but have shown recent and sustained improvements generally in their political and economic environment (McKinsey and Company 2017). Examining SME IB relationships under an inadequate or rapidly changing business environment, typical for a transitional economy such as

Tanzania, provides an opportunity for a deeper understanding of the importance of context.

9 Tanzania's Aid Dependence and the Challenge of Self-Reliance

Compared to many African economies, illustrated by East Africa as a region, Tanzania has been experiencing relative stability in its political reforms since it adopted the multiparty system in 1992 (The Economist 2019). However, the country has been reliant on foreign aid, loans, and other development grants from international organisations and other donor countries since independence (The Economist 2019). Like a number of other African countries, this allows international organisations and donor countries to have significant control over the domestic economic and political developments (Sundberg 2019). Tanzania is the second highest recipient of aid in sub-Saharan Africa, especially from the World Bank, USA, the AFDB, the UK, and the EU (Sundberg 2019). In 2019, approximately 33% of government spending was financed by foreign aid. Does foreign aid promote economic development and improve the SME sector? Some argue that foreign aid has no effect on economic growth in African countries, as donor countries often put pressure on developing economies into adopting the social, political, or economic policies against their wishes (Hansen et al. 2018). This can make it impossible for developing economies, such as Tanzania, to achieve sustainable development. In recent years, there is an uncertainty regarding relations between donors and the Tanzanian government.

The government is under increasing pressure from its key donors over its domestic policies (Reuters 2018). Denmark, Tanzania's second biggest donor, withheld USD 10 million worth of aid money due to concerns over gay rights (Reuters 2018). The European Union and the World Bank also announced the suspension of aid to Tanzania due to human right concerns (The Financial Times 2020). However, the Tanzanian government argues that aid and loans undermine the sovereignty of the country on social and economic development (The Economist 2019). The

Tanzanian government states that it will not succumb to pressure from donors' countries when it comes to defending the country's independence and sovereignty. The current Tanzanian government is aiming to move away from aid dependency and to focus on trade and investment. Foreign grants, aids, and loans are in decline, from an average of 45% in 2003/2004, 26.3% in 2010/2011 to 8.3% in 2017/2018 (Tanzania Investment Centre 2020). Tanzania's government has focused increasingly on industrialisation and economic transformation that support its vision, including some major projects, such as construction of a new central railway line to standard gauge, ports, new international airports, and construction of a rapid bus system (The Economist 2019). The majority of these major infrastructure projects are now funded by the Tanzanian government, rather than aid (Ministry of Finance and Planning 2020). Tanzania's journey to self-reliance is becoming a model for other economies in East Africa, and in sub-Sahara Africa at large (Sundberg 2019).

10 SMEs in the Transitional Economy Context

Moving from the macro- to the microeconomic level of analysis, the ability to develop and maintain business relationships has become a competitive requirement for the survival of many SMEs in IB, particularly for those SMEs from transitional economies (Costa et al. 2017). One of the main challenges facing many transitional economies such as Tanzania is the impact of an extremely high level of population growth (IMF 2018). Tanzania's population grew from 10 million in 1960 to 49 million in 2018, and the country's population is likely to be around 60 million in 2020, with a current population growth rate of 3% annually (see Fig. 12.2). Rapid population growth in Tanzania directly affects the SME sector, with lack of reliable policy initiatives from the government, capital support to SMEs, and rising unskilled labour leading to increasing unemployment (Djimeu 2018).

Costa, Soares, and Sousa (2017) argue that the extant literature views SMEs solely through the lens of a destination country perspective, but

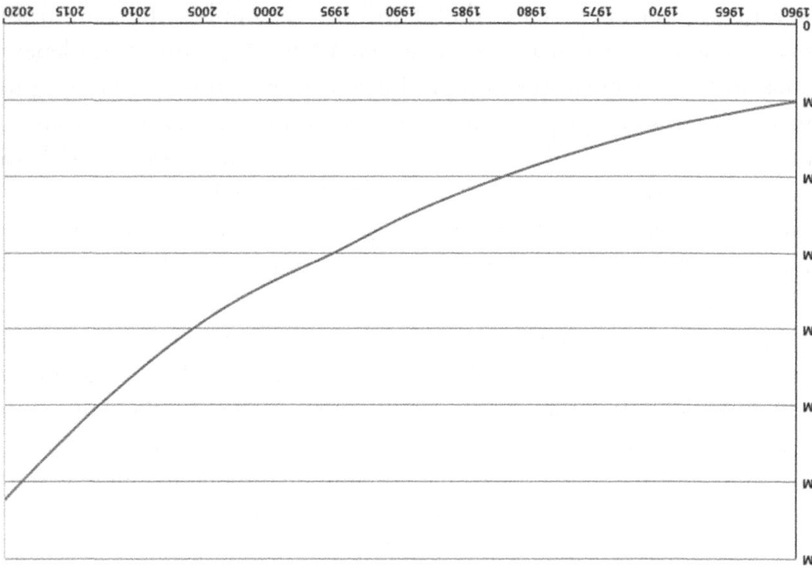

Fig. 12.2 Tanzanian population growth: 1960–2019. (Source: AFDB Socio Economic Database 2018)

rarely from an origin country perspective. In other words, most of the studies on the internationalisation of SMEs have been between emerging and advanced economies (Maksimov et al. 2017). For example, Bangara et al. (2012), Yamakawa et al. (2008), and Liu and Vrontis (2017) examine the behaviour of SMEs during internationalisation from emerging economies into advanced economies. On other hand, Child et al. (2017) investigate the expansion of advanced economy SMEs into emerging economies. Maksimov et al. (2017) suggest that there is scarce literature on the nature of SMEs in transitional economies, an important global trading group. The role of SMEs in transitional economies is considered important due to the increasing internationalisation of these firms, which contribute increasingly to world economic growth and competitiveness (Leonidou et al. 2017), and how they deal with their counterparts from advanced and emerging economies.

Definitions and the significance of SMEs vary across contexts and are generally based on the total number of employees and/or firm profitability (Costa et al. 2017). The World Bank defines SMEs as firms with fewer

Table 12.2 Definition of SMEs in Tanzania

Category	Employees	Characteristics
Micro-sized firms	1 to 4	• One or two family members are actively involved in business activities and rely on individual initiatives and knowledge about business • Fall under the informal sector—most of these firms are not formally registered with the government authorities • Lacking business relationships with other firms
Small firms	5 to 49	• The majority of business controls lie within a family • Mostly have formalised processes and procedures in their business dealings • Are more likely focused on increasing their market presence in domestic markets and international markets • Specialisation in niche markets
Medium firms	50 to 99	• Owners and experts are in key roles and they are making all decisions about business dealings • Most are formally registered in the government systems • Focus on international markets, with diverse business partners

Source: MIT (2014)

than 250 persons employed. This definition allows consistency and is comparable to the meaning of SMEs in most transitional economies. In the case of Tanzania, SMEs generally range between micro, small, and medium enterprises (refer to Table 12.2), where micro-sized firms employ up to 4 employees, small firms have at most 49 employees, and medium-sized firms consist of up to 99 employees (MIT 2014).

The introduction of the Small and Medium Enterprises Development Policy (2002–2025) by the Tanzanian government is a key landmark for the SME development process and their involvement in IB. This trade policy aims to stimulate development and growth of the SME sector by promoting open markets, enhanced trade liberalisation, and competitiveness (Berger et al. 2017). The SME Development Policy (2002–2025) is consistent with the TDV 2025 vision and estimates that the number of formally registered SMEs keeps increasing and it suggests that the SME sector will continue to be a major contributor towards Tanzania becoming a middle-income country by 2025. The SME Development Policy indicates that the number of SMEs is expected to grow from 3 million to 10 million by 2025. Efforts have been made by the Tanzanian government in supporting the SME sector by implementing market-based strategic plans such as the encouragement of subcontracting arrangements between foreign firms and local SMEs; this provides useful linkages for SMEs (Tanzania Investment Centre 2020). In their Small and Medium Enterprises Development Policy, the Tanzanian government states that by 2025:

> *Tanzania should have created a strong, diversified, resilient and competitive economy, which can effectively cope with the challenges of development and, which can also easily and confidently adapt to the changing market and technological conditions in the regional and global economy.* (MIT 2002, p. 1)

To implement the Small and Medium Enterprises Development Policy for 2002–2025, the Tanzanian government is relying on the following strategies:

1. Rural Development Strategy—aims to bring sustainable development for SMEs in the rural areas in Tanzania.
2. Agricultural Sector Development Strategy—aims to provide linkages between SMEs and their stakeholders.
3. Business Environment Strengthening for Tanzania (BEST) Programme—aims to improve the SME business environment.
4. Micro-Finance Policy and Poverty Alleviation Strategies—aims to provide financial services, credit, and other financial support to SMEs.

By pursuing policy reforms and adhering to them, transitional economies have created more opportunities for firms, particularly SMEs, by facilitating SMEs' access to different IB activities including international investment, trade, and engaging in business networks and partnerships (Maksimov et al. 2017). Engaging in a global market is of particular importance for SMEs from transitional economies (Maksimov et al. 2017) due to the increasingly competitive environment, environmental uncertainty, and resource constraints in their local markets (Berger et al. 2017). Many transitional economies, such as Tanzania, are still moving towards a free market system, emphasising more entrepreneurial activities, and SMEs play an important role during this process of social, political, and economic transformation. Understanding how such SMEs create and develop their business relationships with their counterparts in such a challenging and risky environment is of critical importance. Moreover, understanding how these firms take advantage of new growth opportunities in a transitional economy remains unexplored (Maksimov et al. 2017; Matanda and Freeman 2009).

11 Characteristics of SMEs in a Transitional Economy

SMEs generally contribute more than 90% to job creation and business economic outputs, and stimulate the presence of transitional economies in the IB arena (Maksimov et al. 2017). As such, SME IB relationships emerge as a key instrument in economic growth in transitional economies (Costa et al. 2017). SMEs in transitional economies are generally smaller in terms of size, market, and financial capability compared to their counterparts in other economies (Chit 2017). These firms are typically family-owned, where family members are actively involved in the day-to-day operation of a firm, and the owners and managers are usually committed and involved in the firm's internationalisation process (Leonidou et al. 2017). Thus, the personalities of the founders/owners can determine the success or failure of these firms in their business relationships. SMEs in a transitional economy operate in a relatively high-risk and unstable environment and this has a pivotal impact on their competitiveness in IB. Due to the pressure of the market, many SMEs in transitional economies consider being involved with trusted business partners as a way of minimising the challenge of the domestic market (Child et al. 2017; Mainela 2007). According to Maksimov et al. (2017), firms from transitional economies are regarded as latecomers in global business as they lack the international experience and knowledge of other local markets. Thus, engaging with reliable business partners from other economies demonstrates how these firms compensate for their lack of financial and managerial capabilities (Child et al. 2017). Previous studies often overlook the challenges that affect the business decisions of SMEs in transitional economies. Tanzania still faces several challenges in improving its business environment and the SME sector; the progress of the Tanzanian SME sector is still not convincing and remains tenuous, mostly characterised by uncertainty, where SMEs are often left behind the current global economic growth trajectory (The World Bank 2017). The financial and regulatory challenges faced by SMEs in starting business and taking their business globally have a negative impact on the Tanzanian SME sector, especially the lack of transparency among regulatory agencies on what is involved in the implementation of regulations on SMEs (The World Bank 2017).

12 Conclusion

This study has provided a comprehensive understanding of the transitional economy context from a broader macro perspective, taking a regional, East African, and then an illustrative economy perspective, Tanzania. Due to extensive research, there is a good understanding of SMEs in advanced and emerging economies. However, research on SMEs in transitional economies, especially those in Africa, an important and significant continent for its expected growth, remains inadequate (Maksimov et al. 2017). We have limited knowledge regarding transitional economies, such as Tanzania, and their SME development; we need to do more exploratory research to get a better understanding of this context. Since the inception of transitional processes towards an open market and the development of the SME sector, transitional economies, such as Tanzania, have attracted enormous investment and establishment of business relationships. Due to this rapid growth in transitional economies globally, new consumption and domestic demand patterns continue to demonstrate noticeable increases (Chit 2017). The emerging middle class has contributed towards this economic transformation and growing demand, and is expressing its support for business growth (Cavusgil et al. 2015; McKinsey and Company 2017). It is less clear, however, to what extent IB relationships are sustained in transitional economies. Thus, examining the conditions underlying the existence of business relationships in transitional economies is important. The challenging business environment at home, a competitive market due to its size, and other social, political, and economic challenges suggest that SMEs in a transitional economy need to possess unique competencies for implementation in foreign markets (Chit 2017). Their unique competencies, such as the adaptability and speed of response to changing business environments (Alemayehu and Van Vuuren 2017), allow these firms to create value to business relationship building. Therefore, the extent of diversity of SMEs in transitional economies provides a valid context by which to understand the phenomenon under study (Costa et al. 2017). Moreover, the lack of proper institutional systems continues to create a challenging environment for SMEs to develop and maintain their business relationships. This provides an ideal context for examining the nature of SME IB relationships, while allowing for regional and individual economy heterogeneity, typical of Africa.

References

AFDB Socio Economic Database. (2018). United Republic of Tanzania. Retrieved from https://dataportal.opendataforafrica.org/apps/atlas/United-Republic-of-Tanzania.

Alemayehu, B., & Van Vuuren, V. (2017). Munificence Contingent Small Business Growth Model (Special Emphasis to African SMEs' Context). *Journal of Small Business and Entrepreneurship, 29*(4), 251–269.

Aminzade, R. (2013). The Dialectic of Nation Building in Postcolonial Tanzania. *Sociological Quarterly, 54*(3), 335–366.

Amoako, I. (2019). *Trust, Institutions and Managing Entrepreneurial Relationships in Africa An SME Perspective*. Hampshire: Palgrave Macmillan.

Bagachwa, M. (1992). Choice of Technology in Small and Large Firms: Grain Milling in Tanzania. *World Development, 20*(1), 97–107.

Bangara, A., Freeman, S., & Schroder, W. (2012). Legitimacy and Accelerated Internationalisation: An Indian Perspective. *Journal of World Business, 47*(4), 623–634.

Bank of Tanzania. (2017). Annual Report. Retrieved from https://www.bot.go.tz/.

Berger, R., Herstein, R., Silbiger, A., & Barnes, B. (2017). Developing International Business Relationships in a Russian Context. *Management International Review, 57*(3), 441–471.

Cavusgil, S., Knight, G., Riesenberger, J., Rammal, H., & Rose, E. (2015). *International Business: The New Realities*. Melbourne, VIC: Pearson Australia.

Child, J., Hsieh, L., Elbanna, S., Karmowska, J., Marinova, S., & Puthusserry, P. (2017). SME International Business Models: The Role of Context and Experience. *Journal of World Business, 52*(5), 664–679.

Chit, M. (2017). Political Openness and the Growth of Small and Medium Enterprises: Empirical Evidence from Transition Economies. *Empirical Economics, 55*(2), 781–804.

Costa, E., Soares, A., & Sousa, J. (2017). Institutional Networks for Supporting the Internationalisation of SMEs: The Case of Industrial Business Associations. *Journal of Business and Industrial Marketing, 32*(8), 1182–1202.

Deloitte. (2017). Tanzania Economic Outlook: Joining the Dots, Deloitte. Retrieved November 20, 2017, from www2.deloitte.com/content/dam/Deloitte/tz/Documents/tax/tz-budget-economicoutook-2017.pdf.

Department of Foreign Affairs and Trade (DFAT). (2017). Budget *2017–2018: Foreign Affairs and Trade Portfolio*. Retrieved January 12, 2018, from https://dfat.gov.au/about-us/corporate/portfolio-budget-statements/Documents/2017-18-foreign-affairs-and-trade-pbs.pdf.

Djimeu, E. (2018). The Impact of the Heavily Indebted Poor Countries Initiative on Growth and Investment in Africa. *World Development, 104*, 108–127.

EAC. (2017). *The EAC Industrial Competitiveness Report*. The East African Community, Arusha, Tanzania.

FAO. (2019). The United Republic of Tanzania Resilience Strategy 2019–2022. Rome. p. 32

Freeman, S., Hutchings, K., Lazaris, M., & Syngier, S. (2010). A Model of Rapid Knowledge Development: The Smaller Born-Global Firm. *International Business Review, 19*(1), 70–84.

Freeman, S., Deligonul, S., & Cavusgil, T. (2013). Strategic Re-structuring by Born-Globals Using Outward and Inward-Oriented Activity. *International Marketing Review, 3*(2), 156–182.

Gulati, R., & Sytch, M. (2007). Dependence Asymmetry and Joint Dependence in Interorganizational Relationships: Effects of Embeddedness on a Manufacturer's Performance in Procurement Relationships. *Administrative Science Quarterly, 52*(1), 32–69.

Hansen, U., Nygaard, I., Romijn, H., Wieczorek, A., Kamp, L., & Klerkx, L. (2018). Sustainability Transitions in Developing Countries: Stocktaking, New Contributions and a Research Agenda. *Environmental Science and Policy, 84*, 198–203.

Hofstede, G. (2017). *Cultural Tools Country Comparison*. Retrieved December 25, 2017, from https://www.hofstede-insights.com/product/compare-countries/.

International Monetary Fund. (2018). *Republic of Tanzania: Seventh Review under the Policy Support Instrument-Report*. Washington, DC: International Monetary Fund.

Kohtamäki, M., Rabetino, R., & Möller, K. (2018). Alliance Capabilities: A Systematic Review and Future Research Directions. *Industrial Marketing Management, 68*(1), 188–201.

Leonidou, L., Aykol, B., Fotiadis, T., Christodoulides, P., & Zeriti, A. (2017). Betrayal in International Buyer-Seller Relationships: Its Drivers and Performance Implications. *Journal of World Business, 52*(1), 28–44.

Liu, Y., & Vrontis, D. (2017). Emerging-Market Firms Venturing into Advanced Economies: The Role of Context. *Thunderbird International Business Review, 59*(3), 255–261.

Mainela, T. (2007). Types and Functions of Social Relationships in the Organizing of an International Joint Venture. *Industrial Marketing Management, 36*(1), 87–98.

Maksimov, V., Wang, S., & Luo, Y. (2017). Reducing Poverty in the Least Developed Countries: The Role of Small and Medium Enterprises. *Journal of World Business, 52*(2), 244–257.

Matanda, M., & Freeman, S. (2009). Effect of Perceived Environmental Uncertainty on Exporter–Importer Inter-Organisational Relationships and Export Performance Improvement. *International Business Review, 18*(1), 89–107.

McKinsey and Company. (2017). Dance of the Lions and Dragons: How Are Africa and China Engaging, and How Will the Partnership Evolve? *New African, 575*, 27.

Ministry of Finance and Planning. (2020). Revised Medium Term Strategic Plan 2017/18 - 2021/22. *Tanzania's national development agenda*. United Republic of Tanzania. Retrieved from https://www.mof.go.tz/docs/REVISED%20STRATEGIC%20PLAN.pdf.

Ministry of Industry and Trade (MIT). (2002). *Small and Medium Enterprises Development Policy 2002–2025. The Ministry of Industry and Trade of the United Republic of Tanzania.*

Ministry of Industry and Trade-MIT. (2014). *Integrated Industrial Development Strategy 2025*. The Ministry of Industry and Trade of the United Republic of Tanzania.

Narooz, R., & Child, J. (2017). Networking Responses to Different Levels of Institutional Void: A Comparison of Internationalizing SMEs in Egypt and the UK. *International Business Review, 26*(4), 683–696.

Ndulu, B. (1987). *Stabilisation and Adjustment Policies and Programmes*. Helsinki: World Institute for Development Economics Research.

Ndulu, B. (2006). Infrastructure, Regional Integration and Growth in Sub-Saharan Africa: Dealing with the Disadvantages of Geography and Sovereign Fragmentation. *Journal of African Economies, 15*(2), 218–242.

Ong, X., & Freeman, S. (2017). Understanding the Chinese in Prato's Industrial District: Benefits to Local Entrepreneurs. In S. Guercini et al. (Eds.), *Native and Immigrant Entrepreneurship. Lessons for Local Liabilities in Globalization from the Prato Case Study* (pp. 209–217). Cham: Springer International Publishing. Chap. 11.

Prange, C., & Pinho, J. (2017). How Personal and Organizational Drivers Impact on SME International Performance: The Mediating Role of Organizational Innovation. *International Business Review, 26*(6), 1114–1123.

Ramaswamy, K., Purkayastha, S., & Petitt, B. (2017). How Do Institutional Transitions Impact the Efficacy of Related and Unrelated Diversification Strategies Used by Business Groups? *Journal of Business Research Vol., 72*, 1–13.

Reuters. (2018). Under Pressure from Western Donors, Tanzanian Leader Prefers Chinese Aid. Retrieved from https://www.reuters.com/article/us-tanzania-china-aid/under-pressure-from-western-donors-tanzanian-leader-prefers-chinese-aid-idUSKCN1NW1SB.

Southern African Development Community-SADC. (2017). Regional Vulnerability Assessment and Analysis Synthesis Report. *Southern African Development Community*.

Sundberg, M. (2019). Donors Dealing with 'Aid Effectiveness' Inconsistencies: National Staff in Foreign Aid Agencies in Tanzania. *Journal of Eastern African Studies, 13*(3), 445–464.

Tanzania Investment Centre. (2018). *Tanzania's Investment Promotion Agency Call for Chinese Investors*. Retrieved April 20, 2018, from http://www.tic.co.tz/.

Tanzania Investment Centre. (2020). Tanzania Development Plan, Vision and Investment Priorities to Achieve Middle Income Status by 2025. Retrieved

January 10, 2020, from https://www.mcci.org/media/154357/tanzania-developemnt-plan-booklet.pdf.

Temu, A., & Due, J. (2000). The Business Environment in Tanzania After Socialism: Challenges of Reforming Banks, Parastatals, Taxation and the Civil Service. *The Journal of Modern African Studies, 38*(4), 683–712.

The Economist. (2019). John Magufuli's Follies: Tanzania's President Loves Mega-Projects. Careful Planning, Less So. Retrieved from https://www.economist.com/middle-east-and-africa/2019/06/08/tanzanias-president-loves-mega-projects-careful-planning-less-so.

The Financial Times. (2020). World Bank Delays Vote on $500m Tanzania Loan after Public Pressure. Retrieved from https://www.ft.com/content/f20cab8a-41c0-11ea-a047-eae9bd51ceba.

The World Bank. (2017). Improving Access to Finance for SMEs in Tanzania: Learning from Malaysia's Experience. Retrieved from http://blogs.worldbank.org/eastasiapacific.

Yamakawa, Y., Peng, M. W., & Deeds, D. L. (2008). What drives new ventures to internationalize from emerging to developed economies?. *Entrepreneurship Theory and Practice, 32*(1), 59–82.

Young, C. (1995). The Heritage of Colonialism, Harbeson, J. W. and Rothchild, D. (eds.), *Africa in World Politics: Post-War Challenges*. Westview Press, Boulder, San Francisco and Oxford.

13

The Evolution of Relational Governance Mechanisms in International Joint Ventures (IJVs): Trust and Communication in IJVs in Morocco

Dora Triki and Btissam Moncef

1 Introduction

In the past 20 years, globalisation has fostered the development of emerging markets. More and more businesses are attracted to these markets, seeing them as a promising investment in view of their rapid economic growth and liberalised investment policies (Wang et al. 2017; Kwok et al. 2019). When expanding in emerging and developing markets, firms often choose to set-up international joint ventures (IJVs) with local partners (Meschi and Riccio 2008; Triki and Mayrhofer 2016; Wang et al.

D. Triki (✉)
ESCE International Business School, INSEEC U Research Center, Paris, France
e-mail: dora.triki@esce.fr

B. Moncef
ISC Paris, Paris, France
e-mail: bmoncef@iscparis.com

S. M. Apitsa, E. Milliot (eds.), *Doing Business in Africa*, Palgrave Studies of Internationalization in Emerging Markets,
https://doi.org/10.1007/978-3-030-50739-8_13

2017). In such context, IJVs are generally regarded as a collaborative strategy to confront the liability of foreignness encountered in an unfamiliar, unstable and challenging environment. IJVs are "organisational arrangements where two or more independent organisations establish and maintain a separate legal organisational entity to collaborate for mutual strategic interests under an incomplete contract, wherein at least one of the entities (i.e., parent firms or venture) is located in another country" (Nippa and Reuer 2019, p. 566). IJVs thus offer their partners a number of advantages but remain an unstable organisational structure with a high rate of failure, particularly due to governance problems (Nemeth and Nippa 2013; Cheriet and Dikmen 2014; Ali and Larimo 2016). Consequently, the governance of IJVs is a major issue for partners (Inkpen and Curall 2004; Lin and Wang 2008). It is presented as a determining factor, which can influence IJVs' outcome in terms of performance (Lin and Wang 2008; Cheriet and Dikmen 2014). In the majority of studies on alliances and IJVs, two modes of governance have been observed: on the one hand, relational governance and, on the other, formal governance (Poppo and Zenger 2002; Hoetker and Mellewigt 2009). An analysis of the literature shows that available studies concentrate on the complementarity or the substitution of relational governance and formal governance within interfirm relations, without actually focusing on one or the other (Poppo and Zenger 2002; Zhou and Xu 2012; Cheriet and Dikmen 2014). In addition, it is worth noting that studies on governance traditionally rely on formal governance mechanisms (Dong et al. 2008; Hoetker and Mellewigt 2009). Only recently has research begun to take an interest in the role played by relational governance mechanisms (Dong et al. 2008). In this regard, it is important to note that research into the impact of relational governance on IJVs' performance has often been limited to the study of trust (Boersma et al. 2003; Ertug et al. 2013). As a result, several authors have confirmed that relational governance in IJVs deserves further investigation by researchers (Inkpen and Curall 2004; Nemeth and Nippa 2013). Indeed, the adverse impact of the lack of relational governance mechanisms is likely to worsen in the context of an IJV set-up between firms from the developed and emerging markets, due to the differences between the organisational cultures of the parent firms (e.g. Kwok et al. 2019). Furthermore, in the context of emerging economies, where formal institutions are not fully developed, contracts are "ineffective" in reducing opportunism, and relational governance intercedes as a proxy for legal institutions in ensuring the contract is respected (Zhou and Xu 2012).

This research attempts to fill this gap. The objective of this chapter is to determine how relational governance operates in IJVs over time. Indeed, despite the growing importance of relational governance mechanisms for the performance of IJVs, there is little research on the impact of elements such as trust and communication on the success of IJVs in the context of an emerging market. These mechanisms are considered key factors that reduce opportunism in IJVs and thus drive performance in the emerging markets.

To meet this objective, we draw on three case studies of IJVs based in Morocco and created with one or more foreign partners. Morocco was the fourth largest FDI (foreign direct investment) recipient in Africa in 2018 (Unctad 2019). The country has for several years focused efforts on liberalising the economy and implementing structural reforms in order to attract foreign direct investments (FDIs). In addition, the country benefits from relatively stable economic performance and a diversified economy (Gomez-Miranda et al. 2015; Unctad 2019). These advantages have enabled Morocco to attract multinational enterprises (MNEs) by the setting up of subsidiaries and IJVs particularly (World Bank 2017). The joint ventures selected in our study operate in dynamic sectors, namely, aeronautics and mining.

We will first present the theoretical foundations on relational governance in IJVs and the role of trust and communication for the performance of the IJV. Then, we explain the methodology. Finally, the main findings of the empirical study are analysed and discussed.

2 Theoretical Foundations: Relational Governance in IJVs

Governance is a crucial element in an IJV, providing parents with a means to ensure their organisation conforms to their interests and their objectives. The literature on IJVs identifies two types of governance: formal governance on one hand, and relational governance on the other (Hoetker and Mellewigt 2009; Cheriet and Dikmen 2014).

Formal governance refers to the use of formal mechanisms, or a set of "standards", "codified rules" or "procedures", which enable parents to pursue mutually compatible objectives (Schaan and Beamish 1988; Hoetker and Mellewigt 2009). It helps in "clarifying the roles and responsibilities of each party and specifying monitoring procedures and penalties for opportunistic behaviors at the onset of the relationship" (Wang et al. 2017, p. 101). However, relational governance indicates the extent to which exchanges between partners are coordinated via social relationships and shared norms (Poppo and Zenger 2002; Zhou and Xu 2012; Wang et al. 2017). In order to achieve this, the partners set up these mechanisms defined as "mechanisms that enhance the building of trust and social identification" (Hoetker and Mellewigt 2009, p. 1028) such as setting up teams, working groups, meetings and business trips. In fact, thanks to the interactions between the employees, managers get to know each other and personal links between them increase. These mechanisms help mitigate opportunism and may resolve conflict through open communication, information sharing and improved cooperation and coordination between the parties (Hoetker and Mellewigt 2009).

In the context of emerging markets, IJVs present several asymmetries in terms of the partners' resources and skills. According to Meschi and Riccio (2008), the foreign partner contributes upstream resources, providing funding, expertise or technology, for example, while the local partner contributes downstream resources, such as local market knowledge, access to distribution networks and a skilled workforce at competitive cost. The resources are therefore complementary in nature (Khalid and Ali 2017). The transfer of knowledge from the foreign partner to the IJV is vital for meeting objectives, and ultimately for the success of the relationship, especially when based in emerging markets (Luo 2008).

In addition, literature in international business demonstrates the crucial role played by communication (formal and informal) in strategic alliances and especially IJVs (Ali and Larimo 2016; Khalid and Ali 2017). According to Hofstede (2001) and House et al. (2004), Moroccan society is hierarchical and collectivist. Thereby, collective achievements are held in higher esteem than individual ones (Gomez-Miranda et al. 2015).

These cultural patterns have an incidence on communication and the exchange of information within Moroccan-foreign IJVs. They can lead to misunderstandings and may lower business relationship quality (Barkema et al. 1997). Therefore, to run IJVs formed in emerging economies effectively, partners from different cultures strive to coordinate activities via communication strategies (Zeybek et al. 2003) in order to succeed when operating in such context.

2.1 Trust in IJV Relationships

Trust "concerns the willingness of a partner firm to accept the vulnerability of another partner firm in an IJV relationship, based on the positive expectations/beliefs of the counterpart's reliability" (Khalid and Ali 2017, p. 492). Many studies have shown that trust in IJVs is fostered by a social process based on prior experiences and by interaction between partners (Khalid and Ali 2017). In emerging markets, formal institutional support is often lacking (Lin and Wang 2008), thus creating a challenging and unstable environment for firms (Wang et al. 2017). In this case, trust may be used as a tool to reduce negotiation costs and conflicts. As a result, trust is considered crucial in determining IJVs' performance (Boersma et al. 2003; Ertug et al. 2013; Nippa and Reuer 2019). In their study of IJVs established in Asia, Ertug et al. (2013) find that interorganisational trust in cross-border relationships is influenced by the partner firms' countries of origin. In a longitudinal study, Gulati (1995) demonstrates that firms that have been previously involved in alliances tend to go on to engage in future ones. Indeed, the repeated links and collaborative experiences imply a good level of cooperation and understanding, contributing to a climate of trust between the partners (Ring and Van de Ven 1992). This initial or a priori trust, describing positive relationships in the past, tends to reduce both opportunistic behaviour (Ali and Larimo 2016; Khalid and Ali 2017) and the likelihood of resorting to formal mechanisms. Therefore, the availability of information to each partner plays an important role in ensuring the success of the partnership. Information concerning the trustworthiness of a partner and its operations elicits confidence in the parent. It follows, then, that the partner's reputation accrues trust. This makes it possible to overcome difficulties in the inception phase of the relationship (Delios and Beamish 2001). This initial trust evolves over time (Boersma et al. 2003). Regarding this, several authors emphasise that trust is a multidimensional construct (Inkpen and Curall 2004; Luo 2008; Robson et al. 2008), which may be analysed at different levels: interpersonal, interpartner and interorganisational. Few studies focus on the different levels of trust analysis (Boersma et al. 2003; Robson et al. 2008). Robson et al. (2008) define interpartner trust as an outcome of the parents' behaviour and beliefs. So-called behavioural trust includes, on the one hand, a "calculative" dimension, and, on the other, an affective one (Robson et al. 2008). Calculative trust is "opportunistic" to the extent that the choice of trusting is based on what is considered beneficial for the partners (e.g. the existence of costly penalties or potential rewards). However, affective trust takes the form of loyalty towards a partner, mainly brought about by repeated ties. The authors have also identified two trust behaviours, namely, "influence receptiveness denoting the degree to which an alliance partner voluntarily changes its behavior to accommodate the wishes of the counterpart and forebearance, which constitutes an alliance partner acting in the spirit of cooperation without cheating or withholding actions helpful to the counterpart" (p. 649).

There is much debate in the literature about the complementarity and substitution of formal governance mechanisms (e.g. monitoring, contract specificity) and trust. Indeed, at the outset of a partnership, the contract works to formalise the partners' expectations (Brulhart and Favoreu 2006). A number of authors defend the idea that contract and trust are complementary mechanisms (Poppo and Zenger 2002; Luo 2008; Cheriet and Dikmen 2014). Das and Teng (1998) regard trust and control as parallel phenomena that act together and influence confidence in partner cooperation. According to Cheriet and Dikmen (2014), there is an inverse relationship between trust and control in asymmetric[1] alliances. However, other research found that formal governance

[1] Asymmetric alliances involve companies of different sizes, different resource levels and different capacities (Mouline 2005).

mechanisms are more important than trust in the determination of the performance of the IJV (Dyer and Singh 1998).

2.2 Communication in IJV Relationships

Communication is defined as "formal and informal sharing of meaningful and timely information between firms" (Anderson and Narus 1990, p. 44). Communication between partners is often employed as a tool to enhance partners' trust of each other, to build commitment and reduce conflicts among partners (Jolly 1995; Luo 2008; Ali and Larimo 2016; Khalid and Ali 2017). Zeybek et al. (2003) show that a formalised communication strategy implemented by an IJV partner leads to a great self-reported partner performance. In a recent study analysing 89 IJVs involving Scandinavian companies in Asia, Europe and the USA, Khalid and Ali (2017) base their reflection on the theory of social exchange and find that communication is an antecedent of trust. Ali and Larimo (2016) add that communication allows partners to gain a better understanding of their respective internal processes and external market conditions, at the same time as reducing the asymmetry of information and opportunism. According to Jolly (1995), information sharing increases partner satisfaction and in so doing maximises the chances of the partnership's success. He concludes that managing the exchange of information is vital for the alliance.

Managing communication can help reduce differences between partners, on the one hand, and management teams, on the other. There are numerous tools for interactive communication including meeting places, informal meetings and social events. Formal and, above all, informal communication between partners and management teams form an essential part of conflict resolution. This is especially true of partnerships in emerging markets, where the quality and extent of interpersonal relations carry more weight than legal or contractual considerations (Schaan and Beamish 1988).

In summary, communication is vital in ensuring the smooth working of the IJV and is especially important in helping to resolve problems when they arise.

Ultimately, our study sets out to answer the following question: how does relational governance, perceived through trust and communication, operate in IJVs over time? We approach this question in the context of IJVs established in Morocco, an emerging economy.

3 Methodology and Presentation of Empirical Study

In order to understand the evolution of governance mechanisms during the development of IJVs in an emerging market, we conducted a qualitative case study research. This approach helps scholars learn about complex, new and context-specific phenomena (Eisenhardt 1989; Yin 1994; Miles and Huberman 2003). Indeed, our research objective is to describe how IJVs evolve and operate over time and the influence of trust and communication in such a process. In addition, this method enables us to provide contextual details and develop causal explanations (Welch et al. 2011).

3.1 Selection of IJV Sectors

To do so, we set out to study IJVs created by a Moroccan state partner and involving one or more foreign partners. We selected three IJVs led by leading Moroccan firms in growth sectors. The partnerships were vertical and established between partners operating in different sectors. Thus, two of the IJVs operate in the aviation sector, while another is part of the mining industry. For reasons of confidentiality, we will call them, respectively, Aero A, Aero B and Mine. Our choice of the aeronautics industry and the mining sector is justified as follows. Firstly, the aeronautics sector in Morocco has flourished in the last ten years, thanks to the Moroccan government's industrial acceleration plan (2014–2020). The plan sets out to increase the manufacturing value-added share of GDP from 14% in 2014 to 23% in 2020, and create 500,000 jobs. Thanks to the positive dynamics in the sector supported by public policy (World Bank 2017;

Unctad 2019), Morocco is attracting more and more major aeronautical companies, including Safran, Airbus Group, Bombardier and Boeing.

For the mining sector, Morocco supplies a wide range of minerals (phosphates, zinc, copper, etc.) in major quantities. An ecosystem network bringing together integrated industry projects is emerging to promote the development of mines and hydrocarbons (World Bank 2017). This strategy has led to the modernisation of local players and has resulted in Morocco becoming a world leader in the sector. Local funding is often limited in Morocco and the bulk of the investment is provided by foreign companies (World Bank 2017). Only leaders in these sectors are able to provide the necessary capital to form IJVs with foreign partners. It is this criterion which led us to study three IJVs, Aero A, Aero B and Mine, all created with the Moroccan leaders in their respective sectors. Our analysis concerns both senior directors of the IJV and those with responsibility for managing it.

3.2 Data Collection

We collected retrospective data through interviews with people who were very closely involved in the management of the IJV. Furthermore, we thought it was essential to analyse the points of view of local and foreign partners in order to check and compare their perspectives. Nevertheless, this approach was not possible in the case of Aero B, since those questioned are exclusively employed by the IJV. We conducted a total of ten interviews lasting an average of two and half hours from a sample of nine people (see Table 13.1). To ensure diversity in the profiles of respondents, four people represented the local partners, three represented the foreign partners and two were employed directly by the JV. The same semi-structured questionnaire was used in all the interviews. However, we approached the themes differently according to the profile of the respondent, their degree of openness and their responsiveness. The interviewees chose the interview locations (inside company premises or outside, in hotel lobbies or cafés). We drew their attention to the confidential nature of the interviews, given the importance of the information under discussion. At the request of the respondents, we relied for the most part on note-taking. When the interview was over, we immediately reviewed our notes, structuring them in order to describe the story in each case. Secondary data was also collected in order to complete our understanding of the three cases (e.g. national economic news media, websites of the partners). In addition, we attended a number of trade conferences held in Morocco. We talked informally with experts who either had been involved in the IJV in question or had observed it (experts, consultants and former managers of the IJV or its partners.). These informal exchanges were very useful, particularly in Morocco, where it is difficult to access internal data. Primary and secondary data were collected between 2009 and 2010. Certain elements (e.g. turnover) were updated by collecting secondary data between 2016 and 2017. Table 13.1 gives a description of the cases studied and the profiles of respondents.

3.3 Data Analysis

Primary data were assigned a prearranged code, prior to an analysis of their thematic content (Miles and Huberman 2003). In the first phase, we conducted a content analysis manually. We drew up an initial list of codes covering all the themes which concerned our theoretical subject. Thus, some code categories matched the literature while others emerged from our interviews. The transcripts were therefore divided according to selected themes. In addition, following the recommendations made by Miles and Huberman (2003), we annotated a certain number of comments for each previously coded unit of analysis. These comments were extremely useful in providing a general understanding of the research subject and for unifying the coding criteria. As we worked through the transcripts, the list of codes was condensed as some redundancy became apparent. By the end of this phase, we had coded our data and grouped them into the dimensions of trust and communication (initial/prior trust, interpartner trust, informal communication, etc.). The result of this step was the convenient arrangement of the interview's segments.

The other sources (observations, discussions and so on) allowed us to cross-check the data. Based on this coding, we analysed the cases.

Table 13.1 Presentation of the case studies

Industry	Creation	Partner's origin and strategic objectives	Ownership structure	IJV's objectives	Respondents
Aeronautics	Aero A (1999)	Morocco: Political considerations	MP1 49%	Maintenance and repair of aircraft engines	General manager (PE1)
		France: International growth	FP1 51%		Quality manager (PE1)
					Quality manager (MP1)
	Aero B[a] (2001)	Morocco: Activities growth	MP2 33%	Aeronautical cabling manufacturing	Management controller (IJV)
		USA sell aircraft to its Moroccan client	AP2 33%		Production manager (IJV)
		France: Establishment in Morocco and Africa	FP2 33%		
Mining	Mine (1997)	Morocco: Securing exports	MP3 50%	Production and export of phosphate	Partnership manager[b] (MP3)
		India: Guaranteeing supplies of raw materials	IP3 50%		R&D manager (MP3)
					Partnership manager (MP3)
					Former expatriate (IP3)

Source: Authors' creation
[a]In 2011, MP2 was no longer a partner in the IJV; however, the IJV still exists
[b]MP3 was interviewed twice

It is usual in the literature to describe the development of IJVs in terms of three different phases: (a) the IJV's inception (b) the IJV's management and (c) the adjustment phase. The people interviewed also used equivalent terms to describe the IJV's development. For each of these phases, we analysed the different themes they encompassed.

3.4 Presentation of the Case Studies

Case Study 1 Created in 1999, the IJV Aero A specialises in the maintenance and repair of aircraft engines built by leading manufacturers. The Moroccan company (MP1) is a well-known airline and is considered one of the driving forces of the Moroccan economy. The group is built around six growth areas in the transport sector. The foreign partner (FP1) is an international engine manufacturer which provides a large range of engine maintenance and repair services to different operators (airlines, the armed forces, etc.). The primary objective of the foreign partner was international expansion. The Moroccan partner, however, was motivated both by profit and by political considerations. Aero A still operates in Morocco.

Case Study 2 Inaugurated in 2001, Aero B specialises in the fabrication of aeronautic wiring for various aircraft manufacturers (Boeing, Airbus, Dassault aviation, etc.). The wiring is exclusively for commercial aircraft. The IJV brings together three industry partners of different nationalities: MP2, a Moroccan airline (and the same partner as in JV Aero A, MP1); AP2, an American partner, a worldwide aircraft manufacturer; FP2, a French partner at the core of Aero B's business, itself a subsidiary of an engine manufacturer. Here, the aim of the Moroccan partner was to develop the aircraft wiring sector with its foreign partners. For the American partner, the set-up of the IJV allowed it to sell its aircraft to its client MP2. As for FP2, it sought a base in Morocco and, more generally, in Africa. In 2011, MP2 withdrew from the capital of Aero B in order to focus on its core business thanks to a large financial transaction. The IJV is still active, however.

Case Study 3 Mine was created in 1997 and involved collaboration between a Moroccan partner (MP3) and its client, an Indian company, owned by a large private group (IP3). MP3 specialises in the extraction, upgrading and sale of ore and its by-products; its reserves represent the equivalent of three quarters of the world's reserves. MP3 approached the Indian company with a view to securing a share of its exports and diversifying its alliances. In 2005, the IJV was strengthened when another private Indian group acquired a stake in the capital. MP3 hoped to diversify its markets through this IJV. For IP3, the main aim was to guarantee supplies of raw materials, given that all the ore extracted was destined to go to IP3.

3.5 Research Results

Our chosen framework of analysis leads us to examine the evolution of relational governance in IJVs, as perceived through trust and communication during three successive phases, namely, the inception phase, the management phase and the adjustment phase.

The Inception Phase

There can be many reasons for setting up an IJV, including access to new markets or the acquisition of new technology. In the case of Aero A, the foreign partner's main aim was one of international expansion. It therefore set out to develop in Morocco through the JV, taking advantage of a low-wage, skilled workforce. The quality control manager told us: "FP1 wanted to keep such an important client, since MP1 sometimes still subcontracted elsewhere. It also wants to retain a large share of the African market." As for the Moroccan partner, profit was the motivation for the choice of the IJV. The quality control manager explained further: "MP1 didn't have any problems of a technical nature. The equipment is very expensive, oversized and underexploited." In fact, FP1 was aware that its partner had no real choice in the creation of the IJV. With no alternatives, MP1 felt obliged to work with its partner, potentially causing an asymmetry in the initial relationship with the potential to affect satisfaction of the partners subsequently.

In the case of Aero B, the inception phase was characterised by differing strategic aims. The two foreign partners, FP2 and AP2, sought to set up a base in Morocco and ultimately establish their respective positions in the African market. However, for MP1, the partnership was a strategic one for the Moroccan government, hence its commitment to the JV.

In the case of Mine, the strategic intentions were compatible: "We need to secure production for MP3 and supply for IP3," the head of the partnership management team explained.

The parents of all three IJVs had previous experiences with their Moroccan partners (customer-supplier or subcontractor relationships). These experiences helped with the launch of the IJV. The trust generated at the outset was for the most part based on the partners' reputations and on those past relationships, as illustrated in comments by the Aero A's chief executive: "In order to attract new clients, we needed the support of someone who had an image and a reputation. Engines require pretty sophisticated technology."

However, while initial trust is essential for choosing a partner and establishing a relationship, it does not reduce the time needed for negotiating and formalising the partnership: "You can act in good faith, but you have to stick to the facts and not rely on feelings" (Management accountant, Aero B). In addition, it is apparent that trust is based on a mutual sense of economic and opportunistic utility: "There's trust in the sense that there's a common interest: strategic interest and financial interest" (Production manager, Aero B).

Trust in skills and competences was also an issue that emerged during this phase. In the case of Mine, trust in MP3 skills was decisive in the selection of a partner. "Before starting our collaboration, we had to know our partner. They have the market knowledge. After all, they're our client before anything else," pointed out the senior manager in charge of the MP3 partnership team. Thus, reputation and trust in skills are essential conditions for launching an alliance. Beyond having good faith, there is a strong need to feel confident in the partner's skills at the outset of the relationship. However, IJV managers do not base their choice on a priori trust and trust in skills alone: they also conduct numerous technical studies to ensure the collaboration is worthwhile. Once they have probed these elements, the partners formalise their cooperation through the contract. The contract varies from one IJV to another. Trust and contract therefore coexist alongside each other in a relationship. While trust may exist between partners, that does not rule out opportunism at some stage by one or the other partners. The contract stipulates all the elements in the running of the partner relationship (anticipated outcomes, exit clauses, etc.). Aero A's chief executive explained how each partner had legal experts go over the contract in minute detail, looking especially for sources of disagreement: "In every contract, we talk about unpleasant things, [...] the contract is drawn up in a very professional, very detailed manner." This reflects the importance of formal control in the IJV during its outset phase.

The Management Phase

The second stage in the relationship is symbolised by the management phase of the IJV. The aims and strategic intentions agreed by each of the partners influence their level of involvement in the partner relationship. In the case of Aero A, the parents' strategic incompatibility, as outlined in the presentation of the case study, gave rise to conflicts over human resource management. They particularly revolved around job descriptions, recruitment policy and employee remuneration. The example of defining tasks and jobs serves as a good illustration of the differences between the two parents: "The problem with business at MP1 is reducing costs. For them, reducing costs automatically means shedding staff" (Quality control manager, Aero A). This obsession with managing costs led to the positions of sales director and production manager being merged into a single role, that of technical manager. For the foreign partner, these two roles are quite different. This situation led to some dissatisfaction in the French partner company.

In Aero B's case, operational management was run by FP2, which had the technical skills. Management and oversight problems on its part resulted in the IJV running at a deficit for several years. The incompatibility of MP2 and AP2 in terms of their strategic aims in the IJV led to a lack of communication about the aims of the common entity. Moreover, the contract agreed during the outset phase turned out to contain omissions. This had an impact on the motivation of IJV employees. The production manager of Aero B explained: "You can sometimes feel frustrated if you work in a company without knowing its aims. How do I go about fulfilling its strategies? How do I know how to contribute to those strategies? Communication is very important." After five years of deficit, several measures were taken to reorganise the joint venture, after which, in 2007, Aero B became the world leader in engine wiring. The financial controller of Aero B recalls the directives taken, and the impact they had: "There was a change of executive management, with an action plan to respond to all the managers' questions. An evaluation system was also brought in. What do you know, there was a positive result in the 5th year and managers became more motivated. [...]. After that reorganisation, you felt you were accountable." Joint learning with good management in the IJV made it possible to achieve economic progress, and contributed to an improvement in the partnership.

As with Aero B, the operational management of Mine was mostly handled by the Moroccan partner. We did not identify any conflicts during Mine's operational phase. That might be explained in part by the low interaction between the two parents, and the introduction of a sufficiently detailed contract establishing the IJV. Whenever our respondents brought up the subject of conflicts of interest or opportunism, they referred to the possibility of them being handled by the contract mediator: "If a conflict ever comes up, there is arbitration. We've never had to resort to arbitration, things work out before that stage since the contract is very detailed" (R&D manager, Mine). This is an example of an IJV in which formalisation is at the heart of the relationship. In addition, communication is an element that facilitates exchanges between the parents in order to ensure the IJV's success.

Once the IJV is operational, interpersonal trust between the partners becomes progressively more important, taking precedence over confidence in skills. Indeed, there needs to be mutual trust for employees to work together, and, in the long run, their common experience consolidates their trust in each other. Trust grows and is strengthened by personal relationships. The quality control manager points out: "[T]he director of Aero A (who came from MP1) has only shaken my hand once. I don't report to him and he adds nothing to the JV." Nevertheless, growth in activity by Aero A seems to have fostered interpartner trust at certain levels of management: "Getting the business up and running cemented trust between the partners," observed Aero A's chief executive. This trend was also noticed in Aero B, where the growth in activity boosted the feeling of belonging and therefore trust, both interpersonal and between the partners: "[T]he trust built within the teams created a will to work together" (Production manager, Aero B).

Trust can also affect the distribution of power. In the case of Mine, IP3 had trust in its partner and so progressively repatriated its staff, leaving Mine's operational management in the hands of MP3. Delegating responsibility to the Moroccan partner can be explained by its competence in this area. Certainly, "in the beginning, the partner is frightened of us. They protect themselves because they do not know us. They don't know Moroccan practices in terms of management." Several years on, "the partner has complete trust in PM3. He starts to withdraw and leave just 1 or 2 people" (a former expatriate of Mine). With time, trust is established and leads to the withdrawal of expatriate staff.

The Adjustment Phase

Relational governance plays a central role in the adjustment phase, since it enables the partner relationship to grow. In the first instance, we observed that communication has an impact of reducing the conflicts that can crop up during this phase. The proliferation of informal meetings, emails and conference calls plays a crucial role. In Aero B's case, "communication management operates at two levels: firstly, at board level, with all the group directors meeting once a year, then at other levels, where bilateral relations enable the IJV to work" (Production manager, Aero B). This management also takes the form of cross-training schemes. In fact, FP2 and AP2 employees visit Aero B regularly. Similarly, JV employees are regularly sent for training with the American and French partners. The IJV cases we studied also make use of formal communication to ensure that key information is traceable and is conveyed through the hierarchy: "Everything we do leaves a trace. Informal is formal, here" (Senior partnership manager, Mine). While formal communications make it possible to manage the flow of information, informal communication helps cultivate a team spirit: "Informal exchanges are a sign that the relationship is improving, taking the form of cultural details and information. That's how you build a working relationship between people" (Senior partnership manager, Mine). We noticed how informal elements had a favourable influence on the existing organisation while reducing conflicts in the different case studies. In Aero A's case, the chief executive recalled the effort needed to create a positive relationship between the partners inside the JV: "We had to try and convince them and explain things regularly." In this way, the foreign partner, via the chief executive, set up weekly meetings with the leader of the board of directors and the technical manager, "to update each other and discuss the different problems that week" (Quality manager, Aero A). Over time, this initiative led to the reduction of conflicts.

The development of communication in the relationship enables partners to learn about each other and their work methods.

4 Discussion

The study of three vertical IJVs, based in Morocco and created by a Moroccan state partner and one or more foreign partners, highlights the evolution of relational governance, as perceived through trust and communication during the development of the relationship.

The multidimensional aspect of trust emerges clearly in our study. Firstly, initial or a priori trust plays a crucial role in the inception phase and in formalising the partnership. This trust is, in fact, the result of prior experience between the parents and their respective reputations. The parents of the three IJVs analysed all had experience prior to partnership (client-supplier or sub-contractual relations). Our findings support those of Gulati (1995) and Boersma et al. (2003). According to the authors, interfirm cooperation is a relational contract, which often assumes a prior relationship, thus helping reduce opportunistic behaviour by the parents and ensuring the success of the IJV partnership (Ali and Larimo 2016; Khalid and Ali 2017). In addition, reputation-based trust is essential when selecting a partner (Ring and Van de Ven 1992). It therefore reduces uncertainty. In the interviews we conducted, it is apparent that trust-based reputation is linked to a trust in skills and competences. In fact, the partner's achievements, history and potential for future development also influence the selection of the partner. The choice of the right partner determines the parents' satisfaction. This trust also acts to guarantee the partners' interests: in this way, it is based on behaviour which is "implicitly" opportunist and calculating. This aspect of trust was put forward in the work of Robson et al. (2008) and is called calculative trust.

In the inception phase and the setting up of the IJV, it is recognised that the contract supports the formalisation of the partners' expectations (Brulhart and Favoreu 2006). Several authors have highlighted the importance of interpersonal relationships within IJVs based in emerging markets (Schaan and Beamish 1988). They regard these relationships as even more important than legal and contractual considerations. Thus, partners tend to adopt less formal governance mechanisms. However, the results of our study, carried out with IJVs in Morocco, do not bear this out. In fact, formal governance (e.g. the contract) is needed for the relationship to work from the outset. It is a prerequisite for trust to develop. In addition, partners sometimes need to rely on the contract in order to overcome the problems and conflicts which may arise as the relationship evolves. For example, the contracts signed by Aero A and Mine are exhaustive compared to that of Aero B. This enabled the former to resolve problems by turning to an extremely detailed contract. Thus, relational and contractual governance coexist together throughout the JV's lifecycle. This study provides additional empirical validation for the work on IJVs by Cheriet and Dikmen (2014), and Das and Teng (1998) in particular, as well as that of Poppo and Zenger (2002), conducted within the framework of client-supplier relationships. According to these authors, contract and trust are complementary mechanisms which interact throughout the development of the partner relationship. However, these findings do not support those of Zhou and Xu (2012), who stipulate the predominance of relational governance over contractual governance in emerging markets.

In the adjustment phase, other levels of trust had an influence in the three case studies: interpersonal and interpartner trust. As the parents worked together and the IJV met its objectives, a climate of trust concerning the collaboration was established. This supports studies dealing with trust as a multidimensional construct that evolves during the development of the relationship (Boersma et al. 2003; Luo 2008; Robson et al. 2008).

Communication contributes to the development of bilateral relations by strengthening trust and fostering learning between partners (Jolly 1995; Ali and Larimo 2016; Khalid and Ali 2017). In so doing, it ensures the IJV operates effectively, as in the example of Mine.

From the inception phase, communication was fundamental for the partners, allowing them to speed up the decision-making process. This was made possible for two reasons: on the one hand, the strategic intentions were compatible from the outset of the collaboration, and, on the other, an exhaustive contract had been drawn up. The other two cases also relied on a formalised exchange of information across various platforms (meetings, emails, reports etc.), thus ensuring the traceability of information. Informal communication often improved interpersonal relations and complemented formal information within the IJV, through business trips, visits, international conferences, and so on. However, it is worth noting that Aero B ran at a deficit for five years, characterised by a lack of exchanges between the partners. Following the introduction of strategic measures in 2007, the partner relationship improved and communication was resumed during the management phase. Our findings support previous analyses on the importance of communication and its influence on trust (Khalid and Ali 2017). In addition, in the context of IJVs operating in Morocco, we see that formal communication is predominant over informal communication. This result may be explained by the high power distance culture in Morocco (Hofstede 2001; Gomez-Miranda et al. 2015). Managers require hierarchical authority in order to act, hence the importance of formal communication.

The results of our empirical study also demonstrate the importance of strategic compatibility from the outset and its influence on relational governance. For example, we observed that the advantages associated with trust could be limited where strategic incompatibility existed between the partners. Indeed, the latter creates disparities in the partners' commitment and leads to conflicts. These conflicts may take the form of divergences in understanding about the environment of the IJV, as seen particularly in the case of Aero A.

5 Conclusion

Our study provides several theoretical implications. First, we contribute to a better knowledge of relational governance mechanisms that need to be correctly addressed by multinational firms intending to set-up IJVs in Morocco. Second, these mechanisms are subject to evolve in a dynamic way throughout the partnership's development (Boersma et al. 2003). Indeed, our study confirmed that trust is "a multifaceted construct" (Robson et al. 2008, p. 648). For instance, interpartner trust and communication appear to be crucial in the management phase of the IJV. However, at the outset of the partnership, trust in competence, reputation and prior experiences with the local parent seem to be important for foreign investors especially in selecting the partner. Third, it is held that different levels of trust are not sufficient for IJVs to be successful; it is imperative for that trust to be strengthened by good communication that enables the IJV partners to reduce the information asymmetries and the opportunism between the parents in emerging markets (Ali and Larimo 2016). Fourth, our study highlights that, in the context of emerging markets, relational and contractual governance mechanisms coexist together throughout the IJV's lifecycle. Fifth, our findings reveal that the compatibility of the parents' strategic aims at the outset is considered as a key determinant of IJV performance in Morocco.

Our findings also have managerial implications. They suggest that companies need to pay specific attention to both relational and contractual governance mechanisms when they choose to establish IJVs in Morocco. Moreover, prior experiences contribute to the success of IJVs in this context. As revealed in this study, trust and communication evolve as the joint venture progresses. Managers can count on these mechanisms when facing challenges over the period of high environmental instability in emerging markets.

This chapter is not without limitations that can be used as the basis for future research. One of the limiting factors is the study of three vertical IJVs based in Morocco. While it has yielded rich data and enabled us to understand how relational governance evolves during the development of the partnership, these results are not representative of all IJVs due to their contextual bias. It would be interesting to develop further studies comparing the development of relational governance in vertical and horizontal IJVs. Indeed, these IJVs are likely to evolve distinctly. Another limiting aspect of this work concerns the elements of relational governance, which were not included in this research. In the context of future research, commitment and culture as well as conflict resolution mechanisms all merit study. In addition, prolonging this study to focus on the stability of IJVs would provide the literature with new answers about how alliances perform. Indeed, two of the cases we studied present instability as defined by Yan and Zeng (2002). For Mine, a change in the structure of the IJV took place a few years after the alliance was set up. Finally, future studies might look at the role of the state in the conclusion and management of IJVs. The case of emerging markets is particular, inasmuch as the state is heavily involved in the companies. As a stakeholder in the alliance, especially in Morocco, the state needs to be more fully incorporated into an analysis of IJVs.

References

Ali, T., & Larimo, J. (2016). Managing Opportunism in International Joint Ventures: The Role of Structural and Social Mechanisms. *Scandinavian Journal of Management, 32*(2), 86–96.

Anderson, J. C., & Narus, J. A. (1990). A Model of Distributor Firm and Manufacturer Firm Working Partnerships. *Journal of Marketing, 54*(1), 42–58.

Barkema, H. G., Shenkar, O., Vermeulen, F., & Bell, J. H. J. (1997). Working Abroad, Working with Others: How Firms Learn to Operate International Joint Ventures. *Academy of Management Journal, 40*(2), 426–442.

Boersma, M. F., Buckley, P. J., & Ghauri, P. N. (2003). Trust in International Joint Venture Relationships. *Journal of Business Research, 56*(12), 1031–1042.

Brulhart, F., & Favoreu, C. (2006). Le lien contrôle-confiance-performance dans les relations de partenariat logistique inter firmes. *Finance Contrôle Stratégie, 9*(5), 59–96.

Cheriet, F., & Dikmen, L. (2014). Contrat ou confiance? Effets de la gouvernance sur les performances des alliances stratégiques asymétriques. *Revue des Sciences de Gestion, 266*, 43–51.

Das, T. K., & Teng, B. S. (1998). Between Trust and Control: Developing Confidence in Partner Cooperation in Alliances. *Academy of Management Review, 23*(3), 491–512.

Delios, A., & Beamish, P. W. (2001). Survival Profitability: The Roles of Experience and Intangible Assets in Foreign Subsidiary Performance. *Academy of Management Journal, 44*(5), 1028–1038.

Dong, M. C., Tse, D. K., & Cavusgil, T. (2008). Efficiency of Governance Mechanisms in China's Distribution Channels. *International Business Review, 17*(5), 509–519.

Dyer, J. F., & Singh, H. (1998). The Relational View: Cooperative Strategy and Sources of Interorganisational Competitive Advantage. *Academy of Management Review, 23*(4), 660–680.

Eisenhardt, K. M. (1989). Building Theories from Case Study Research. *Academy of Management Review, 14*(4), 532–550.

Ertug, G., Cuypers, I., Noorderhaven, N. G., & Bensaou, B. M. (2013). Trust Between International Joint Venture Partners: Effects of Home Countries. *Journal of International Business Studies, 44*(3), 263–282.

Gomez-Miranda, E. M., Pérez-López, C. M., Argente-Linares, E., & Rodríguez-Ariza, R. (2015). The Impact of Organisational Culture on Competitiveness, Effectiveness and Efficiency in Spanish-Moroccan International Joint Ventures. *Personnel Review, 44*(3), 364–387.

Gulati, R. (1995). Does Familiarity Breed Trust? The Implications of Repeated Ties for Contractual Choice in Alliances. *Academy of Management Journal, 38*(1), 85–112.

Hoetker, G., & Mellewigt, T. (2009). Choice and Performance of Governance Mechanisms: Matching Alliance Governance to Asset Type. *Strategic Management Journal, 30*(10), 1025–1044.

Hofstede, G. (2001). *Culture's Consequences: Comparing Values, Behaviors, Institutions, and Organisations Across Nations*. Thousand Oaks, CA: Sage.

House, R. J., Hanges, P. J., Javidan, M., Dorfman, P. W., & Gupta, V. (2004). *Culture, Leadership, and Organisations: The Globe Study of 62 Societies*. Thousand Oaks, CA: Sage.

Inkpen, A. C., & Curall, S. C. (2004). The Coevolution of Trust, Control, and Learning in Joint Ventures. *Organisation Science, 15*(5), 586–599.

Jolly, D. (1995). Le champ des alliances interentreprises. *Revue Internationale de Gestion, 20*(4), 40–47.

Khalid, S., & Ali, T. (2017). An Integrated Perspective of Social Exchange Theory and Transaction Cost Approach on the Antecedents of Trust in International Joint Ventures. *International Business Review, 26*(3), 491–501.

Kwok, F., Sharma, P., Gaur, S. S., & Ueno, A. (2019). Interactive Effects of Information Exchange, Relationship Capital and Environmental Uncertainty on International Joint Venture (IJV) Performance: An Emerging Markets Perspective. *International Business Review, 28*(5), 101481.

Lin, X. H., & Wang, C. L. (2008). Enforcement and Performance: The Role of Ownership, Legalism and Trust in International Joint Ventures. *Journal of World Business, 43*(2), 340–351.

Luo, Y. (2008). Procedural Fairness and Interfirm Cooperation in Strategic Alliances. *Strategic Management Journal, 29*(1), 27–46.

Meschi, P. X., & Riccio, E. L. (2008). Country Risk, National Cultural Differences between Partners and Survival of International Joint Ventures in Brazil. *International Business Review, 17*(3), 250–266.

Miles, M. B., & Huberman, A. M. (2003). *Analyse de données qualitatives* (2ème éd ed.). Bruxelles: De Boeck Supérieur.

Mouline, A. (2005). "Symétrie et asymétrie des alliances dans une industrie en mutation : le cas des télécommunications", *Management International. Vol., 1*, 75–87.

Nemeth, A., & Nippa, M. (2013). Rigor and Relevance of IJV Exit Research. *Management International Review, 53*(3), 449–475.

Nippa, M., & Reuer, J. J. (2019). On the Future of International Joint Venture Research. *Journal of International Business Studies, 50*(4), 555–597.

Poppo, L., & Zenger, T. (2002). Do Formal Contracts and Relational Governance Function as Substitutes or Complements? *Strategic Management Journal, 23*(8), 707–725.

Ring, P. S., & Van de Ven, A. (1992). Structuring Cooperative Relationships between Organisations. *Strategic Management Journal, 13*(7), 483–498.

Robson, M. J., Katsikeas, C. S., & Bello, D. C. (2008). Drivers and Performance Outcomes of Trust in International Strategic Alliances: The Role of Organisational Complexity. *Organisation Science, 19*(4), 647–665.

Schaan, J. L., & Beamish, P. W. (1988). Joint Venture General Managers in LDCs. In F. Contractor & P. Lorange (Eds.), *Cooperative Strategies in International Business* (pp. 279–299). Toronto: Lexington.

Triki, D., & Mayrhofer, U. (2016). Do Initial Characteristics Influence IJV Longevity? Evidence from the Mediterranean Region. *International Business Review, 25*(4), 795–805.

Unctad. (2019). *World Investment Report 2019 – Special Economic Zones*. New York and Geneva: United Nations Conference on Trade and Development.

Wang, L., Sheng, S., Wu, S., & Zhou, K. Z. (2017). Government Role, Governance Mechanisms, and Foreign Partner Opportunism in IJVs. *Journal of Business Research, 76*, 98–107.

Welch, C., Piekkari, R., Plakoyiannaki, E., & Paavilainen-Mäntymäki, E. (2011). Theorising from Case Studies: Towards a Pluralist Future for International Business Research. *Journal of International Business Studies, 42*(5), 740–762.

World Bank. (2017). *Le Maroc à l'Horizon 2040, Investir dans le capital immatériel pour accélérer l'émergence économique*. Washington, DC: World Bank Group.

Yin, R. K. (1994). *Case Study Research: Design and Methods* (2nd ed.). New York: Sage, 171p.

Zeybek, A. Y., O'brien, M., & Griffith, D. A. (2003). Perceived Cultural Congruence's Influence on Employed Communication Strategies and Resultant Performance: A Transitional Economy International Joint Venture Illustration. *International Business Review, 12*(4), 499–521.

Zhou, K., & Xu, D. (2012). How Foreign Firms Curtail Local Supplier Opportunism in China: Detailed Contracts, Centralized Control, and Relational Governance. *Journal of International Business Studies, 43*(7), 677–692.

14

The Propagation of Online Rumours Slandering Multinational Companies in Egypt

Mona Shehata

1 Introduction

In competitive, changing and unpredictable environments, organisations can easily become victims of multiple rumours which spread on digital platforms and cause a lot of hazards. Colas (2004, p. 21) states that "rumour is one of the oldest threats that an economic actor can face". Today, the spread of online rumours has become more ferocious and has different forms (photos, videos, graphics and visual signs) that amplify the attention of Internet users. These new forms of *e-rumours* are embarking on a multicultural orientation that requires organisations to adapt their communication strategies accordingly, by gaining knowledge on the societal and cultural aspects where they operate. Milliot (2016, p. 134) argues that "the cultural context therefore has a determining influence on the conception and implementation of economic

M. Shehata (✉)
University of Poitiers, Poitiers, France
e-mail: mshehata@poitiers.iae-france.fr

S. M. Apitsa, E. Milliot (eds.), *Doing Business in Africa*, Palgrave Studies of Internationalization in Emerging Markets,
https://doi.org/10.1007/978-3-030-50739-8_14

intelligence". Using the term context, according to Hall's approach (1976), will allow us to comprehend the cultural impact on the diffusion and interpretation of Internet users' interaction during the spread of a specific rumour in the Egyptian context. It seems relevant to study in-depth the commercial rumour propagation to equip multinational companies to face these new challenges proactively and to keep their e-reputation. Thus, the analysis is based on a three-level dynamics (micro-, meso- and macro-environments).

To outline the nature of commercial rumours in the Egyptian context, three concrete case studies belonging to three different economic sectors were executed as follows: politics (Orange), economy (Pampers) and health (Danone). The research question that this chapter tries to answer can then be posed as follows: *Are there distinct socio-cultural factors affecting the mechanism for spreading commercial rumours on Facebook in Egypt?*

This general issue raises three sub-questions:

Q1: What are the factors affecting rumours dissemination on Facebook?
Q2: What is the role of digital platforms, including Facebook, in the process of disseminating rumours?
Q3: To what extent can a country's cultural dimensions be considered as a barrier or leverage to the spread of rumours on social media?

To answer these questions, this chapter is designed into five parts.

1. The definition of a multi-level analysis grid from a literature review base.
2. The pluralism of the method adopted.
3. A detailed overview of the three case studies selected.
4. The main findings and the analysis of the cases.
5. Conclusion.

2 A Multi-level Analysis Grid

The analysis is carried out on the micro-, meso- and macro-environmental levels to determine the variables from the field study conducted in Egypt which act as dissemination vectors. The delivery of these three levels will make it possible to assess the dynamics that ensure the creation, circulation, propagation, survival and death of rumours. Taking Difonzo and Bordia's (2007, p. 283) analysis into consideration, we find that these three levels are mentioned in their study and it states that "real-life rumours (transmission, belief, distortion) almost certainly involve multi-level dynamic processes—micro, meso and macro".

We begin with the micro-environmental level, which focuses on the mechanism of spreading rumours among Internet users in Egypt. In this section, we pinpoint the cultural dimensions that are associated with Internet users to find relevant answers to the sub-question Q1, and the researcher analyses four variables related to the dissemination mechanism at the micro level:

- The first variable focuses on the nature of the source that starts the rumour. Here we analyse the nature and type of profile on social media.
- The second is related to the timing and frequency of diffusing a rumour. According to Ploux (2001), the way rumours circulate is influenced by the gap between the scarcity of information and people's thirst for information. This may explain the variation in the frequency of rumour transmission to fill an information gap.
- The third variable is the trust and beliefs of "famous" people who play an undeniable role in spreading rumours if involved in the propagation process. In the field study, it is observed that a verified account of celebrities, for example, in the course of propagation of a rumour, intensifies its effect by boosting the sharing action of the rumour due to the confidence and trust that Internet users have in them.
- The fourth and last variable tackles Internet users at the micro level, and it is related to conducting a sentiment and semantic analysis of their feelings as they share a rumour. Through this analysis, it is detected that some Internet users write comments on the original

Facebook post before sharing it on their wall as a means of expressing themselves. These added messages represent a form of over-specification (Rouquette 1975, 1979). They play the role of augmenting the spread of rumours, thus reinforcing the basic functionalities of digital platforms such as like, comment and share. According to Milliot's study (2016, p. 135 adapted from Hall 1976), Egypt—situated amongst North African countries—is considered as a high cultural context, a country where cultural framework conditions communication schemes. Milliot (2016, p. 135) adds: "The messages emitted in these cultures, characterized by a highly developed sense of community, are generally interwoven and implicit. One must analyse and decrypt them, according to a particular logic, to comprehend their true meaning".

The meso-environmental level is used to answer sub-question Q2. To conduct this, we analyse Facebook's features to find out how they can leverage the disseminating of rumours. In this respect, Alloing (2013, p. 134) argues: "This production of information inherent to the functionalities of the socio-technical structures specific to the Web 2.0 allows it to develop new forms of relationships, or even to emancipate itself by contributing to the construction of knowledge and by participating in certain collective actions". From a meso-environmental perspective, we have identified four variables relevant to our field study that affect the spread of rumours and are related to the functionality of digital social networks.

- First, it is noted that rumours can be manifested in many forms: photos, videos, written statutes or even URL links (Uniform Resource Locator). Therefore, in each case, we will analyse this variable to determine if there is a repetitive form in all cases.
- The second variable concerns the affective metrics (e.g., likes, comments and sharing) provided by the Facebook platform. According to Kim and Yang (2017, p. 447), "Facebook behaviours also fall into discrete levels. First, like is the lowest. Like requires less commitment than others do. While a click is enough for like, comment and share need additional actions that ask extra commitment or cognitive effort.

Second, share may be a higher level than comment [...] On the other hand, when sharing a post; the post not only appears on News Feed but also goes to user's profile page, suggesting that the shared post constitutes a part of user's self-presentation".

- The third variable, linked to the specific characteristics of digital platforms, lies in the presence of transposable signs and hashtags in the path of rumours (either the initial content or the exchanges between Internet users). Transposable signs are defined by Le Béchec and Boullier (2014, p. 124) as "elementary semiotic forms of the territory that circulate easily on the web. This circulation and transposition produce a new version of what a regional scale is by making it visible and portable". The hashtag is defined according to Bruns and Burgess (2011, p. 1) as "a short keyword, prefixed with the hash symbol '#'—as a means of coordinating a distributed discussion between more or less large groups of users, who do not need to be connected through existing 'follower' networks".
- The fourth variable is related to the traceability feature provided by the ability of digital platforms to archive old exchanged publications (the memory of the Web). Le Béchec (2010, p. 345) highlights that the memory of the Web, of which social media are a part, is "a medium and a repository of memory". This dimension ensures that rumours survive on the platforms leaving behind digital traceability that helped us find and collect some data related to each case.

The macro-environmental level, which answers sub-question Q3, also includes four variables.

- First, we underline the important topics and themes related to the cultural context. The derived values from each topic are crucial for studying the spreading of a rumour.
- Second, we analyse the cultural features translated by the language and semantics used during the interactions between Internet users.
- Third, we extend the analysis to detect clusters formation. According to Latané's (1996) theory of dynamic social impact (DSIT), some cultural elements are more likely to spread and self-organise (i.e., to regroup, correlate and merge) than others.

- The last variable examines the behaviour of multinational companies that are victims of rumours. They show these behaviours in unofficial and/or official debunking statements to counteract the rumours.

It is important to mention that Shibutani's (1966) study inspired this analysis, which incorporates the notion of a situation into the definition of the circulation of a rumour (1966, pp. 8–9). He also underlines a collective sense-making explaining that the circulation of a rumour is a transaction inside a group. Shibutani (1966, p. 17) explains that this allows rumours to aggregate all the understandings distributed within the community. Rumours are attempts to raise collective awareness. In this perspective, Shibutani (1966) considers the degree of emotional arousal that a rumour can trigger (cited by Brodin and Roux 1990, p. 53).

3 The Method of Data Collection on Facebook

The choice of the Facebook platform to study the spread of rumour in Egypt was not selected randomly, but was linked to two reasons. Firstly, Facebook is the most used platform in Egypt (72.12% compared to 22.17% for YouTube and 2.96% for Twitter in September 2019).[1] Moreover, the total number of active Egyptian Facebook users reached 41,930,000 (or 40.9% of the total population).[2] Second, 81% of the users in Egypt claim to have witnessed false information on the platform according to a study conducted by Ipsos Global Survey (p. 37 of the report).[3] To collect data on exchanges between Internet users, we

[1] According to the statistics of the study of the stat counter site. Link to the study: https://gs.statcounter.com/social-media-stats/all/egypt/2019 retrieved on 30 October 2019.

[2] Study conducted statistically by Napoleon Cat, link to https://napoleoncat.com/stats/facebook-users-in-egypt/2019/09 retrieved on 30 October 2019.

[3] Survey conducted by Ipsos on behalf of the Centre for International Governance Innovation (CIGI) between 21 December 2018 and 10 February 2019. The survey was conducted in twenty-five economies—Australia, Brazil, Canada, China, Egypt, France, Germany, Great Britain, Hong Kong (China), India, Indonesia, Italy, Japan, Kenya, Mexico, Nigeria, Pakistan, Poland, Russia, South Africa, Republic of Korea, Sweden, Tunisia, Turkey and the United States—and involved 25,229 Internet users. Available on 2019 CIGI-Ipsos Global Survey—Part 3 Social Media, Fake

conducted a virtual ethnography (netnography). According to Kozinets (2002, p. 2) "netnography, or ethnography on the Internet, is a new qualitative research method that adapts ethnographic research techniques to the study of cultures and communities emerging through computer-mediated communications".

To concretise this study, the multiple case study method is used; it involves "intensive study of a unit for the purpose of understanding a larger class of (similar) unit observed at a single point in time or over some delimited period of time" (Gerring 2004, p. 342). The multiple case (multi-case) approach is relevant for "giving a broader picture of a complex phenomenon" (Stake 2006) and for comparing different realities in different industries.

4 The Presentation of the Three Case Studies

4.1 Danone Egypt

Rumour: "*Danone yoghurts contain pork gelatin*"

Presentation of the Case

In 2016, the dairy company Danone was hit by a rumour on social networks in Egypt accusing it of using gelatin from pork skin in the manufacture of its yoghurts.

The Origin of the Rumour

The theme of the rumour concerns religious morals and beliefs of Muslim communities since the consumption of pork and all its derivatives is

News & Algorithms. Source available on https://www.cigionline.org/sites/default/files/documents/2019%20CIGI-Ipsos%20Global%20Survey%20%20Part%203%20Social%20Media%2C%20Fake%20News%20%26%20Algorithms.pdf retrieved on 17 June 2019.

prohibited in Islam. In 2016 the rumour started in Egypt, when it was spread by a public page on Facebook called "Alexandria 24 Hours". This is an Egyptian tabloid-type page that shared the rumour as a photo that was widely circulated. It contained the pots of Danone yoghurt with a photo of a pig and a brief narrative of a text written in Arabic. This text begins with a religious expression generally used in times of disappointment to generate feelings of empathy with the Muslim community that has been deceived and causes resentment against Danone. It ends with a call for action to boycott the products (the translation of the text in the footnote). In addition, an indexed hashtag in Arabic: #زبادي_دانون (#yaourt_Danone) had been added to the publications.

It is important to mention that the roots of the rumour date back to 15 September 2012 when it first appeared on the Web in a video[4] on YouTube entitled هل[5] بهما DANETTE ودانيت DANONE زبادى دانون جيلاتين الخنزير؟ (translation: Do Danone and Danette yoghurts contain pork gelatin). This video was downloaded by a religious page called *HolyQuranbyHosary*. The source is a YouTube channel with 1.38 K subscribers. This page broadcast the video in French, but with Arabic subtitles, with the intention to target a Franco-Arabic community. The total number of views on YouTube exceeded 100,000, exactly 115,960 views, 26 comments from 2012 to 2019 and 343 likes until 17 October 2019. The rumour continued its life cycle on Facebook and Twitter from 2012 until September 2018 through international interactions among Internet users.

By observing the timestamp of the dissemination of publications that spread the rumour over the years, we can notice a cyclical diffusion. For example, in Egypt the rumour appeared just before the month of Ramadan, known as the yogurt consuming season. The rumour on Facebook lasted two years and five months.

The reaction of Internet users on Facebook was mainly sharing this rumour more than liking it or commenting on it. Some messages written in Arabic were added to these shares by Internet users, and contained

---

[4] Link to the video, https://www.youtube.com/watch?v=Ew65Tds3a_o&feature=youtube_gdata_player retrieved on 17 October 2019.

[5] The title was scripted using Arabic and English words on the original video on YouTube.

religious expressions such as "Allah is sufficient for me, he is the best protector" to express their dissatisfaction.

Rumour Management/Debunking?

The public page on Facebook called *Da begad* played the role of fact-checking in Egypt and denied the rumour three days after it appeared on Facebook.[6] The Danone Company has not published anything and has not reacted.

4.2 Pampers Egypt

Rumour: "Pampers prices are rising in Egypt after applying the new VAT"

Presentation of the Case

This rumour was launched on the 19 July 2016 on Egyptian social media, on the occasion of government announcements concerning economic reforms aimed at changing the value-added tax (VAT) of some goods and services in Egypt. A public page called "Porto Tora for you"[7] on Facebook published a photo containing Arabic text and hashtags indexed by a fake account under the name of "Nesma Alaa". We analysed the social media platforms, including Facebook, and found that this publication was the first to disseminate this topic. We therefore believe that this was what triggered the rumour. The name of the page already reveals that it is a page opposing the regime, because it holds the name of a prison in Egypt called "Tora". The translation of the name of the public page is "Porto

[6] Link of the debunking published on Facebook by "Da begad". Retrieved on 30 April 2018. https://www.facebook.com/DaBegad/photos/a.178588762292398/644216762396260/?type=3&theater.

[7] Link to the rumour on Facebook, retrieved on 30 April 2018: https://www.facebook.com/tora.for.u/photos/a.139055169499755/1157449647660297/?type=3&theater.

Tora prison is made for you" implicitly to ironically mean that all those who oppose the regime will end up in prison.

On the occasion of the new law, the rumour found a favourable ground to emerge and to trigger dismay in society even though these legislations had not yet been made official. It's also important to mention that Procter & Gamble effectively raised Pampers' prices six months after the rumour spread in January 2017 following the devaluation of the Egyptian pound, which caused exchange rate fluctuations.

In the content of the rumour, we note two hashtags indexed in Arabic with an Egyptian dialect: #Taxe_added and #Piss_on_Egypt_my_baby. The public page also added a sarcastic comment to the photo: "even Pampers + laughing emoticon". We suggest that the insertion of a laughing emoji along sarcastic hashtags can capture the attention of Internet users and make the rumour more engaging.

Translation of the publication

The Pampers box costs 97 L.E. two weeks ago … Today, it costs 158 L.E.[8]

#Added_tax

#Piss_on_Egypt_my_baby.

It was noticed on Facebook that the most common reaction of Egyptian Internet users was the likes, not the sharing of the publication of the rumour. Messages written in Arabic, which were added to the shares by Internet users, were also analysed; 63% of the messages belonged to the category of irony and sarcasm, in accordance with the initial content of the rumour and its sense of humour.

The rumour was last spotted on social media platforms a few days later, precisely on 24 July 2016 on Facebook. Despite the enormous reaction rate reaching 10,113 interactions, it only persisted for a few days. The rumour circulated only for a month on Facebook. This may be related to the presence of official declarations concerning these economic reforms putting an end to the rumour.

[8] Equivalent to $9.

Rumour Management/Debunking

The *Da begad* public page also played the role of fact-checking for this rumour and denied the rumour six days after it appeared on Facebook with screen shots of actual price tags of Pampers showing that prices didn't change. The reach of this denial reveals its effectiveness in combating and curbing the spread of rumour. No announcement from P&G was officially published to deny the rumour.

4.3 Orange Telecom

Rumour: "*Orange is an Israeli company that sponsors Israeli military units*".

Presentation of the Case

In 2015, Orange acquired Mobinil, an Egyptian mobile phone giant with the largest number of customers in Egypt. Before the announcement of the acquisition and the change of the company's name from Mobinil to Orange, a wave of rumours was launched on Facebook and Twitter. Boycott campaigns against the companies Mobinil and Orange were also conducted.

According to our observations, the public page called BDS Egypt on Facebook launched the rumour and spread it to Egypt on 23 May 2015. This rumour is considered a sensitive political matter for Egyptians since the state of war between the Arab Republic of Egypt and Israel, which dates back to the 1948–1949 Arab-Israeli war. Despite the signing of the Israeli-Egyptian peace treaty in 1978, the rate of investment and trade is still low: 117 Israeli organisations exported their products to Egypt in 2015 for a total amount of only US$236 million (Darmon 2016).

The spread of this rumour was characterised by numerous indexed hashtags present in the content of publications disseminating the rumour, in Arabic and French, as follows[9]:

> #مصر_تقاطع# (translation: #Egypt_boycott),
> #قاطع_موبينيل (translation: #boycottMobinil),
> #مليونيه_مقاطعه_شركات_الاتصالات (translation: 1 million telecommunication company boycotts), #OrangeApartheid, #Orange_Sanguine.

It is noteworthy that the design of the Arabic-indexed hashtags was similar to the jargons used in 2011 during the Arab Spring Revolution, which were designed to mobilise the masses. Using these indexed hashtags as keywords in the Facebook search section, twenty-five public pages on Facebook were found and were involved in spreading the rumour and linked to the BDS Egypt page. Of these Facebook pages, seven became inactive after an average of four months. These seven ephemeral pages played the role of a kind of astroturfing, a term that often describes actions taken by states or political groups to influence public opinion, the media or the vote as described by Gautreau (2019). The political organisation BDS wanted to give the impression of a massively amplified boycott movement, when in fact it was orchestrated and coordinated by them alone.

Regarding the timing of the distribution of rumour publications, the BDS Egypt page followed a well-organised agenda that targets the hours when Egyptian Internet users are likely to be more active.

The photo launched by BDS Egypt, which caused the highest reaction rate, has been shared more than 2000 times thanks to its design with little written content, the two logos of Mobinil and Orange, clearly visible and the Israeli flag in the middle of the page. It was launched on 23 May 2015, accompanied by all the main hashtags of the boycott campaign.

The reaction rate of Internet users to this publication on Facebook was marked by a volume of sharing that exceeded the volume of likes and comments.

---

[9] All hashtags were copied as they were launched originally even if they may contain some spelling mistakes.

The analyses of the messages, added before sharing the publication by Internet users, identify requests for a boycott of Orange.

During the propagation of this rumour, the existence of the account of a famous person in the circuit of the propagation reinforced the plausibility of the message transmitted. It was the account of an Egyptian politician named Mr. Sabahy—a former presidential candidate in Egypt and currently leader of a political party—who began to support the attack campaign against Mobinil/Orange Egypt with a tweet containing the hashtags indexed from his certified account.

Rumour Management/Debunking

Two approaches have been adopted:

- Even if we are only interested in the Facebook platform, Orange's crisis management on Twitter deserves our attention. On Twitter, the company has been very active and has responded directly to comments from Internet users and BDS Egypt. The Orange Egypt community manager has given a lot of importance to Mr. Sabahy's Tweets. He responded to these tweets within ten minutes of their broadcast. Orange Egypt's interactive tempo shows that its reaction was the fastest when a famous person relayed the rumour than when the source came from other users.
- On Facebook, the public page *Da begad* took the initiative to post an official denial from Orange Egypt.

5 The Main Findings and the Analysis of the Cases

In this section, we identify the patterns that highlight the specificities of the dissemination of rumours in Egypt and the elements that feed them on social media. To perform this, we will study the three cases presented through the multi-level analysis grid presented earlier.

5.1 At the Micro-environmental Level

Four variables are taken into consideration here.

The Beginning of the Process of Dissemination to the Public
Finding the person responsible for a rumour campaign is complicated. In our empirical research, the launching source of the rumour has been noticed to be isolated individuals, hidden behind public pages on Facebook; they have never used individual accounts. One of the members of the BDS organisation in Egypt, which sponsored the launch of the rumour against the Orange company, explained to us, during a semi-directive interview, the coordinated effort of several actors acting at different levels to effectively manage the sustainability of the rumour. Steps pretty similar to a publicity campaign.

Frequency of the Propagation
According to our observations, the frequency of dissemination of a rumour varies according to three situations.

- Rumour already has ancient roots on the Web. This was the case for Orange and Danone. The frequency with which these rumours are spread was cyclical throughout the years.
- Rumours intensify according to specific events: Ramadan for Danone yoghurts, the acquisition of Mobinil by Orange.
- The rumour is associated with the promulgation of a new economic law. This was the case for Procter & Gamble when a new VAT was applied. Here, the rumour resonates with the mistrust, anxiety or even resistance to change of the members of a society.
- *Involvement of celebrity accounts in the propagation process*
  This situation was observed only in the case of Orange, but only on the Twitter platform when certain "famous" individuals get involved in the rumour circuit, which can boost the effect of its propagation on social media.

Sentiment and Semantic Analysis of Internet Users
It is important to note that the functionality of Facebook allows Internet users to add written texts and comments before sharing a publication which allows them to express their own feelings and opinions. This behaviour was observed in all the three cases presented.

During the spread of the rumours studied in Egypt, three categories of feelings were observed: religious beliefs, the call for action to boycott (call for action) and sarcasm. For Danone, the messages added by Internet users are characterised by religious expressions such as "Allah is enough for me, he is the best guarantor". These religious expressions serve to express deep discontent and reflect the emotional state of the individuals concerned. For Pampers, the sentiment expressed is linked to sarcasm and/or a sense of humour. It is important to mention that this feeling was already embedded in the content of the rumour on Facebook. We deduce from this that the initial message used for the rumour conditions, at least partially, the reactions of Internet users.

5.2 The Meso-environmental Level

Here as well, four dimensions must be taken into account.

The Form of the Most Widely Disseminated Rumour
Our analyses reveal that, during the launch of a rumour, Internet users' reactions are particularly strong when photos are shared. This confirms that the spread of a rumour is partly motivated by visual messages. These photos contain transposable signs that evoke certain impulsive emotional reactions (such as a picture of a pig for a community who follows a religion that prohibits its consumption), which incite Internet users to spread the rumour.

Affective Metrics Reflecting Reactions
The aim here is to assess the nature of Internet users' engagement. According to our analyses, Egyptian Internet users had three reactions:

sharing the publication, liking and writing comments. For Orange and Danone, we found that the first reaction was the most frequent. This observation contradicts the trends normally followed on Facebook where the likes rate exceeds the rate of sharing and comments.[10]

Rumour Design: Transposable Signs and Hashtags

A wide variety of transposable signs were found: added symbols (e.g., a flag) or integrated elements (e.g., images). The content of the rumours also included indexed hashtags calling for boycotts, as in the case of Pampers and Orange. These various indexed hashtags, which were specifically created for these boycott campaigns, played a vital role in the rumour reach on social media. Hashtags are symbols that reinforce the sense of belonging to a group that defends a cause; this reinforces the credibility of rumours in the minds of Internet users.

Digital Traceability and Web Memory

In the case of Orange, for example, thanks to the digital traceability provided by the Web memory, new public pages on Facebook have been detected. Exactly twenty-five public pages were created to increase the spread of rumours by multiplying sources. This variable characterising the Web 2.0 was pivotal to help us conduct our data collection and through netnography and using data retrieval softwares such as Netvizz, NodeXl and Gephi.

5.3 Macro-environment Level

At this last stage of analysis, the four variables to be considered are as follows.

[10] Link to the study: https://www.quintly.com/blog/new-facebook-reaction-study. Accessed on 17 September 2018.

Topics and Themes Related to the Cultural Context

The themes of the rumours studied are closely linked to the culture in Egypt. They concern health and religion (Danone), politics (Orange) and the economy (Pampers). Thanks to the three axes proposed by the sociologist Shibutani (1966), we were able to establish a link between the themes and the situational contexts that led to the emergence of rumours.

The first axis focuses on the relevance of the situational context observed. For example, during the rumour about Pampers, it appeared just after the economic reforms announced in Egypt in 2016. The latter provided a favourable situational context to support the plausibility of the rumour. Another example, demonstrating the relevance of the situational context, concerns the rumour about Danone yoghurts just before Ramadan in a rather Muslim context.[11]

The second axis is concerned with the collective interpretation of a rumour. Rumours seem more plausible if there is a collective and shared meaning and consciousness. This triggers an emotion of belonging (emotional activation). This was observed with the rumour about the Orange company. The reaction of Internet users was to write comments before sharing the rumour on their Facebook walls.

The third axis reflects the degree of emotional activation (arousal). The emotions activated by the rumours studied are associated with the themes discussed and translated into the written messages. In the case of rumours based on a political theme, the messages called for a boycott action. Regarding the theme of health, Internet users expressed themselves through messages containing religious terms. For the economic theme, the messages were sarcastic to criticise the new laws. Rumours can thus create an emotional shock that encourages users to share frustration or anger on their Facebook walls.

[11] In the Egyptian Constitution (URL link: https://www.constituteproject.org/constitution/Egypt_2014.pdf), according to article 2, "Islam is the religion of the State and Arabic its official language. The principles of the Islamic Shariah are the main source of the legislation". The preamble states that "their interpretation derives from the jurisprudence of the Supreme Constitutional Court". Retrieved on 16 February 2019.

Language Used During the Interactions

In the three cases studied, particularly during the appearance on Egyptian territory, the language used was Arabic with an Egyptian dialect. The interactions of Internet users, in the form of comments or messages added before the act of sharing, have used this language, with the exception of the rumours about Danone and Orange, since the traces on the digital platforms showed that they were launched from another territory before coming to Egypt. These "extraterritorial", as we suggest naming them, have adapted the language and dialect to each country.

Cluster Formation

The data treated from the study data set revealed the existence of cluster formation. This variable is well linked to culture since clusters appeared as social representations distributed in space and strongly linked to local/national values according to Latané's theory of dynamic social impact (1996).

According to our analysis, the public pages on Facebook that form the clusters are managed by people from different countries. The resulting cultural diversity thus reinforces the need for a communication style adapted to each cultural context.

Rumour Management/Debunking

In the three cases, the rumours were denied by a verified public page on Facebook entitled *Da begad?* (ده بجد؟). This page plays the role of a fact-checker and is followed by more than 1 million subscribers. It is important to note that the option, which exists on Facebook in different countries, to report that a piece of information is false is not active in Egypt. This option, proposed by the platform, invites users to signal false content in order to correct the information transmission algorithm. However, Egyptian Internet users have no reliable source other than the *Da begad* page to check the veracity of publications.

6 Conclusion and Modelling of the Analysis Grid

Our observations and analysis suggest that the process of launching a commercial rumour is far from a natural or random phenomenon. To study the rumours in Egypt in depth, we proposed an analysis grid based on twelve variables at three levels: micro-, meso- and macro-environment. This grid allows us to claim that the initiators of rumours on social media carefully plan their entry through public accounts and pages. Internet users, by spreading false information, can be indeed considered as active stakeholders.

The twelve variables proposed to identify the process of spreading a rumour functioned as leverages to facilitate the achievement of certain goals, slandering the e-reputation of companies. Thus, with a minimum knowledge of the cultural particularities of a country, the act of propagation can have more or less long and more or less negative effects. By providing insights into the tactics used, our research aims to help companies understand this propagation phenomenon in order to better combat these attacks, which tend to increase in number.

We can conclude that rumours dissemination depends on socio-cultural factors. Ignoring the effects of these factors on Internet users' behaviour can discredit the image of companies on social media. To contextualise the applied analysis grid, we summarise it in Fig. 14.1.

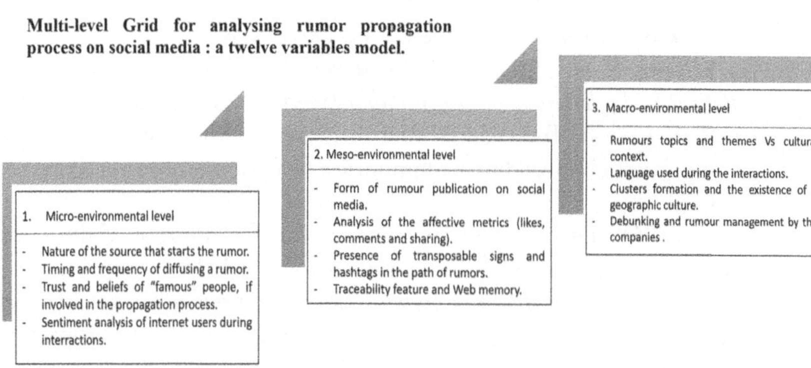

Fig. 14.1 Summary of analysis: multi-level grid for analysing rumour propagation process on social media, a twelve-variable model. (Source: Author's creation)

References

Alloing, C. (2013). *Processus de veille par infomédiation sociale pour construire l'e-réputation d'une organisation. Approche par agents-facilitateurs appliquée à la DSIC de La Poste.* Doctoral dissertation, Université de Poitiers.

Brodin, O., & Roux, E. (1990). Les recherches sur les rumeurs: courants, méthodes, enjeux managériaux. *Recherche et Applications en Marketing (French Edition), 5*(4), 45–70. https://doi.org/10.1177/076737019000500403.

Bruns, A., & Burgess, J. E. (2011). *The USE of Twitter Hashtags in the Formation of Ad hoc Publics.* Proceedings of the 6th European Consortium for Political Research (ECPR) General Conference, University of Iceland, Reykjavik.

Colas, F. (2004). *Introduction au renseignement extérieur d'entreprise.* Paris: l'esprit du livre éditions.

Darmon, A. (2016, août 24). *Hausse des investissements étrangers en Égypte.* From Israël Export & International Cooperation Institut, Israël Magazine. Retrieved October 25, 2018, from http://israelmagazine.co.il/hausse-investissements-etrangers-Egypte/.

Difonzo, N., & Bordia, P. (2007). Rumours Influence: Toward a Dynamic Social Impact Theory of Rumour the Science of Social Influence: Advances and Future Progress. In A. R. Pratkanis (Ed.), *The Science of Social Influence* (pp. 281–305). Philadelphia, PA: Psychology Press.

Gautreau, E. (2019). Expliquez-nous... L'astroturfing. Retrieved March 15, 2019, from https://www.francetvinfo.fr/replay-radio/expliquez-nous/expliquez-nous-lastroturfing_3119383.html.

Gerring, J. (2004). What Is a Case Study and What Is It Good For? *American Political Science Review, 98*(2), 341–354.

Hall, E. T. (1976). *Beyond Culture.* New York: Doubleday.

Kim, C., & Yang, S. U. (2017). *Like, Comment, and Share on Facebook: How Each Behaviour Differs from the Other. Public Relations Review, 43*(2), 441–449.

Kozinets, R. V. (2002). The Field Behind the Screen: Using Netnography for Marketing Research in Online Communities. *Journal of Marketing Research, 3*(1), 61–72.

Latané, B. (1996). Dynamic Social Impact: The Creation of Culture by Communication. *Journal of Communication, 46*(4), 13–25.

Le Béchec, M. (2010). *Territoire et communication politique sur le web régional breton.* Doctoral dissertation, Université Rennes 2; Université Européenne de Bretagne.

Le Béchec, M., & Boullier, D. (2014). *Communautés imaginées et signes transposables sur un "web territorial". Études de Communication, 42*, 113–126.

Milliot, E. (2016). The Pivotal Role of Guanxi for Economic Intelligence in the People's Republic of China. *Management International, 20*(4), 133–145.
Ploux, F. (2001). Bruits alarmants et fausses nouvelle dans la France du XIXe siècle (1814–1870). *Hypotheses, 4*(1), 303–314.
Rouquette, M. (1975). *Les Rumeurs* (pp. 79–89). Paris: PUF.
Rouquette, M. (1979). *Les Phénomènes des Rumeurs.* Thèse de doctorat en Psychologie, Université de Provence, p. 117.
Shibutani, T. (1966). *Improvised News: A Sociological Study of Rumour.* Indianapolis: The Bobbs-Merrill Company.
Stake, R. (2006). *Multiple Case Study Analysis.* New York: The Guilford Press.

[illegible]

15

General Conclusion: The Managerial Challenges for a Societal Development in Africa

Suzanne M. Apitsa and Eric Milliot

The different chapters of the book identify five types of challenges facing national and international companies. These are cultural, economic, institutional, ecological and technological challenges. The study of these challenges, even if the fields of investigation remain numerous and varied, allows three types of contributions: theoretical, methodological and managerial.

S. M. Apitsa (✉)
University of Poitiers, Poitiers, France

E. Milliot
University of Nantes, Nantes, France
e-mail: emilliot@poitiers.iae-france.fr

S. M. Apitsa, E. Milliot (eds.), *Doing Business in Africa*, Palgrave Studies of Internationalization in Emerging Markets,
https://doi.org/10.1007/978-3-030-50739-8_15

1 Theoretical Contributions

Africa is made up of 55 sovereign states. The research presented directly concerns 11 countries: Algeria, Benin, Burkina Faso, Cameroon, Egypt, Ethiopia, Madagascar, Morocco, Niger, Nigeria and Tanzania. Among these countries, four represent important economies already involved internationally (Algeria, Egypt, Morocco, Nigeria). The others, of various sizes, are beginning to structurally develop their activities abroad.

The research presented in this book highlights several themes related to the challenges of market globalisation.

- First of all, they confirm the desire to develop reticular economic structures. The resulting networks are varied in nature. They are sometimes built on the basis of contradictory logics (e.g. the status of competitor-partner). In addition to these paradoxical structures, there are more traditional forms of inter-organisational relations that make it possible to circumvent certain obstacles to development and international trade.
- Secondly, they underline the need for south-north and south-south internationalisation. This internationalisation is associated with Africa's emergence on the international scene. It shows that, between the global and the local, international trade flows are also developing on a continental/regional scale. From a strategic point of view, this calls for a geographical reorientation of the deployment of organisations. In terms of implementation, this reorientation calls for continuous adjustments in organisational patterns and calls for special attention to African contingencies. In this context, where the dynamics of expansion and the search for profitability are at stake, it is necessary to identify suitable performance indicators (e.g. those of sustainability). Of course, obstacles have to be overcome (e.g. the domination of large global operators in port and maritime logistics chains), because they limit the international ambitions of players based in Africa.
- Some analyses highlight the importance of digitisation in economic activities. Information and communication technologies (ICTs), which bring peoples closer together, multiply the links between the territories of the different subregions of the continent. The analyses underline that innovation must also integrate local cultural characteristics in

order to understand the conduct of the actors and avoid nuisances that are sometimes difficult to control (case of the spread of online rumours).
- Similarly, there is a growing need to become aware of the challenges of ecological transition in Africa. Africa is a victim of climate change (droughts, floods, cyclones, urbanisation problems, non-recycled waste, and so on), which has consequences on production and the well-being of the population and sometimes causes migration. The ecological transition suggests greater corporate social responsibility (CSR). However, this CSR is still too often misunderstood and poorly perceived by African managers.
- A final trend identified in the book is the need to better understand and manage institutional and cultural phenomena. These are very specific and sometimes constitute major obstacles to investment in Africa (e.g. problems caused by corruption). There is a need to better assess their impacts. This imperative suggests a better mastery of their distinctive characteristics. Cultural aspects studied through the prism of ethnicity contribute to a better knowledge of the diversity of cultures in Africa. They allow, for example, a better understanding of the intra- and inter-organisational logics developed.

The depth of the various works presented by the authors is great. The authors invite a collective reflection on the renewal of the themes. These key themes invite us to propose fine analyses and appropriate modelling. This book proposes some of them (e.g. the concept of integrated cooperation and the model of cooperative integration).

2 Methodological Contributions

The proposed chapters make use of different methodologies: surveys, archive analyses, observations, interviews, and so on.

- The quantitative approaches in this book allow a large-scale assessment of certain organisational behaviours. They are essential for identifying trends that emerge over time. Often based on hypotheses, they make it possible to invalidate or confirm abstract representations of reality and to put into perspective the evolution of certain observed realities (e.g. SMEs' commitment to export).

- Qualitative approaches are favoured in many chapters. They allow new phenomena to emerge (e.g. the use of social networks for managerial purposes) or to be developed. Without opening the way to generalisations, they make it possible to identify—through each geographical, managerial, sectoral and cultural reality—the diversity of elements that need to be taken into consideration. Indeed, they facilitate the in-depth study of certain complex phenomena and emphasise the meaning that actors give to particular situations (e.g. intra-ethnic solidarity or respect, which is a value linked to ethics).
- Finally, some research—few in number—adopts a mixed methodology combining quantitative and qualitative approaches. This approach allows a better understanding of phenomena in which cultural, institutional, economic, social and societal dimensions are intertwined (e.g. analysis of performance indicators in the local port supply chain).

The use of these methodological approaches inspires the construction of appropriate conceptual frameworks to better describe the phenomena and developments observed.

3 Managerial Contributions

Using different methodologies, the study of the five challenges of international business development in Africa leads to the definition of new logics of action.

- Economic actors need, more than ever, to better understand the transformations that characterise the African continent (e.g. the development of a middle class with discretionary income). These transformations require a better understanding of the expectations of internal and external stakeholders. They also call for the identification of trends in environmental conditions, the development of monitoring systems and the adoption of contingent plans.
- Africa is characterised by institutional weaknesses. The African Union devoted the year 2018 to the fight against corruption. Even if some African countries are well placed in the Transparency International

ranking, the fight against corruption and illicit financial flows continues (for the latter, Africa loses US$50 billion annually). These institutional weaknesses are obstacles to investment. For this reason, this book focuses on societal development.

- Research shows that economic actors are developing new governance structures (e.g. cooperation). These structures are based on more or less formal networks that make it easier to adapt to a competitive and changing environment.
- In view of the particularities of Africa, the choice of a strategy and a management mode must often be adapted. This adaptation leads to the creation of appropriate tools and methods (e.g. more or less implicit communication tools). It is based on respect for traditional African values (e.g. ethnic solidarity).
- On the basis of the digital transformations observed, the work presented highlights an economic dynamic that needs to be inclusive. This dimension is essential for achieving societal development in Africa. The realisation of the opportunities offered by digital technology places the responsibility of companies and states at the heart of the success of the ecological transition.

This book opens up many research perspectives. The five challenges identified each relate to a multitude of issues. It is up to African researchers or those interested in Africa to continue exploring them. Their work will help to better identify ways to ensure societal development on the African continent.

Index[1]

[1] Note: Page numbers followed by 'n' refer to notes.

S. M. Apitsa, E. Milliot (eds.), *Doing Business in Africa*, Palgrave Studies of Internationalization in Emerging Markets,
https://doi.org/10.1007/978-3-030-50739-8

The manufacturer's authorised representative in the EU is Springer Nature Customer Service Centre GmbH, Europaplatz 3, 69115 Heidelberg, Germany. If you have any concerns regarding our products, please contact ProductSafety@springernature.com

Printed and bound by CPI Group (UK) Ltd, Croydon, CR0 4YY
22/09/2026
02220984-0004